AARDVARK TO ZEBRA

AARDVARK TO ZEBRA

Complete Patterns & Instructions for Making
Original & Unusual Stuffed Animals

Lois Boncer

NEW CENTURY PUBLISHERS, INC.

Copyright © 1984 by Lois Boncer

All rights reserved. No part of this book may be used or reproduced in any manner whatsoever without prior written permission from the publisher except in the case of brief quotations embodied in critical reviews and articles. All inquiries should be addressed to New Century Publishers, Inc., 220 Old New Brunswick Road, Piscataway, New Jersey 08854.

Printing Code
11 12 13 14 15 16

Library of Congress Cataloging in Publication Data

Boncer, Lois.
   Aardvark to zebra.

   1. Soft toy making. 2. Sewing. I. Title. II. Title: Stuffed animals.
TT174.3.B66 1984   745.592'4   84-6899
ISBN 0-8329-0306-X (pbk.)

CONTENTS

Introduction vii

AARDVARK 2

ANTEATER 18

BISON 32

DODOS 50

DUCK 70

ELEPHANT 78

KOALA 92

MOOSE 120

PIG 134

PETER RABBIT FAMILY 146

SLOTH 172

SNAKE 184

SPIDER 196

UNICORN/HORSE 202

ZEBRA/DONKEY 218

HOBBY CAMEL 232

HOBBY HORSE/UNICORN 242

HOBBY RABBITS 252

Introduction

The designs in this book vary from very simple to quite complex. Some are basic, with variations or optional pieces and procedures that can make them more complicated. All have been tested by home sewers, though, to ensure that their construction is possible using regular sewing techniques, that the pieces fit and the dots and notches are correctly placed, and that the instructions are completely and clearly written.

The photographs show the animals made in materials that were available at the time they were designed. Since types and colors of fabrics come and go, you may not be able to find precisely these materials where you are. Use what you can find. These fabrics are only suggestions. You may choose natural colors and textures or any whimsical materials that suit your fancy. Several designs lend themselves to using up scrap materials.

Do use quality materials. You are wasting your time if you don't. An animal made of cheap fabric will look cheap and wear poorly, no matter how good the workmanship is.

The materials and the techniques you choose to use depend also on whom the animal is for. If you are making the animal for a teenager or an adult, as a display piece or decoration, you may choose a more fragile fabric, such as satin or velvet. You might use whimsical buttons or beads for eyes and put wood or wire supports inside. If, on the other hand, you are making it for a young child to use as a toy, you want it to be soft, safe, and washable. It should be made of a strong fabric like acrylic fur, corduroy, velour, cotton velveteen, terrycloth, or some upholstery fabrics that are durable and washable. A long shag fake fur is not suitable for infants or toddlers, as they can pull out the hair and get it in their mouths. Safety eyes are preferable to buttons or beads. There is no way to sew on a button so that it will never come off. You can also embroider or appliqué the features. Don't use wires inside an animal that is to be used as a toy.

After reading the following hints, choose a pattern, gather your materials, and go to it! I hope you have as much fun making and owning these critters as I have.

About Fabrics Cutting and sewing fur fabrics are not difficult. Fur fabrics consist of a pile (furry) side on a backing, usually knit. The direction of the pile is the direction you can stroke the fur (as you would pet an animal). Mark the direction of the pile on the back of the fabric with a chalk arrow. Lay the fabric, one layer thick, pile side down, on the table and pin the pattern pieces to the backing with the arrows on the pattern pieces corresponding to the chalk arrow. Cut through the fabric backing only, using the tips of your scissors, and pull the pieces out to separate the pile. Be sure to reverse the pattern pieces to get a right and left side, as necessary.

When sewing fur fabrics, push the pile into the seam so that the edges of both backings are visible. This allows a more accurate seam and helps prevent too much pile from being caught in the stitching.

Some pile will be caught in the seams nonetheless. After the animal is stuffed and sewn up, take a stout needle or T-pin and scrape along the seams to pull the pile up enough to cover the seams.

Remember, the thicker the fur fabric you choose, the fatter the animal will look.

When sewing vinyl on the right side, it may drag or stick under the presser foot. To prevent this, rub a light coating of sewing machine oil on the top surface. Wipe the oil off after stitching.

If top stitching close to the edge of small pieces of vinyl is frustrating for you, here are a couple of alternatives: (1) Trace around the pattern pieces on the right side of a piece of vinyl. Fold the vinyl double, wrong side together. Stitch just inside the drawn lines and then cut out the pieces close to the stitching. (2) Draw or trace the pattern pieces onto tissue paper. Lay the paper over the doubled vinyl. Stitch, tear away the paper, and cut out the pieces.

If you are using a napped fabric like corduroy, velour, velvet, or velveteen, be sure to lay the pattern pieces all in the same direction. These fabrics usually show a color change if rotated 180 degrees. You could end up with one half of the animal a lighter shade than the other half. Also, some satins are duller when turned 90 degrees, so you should check this before cutting partly on the lengthwise grain and partly crosswise.

Stretch fabrics are not generally recommended for making these designs. As you stuff, the animal gets bigger and bigger, and you can wind up with a shapeless blob. If you have a stretch fabric that you love the color and texture of, you can use it if you line it with a firm fabric. Cut pieces from both fabrics, lay the lining against the wrong side of the stretch fabric, and sew the two pieces as if they were one. Be sure all four edges are aligned as you stitch. It's annoying to think you're finished, turn the animal right side out, and find you have missed an edge somewhere.

It is also advisable to line fabrics that are so thin that the seams show through, and fabrics that ravel badly like satin and velvet. These patterns all use ¼-inch (⅗-cm) seam allowances. Satin and velvet can pull apart at the seams before you finish stuffing them. Backing each piece with muslin and stitching all four layers together reinforces the seams well so the stuffing can be packed in firmly.

You could also use iron-on interfacing to back each piece of stretch or fragile fabric. This leaves the fabric stiffer than I like it, but if you like the effect and the convenience, use it.

More fabric recommendations are found at the beginnings of most of the patterns.

Sewing Techniques

Choose the proper sewing machine needle to go with your fabrics: a heavy-duty needle for furs, a light needle for thin fabrics, a ballpoint for knits.

In making a stuffed animal, the most natural place to start would be the head. But you'll notice that I often don't do this. I have found it easier, sometimes, to make a right side and a left side and then sew them together at the head center, finishing up with the center back and underbelly seams. It is easier to do details like the hooves and the soles of the feet if the piece is less bulky.

In almost every pattern you will be instructed to sew to a dot or between dots instead of to the edge of the piece. It is important to stop at the dot where so instructed. This leaves a seam allowance free to sew to another piece. These dots occur where several pieces come together at a single point—for instance, where the point of a head gusset meets the center back seam:

This row of stitching continues to the dot. The point of the gusset should be folded out of the way when sewing the center back seam. If all lines of stitching stop at exactly the same point, the pieces will meet without having a hole or a pucker. Another instance is where the underbody pieces meet the center back seam:

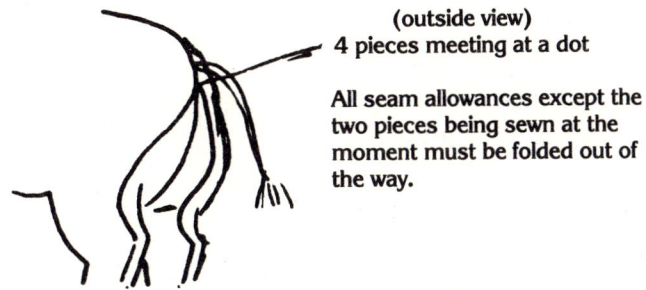

I also recommend double stitching at the inside corners where the fabric must be clipped to the seam line before turning the animal right side out. This does not require a separate operation—just back stitch at the corner, then continue along the seam. I don't double stitch all the seams, as some authors recommend. I just haven't found it necessary.

More sewing techniques are described and illustrated as they are used in a given pattern.

About Stuffing There are many materials that you can use to stuff animals: rags, old nylon stockings, shredded foam, excelsior, sawdust, shredded newspapers, and so on. I don't recommend most of them, but it's your choice. I prefer to use polyester fiberfill. It's clean, nonallergenic, and easy to work with. It washes and dries nicely, better than cotton. It is not cheap, and there are different grades. Some of the cheaper grades wad up into tight little clumps like white bread. With these, it is difficult to get a smooth stuffing job. Some clump up after the animal is put through the washer and dryer. You will have to try the different brands that are available where you live and see which works best for you. A good-quality fiberfill doesn't stick together—it's resilient enough to spring back to size after being squeezed hard.

Stuffing is one of the most important skills in making nice toys—a skill that takes some care and practice. A lumpy, misshapen animal is no joy, so stuff slowly and carefully.

You can stuff an animal softly, firmly, or very firmly. The more firmly the animal is stuffed, the longer it will hold its shape through repeated handling and washing. If you have time, you may want to stuff it as firmly as you can, let it rest overnight, and then work in more stuffing as necessary before sewing it up.

A bamboo chopstick is useful as a pushing tool—it's strong, flexible, and smooth, usually tapered at one end. A sanded dowel is good, too, or the eraser end of an unsharpened pencil. Some people like a table knife. Sharp, pointed instruments like scissors or knitting needles are risky; it's too easy to punch through the fabric. But they may be necessary to get into very narrow places; just be careful.

Start with the parts farthest from the opening. Tear off wads of stuffing and push them into place firmly. A small space requires a small piece of stuffing. Larger areas, like the main body cavity, can take larger wads. As you push with one hand, hold the other hand against the outside of the animal so that you are pushing against your hand rather than against the fabric. This relieves strain on the cloth and seams. Push the stuffing firmly against the seams so there are no gaps or wrinkles.

As you work along, you may discover a place "back there" that is missing sufficient fiberfill. There are a couple of things to try before you pull out your stuffing to get back to the gap: (1) Often, using a chopstick or other pushing tool, you can work a wad along the inside wall of the fabric, past the intervening stuffing and into the empty space. (2) Using a strong needle or T-pin, you can enter from outside the animal and pull stuffing from the surrounding area into the gap.

Shape the animal as you stuff. Push extra stuffing into areas you want rounder, such as cheeks, shoulders, and hip areas. Use less in areas you want thinner, like the neck and waist.

If you want the animal to stand indefinitely as a display piece, you will want to put dowels as support in the legs and perhaps in the neck. (Heavy wire would work, too. Be sure to turn back the ends.) The dowels should be long enough to reach into the shoulder or hip area, but not so long that they'd rub against the back. Pad the bottom of the foot and insert the dowel in the center of the leg. Push small wads of stuffing, first on one side, then the other, keeping it centered. Stuff firmly all around, up the leg and into the body area, making sure the dowel doesn't touch the outside fabric and cannot be felt from the outside.

Alternatively, you could glue and wrap stuffing around dowels (or wires), and then insert them into the legs. You will probably still have to stuff around the edges to fill all the areas.

Don't use wires or wood if the toy is for a young child or if a youngster is apt to get hold of it. Little children are perfectly happy with animals that have bent legs and broken necks; they just want to hold something soft and safe.

To sew up the openings after stuffing, try the ladder stitch:

stitches directly opposite

pull up tightly every few stitches

The needle is inserted directly across from the last stitch, on the seam line. Pull the thread up every few stitches. The seam allowances will turn under as you draw up the thread. If the stitches are directly opposite and you don't pull the thread too tightly, there will be no puckers.

Placement of Features

Placement of features is important in stuffed animals. It makes a big difference in the final look. You can embroider or appliqué features, or use buttons, beads, glass, or plastic safety eyes. Safety eyes are recommended in toys for young children. These can be purchased in craft stores or ordered by mail from doll or craft supply catalogues. They come in various sizes, colors, and types, but all are constructed similarly. They have a shank that is inserted through a small hole in the fabric from the right side. A washer is pushed up the shank on the inside to catch the fabric tightly between the back of the eye and the washer. These must be inserted before the animal is stuffed.

washer — fabric outside

Some fabrics, especially knits and furs with knit backings, tear out or begin to ravel as soon as you cut the hole for the shank. You can hand sew with a running stitch, whip stitch, or buttonhole stitch around the hole to stabilize the edges, or you can apply a small square of iron-on interfacing or mending tape to the back of the fabric before the hole is cut.

For noninfants, safety eyes probably aren't necessary. You can find some interesting buttons to use for eyes and variously get a natural effect, or a whimsical, even goofy one. Since buttons are applied after the animal is stuffed, you can move them around to get the expression or impression you want. Sew with a heavy-duty, buttonhole twist or carpet cord or even dental floss. A dab of clear nail polish helps strengthen the threads.

Noses and mouths can be embroidered. In deep pile fur they'd be lost, so you can omit them. Ball buttons or pompoms can be noses, too. Or cut features from felt and sew or glue them on. Experiment and be creative.

The Patterns

All patterns in this book are full size. No reduction or enlargement is necessary to make any animal. However, it has been necessary to cut some of the patterns into smaller segments to fit onto the book pages. (For example, the body of the Aardvark is one piece 30 inches long, and thus had to be cut into several segments. The segments are labeled to show where to join them.) The pieces should be joined so that lines butt together; don't overlap the pattern segments.

To use the patterns in the book, you have the option of cutting the actual patterns from your book or tracing them from the book onto another piece of paper.

SIX PATTERN PIECES
30" (75 cm) LONG

Cutting Diagram

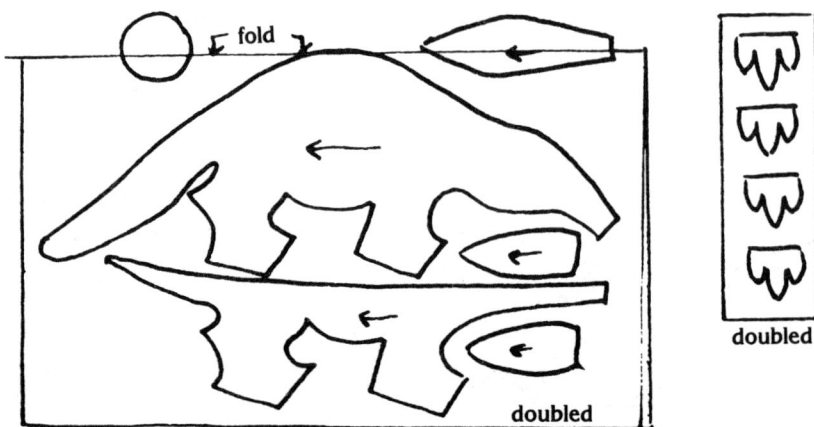

Materials Main fabric: ⅞ yard of 45" material (80 cm of 1 m 15 cm width material)
Felt or vinyl for claws: 6" x 10" piece (15 cm x 25 cm)
Quilt batting or heavy interfacing: 6" x 8" piece (15 cm x 20 cm)
12" (30 cm) satin cord or tubing for tongue (optional)
1 pair safety eyes or 2 buttons or embroidery thread or felt scraps
Felt scraps or embroidery thread for nostrils
1½ lbs. (675 g) of polyester fiberfill for stuffing
4 popsicle sticks or 4 pieces of ¼" (⅗ cm) dowel, 5" (13 cm) long (optional)

1
Aardvark

The aardvark is an African anteater. The word is Dutch for "earth pig." It has scant hair, so the skin shows through; thus, it would be most natural made with a short-napped fabric such as velour, velveteen, or nonwale corduroy, or even a smooth fabric like double-knit (nonstretch). The aardvark has strong claws for ripping open anthills and an extensile tongue to collect the insects. Its large ears are upright, so they should be stiffened.

Cutting Instructions

See the cutting diagram.
Of main fabric, cut two side bodies, two underbodies, four ears (linings may be of same material or contrasting), one head center, and one snout.
Of felt or vinyl, cut eight claws.
Of quilt batt or heavy interfacing, cut two ears.

Sewing Instructions

Use ¼" (⅗ cm) seams unless otherwise instructed.
1. *Claws.* Lay two pieces, wrong sides together, for each claw. Top stitch around, ⅛" (³⁄₁₀ cm) from the edge, leaving straight edge open. Trim close to stitching. Stuff lightly. Set the claws aside. See Figure 1.
2. *Underbody.* Sew the darts in the underbodies and clip at the center of each dart as shown in the pattern and Figure 2. Sew the underbodies to the side bodies from mouth edge to dot A, matching notches 1, 2, and 3, leaving toes open. See Figure 2.
3. *Toes.* Fold the toes on the lines indicated on the pattern so that top and bottom seams meet. Insert the claws in the opening and stitch across through all layers. See Figure 3.

4. *Ears.* Place each ear against ear lining, right sides together, and lay these on the quilt batt or stiffening. Stitch together, leaving the straight edge open. See Figure 4. Trim top, turn right side out. For extra stiffness, top stitch around the edge ⅛" (³⁄₁₀ cm) inside seam line. Fold on center line. Stitch to the side heads between lines shown on the pattern.

5. *Head center.* Sew head center to both side heads, from front edge to dot B, matching notches 4 and 5 and enclosing ear in the seam. See Figure 5. Open the head and lay flat, right side up. Press seams toward side head, and top stitch through all layers close to base of the ears. This will help the ears stand upright. See Figure 6.

6. *Center seams.* Sew center back seam, from dot B to dot A, around tail, matching notches 6 and 7. See Figure 7. Sew center underbody seam from dot A to mouth edge, leaving open between notches 8 and 9 for stuffing. Sew or baste tongue just inside the seam allowance at the mouth edge, at the center underbody seam. See Figure 8.

7. *Snout.* Sew snout into opening, matching top and bottom centers and notches 10. This is easiest if the snout is on the bottom, with the mouth opening spread around with edges meeting. See Figure 9.

8. Clip curves and corners. Turn right side out. If you are using a safety eye, clip a tiny x where indicated on the pattern on each side. Insert the shank of the eyes into the hole, and clamp the washer on inside the head. If you are using buttons, embroidery, or appliqué for eyes, apply them after stuffing.

To support the legs, to keep them from breaking with age, you may want to insert a stick in each. Pad the bottom of the foot well with stuffing. Insert the stick and stuff very firmly all around it so it remains centered and never rubs against the outside fabric.

Stuff the head very firmly, being sure the center head seams are folded toward the side head so ears are upright. Stuff the tail, then the center of the body. Pack it in well, using a chopstick or dowel to push the fiberfill firmly. Sew up center underbody opening.

9. *Finishing.* If you didn't use safety eyes, sew buttons or embroider or use felt appliqué for eyes. Aardvarks have small eyes. Embroider or appliqué felt nostrils on the snout. If the cord you used for a tongue ravels, tie a tight knot at the very end or turn in the ends and stitch.

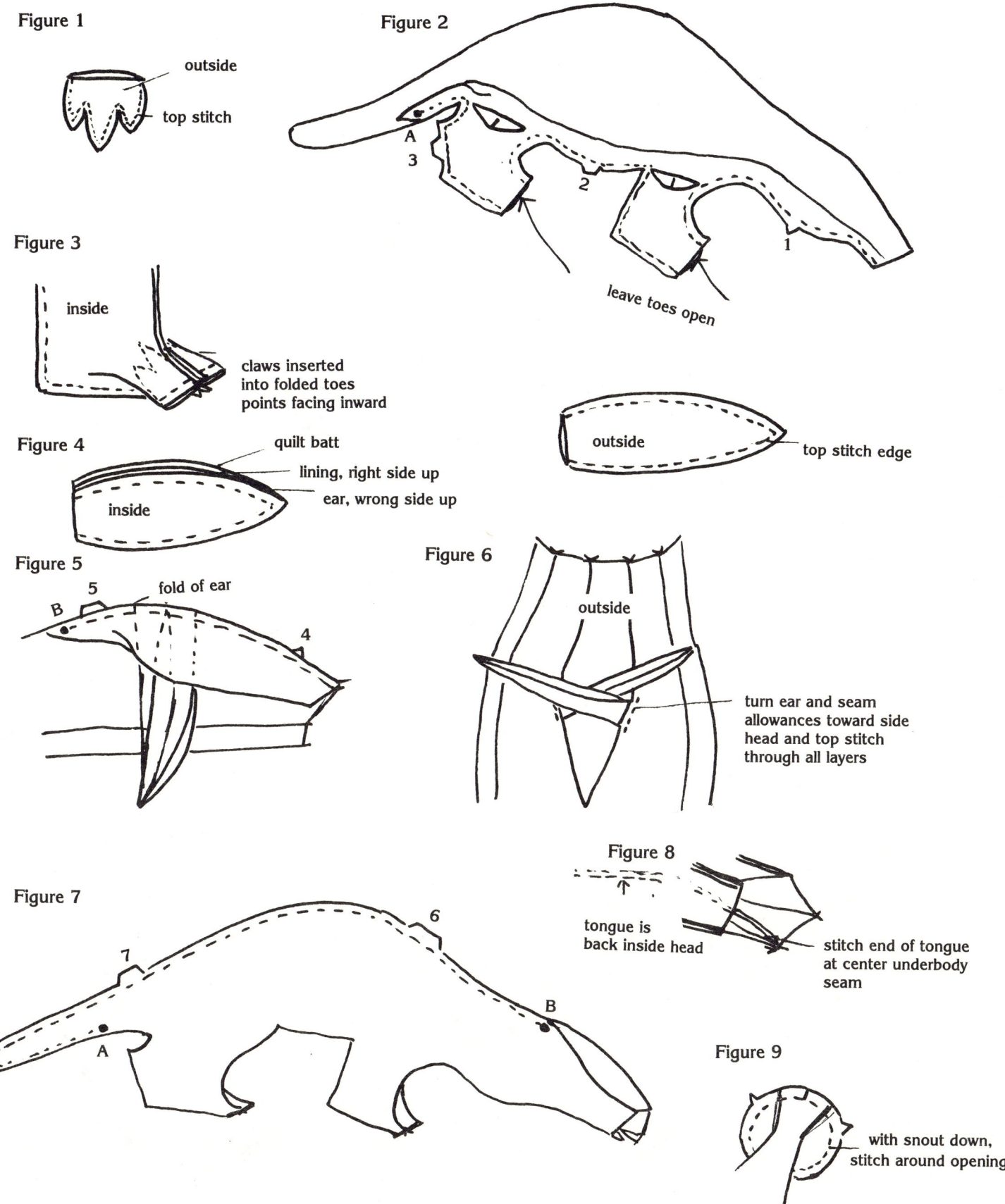

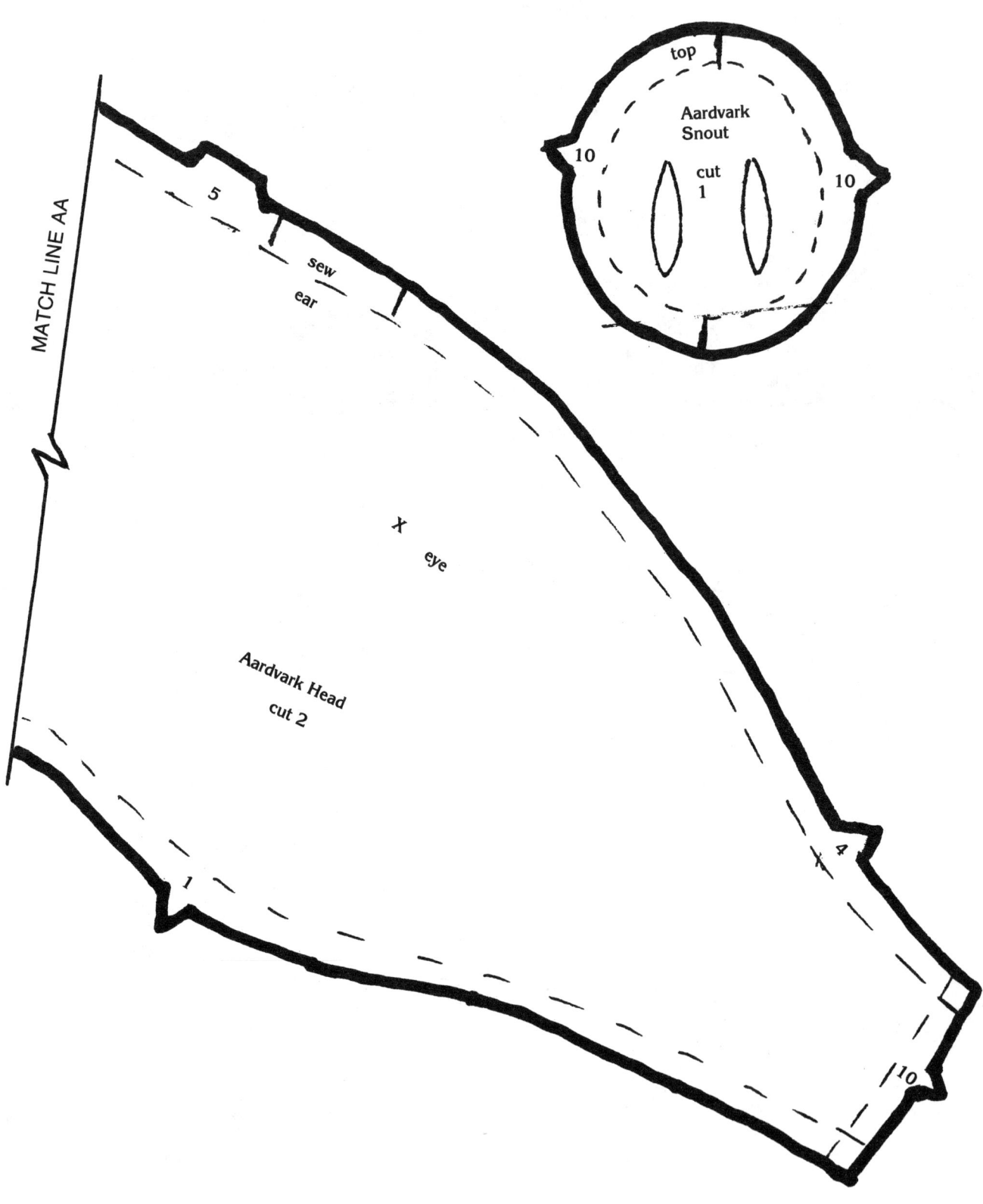

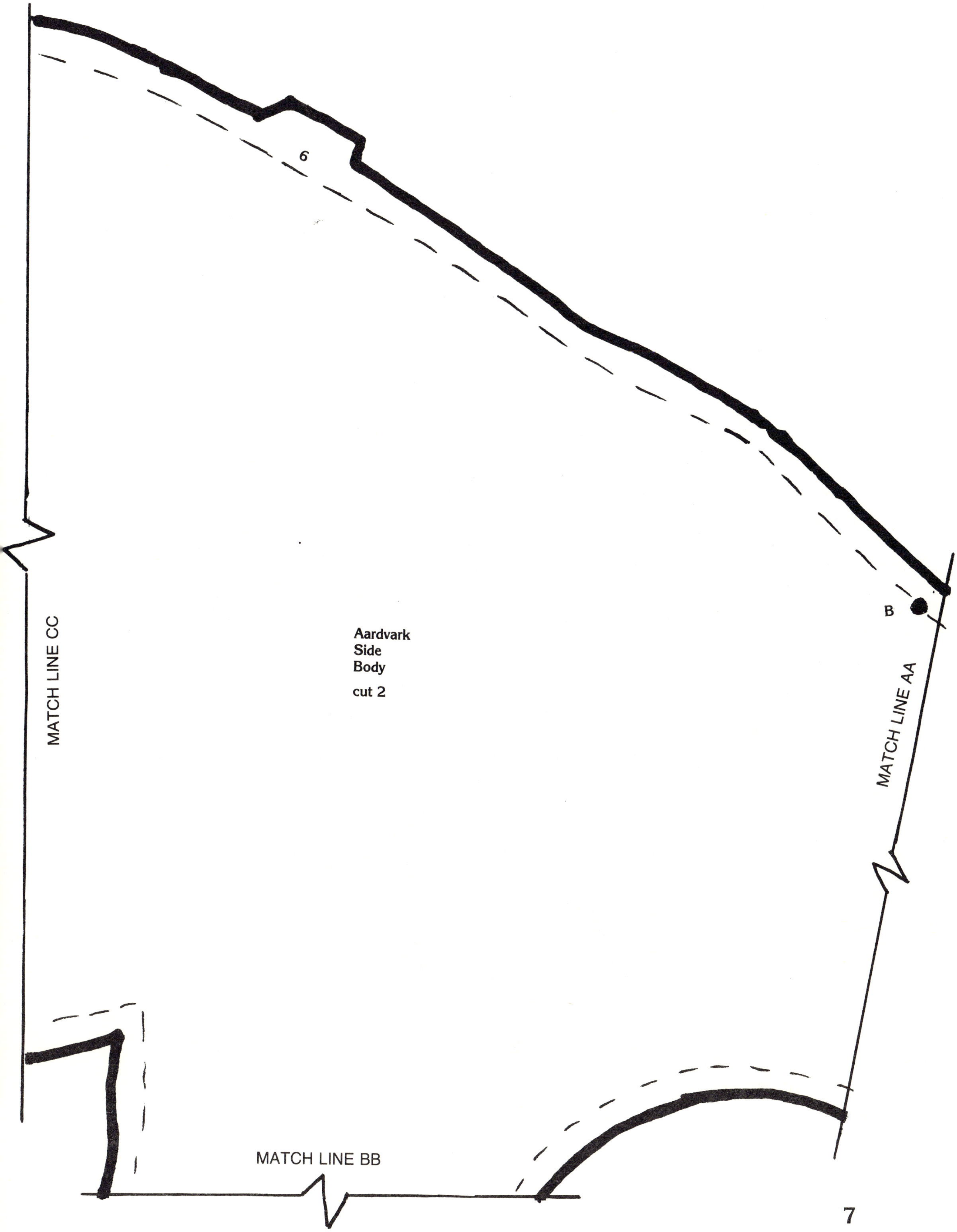

Aardvark
Side
Body

cut 2

MATCH LINE CC

MATCH LINE AA

B

6

MATCH LINE BB

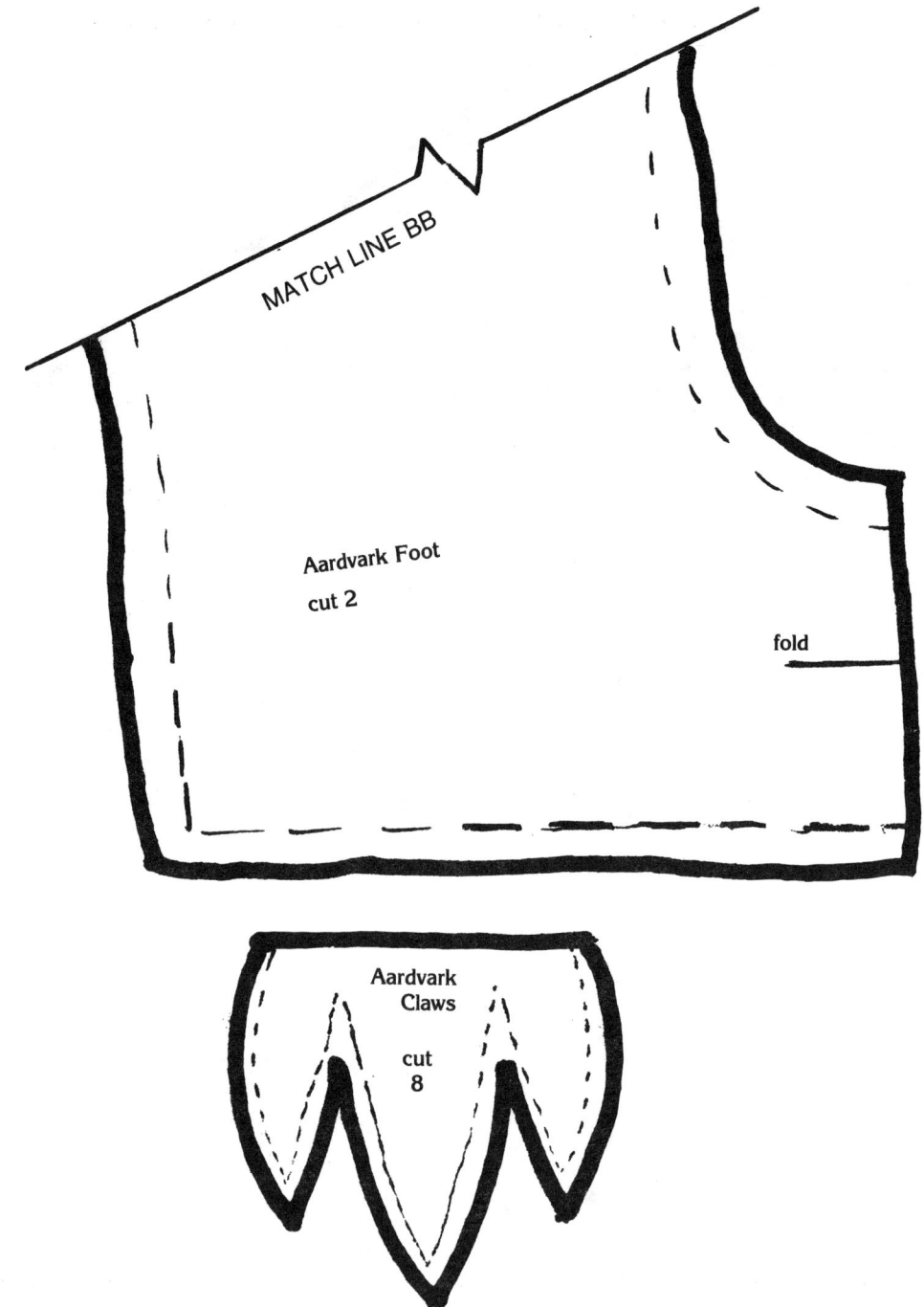

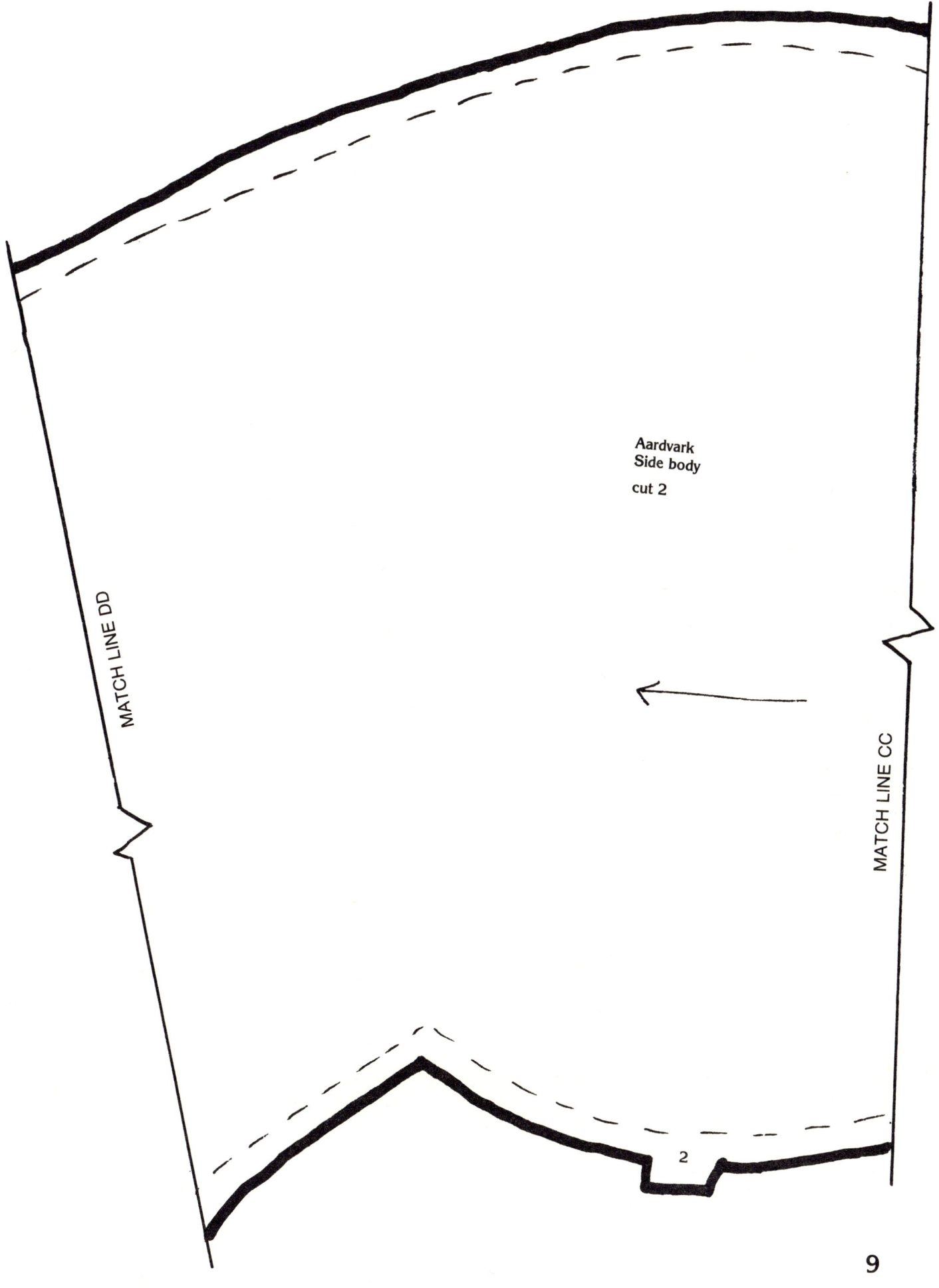

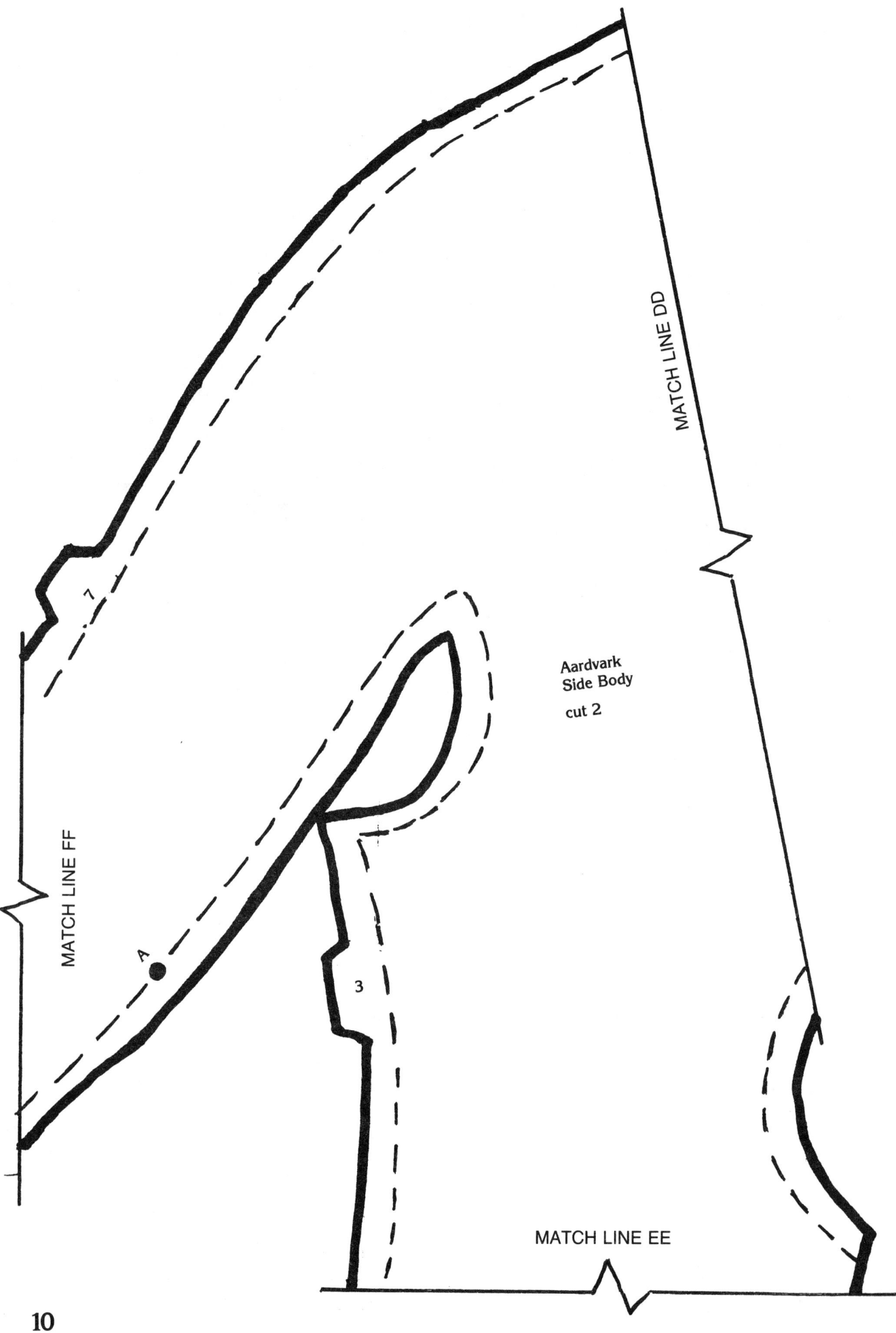

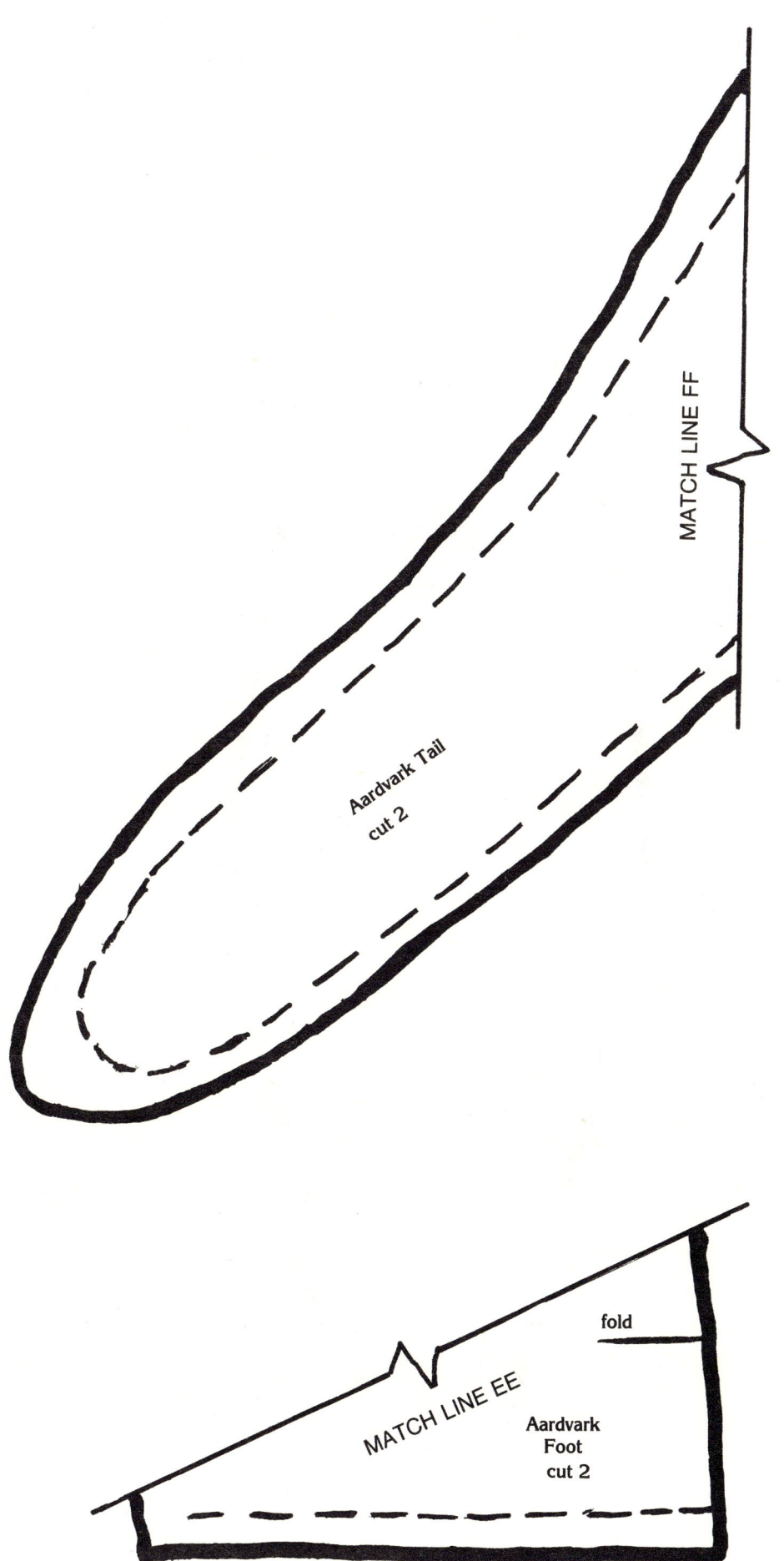

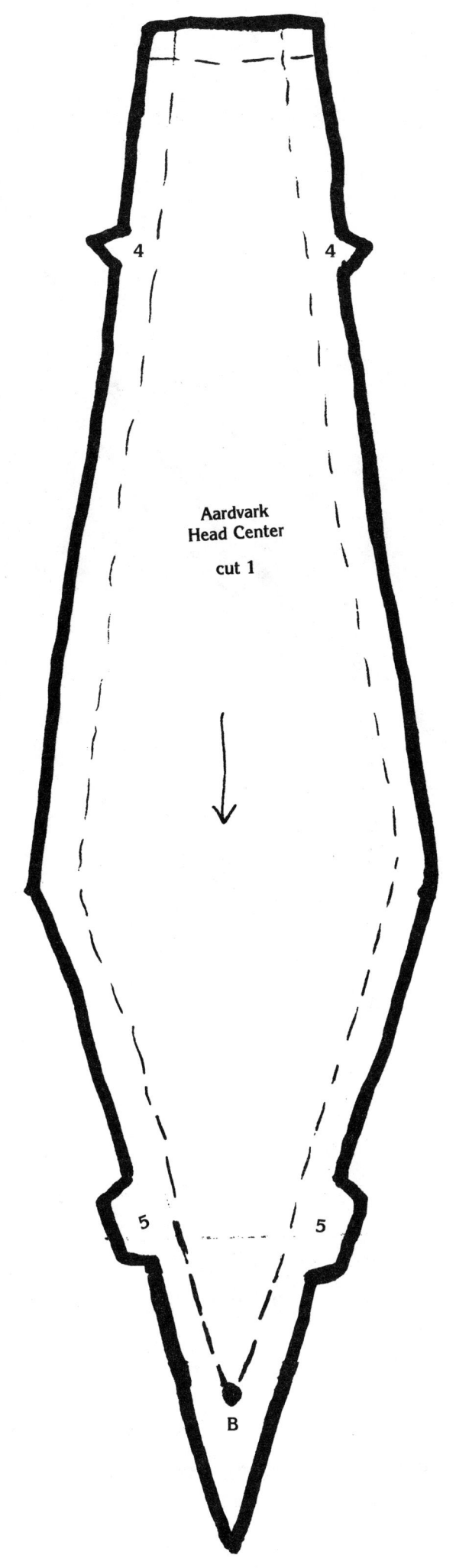

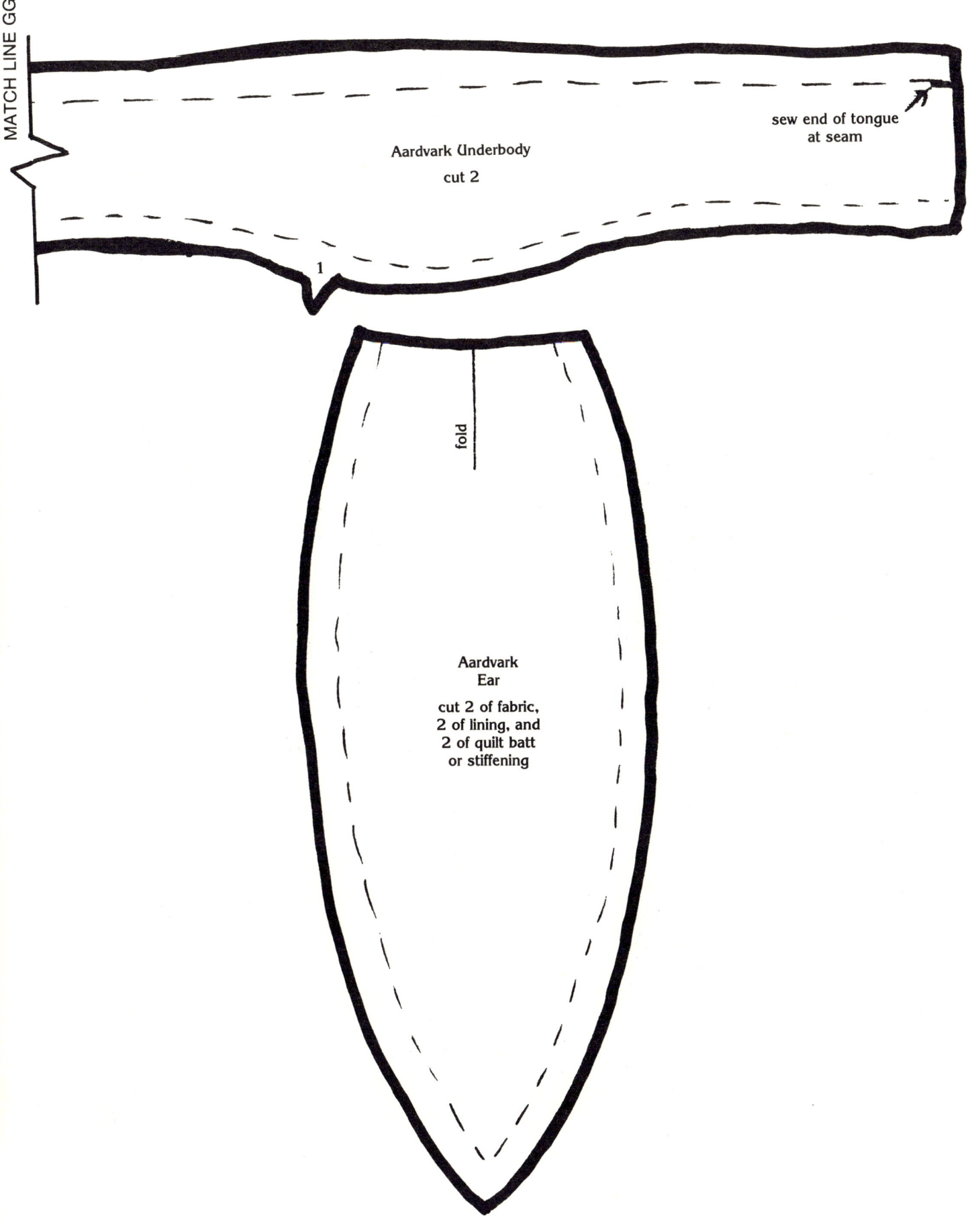

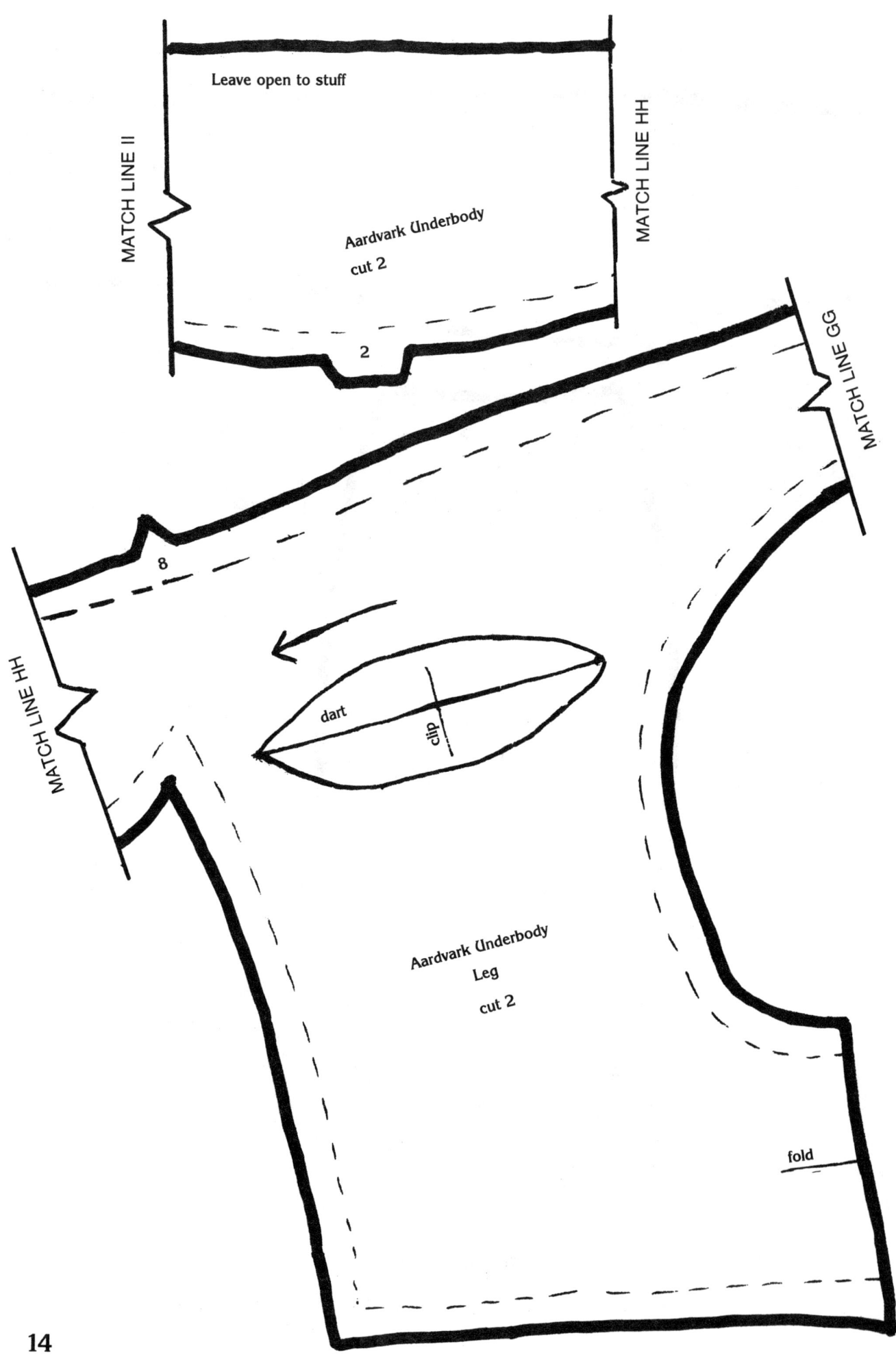

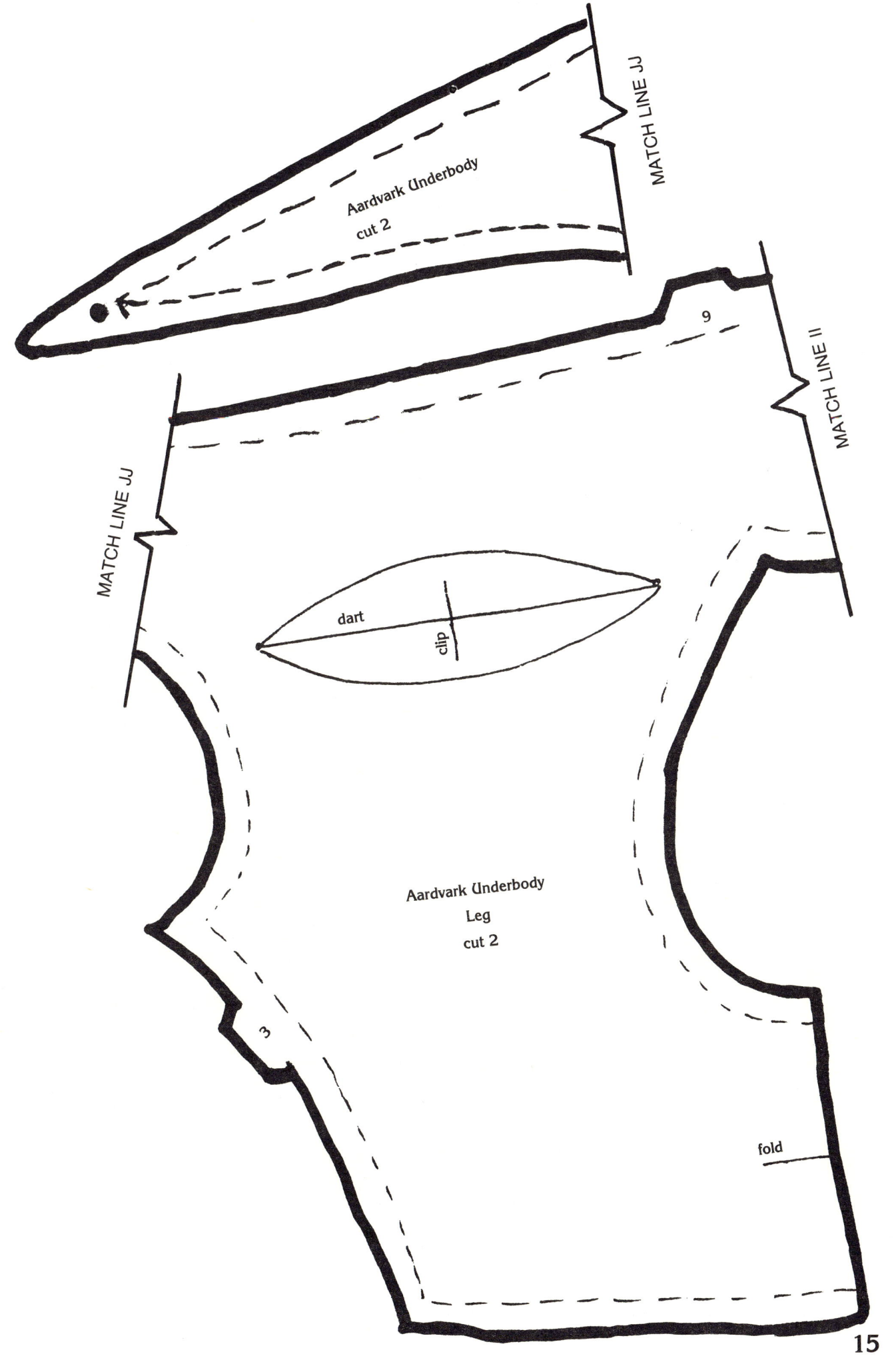

NINE PATTERN PIECES
25" (63 cm) LONG

Cutting Diagram

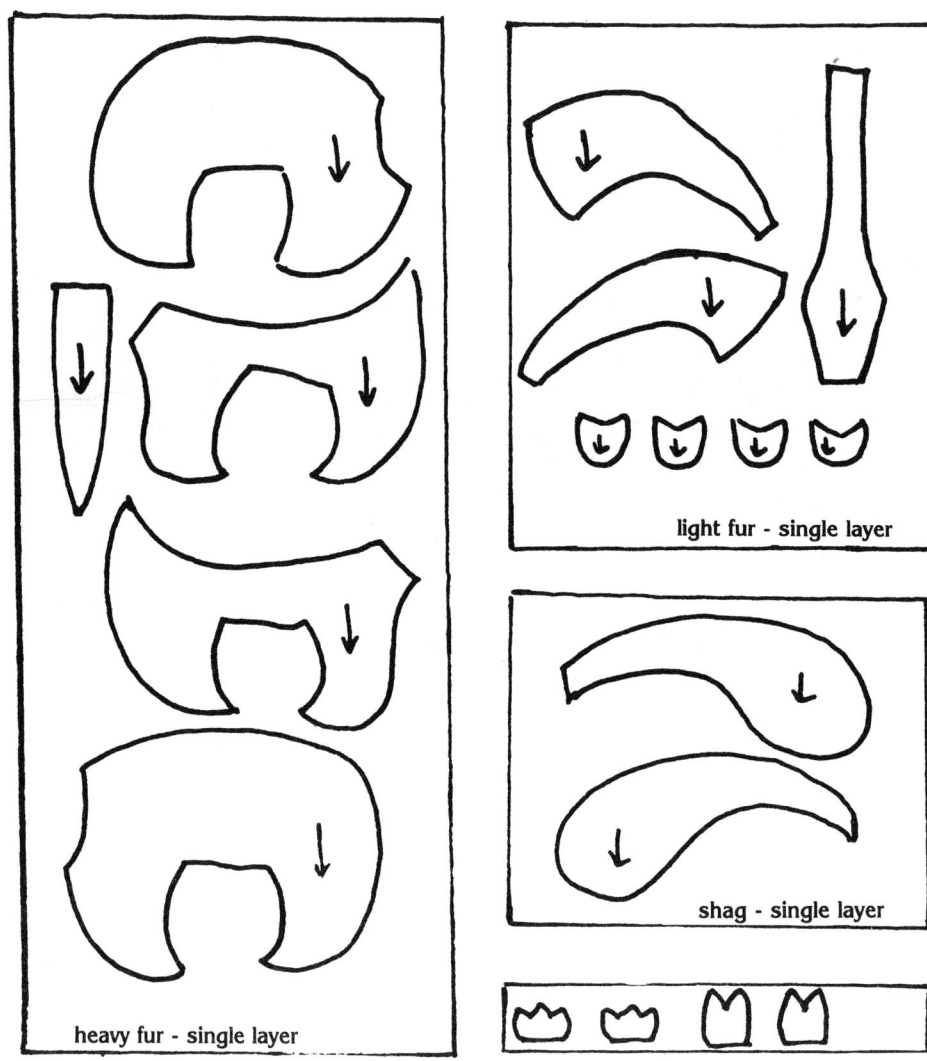

Materials Heavy brown or gray fur fabric: ½ yard of 60" fabric (46 cm of fabric 1m 53 cm width fabric)
Short brown or gray fur fabric: 15" × 15" piece (38 cm × 38 cm)
Dark brown or black shag: 14" × 14" piece (36 cm × 36 cm)
Black vinyl or felt: 5" × 10" piece (13 cm × 25 cm)
Red or pink tubing (vinyl, velvet, satin, etc.): 18" (46 cm) long
1½ lbs. (675 g) polyester fiberfill or other stuffing
1 pair safety eyes or 2 buttons

2
Anteater

There are half a dozen animals in the world called anteaters. This is the shaggy one indigenous to South and Central America, also called the ant bear. These anteaters have powerful front claws that curve backward for ripping open anthills, and a long, sticky tongue for mopping up the ants.

Cutting Instructions

See the Introduction for working with fur fabrics.

Of long brown or gray fur, cut one center tail, two side bodies, and two underbodies.

Of short brown or gray fur, cut two side heads, one center head, and four ears.

Of dark shag, cut two side tails.

Of black vinyl or felt, cut four front claws and four back claws.

Cut tongue of red or pink cord, 18" (46 cm).

If the fur is quite thick and you cannot find short fur to go with it, you can give the fur fabric a crewcut by clipping the fur with scissors close to the backing. Do not clip so closely that the backing shows. Clip the fur on the two side heads, one center head, and four ear pieces.

Sewing Instructions

Use ¼" (⅗ cm) seam unless otherwise specified.

1. *Head.* Sew ears to ear linings, leaving notched edges open. Clip as shown on pattern. Turn ears right side out. Matching notches 1 and 2, turning corner at clip, sew ears to right side of side heads. See Figure

1. Sew side heads to center head, matching notches 2 and 3. If using safety eyes, cut a tiny x (in backing only) where indicated on pattern. Push the shank of the eye through the hole from the right side and clamp the washer on tightly inside. (If using buttons for eyes, sew them on after the animal is stuffed.) See Figure 2.

Turn one end of tongue and hand sew or knot and trim. Sew tongue to head center at center front. See Figure 2. Sew underhead seam, matching notches 4. With strong thread, make a running stitch around the mouth opening and gather tightly to close. Make sure tongue is facing inside before closing. Clip curves, turn head right side out. Set aside.

2. *Claws.* Make darts in two of the foreclaw pieces only. Clip darts in center. Top stitch ⅛" each (³⁄₁₀ cm) darted foreclaw to an undarted foreclaw, wrong sides together, leaving back edge open. Stuff lightly. Top stitch back claws, wrong sides together, leaving back edge open. Stuff lightly. Set aside. See Figure 3.

3. *Feet.* Stitch darts in underbodies. Clip center of each dart. Sew underbodies to side bodies at front and back seams (from A around bottom of foot and from B around bottom of foot). See Figure 4. Open flat, right sides up, and sew claws across seam at bottom of foot. (On foreclaws, side without dart is down, facing the right side of fur.) See Figure 5.

Keeping claws turned inward, stitch underbodies to side bodies between legs, from dots C to D. See Figure 6. Fold openings so seams at C and C match up with seam of foot, and stitch across opening, through all layers, including claws. See Figure 7. (If this is too thick for your sewing machine, sew the opening closed by hand, using strong thread.)

4. *Tail.* Sew center tail to side tails as far as dot E, matching notches 5. Sew under center seam of tail, matching notches 6 and leaving open between small dots for stuffing. Clip curves, turn right side out. Stitch between marks to one side body. See Figure 8.

5. *Body.* Stitch side bodies together along center back seam, from neck to dot B, enclosing tail.

Stitch center underbody seam from neck to dot B, leaving open between notches 7 and 8 for stuffing.

Sew head into neck opening, matching centers and notches 1 (on ears) and 9. Seams will not match.

6. Clip curves, turn right side out. Stuff firmly. Use a dowel or chopstick to push stuffing into far places. Begin with areas farthest from the opening, using small pieces of stuffing for small areas. Pack it in firmly as you go; you cannot push from the center later. Stuff tail tip firmly, rest of tail more lightly.

Sew up underbody and under tail openings, using ladder stitch. Go over seams to pull out pile, using a stout needle. Sew buttons on for eyes if you did not use safety eyes.

Figure 1

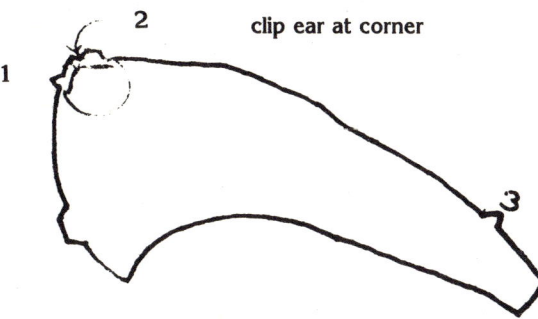

clip ear at corner

Figure 2

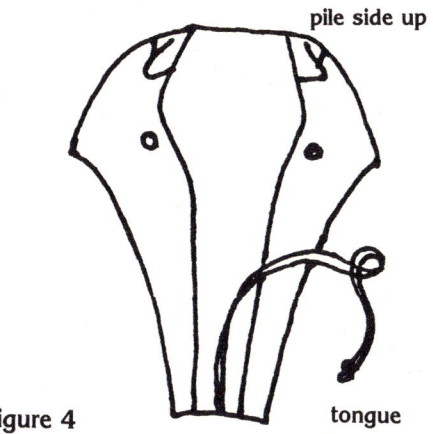

pile side up

Figure 3

top stitch ⅛" (³/₁₀ cm)

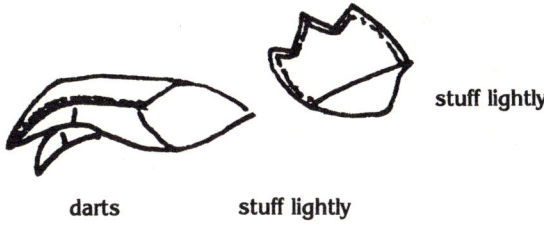

darts   stuff lightly   stuff lightly

Figure 4

tongue

Figure 5

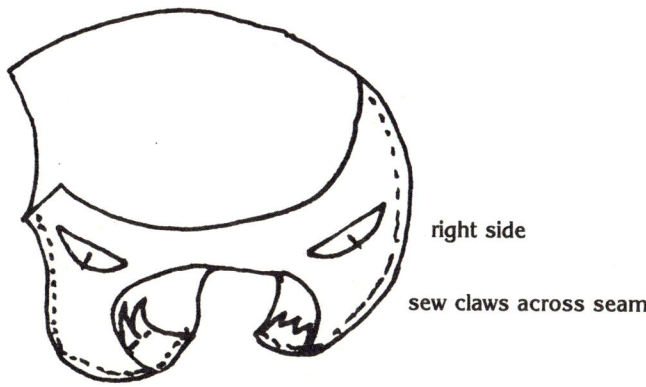

right side

sew claws across seam

Figure 6

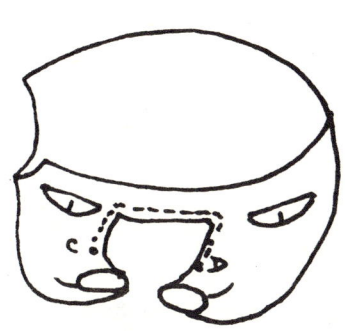

Figure 7

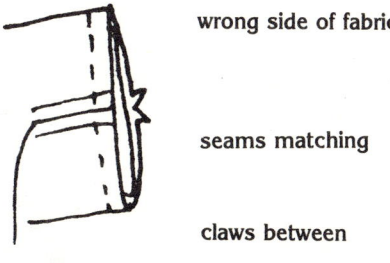

wrong side of fabric

seams matching

claws between

Figure 8

right side of fabric

tail right side out

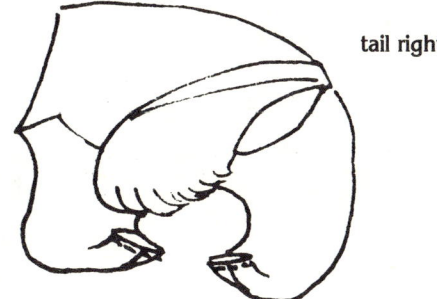

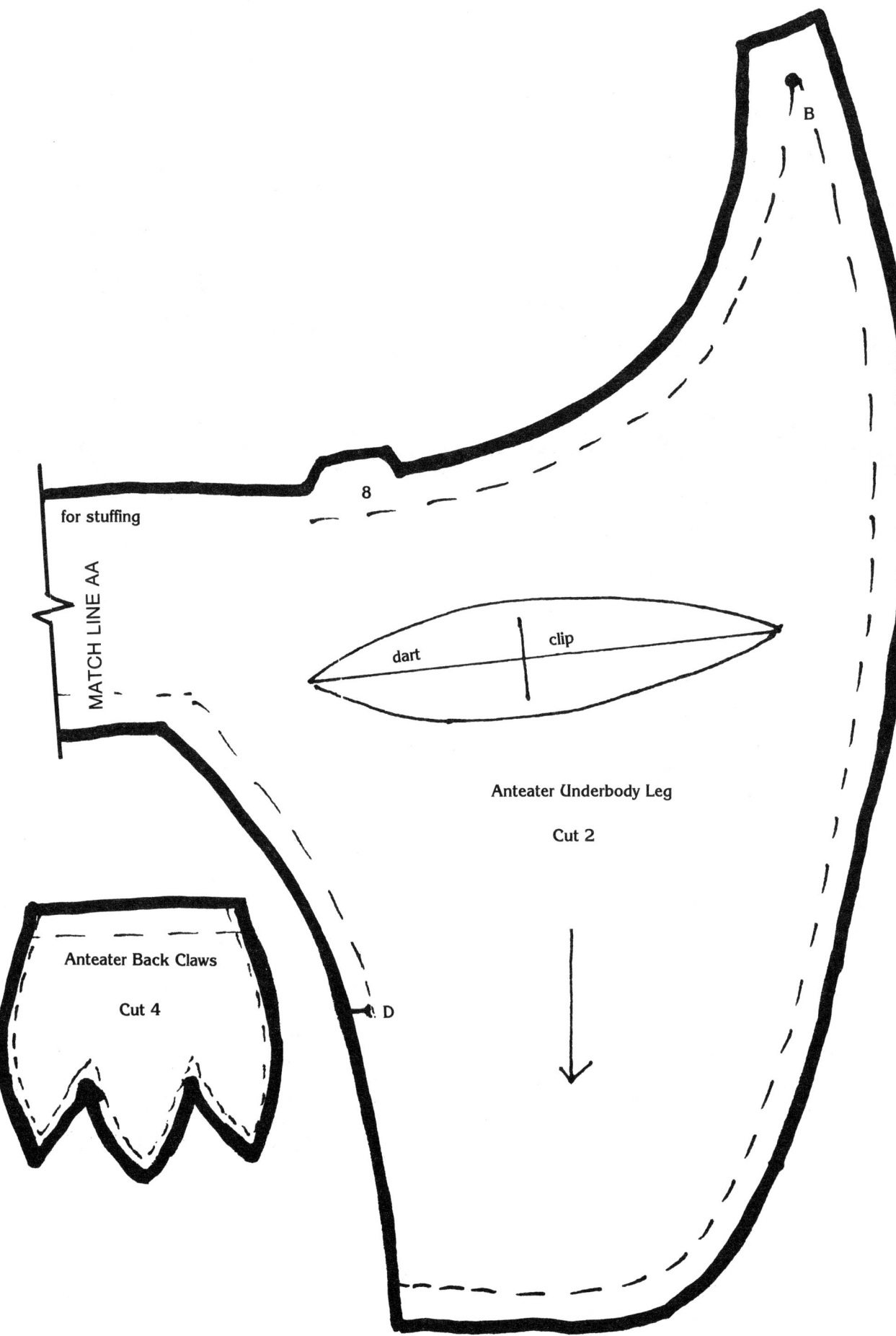

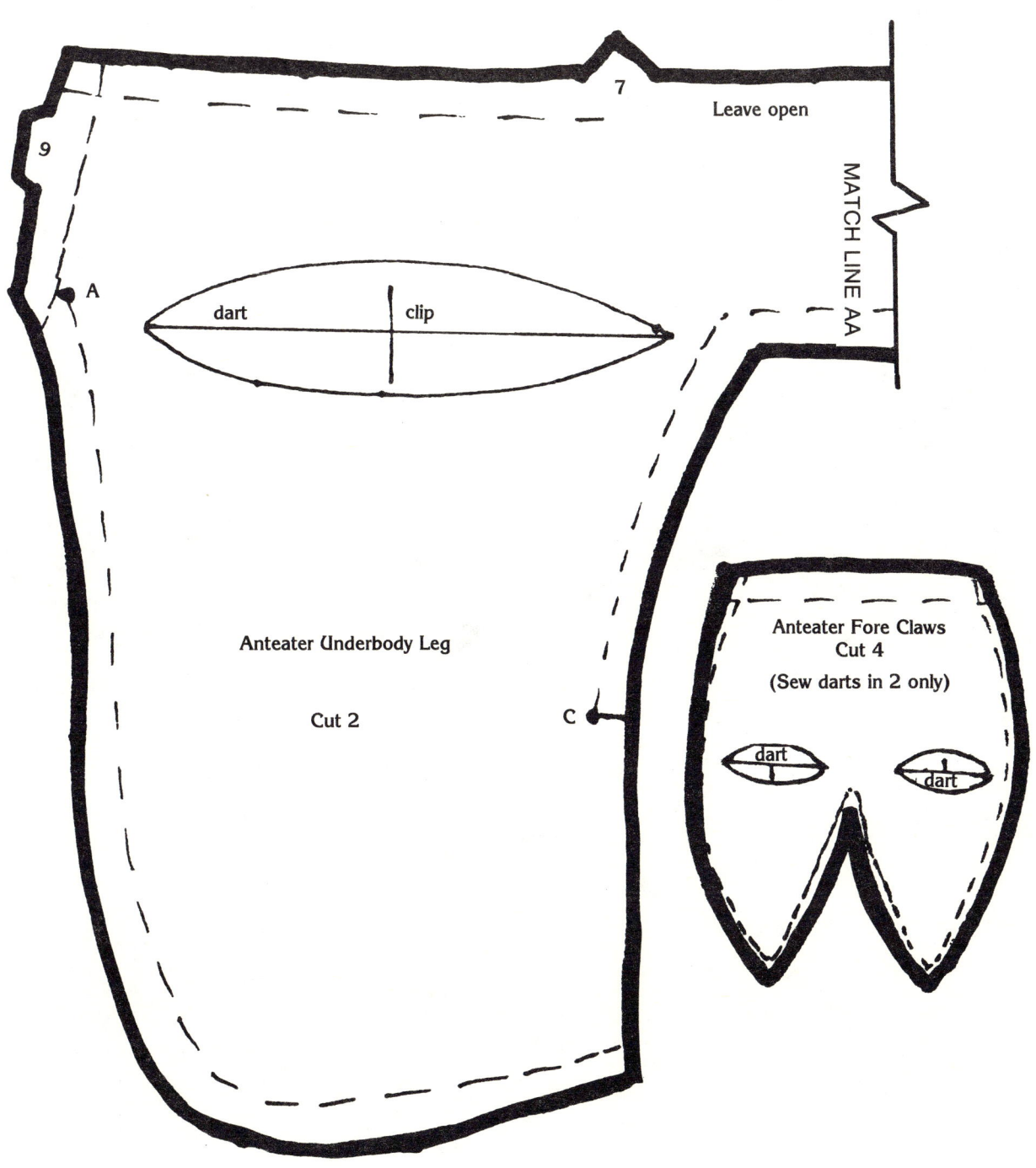

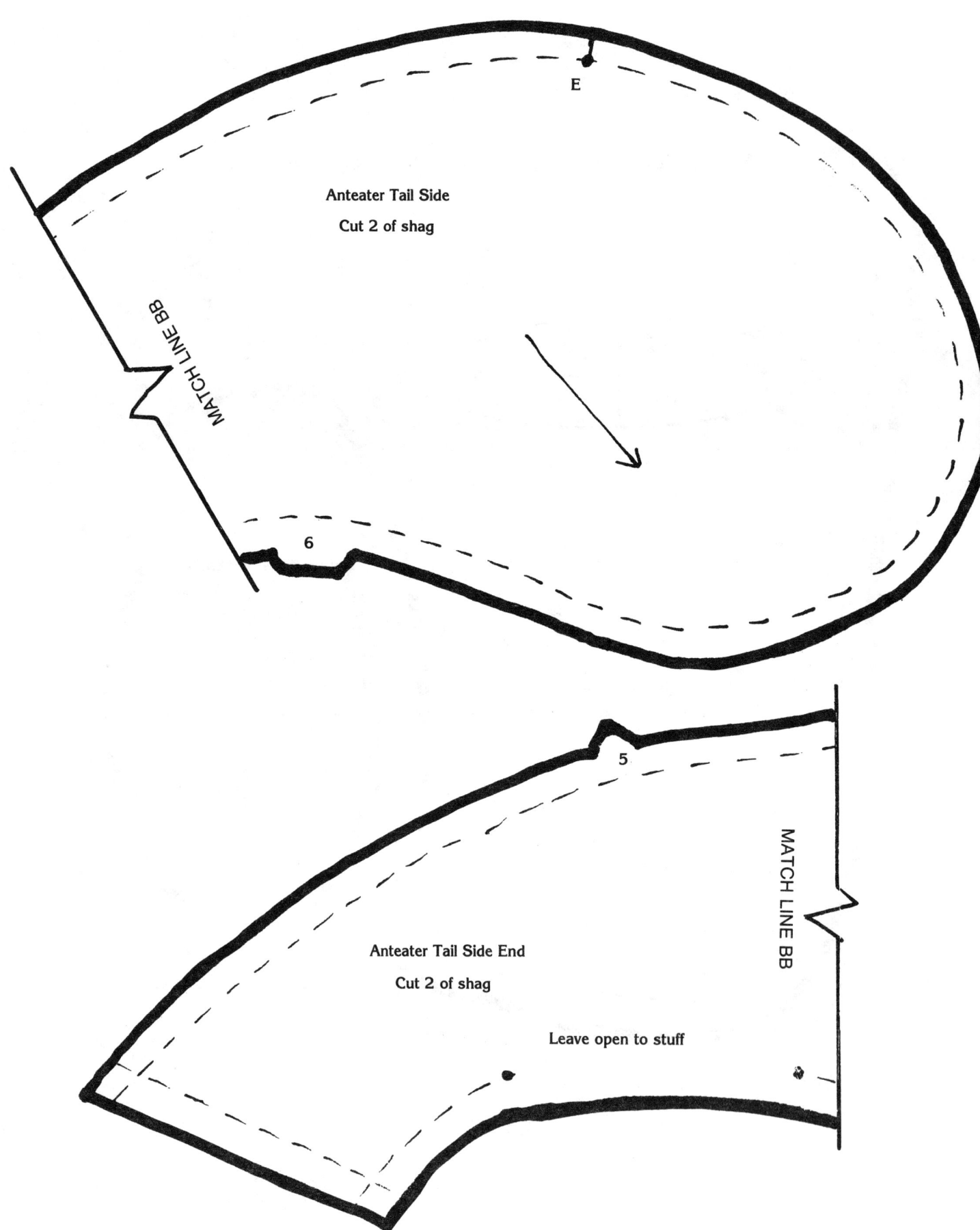

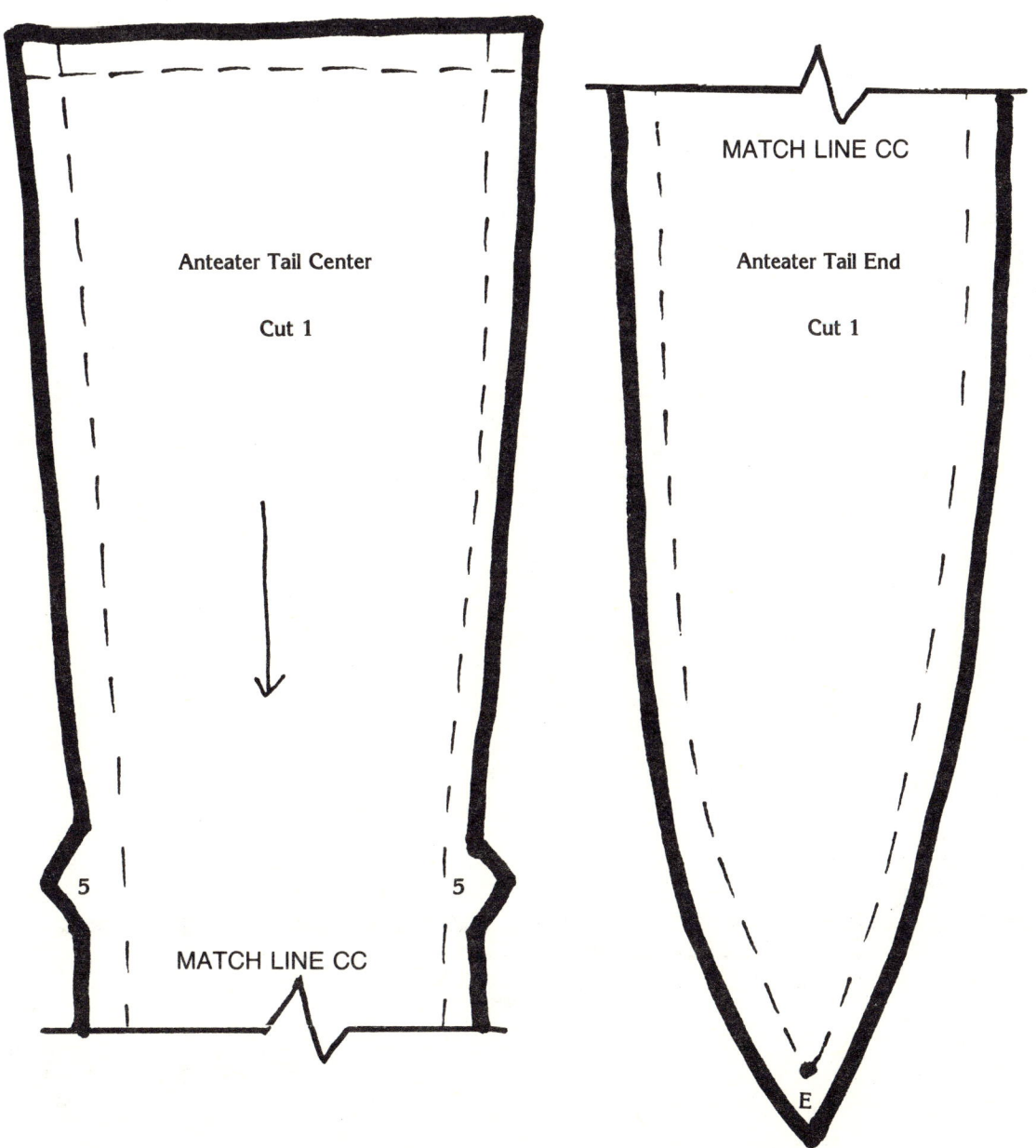

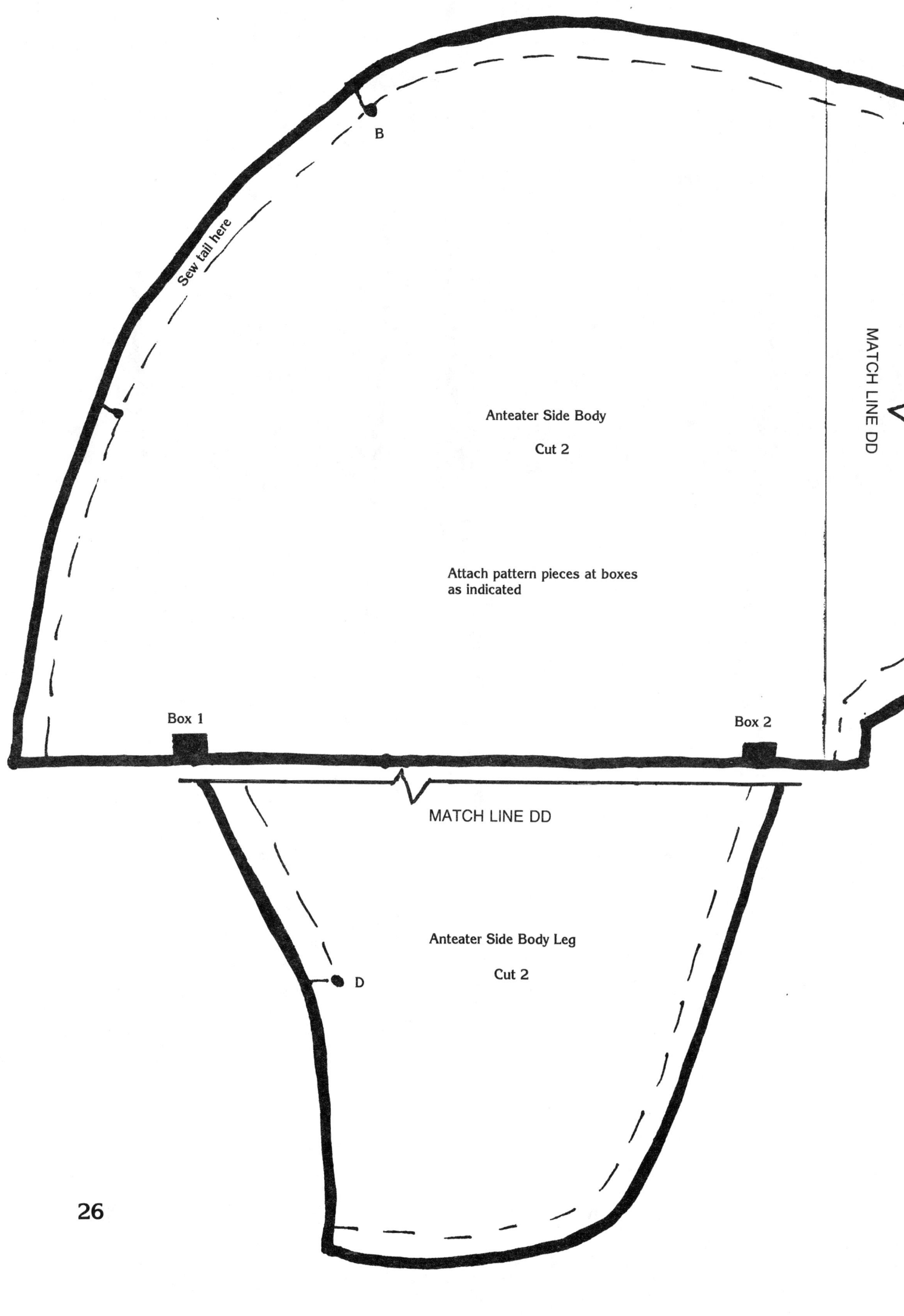

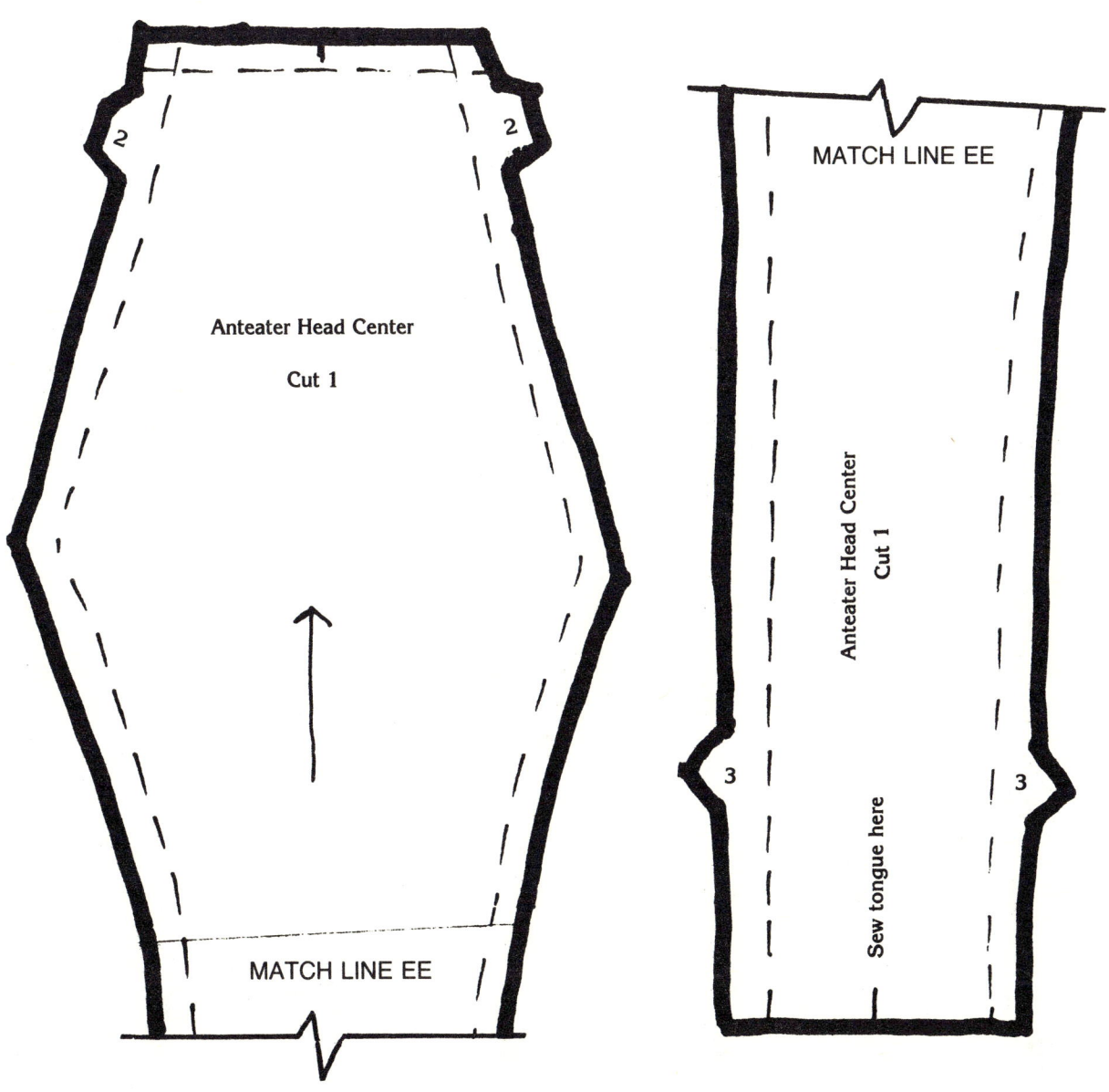

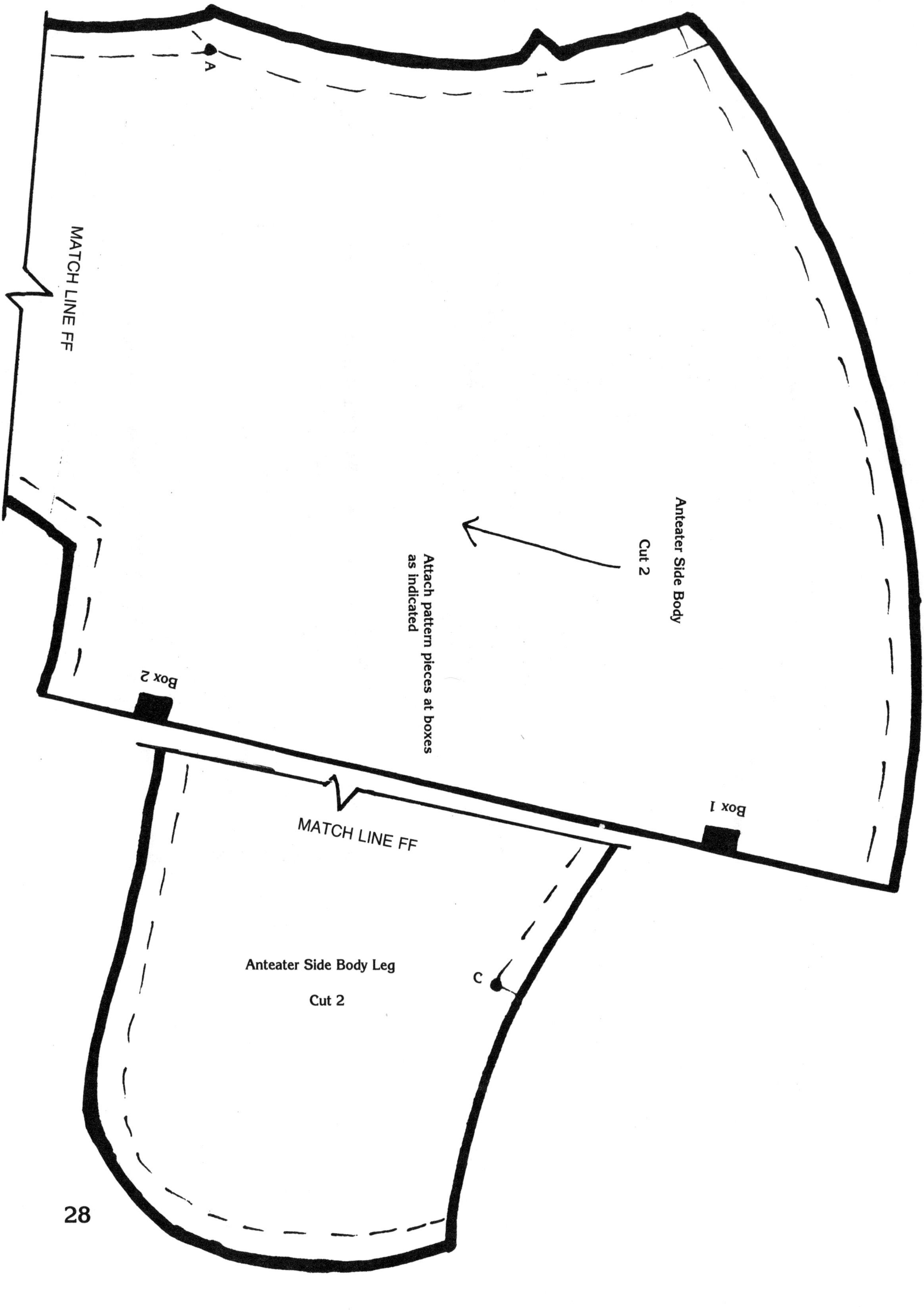

MATCH LINE FF

Anteater Side Body

Cut 2

Attach pattern pieces at boxes as indicated

Box 2

Box 1

MATCH LINE FF

Anteater Side Body Leg

Cut 2

28

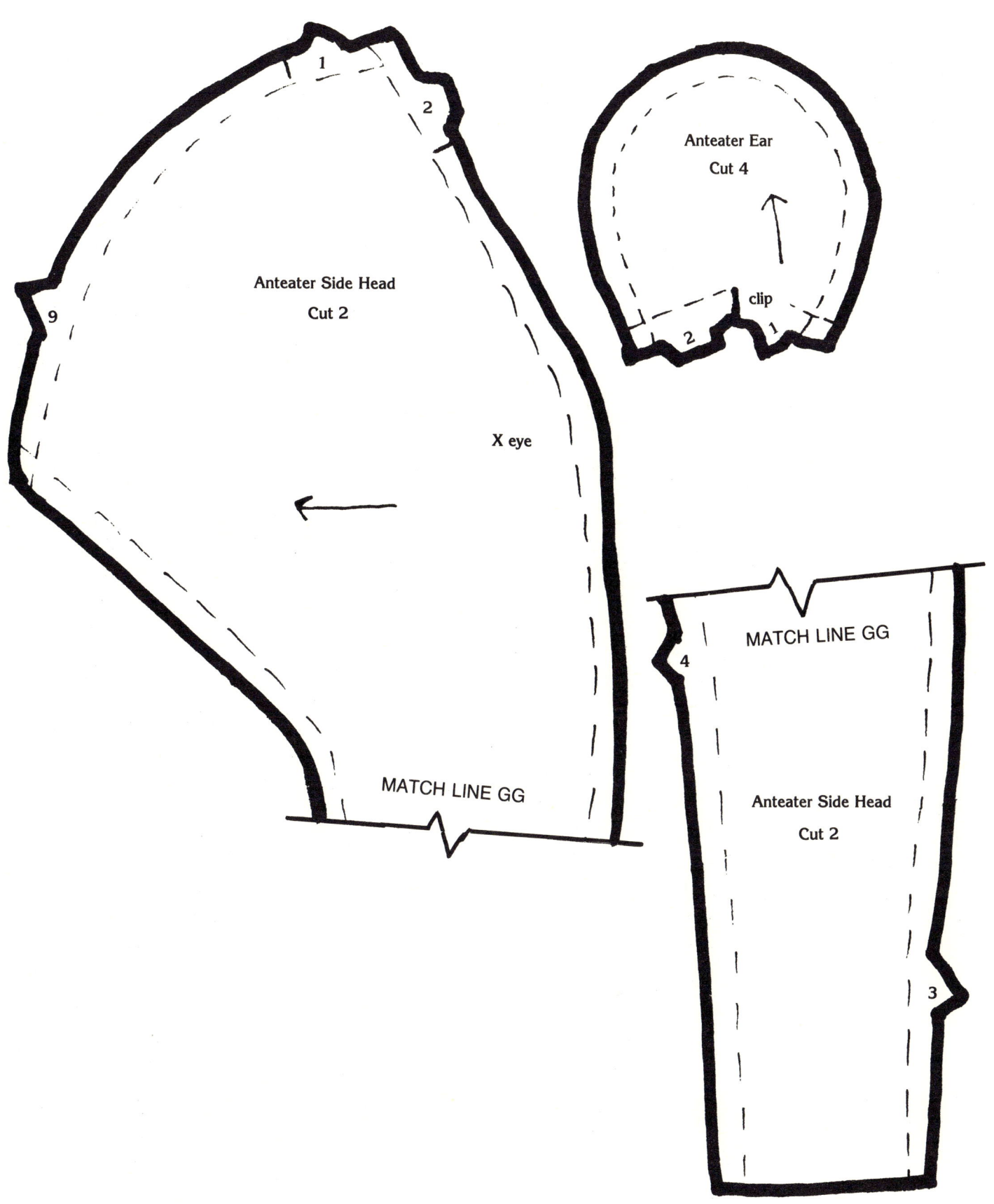

FOURTEEN PATTERN PIECES
LARGE 12" (30 cm) TALL
SMALL 7½" (19 cm) TALL

Cutting Diagram

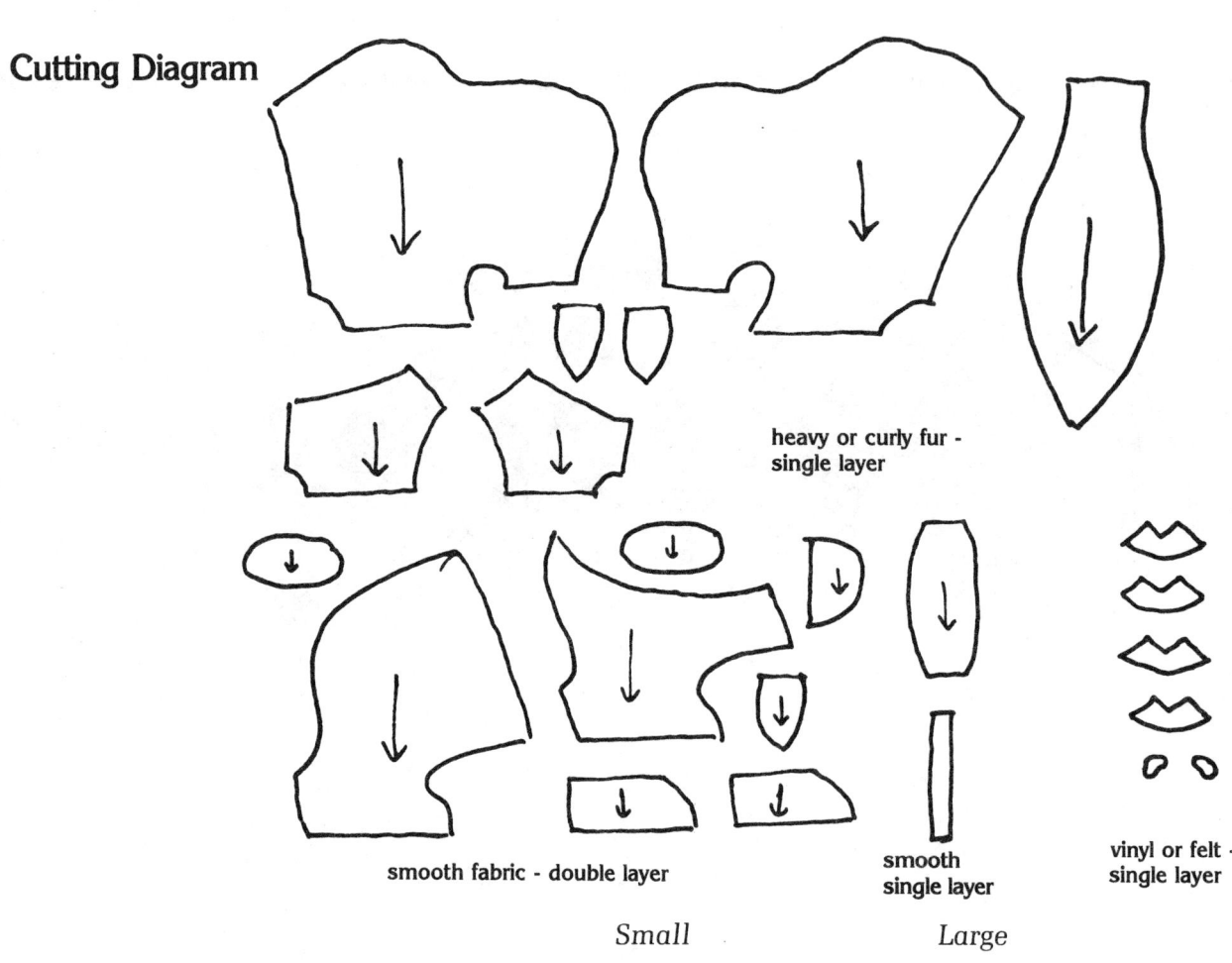

heavy or curly fur - single layer

smooth fabric - double layer

smooth single layer

vinyl or felt - single layer

		Small	Large
Materials	Dark brown or curly fur fabric or heavy fur:	⅓ yard of 60" (⅓ m of 1 m 15 cm width fabric)	½ yard of 60" (½ m of 1½ m 15 cm width fabric)
	Brown velour, corduroy, or thin fur:	¼ yard of 36" (23 cm of 1 m width fabric)	½ yard of 36" (½ m of 1 m width fabric)
	White vinyl or felt:	3" x 4½" piece (8 cm x 11 cm)	5" x 8" piece (13 cm x 20 cm)
	Black vinyl or felt:	1½" x 4" piece (4 cm x 10 cm)	3" x 8" piece (8 cm x 20 cm)
	1 pair safety eyes or 2 buttons		
	Polyester fiberfill:	⅔ lb. (300 g)	2 lbs. (1 kg)
	4 popsicle sticks or ¼" (⅗ cm) doweling		

3
Bison

If you can possibly find it, this bison should be made with dark brown, curly fur fabric (like lamb's wool or fleece) on the head and shoulders and short-nap fabric like velour or nonwale corduroy for the rest of the body. Terrycloth is a possibility. In any case, the fabric for the front should be thicker than that for the back of the animal. Vinyl makes more authentic-looking horns and hooves and is washable, but felt is easier to sew.

Cutting Instructions

See the Introduction for working with fur fabrics.

Of heavy or curly fur fabric, cut two side fronts, two front underbodies, one head center, and two ears.

Of velour or corduroy, cut two ear linings, one center muzzle, two side muzzles, two side backs, four front feet, two back underbodies, one tail, and four soles of feet.

Of white vinyl or felt, cut four horns.

Of black vinyl or felt, cut four hooves and two nostrils.

Sewing Instructions

Use ¼" (⅗ cm) seams throughout unless otherwise stated.

1. *Ears and horns.* Stitch ear facings to ears, right sides together, leaving open at base. Turn right side out. Fold on line.

Lay horns on either side of head slit (see Figure 1) in side front, right sides together. Stitch horns between dots and folded ear just below horn. Fold along slit, right sides together, and stitch dart from top to point, enclosing horns and ears, leaving unstitched between dots (where horns are sewn, to allow stuffing horns from inside). See Figure 2. Repeat for other side of head. With white thread, top stitch horns close to edge, wrong sides together.

2. *Assembling body pieces.* Sew side fronts to side backs, matching notches 1, easing front to fit back. Sew front foot to side front, matching notches 2.

Sew underbody front to underbody back, matching notches 3. Sew front foot to underbody front, as on front side. See Figure 3. Stitch darts in underbody. Clip across center of dart, as indicated on pattern.

3. *Hooves.* The hooves may be stitched on by machine now or hand-sewn on after the bison is stuffed.

To machine stitch: Sew underbody and side body together along front of foot, from dot to bottom. See Figure 4. Clip, open seam flat, and lay right side up. With black thread, top stitch hoof across seam. See Figure 5. Clip curve under neck of side front, as indicated on pattern. Finish sewing underbody to side body, from neck to dot A, leaving bottoms of feet open. See Figure 6. Repeat for other side.

To hand sew hooves later: Just sew entire underbody seam to side body, from neck to dot A, leaving bottoms of feet open.

4. *Soles of feet.* Clip along bottoms of feet, as shown on pattern and in Figure 7. Matching centers, pin sole of foot into bottom opening, spreading clips to make Vs so edges match. See Figure 8. With sole down, stitch around foot just above clips. Repeat for other three feet.

5. *Head center.* Stitch dart in head center and clip at center of dart, as shown on pattern. Sew head center to head sides, from front to dot B, matching notch 4.

6. *Body.* Fold edges of long side of tail to center, fold again on center. Top stitch along edge. Sew small tuft of curly fur to tip. See Figure 9. Baste to side body just above dot A. Sew center back seam from dot A to dot B catching in the tail.

Sew center underbody seam from dot A to front edge, leaving open between notches 5 and 6 for stuffing.

7. *Muzzle.* Nostrils may be machine sewn now or sewn on by hand after stuffing. To sew on by machine, top stitch right side up on side muzzles where indicated in pattern.

Clip muzzle center along long sides, inside seam allowance. Pin to side muzzles, matching notches 7, spreading clips to Vs so edges match. Stitch. Turn right side out. Sew muzzle into front of head, matching centers. (Seams will *not* match.)

8. Clip curves, turn bison right side out. If using safety eyes, cut small xs where shown on pattern. Insert shank of eyes from right side and push washers on tightly inside the head. Stuff, starting with horns. Use small wads of stuffing for the tips and a knitting needle or tapestry needle to push it firmly into tips. Stuff head well, then legs. You may want to put a popsicle stick in each leg to keep them from breaking with age. Stuff bottom of foot, and stuff firmly all around the stick so it doesn't stick out or rub against fabric. Use a dowel or chopstick to press wads of stuffing in. Finish stuffing body and sew up opening.

If you left the hooves and nostrils till now, hand sew them to outside in the proper places. Sew buttons on for eyes, if you didn't use the safety eyes.

Figure 1

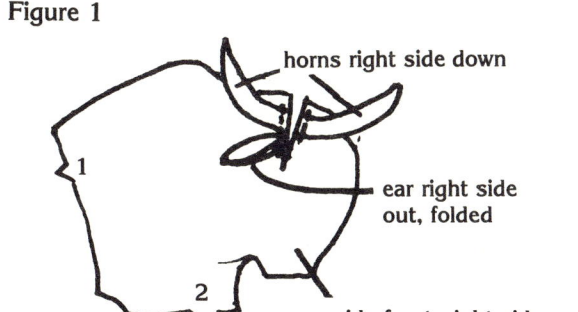

horns right side down

ear right side out, folded

side front, right side up

Figure 2

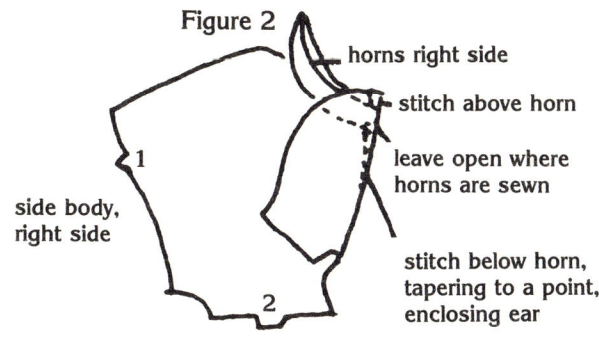

horns right side

stitch above horn

leave open where horns are sewn

side body, right side

stitch below horn, tapering to a point, enclosing ear

Figure 3

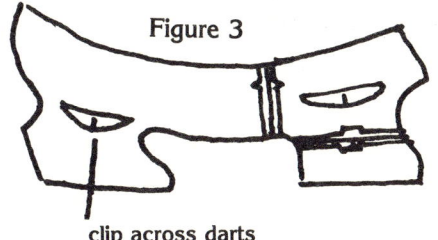

clip across darts

Figure 4

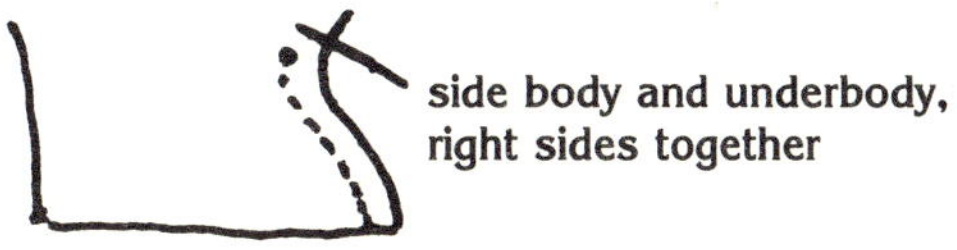

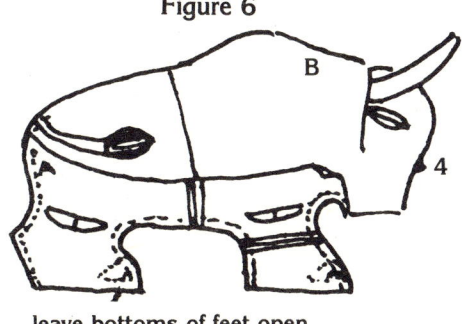

side body and underbody, right sides together

Figure 5

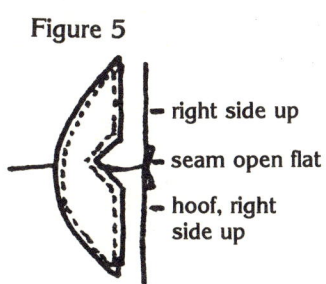

right side up

seam open flat

hoof, right side up

Figure 6

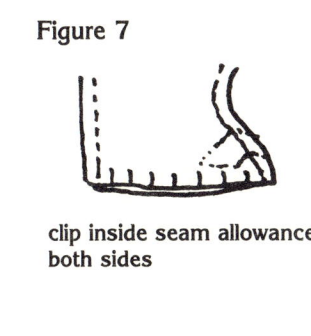

leave bottoms of feet open

Figure 7

clip inside seam allowance, both sides

Figure 8

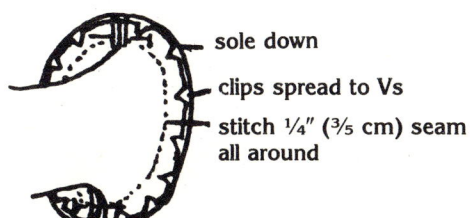

sole down

clips spread to Vs

stitch ¼" (⅗ cm) seam all around

Figure 9

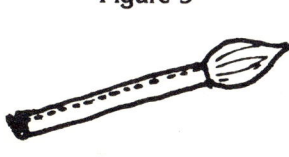

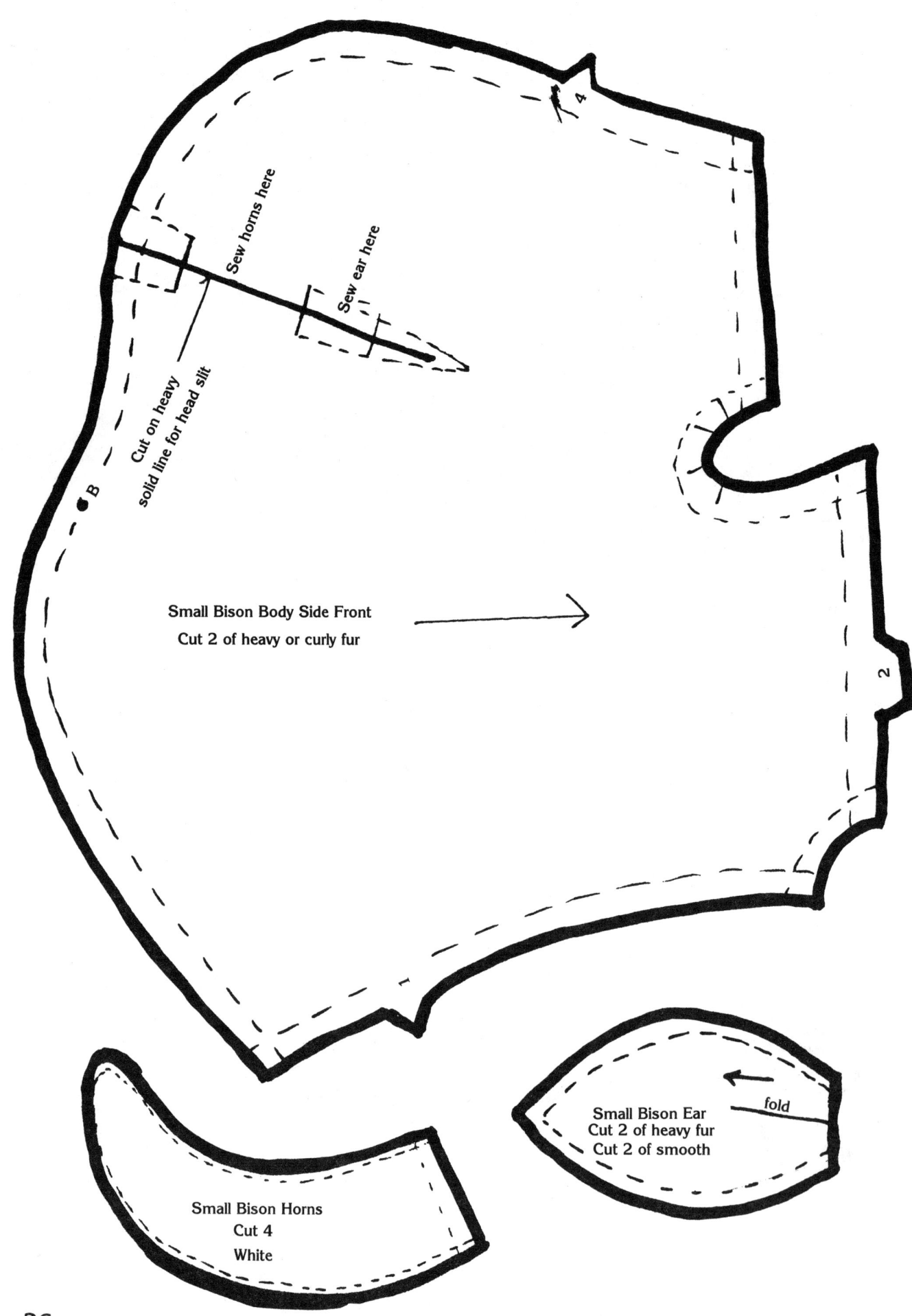

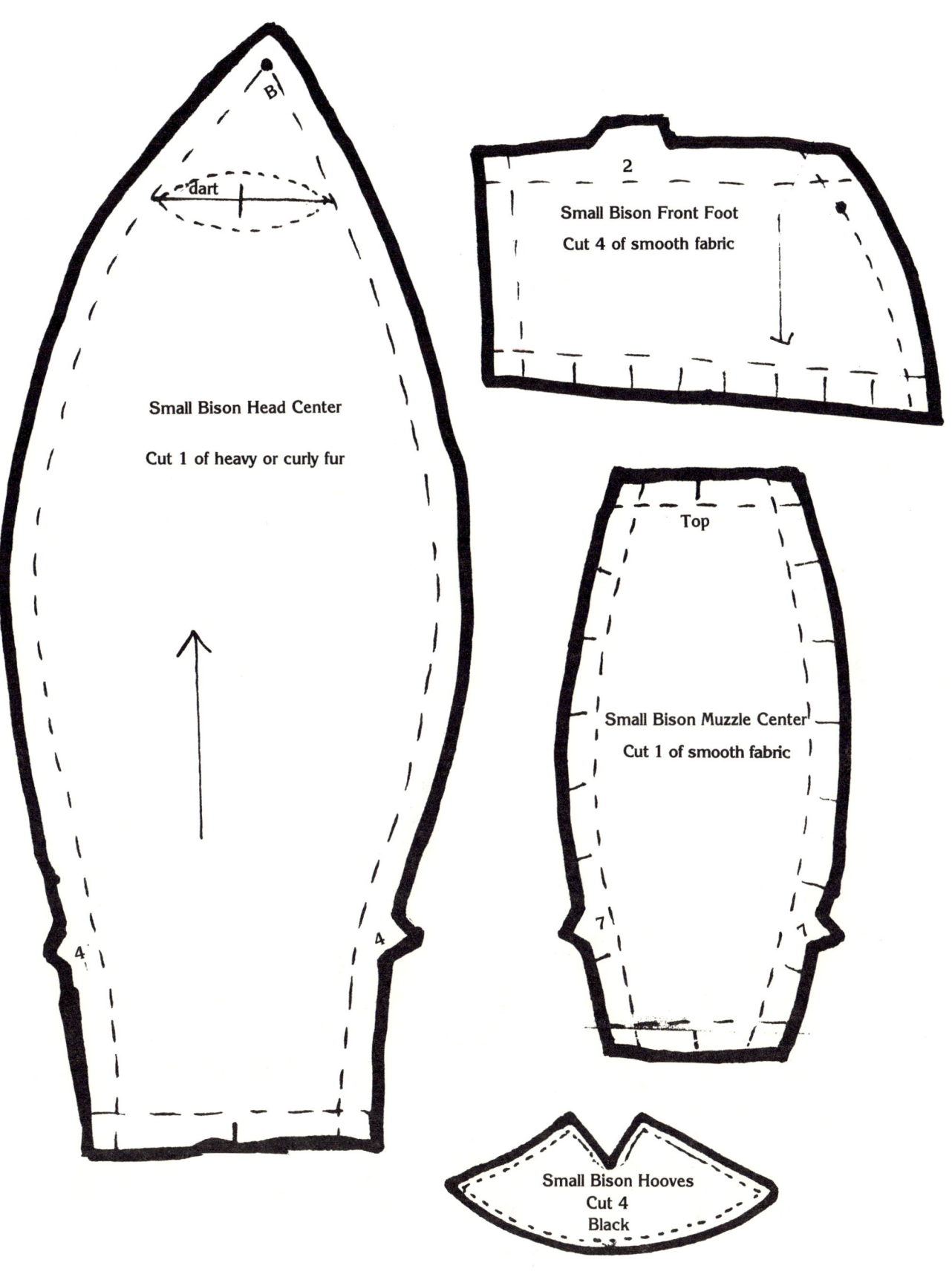

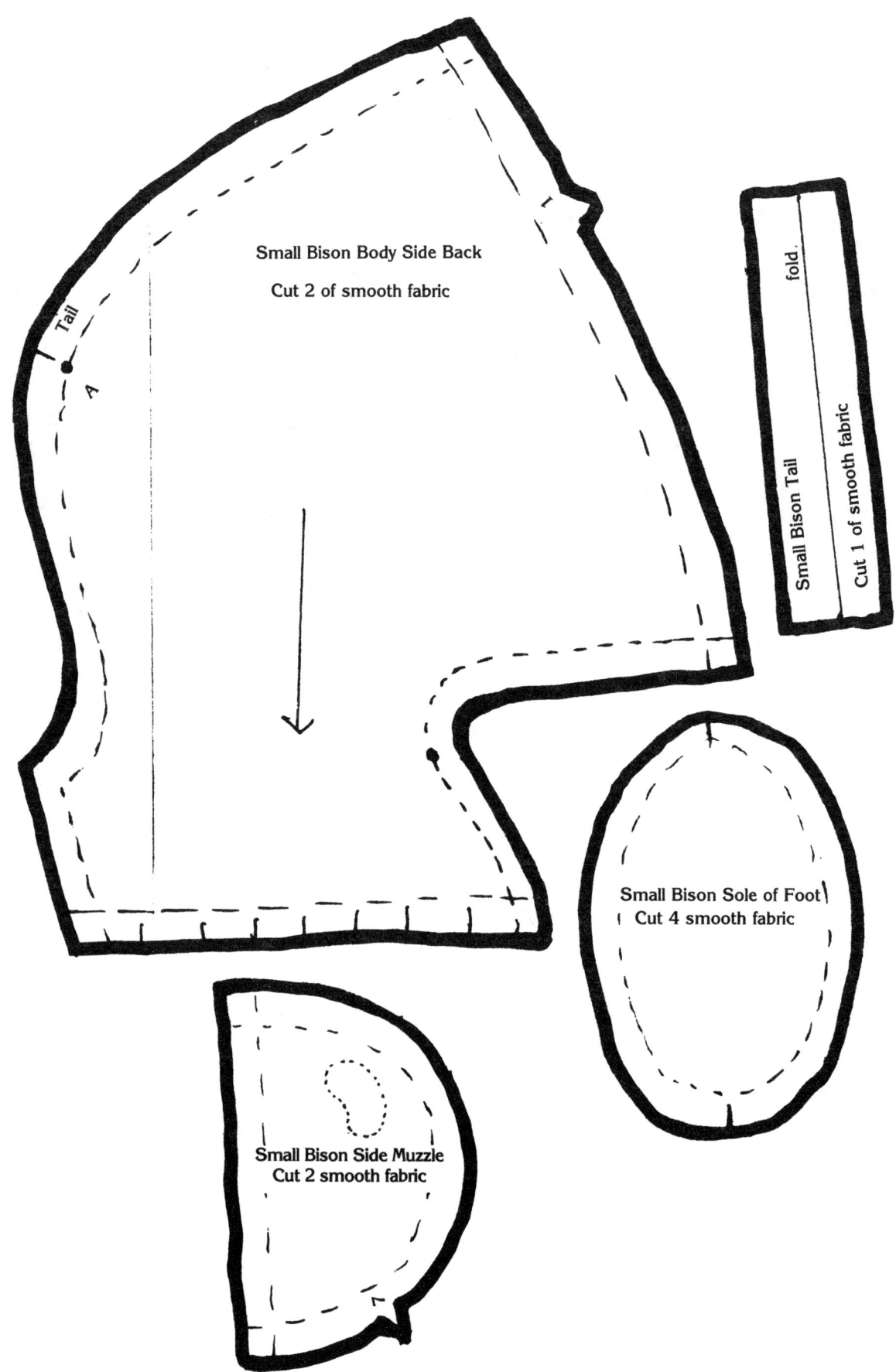

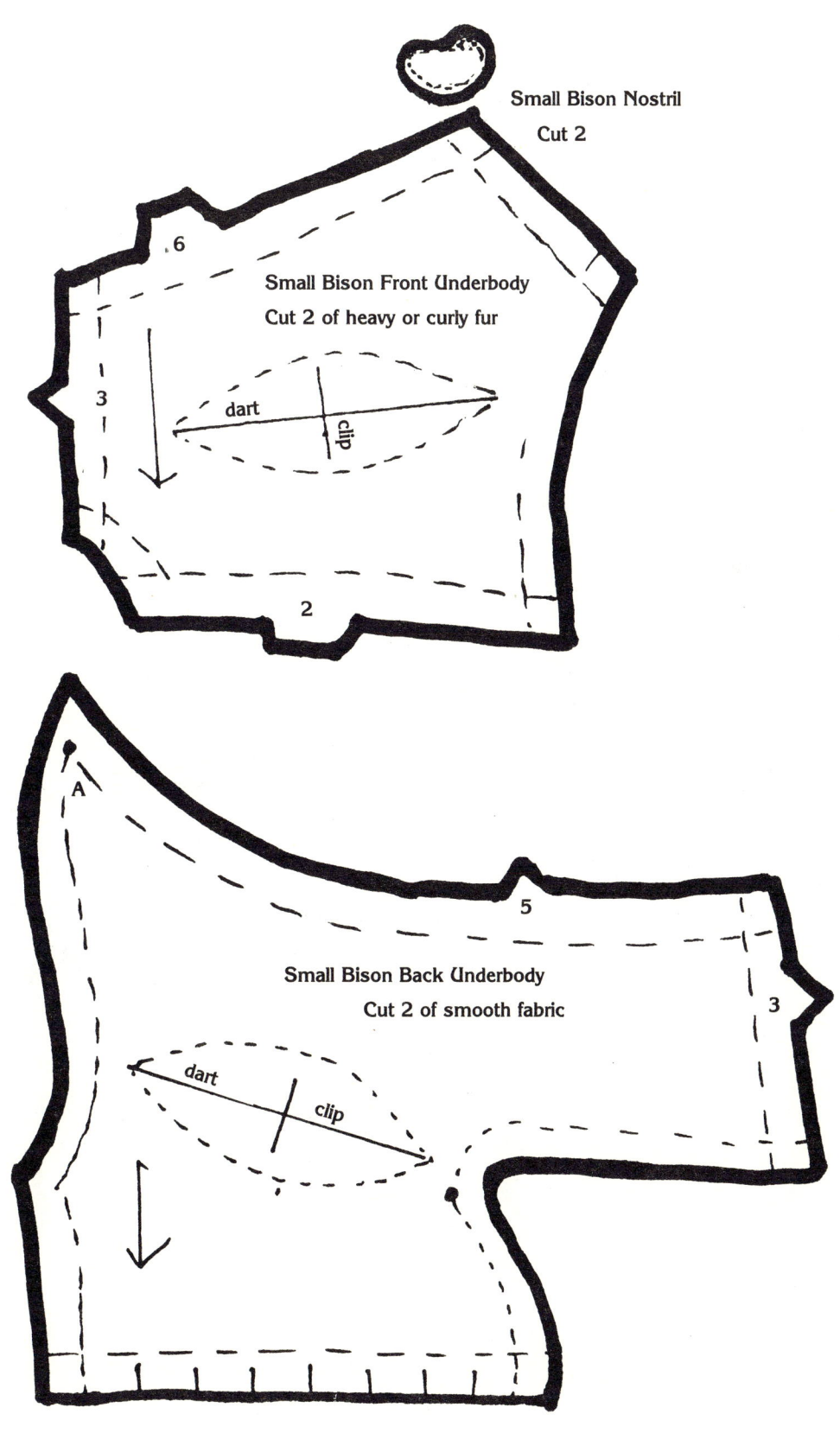

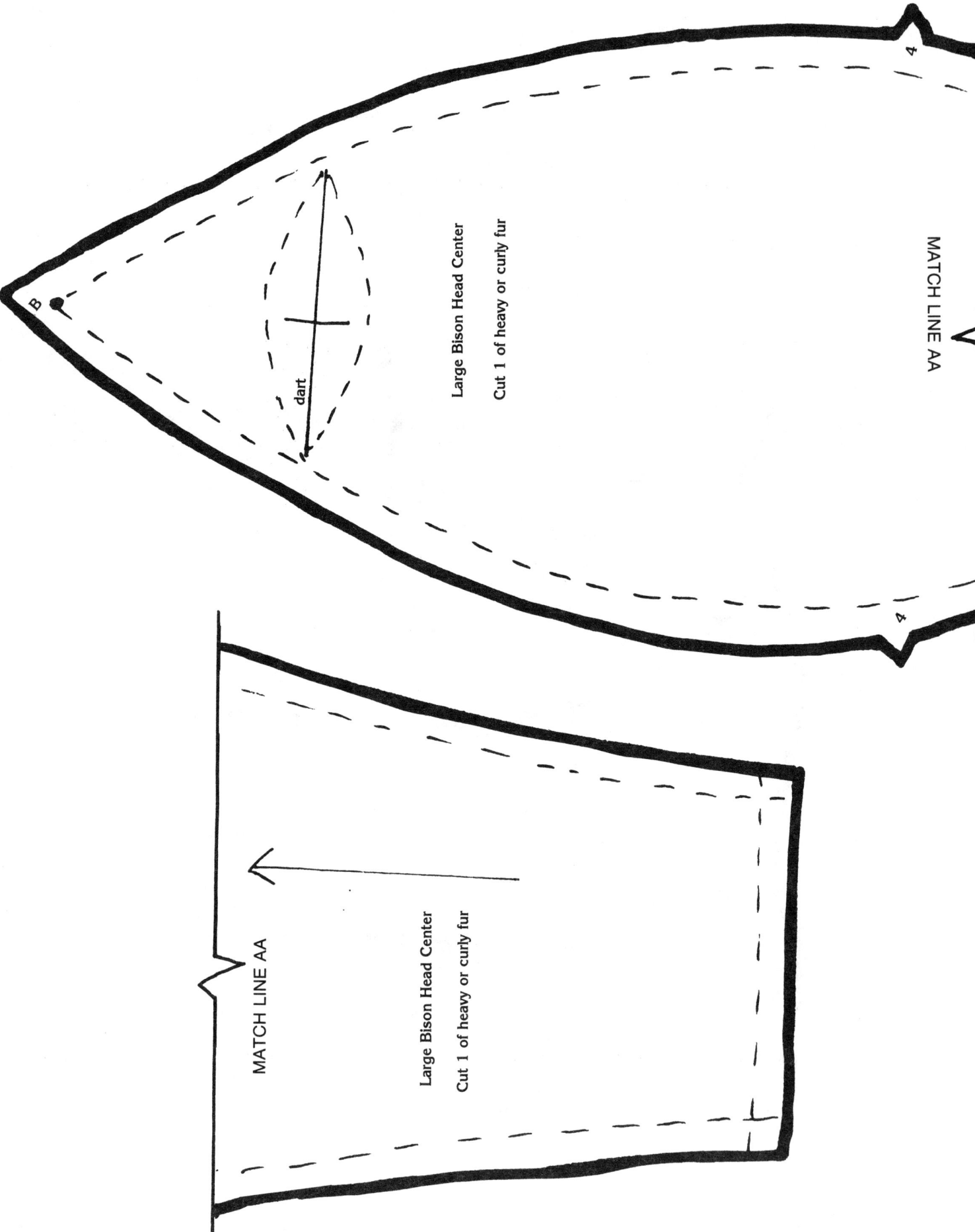

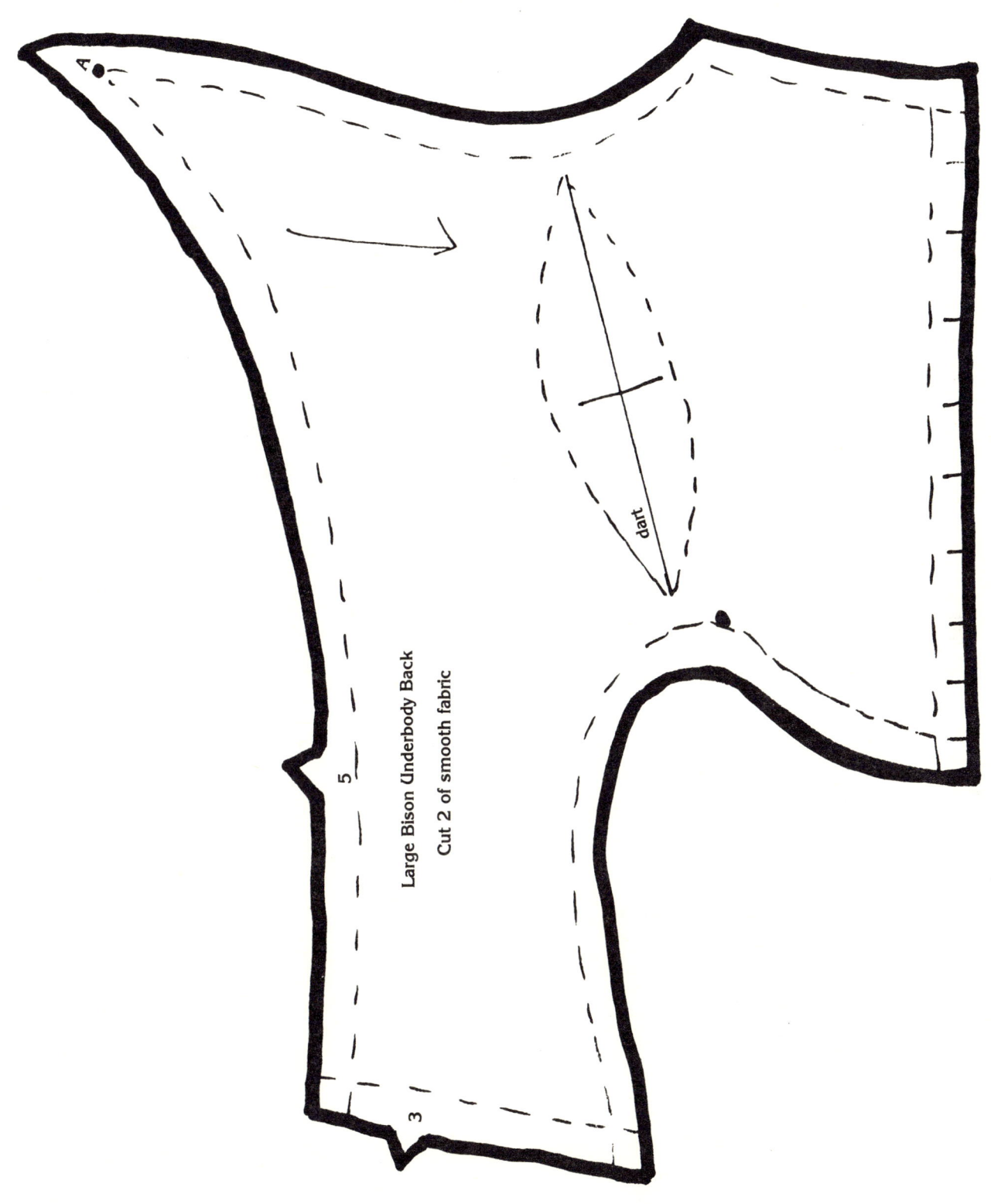

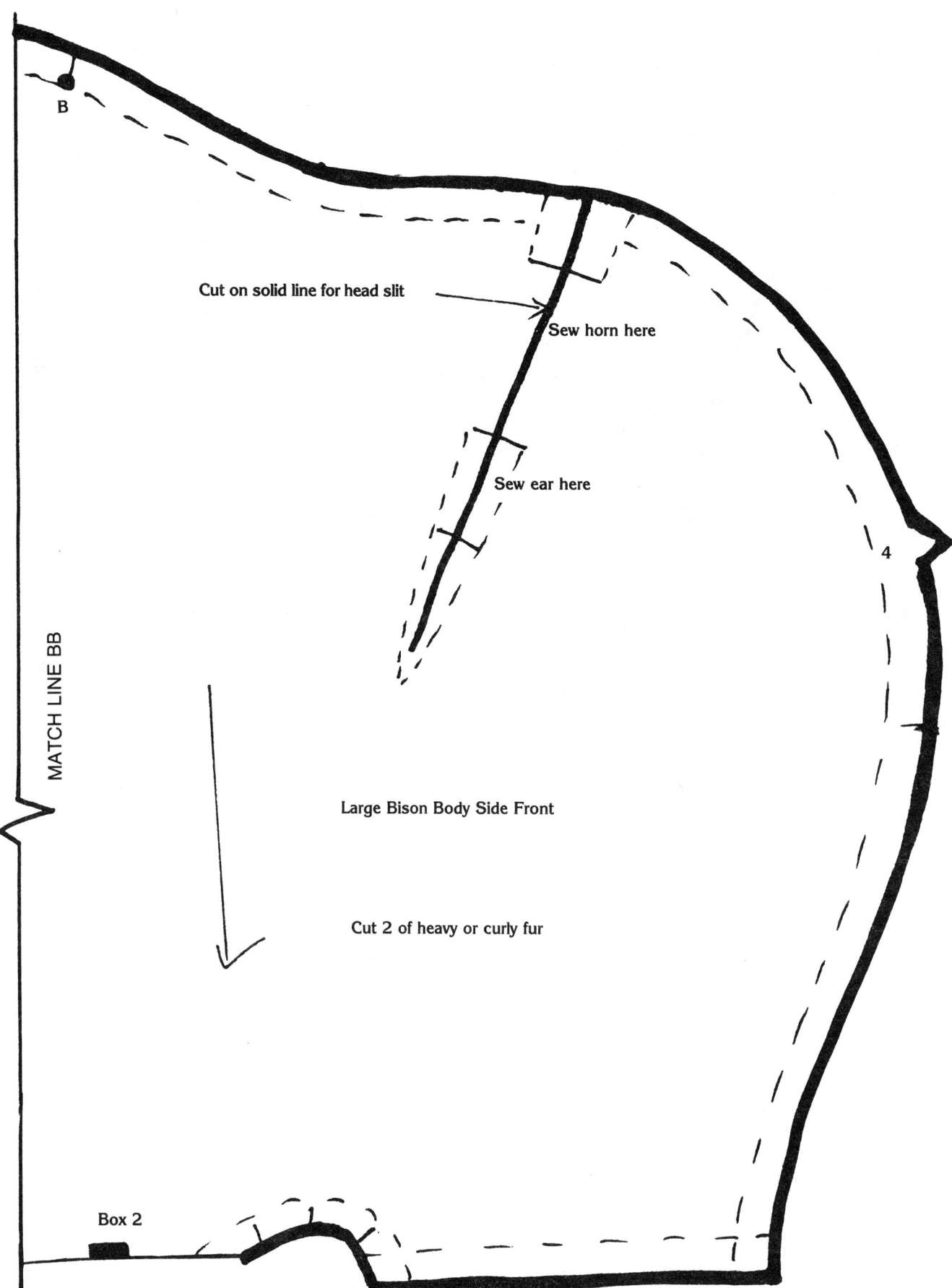

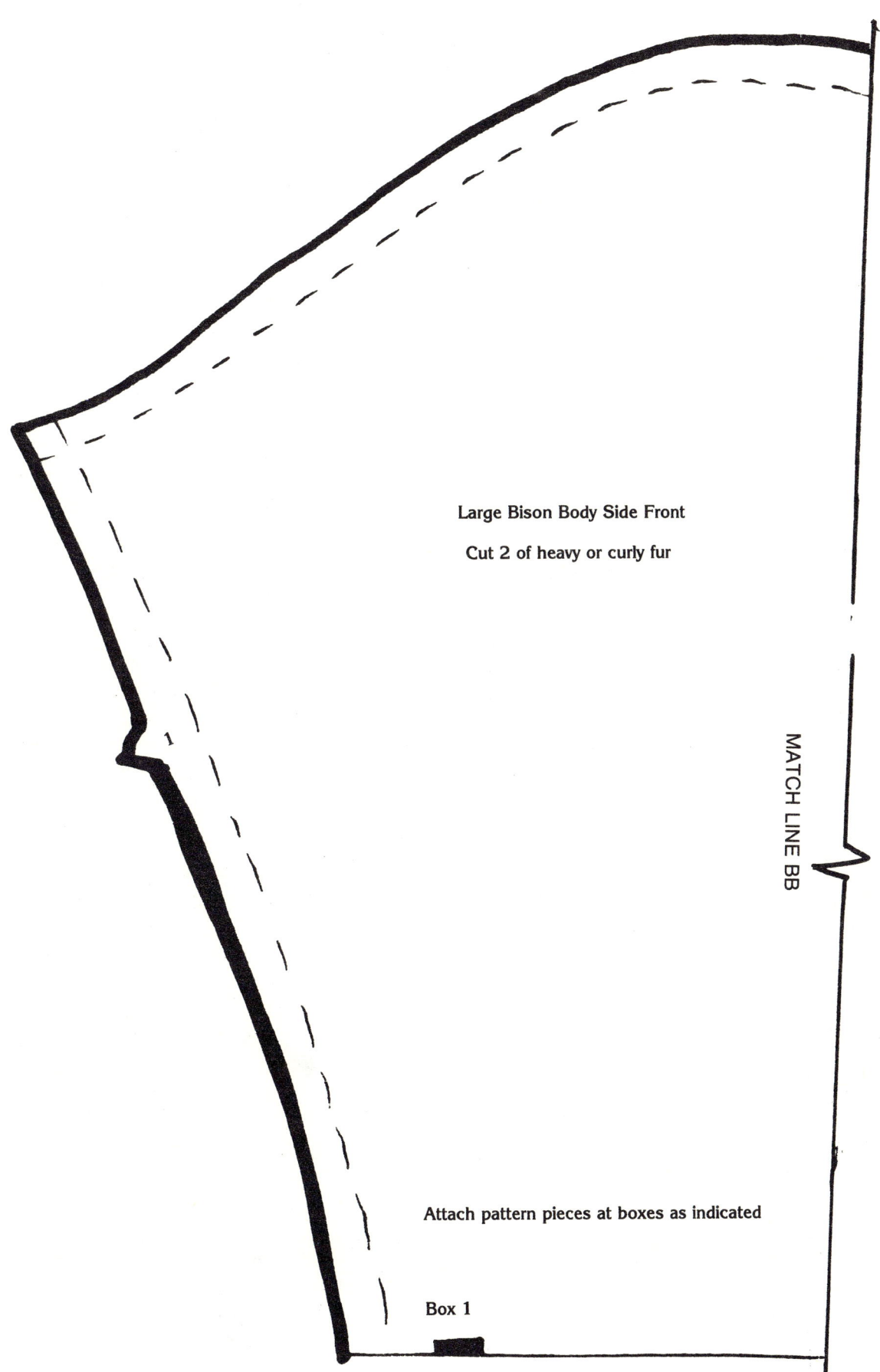

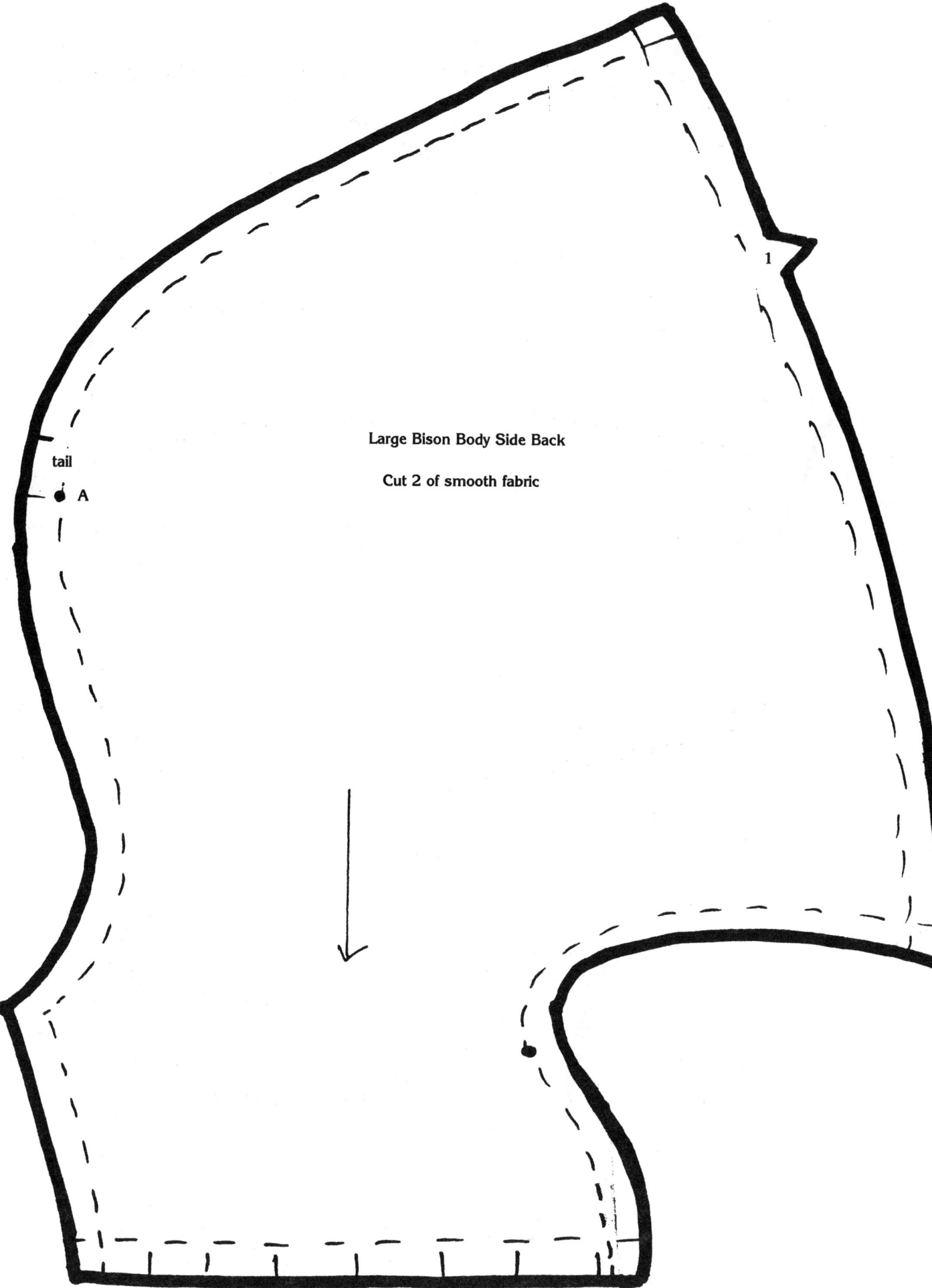

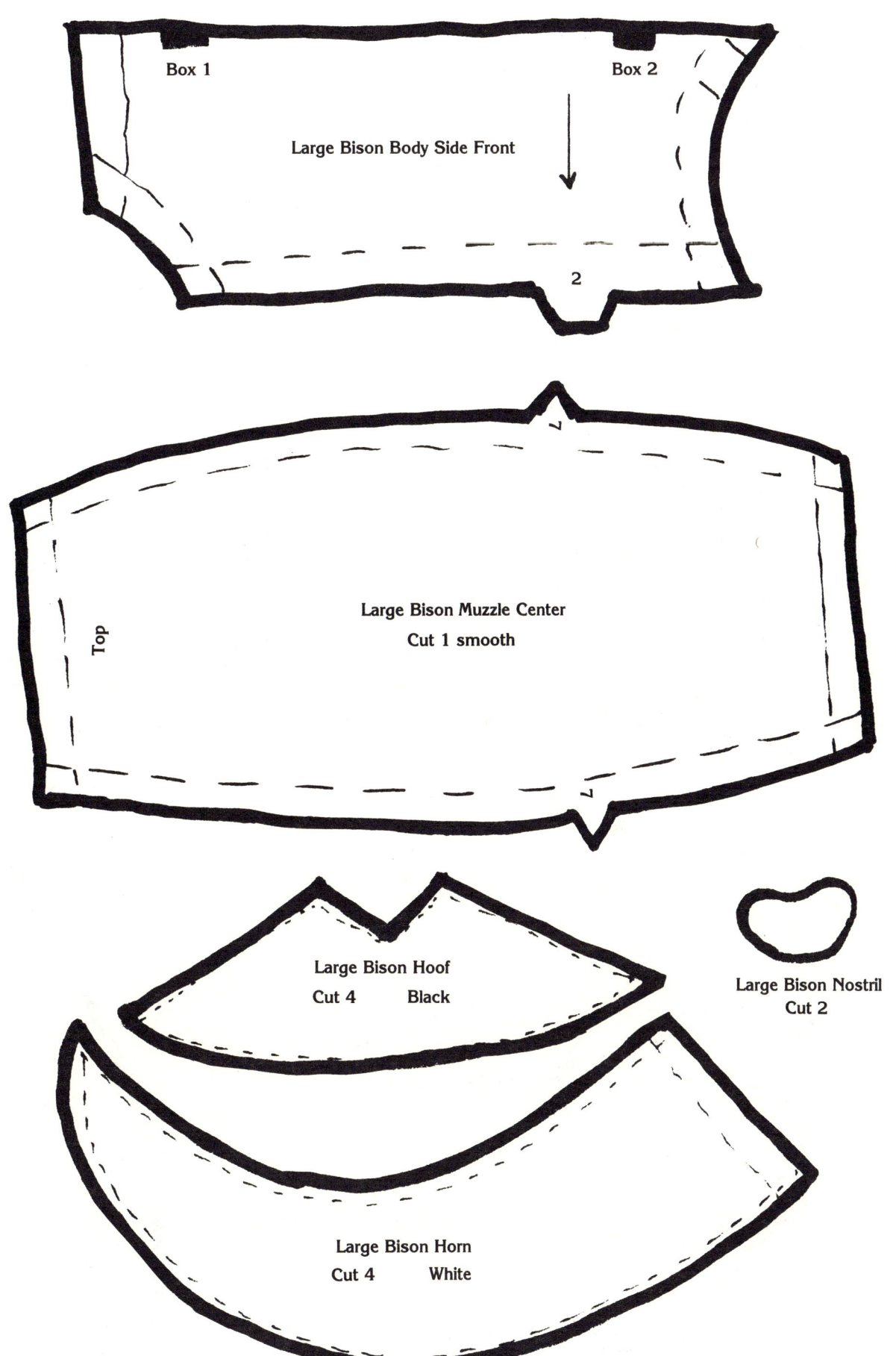

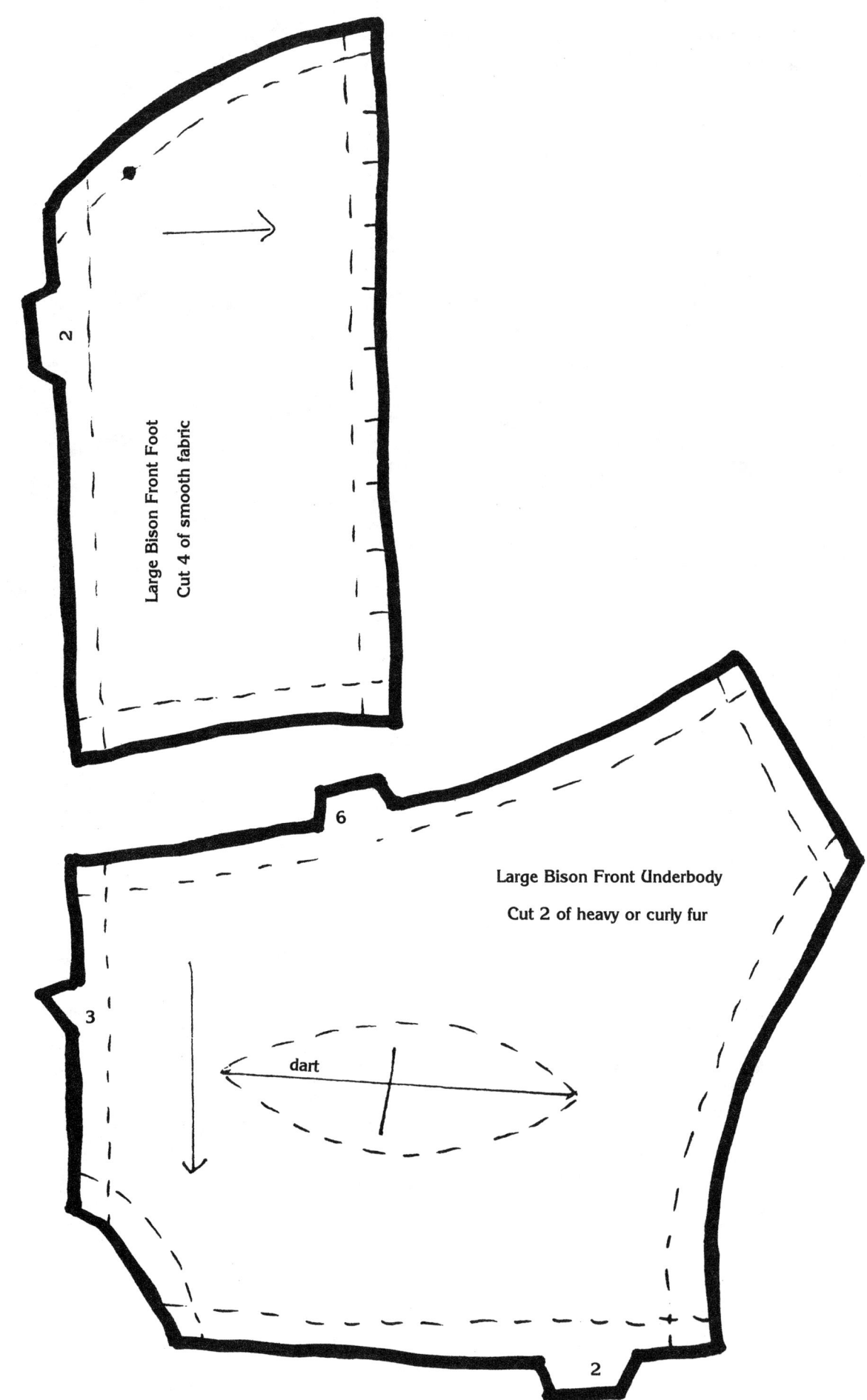

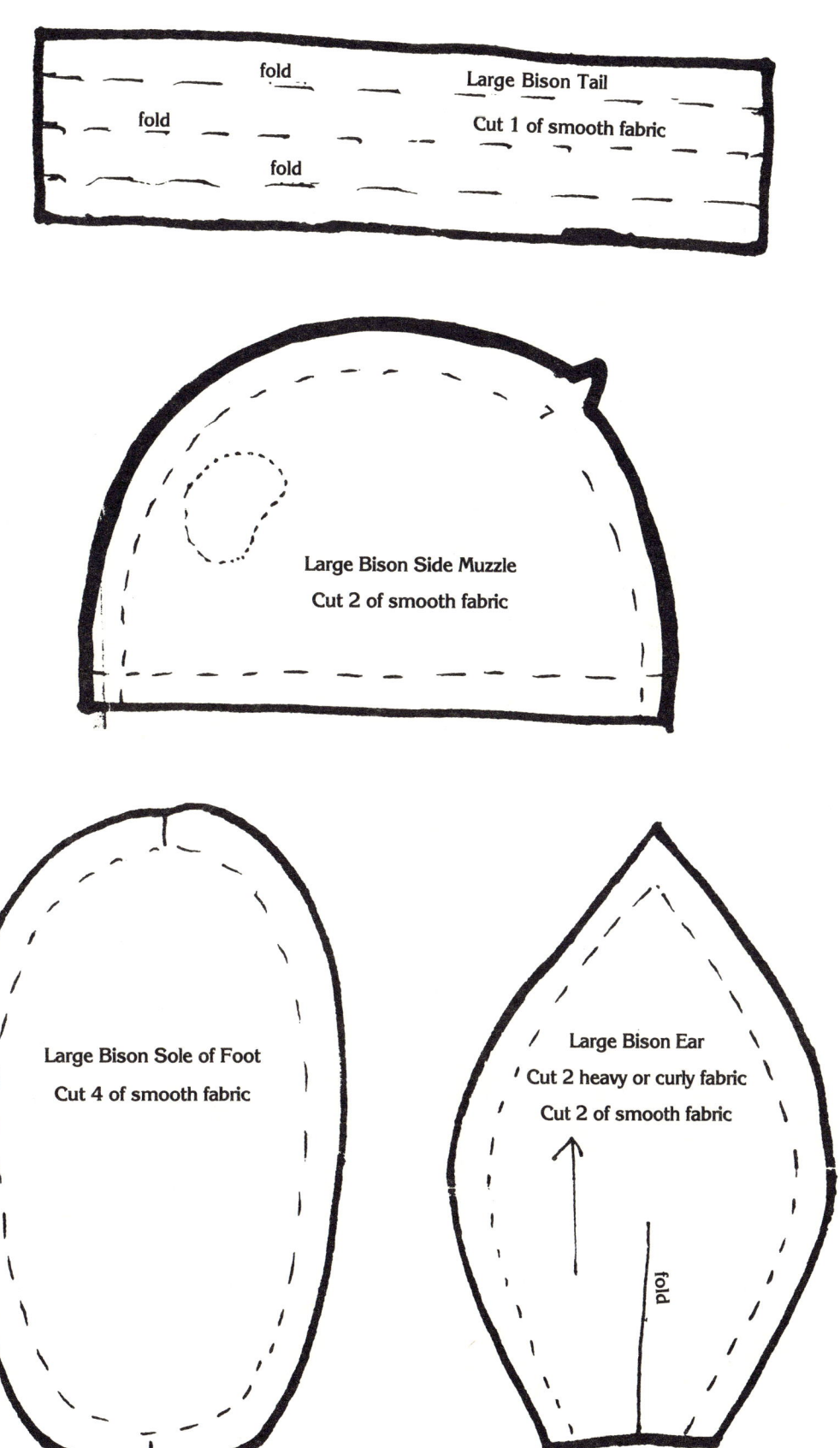

EIGHT PATTERN PIECES
LARGE 22" (56 cm) LONG
SMALL 10" (25 cm) LONG

Cutting Diagram

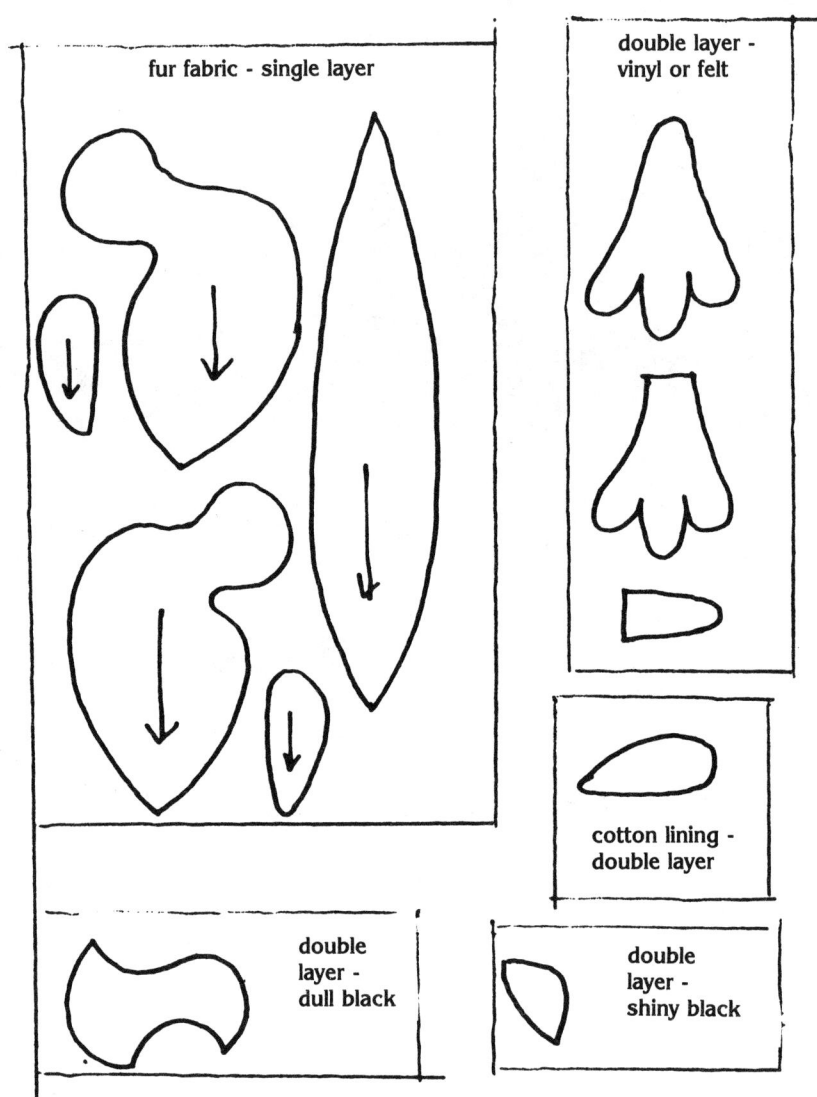

	Small	*Large*
Materials Gray shag or heavy fur fabric:	⅓ yard of 36" (⅓ m of 1 m width fabric)	⅔ yard of 36" (⅔ m of 1 m width fabric)
Gray lining fabric for wings:	6" x 8" piece (15 cm x 20 cm)	5" x 16" piece (13 cm x 41 cm)
Yellow or orange vinyl or felt:	5" x 15" piece (13 cm x 38 cm)	9" x 24" piece (23 cm x 61 cm)

Black dull vinyl:	4″ x 9″ piece (10 cm x 23 cm)	7″ x 17″ piece (18 cm x 43 cm)
Black shiny vinyl:	3″ x 3″ piece (8 cm x 8 cm)	7″ x 12″ piece (18 cm x 30 cm)
Polyester fiberfill:	¾ lbs. (340 g)	2 lbs. (1 kg)

1 pair glass safety eyes or 2 small buttons

9 small curled feathers, white or yellow

4
Dodo

The dodo has been extinct since 1681. There are no photographs, of course, and few surviving drawings of what they actually looked like. Most reports say they were ashen-gray with white or yellowish wings, yellow feet, and a large black bill. There is a report of another species that was silvery-white with yellow wings, feet, and beak. All drawings show stubby wings incapable of flight and tail feathers that curl up over the back. Some drawings show bird feet like a chicken; others show web feet like a duck. I have found the most effective material to simulate feathers is a medium shag or tufted fur fabric. Vinyl makes the most authentic beak and feet but is more difficult to sew than felt. Vinyl is washable, however.

Cutting Instructions

See the Introduction for working with fur fabrics.
 Of gray fur fabric, cut two body sides, two wings, and one underbody.
 Of gray lining fabric, cut two wings.
 Of yellow or orange vinyl or felt, cut two of each of the three feet pieces.
 Of dull black vinyl, cut two beaks.
 Of shiny black vinyl, cut two bills.

Sewing Instructions

Use ¼" (⅗ cm) seam allowance unless otherwise noted.
 1. *Wings.* Sew the wings to the wing linings, right sides together, leaving open between dots. Turn right side out, and sew up opening by hand. Sew to side body, fur side up on both, along curved line indicated

on pattern. See Figure 1. Set side bodies aside.

2. *Feet.* Top stitch front toes to foot bottom, wrong sides together ⅛" (³⁄₁₀ cm) from edge from dot A to dot B. Stitch heel to foot bottom, from dot to dot. Stitch each side of the ankle. See Figure 2. If using vinyl, you may find this difficult. If the vinyl sticks under the presser foot, rub a light film of sewing machine oil on the top surface of the vinyl. Wipe it off, after stitching. Trim close to the stitching with scissors. It is also easier to handle if you use masking tape to hold the two layers together and aligned as you sew, and then tear away the tape after stitching.

Stuff the feet lightly. Stitch to underbody between lines, folding so ankle seams are together. Be sure the feet face forward. See Figure 3.

3. *Body.* Stitch underbody to side bodies from dot C to dot D, catching in feet and leaving open between notches 1 and 2 on one side to stuff. Stitch from dot D around head and down back to tail, dot C. Clip curves and turn right side out. Stuff firmly, sew up opening.

4. *Beak.* Top stitch, close to edge, the shiny bill to tip of beak along line shown on pattern. Align front edge of bill to beak, forming two small pleats to just cover top stitching with excess shiny vinyl. See Figure 4. Repeat for other side of beak. Sew upper and lower seams of beak, matching notches 3 and 4. Leave unnotched side open. Clip curves and turn right side out.

Cut a small x on each side of the beak where the eyes go. Insert the shank of the glass eyes through the hole, from the outside. Firmly push the washer onto the shank on the inside. Stuff the beak and hand sew to the face along the lines indicated on the pattern.

5. *Feathers.* Sew feathers on by hand—three on the tips of each wing and three curving up the back at the tail. Omit feathers if this is for a young child.

Figure 1

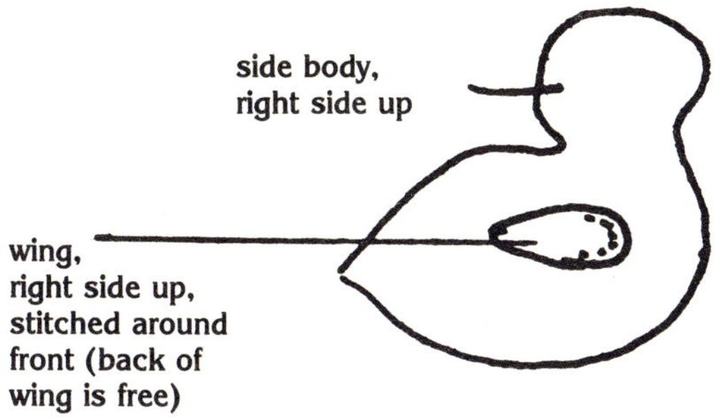

side body, right side up

wing, right side up, stitched around front (back of wing is free)

Figure 2

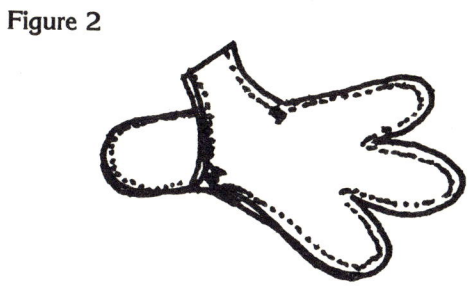

Figure 3

front   ankle seam

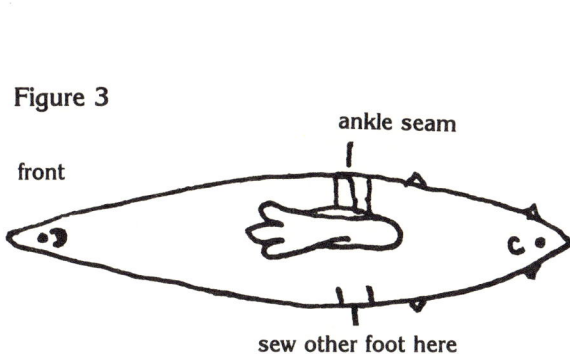

sew other foot here

Figure 4

beak, right side up

bill, right side up

top stitch along this line

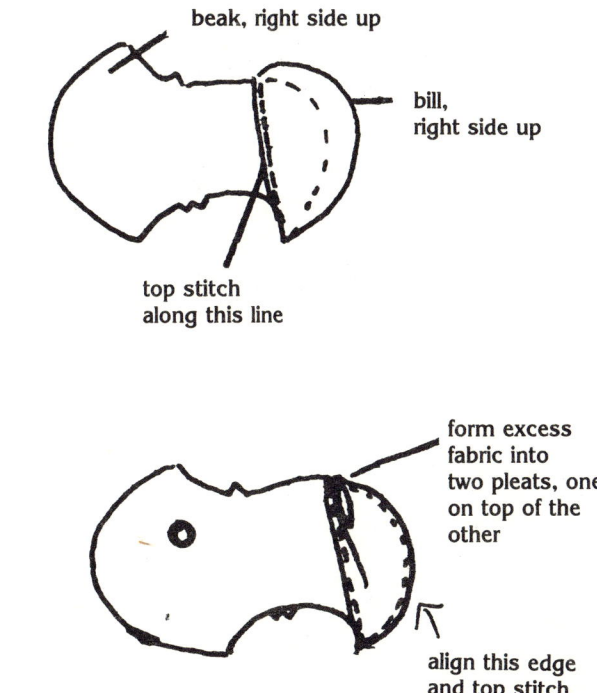

form excess fabric into two pleats, one on top of the other

align this edge and top stitch

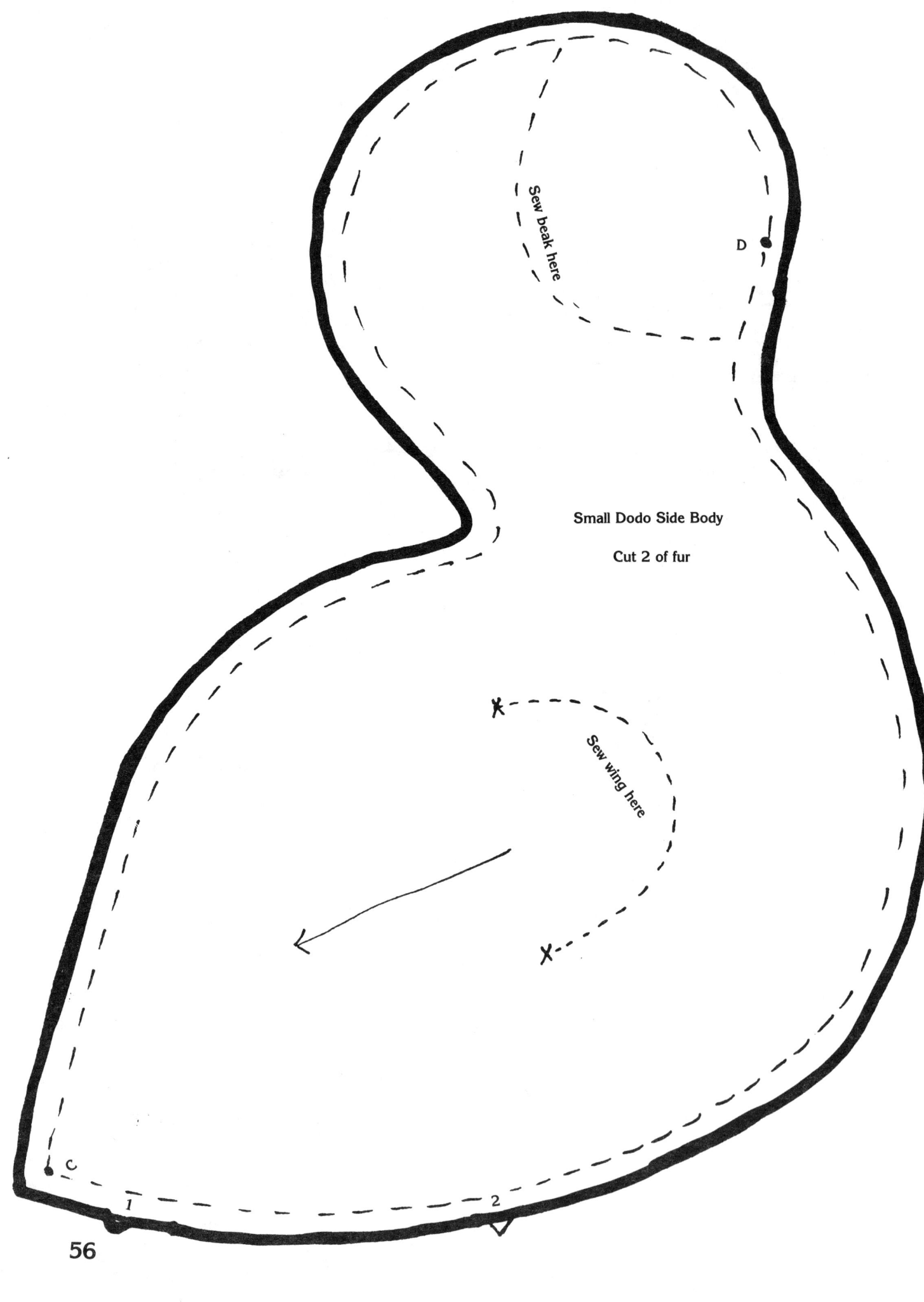

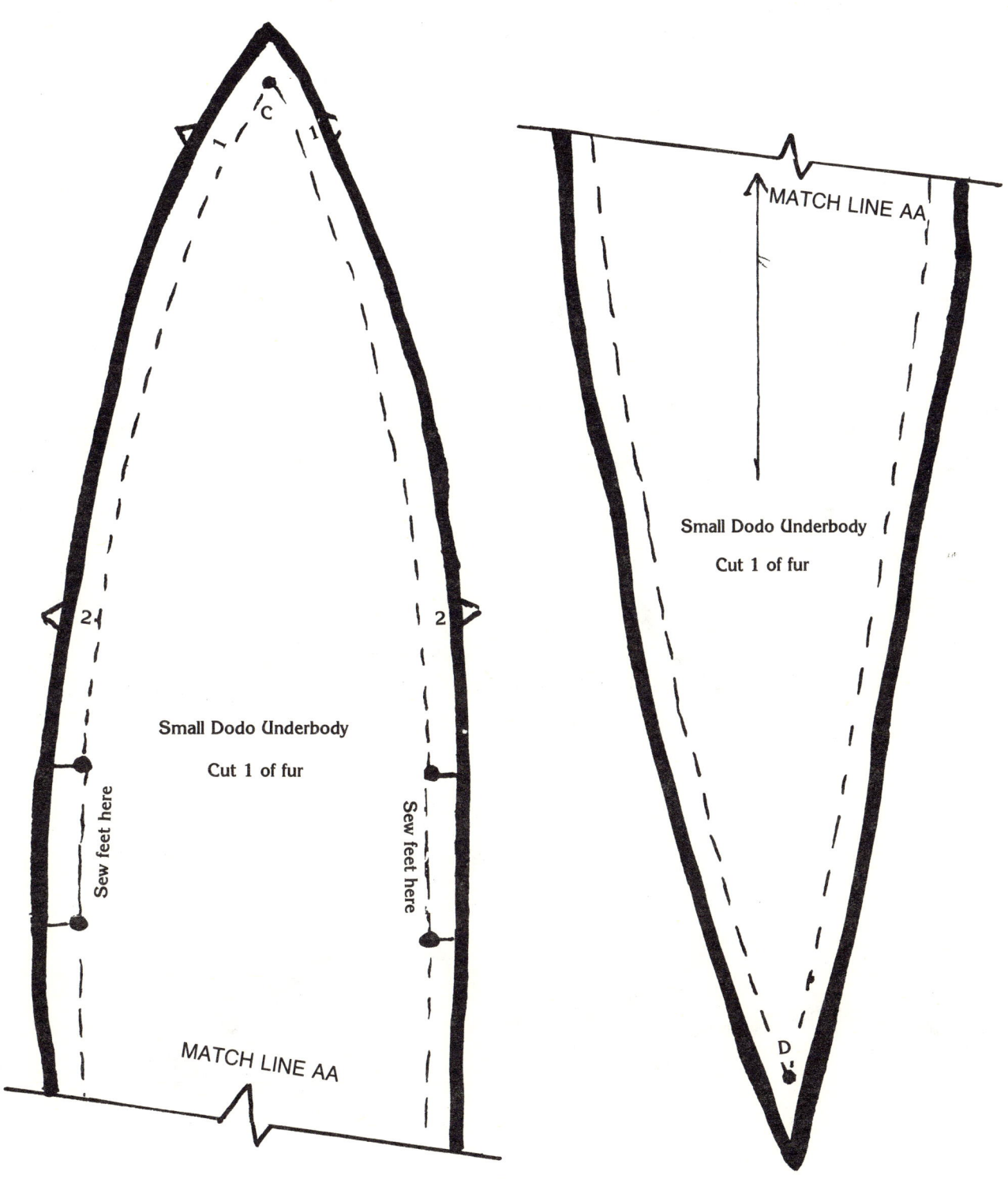

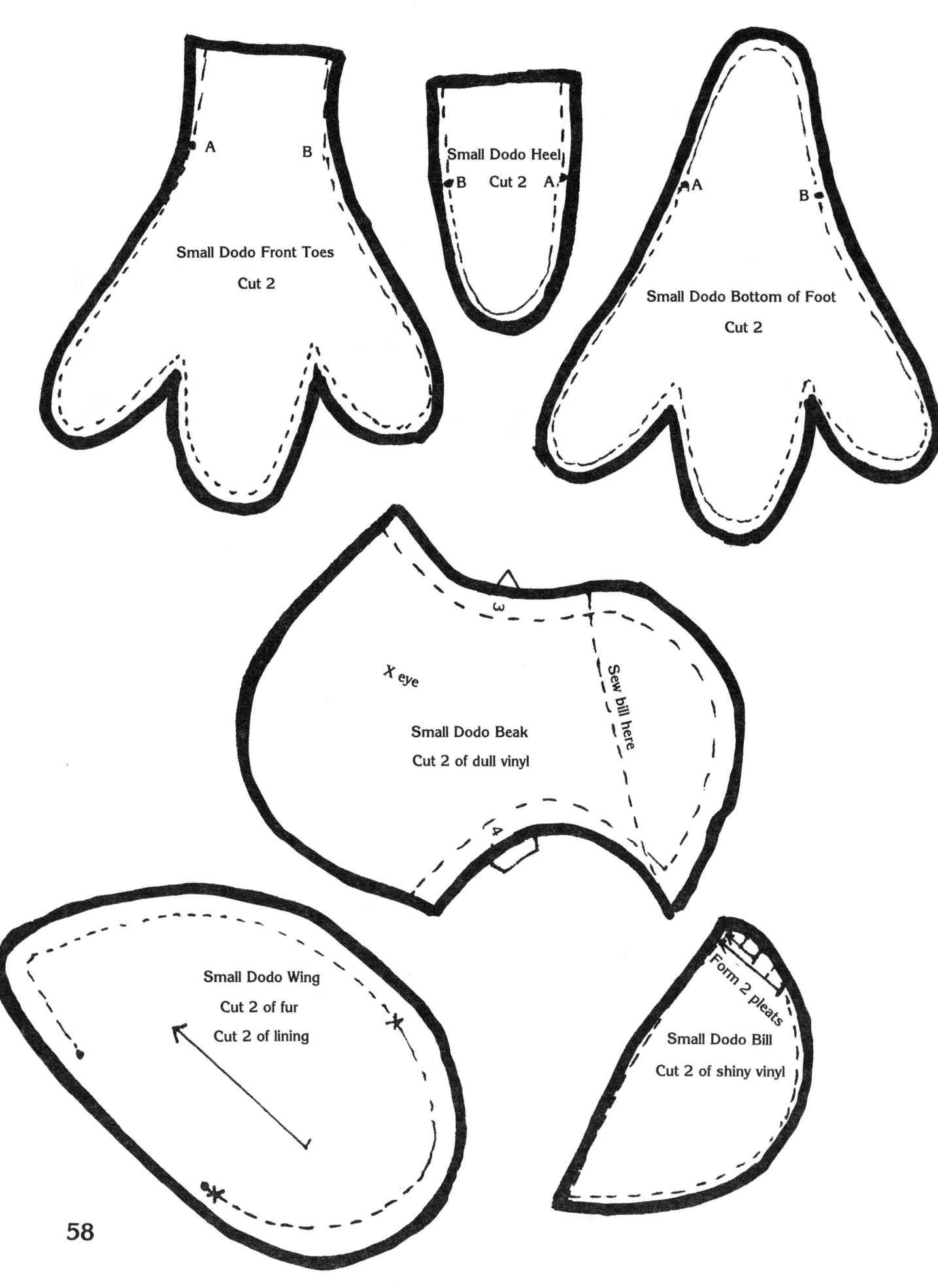

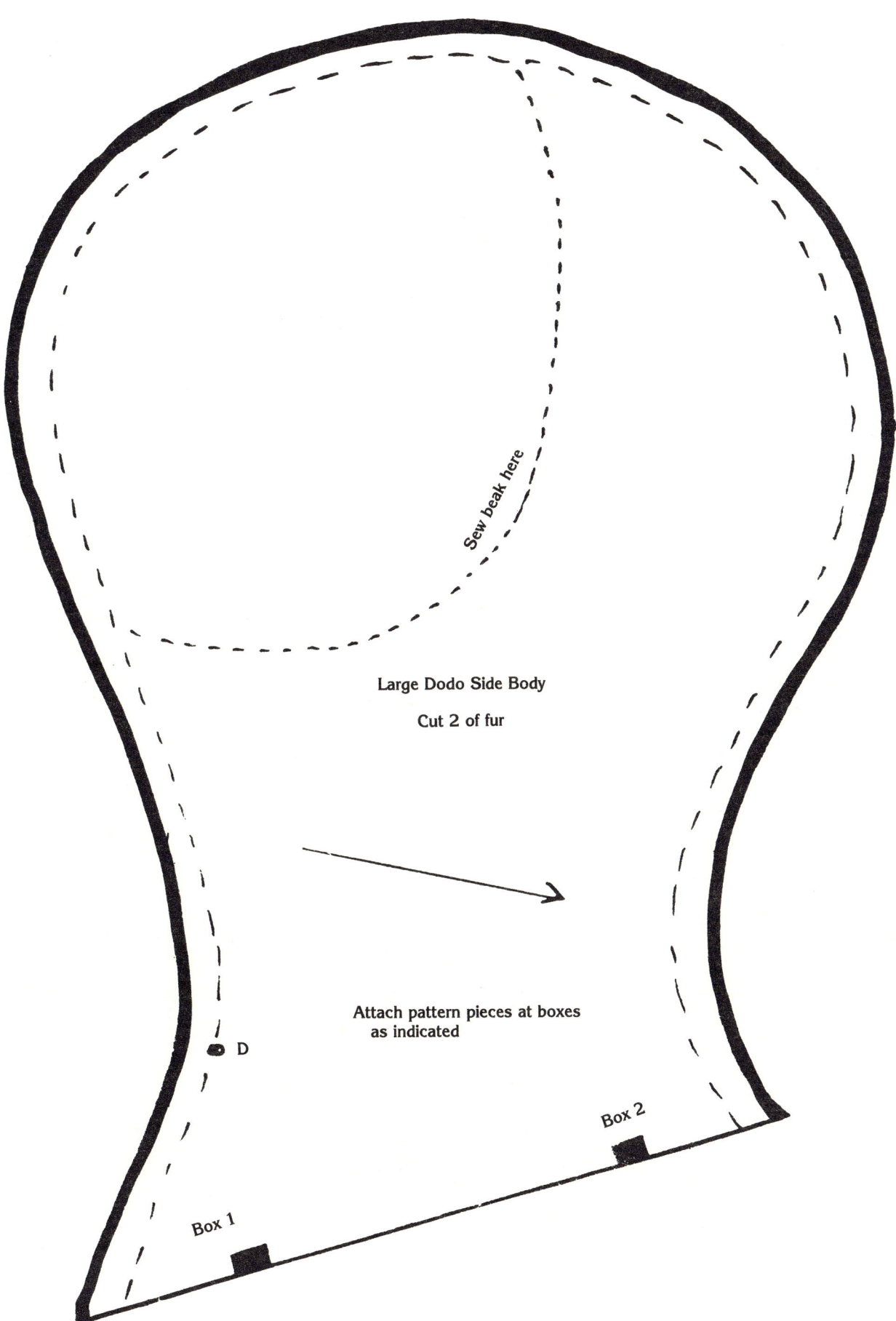

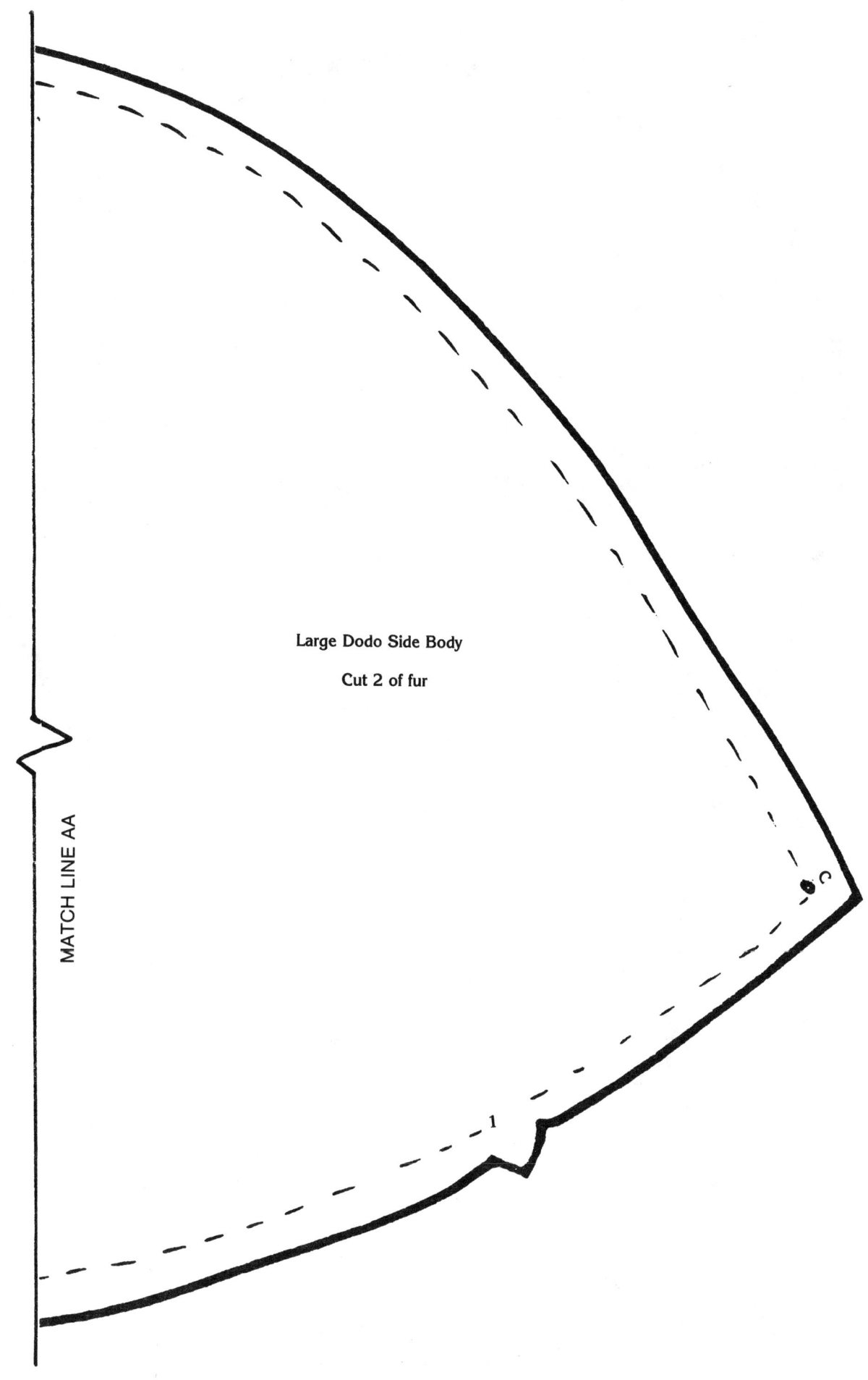

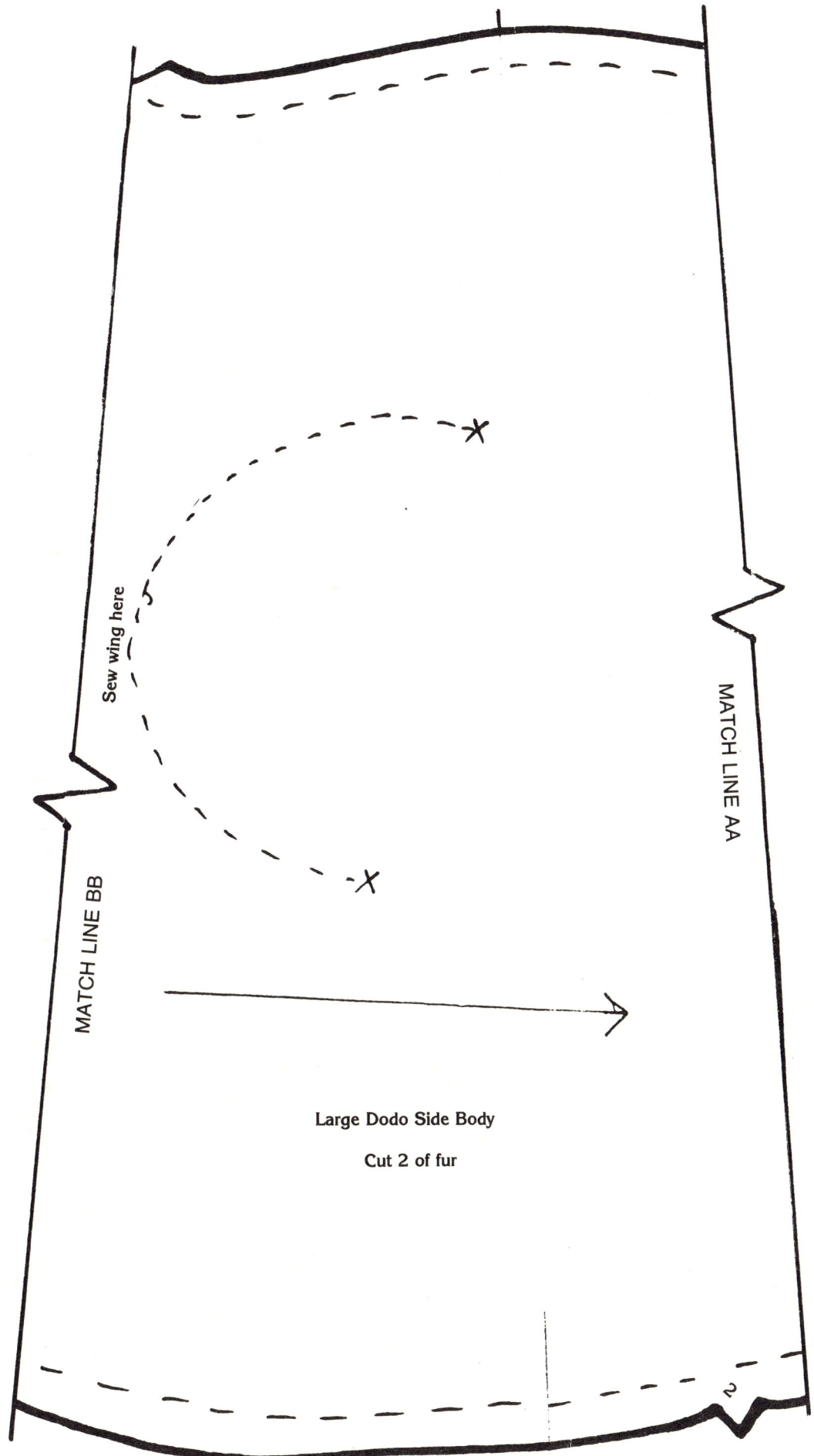

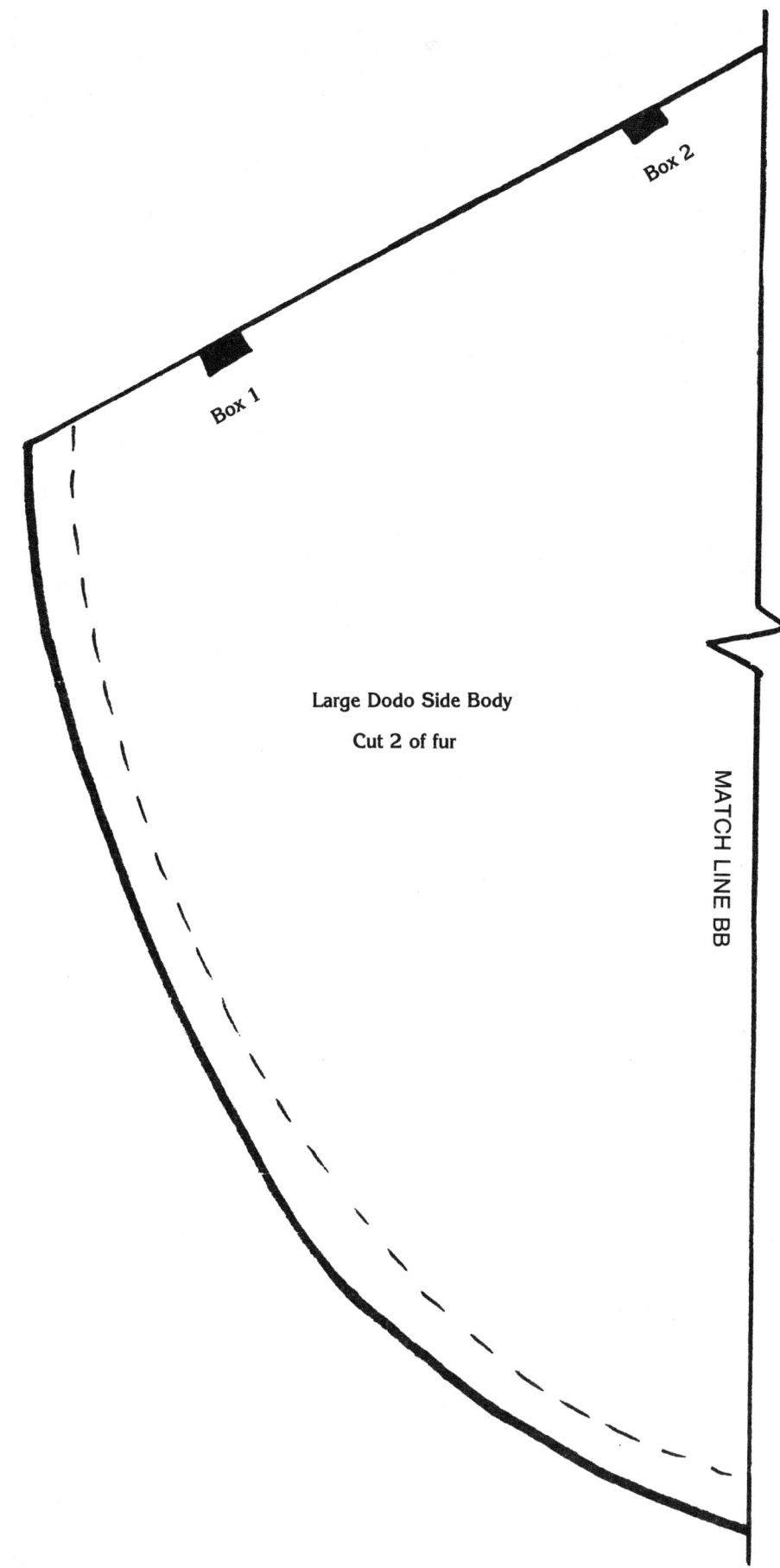

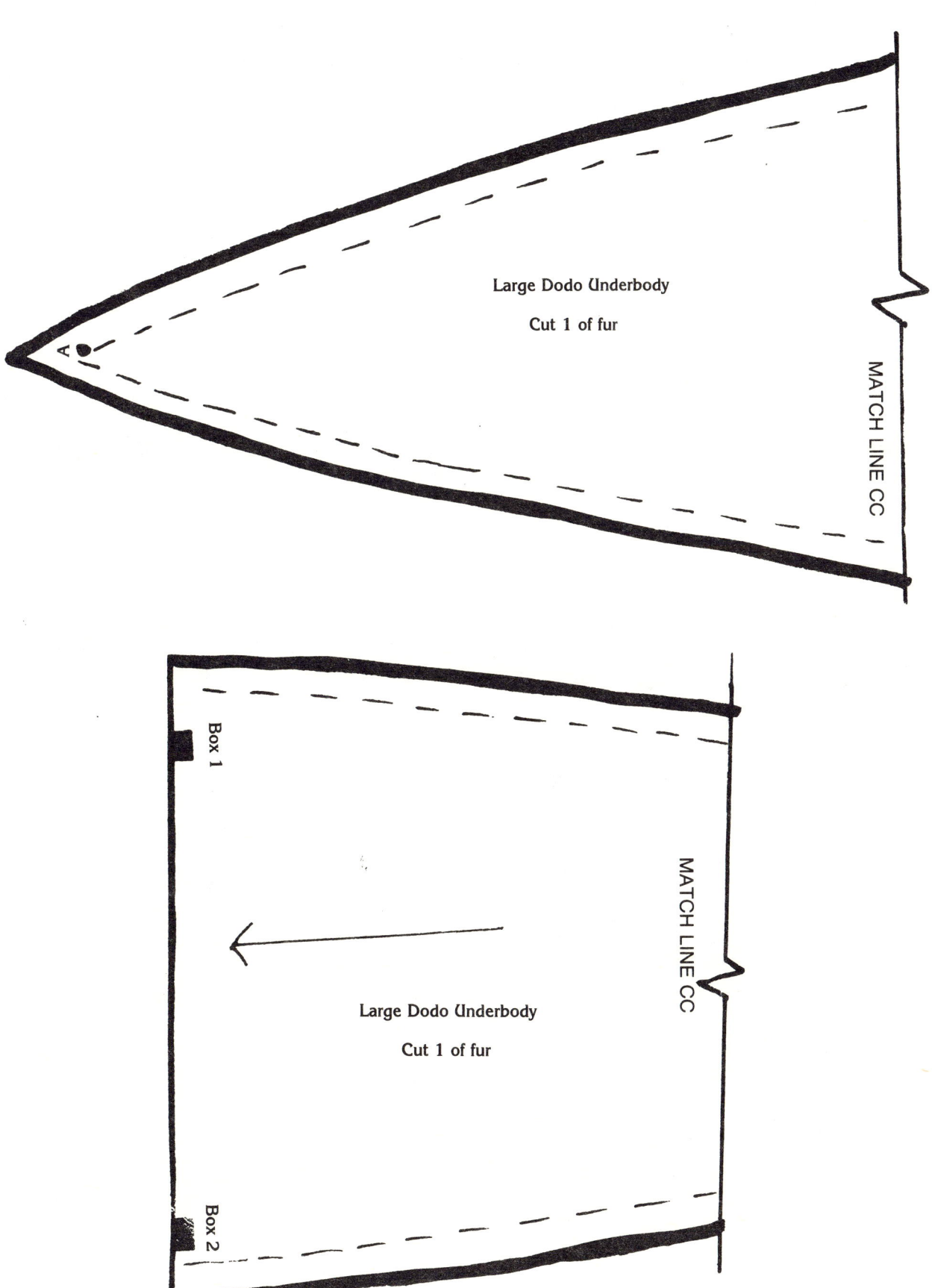

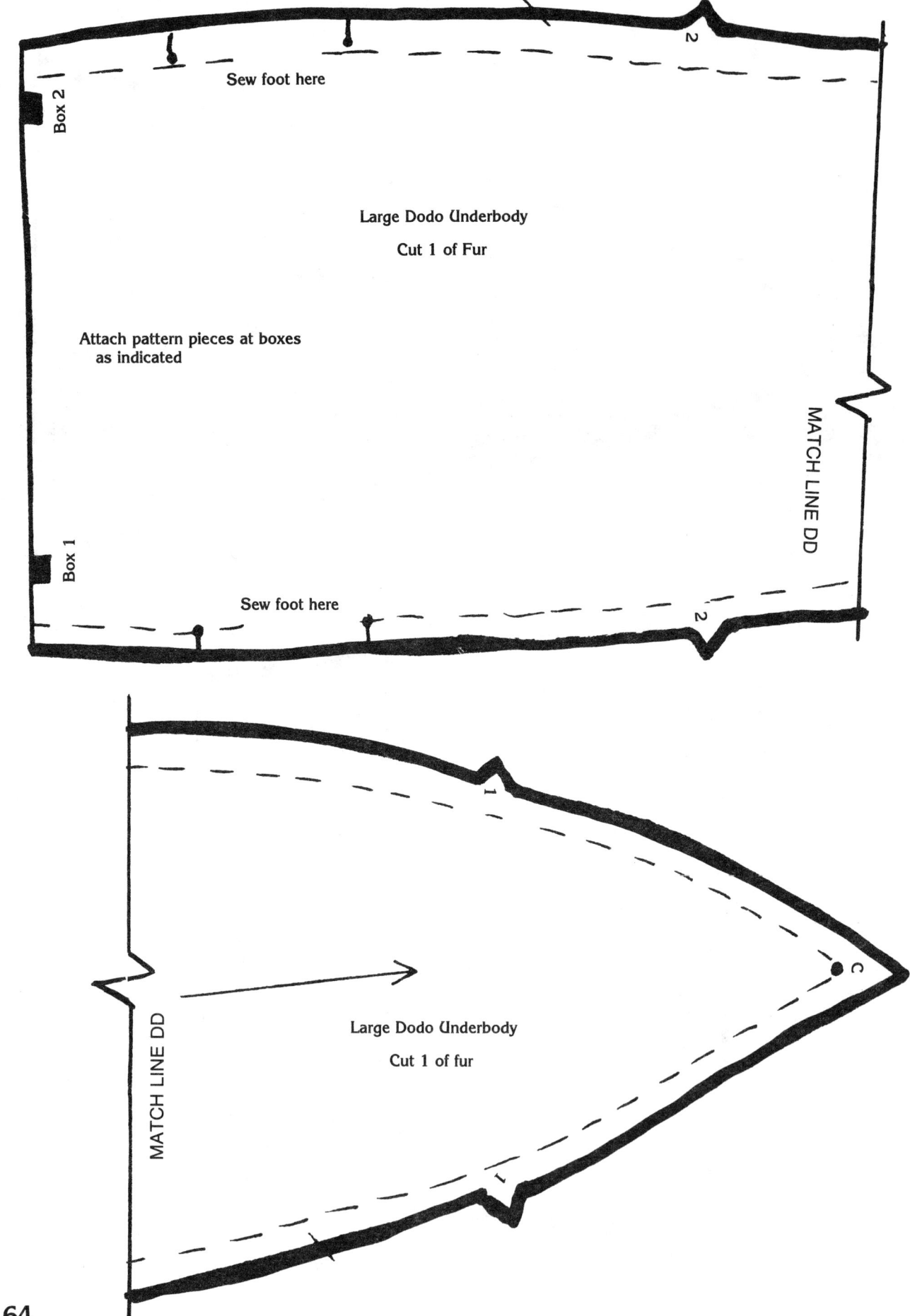

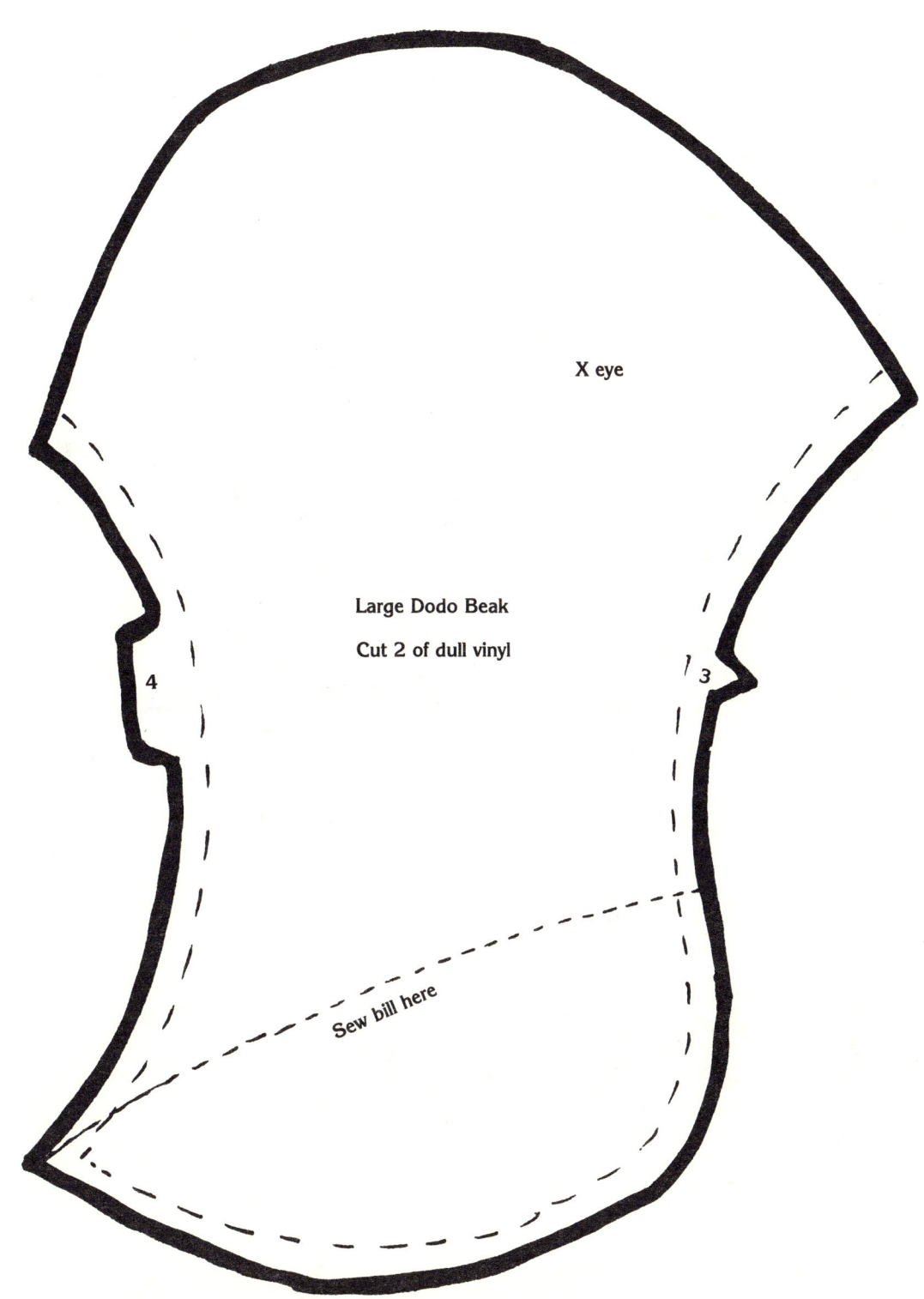

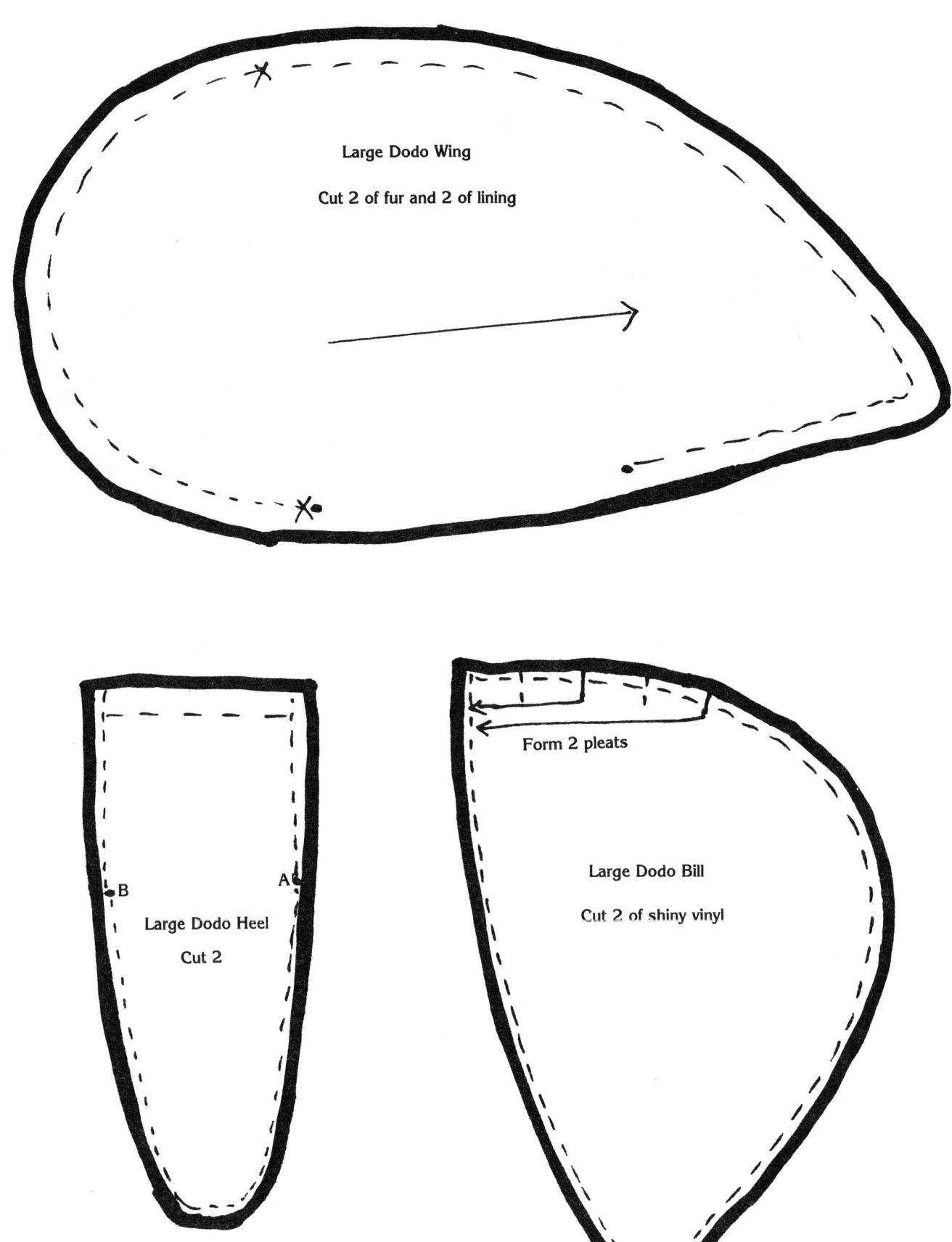

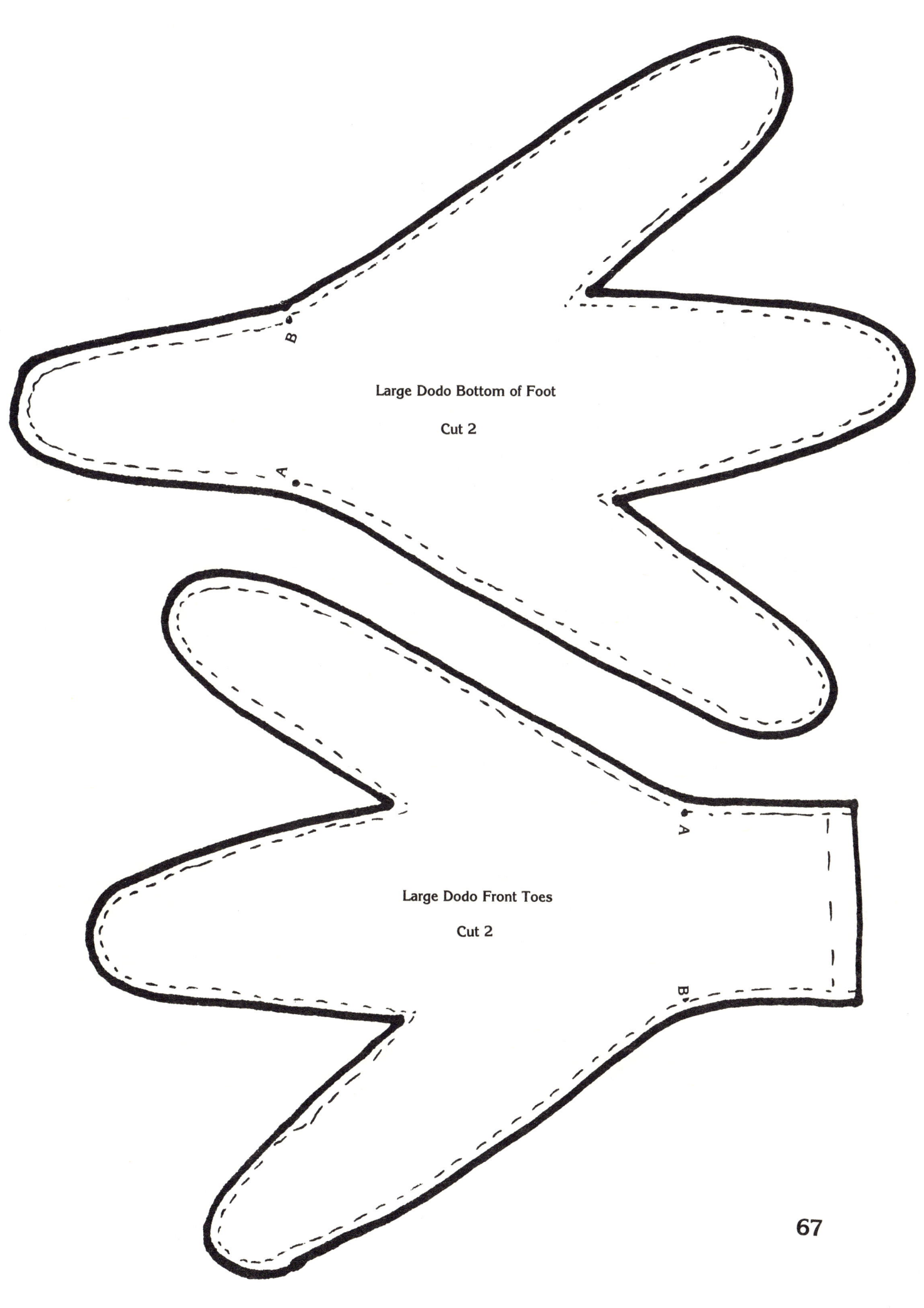

FIVE PATTERN PIECES
10" (25 cm) TALL

Cutting Diagram

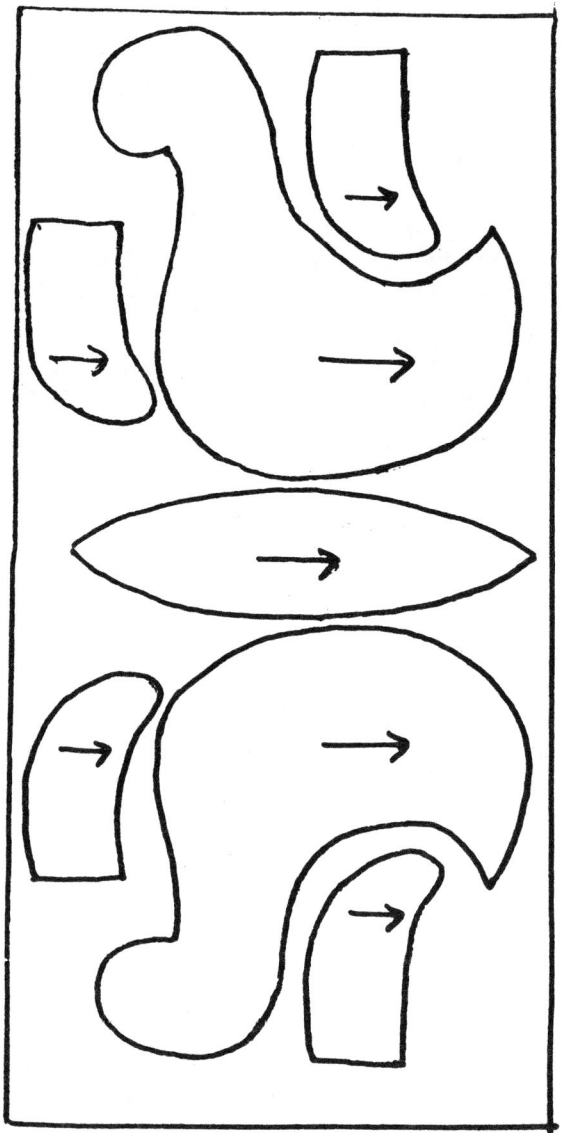

Materials White or yellow fake fur fabric or other sturdy material: ⅓ yard (⅓ m)
Yellow or orange vinyl or felt: 3" × 10" piece (8 cm × 25 cm)
1 lb. (450 g) polyester fiberfill (for stuffing)
1 pair safety eyes or 2 buttons

5
Duck

This duck is cute when made in a soft white or pale yellow fur fabric, although any sturdy material you have may be used. The beak and feet look best in yellow or orange vinyl, which is washable. Felt is easier to sew, however. Safety eyes should be used if this is being made for a small child of button-swallowing age. You may embroider or appliqué eyes if you choose. If washable fake fur, vinyl, and polyester fiberfill stuffing are used, the whole animal may be put through the washer and dryer to clean. This makes a very cute toy for a young child or a bed decoration for a teenager.

Cutting Instructions See the Introduction for working with fur fabrics.

Of fur fabric, cut two side bodies, one underbody, and four wings. See cutting diagram.

The feet and beak may be done either of two ways: (1) Cut out the pieces, place wrong sides together, and top stitch close to the edge. If you are using vinyl, you may find it sticks under the presser foot. A light coating of sewing machine oil on the top surface will prevent this. Wipe the oil off completely after stitching. You may find it helps to tape the pieces together with masking tape to hold them while you stitch, as pins can leave holes in vinyl. Tear away the tape after stitching. (2) Trace the feet and beak patterns on tissue paper, tape the paper to the uncut vinyl (double layer, wrong sides together), and top stitch just inside the outline. Tear away the tissue and cut out the feet and beak just outside the stitching.

Sewing Instructions

Use ¼" (⅗ cm) seams throughout unless otherwise stated.

1. *Feet and beak.* Make two feet and one beak, using either of the methods described under the cutting instructions. Fold the beak lengthwise, and baste to one side of the head as shown in Figure 1. Baste the feet to the underbody between dots as shown in Figure 2.

2. *Wings.* For each wing, sew two pieces, right sides together, leaving the straight edge open. Turn right side out. Stitch wings to side bodies between dots as indicated on pattern and shown in Figure 3. The wings will be tacked down after stuffing.

3. *Body and head.* Sew side bodies, right sides together, from dot A around head and tail to dot B, matching notches 1 and 2.

Stitch underbody to side bodies, right sides together, between dots A and B, catching in feet. Leave open between notches 3 and 4 on one side for stuffing.

4. Clip curves and turn right side out. If you are using safety eyes, attach now. Cut a small x in each side of the head, where indicated on pattern. Push the shank of the eye through the hole from the right side. Slide the washer onto the shank inside the duck. Push together tightly.

Stuff the duck firmly. Use small wads of stuffing, packing them in with a dowel or chopstick. Sew up the opening, using the ladder stitch.

Fold the wings down and tack both front and back edges to cover the raw seam. See Figure 4.

If you are using buttons for eyes, sew them where indicated on the pattern. Use heavy-duty thread or carpet cord to sew them securely. You may want to pass the thread clear through the head, through one button, back through the head, and through the other button, pulling tightly to sink the eyes into the head. Alternatively, you may want to appliqué felt eyes or embroider them.

Figure 1

two beak pieces,
wrong sides together

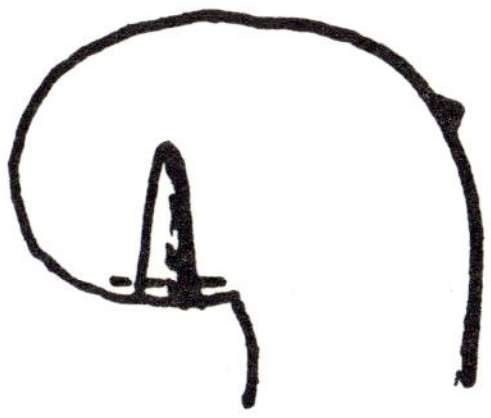

right side

beak, with fold toward
the front

Figure 2

A   B   underbody, right
                      side up

Figure 3

side body,
right side up

Figure 4

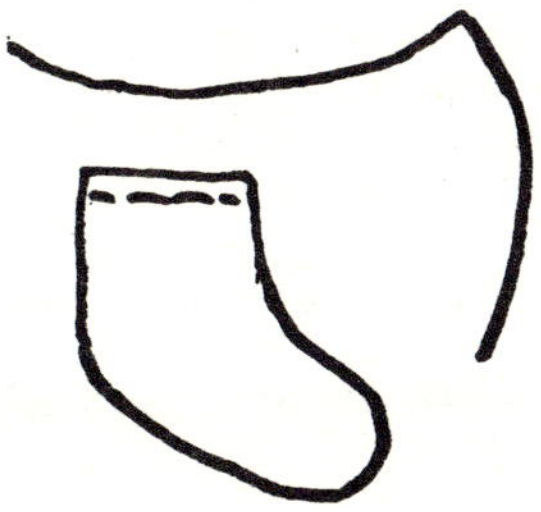

outside
tack wings down here,
so raw seam is covered

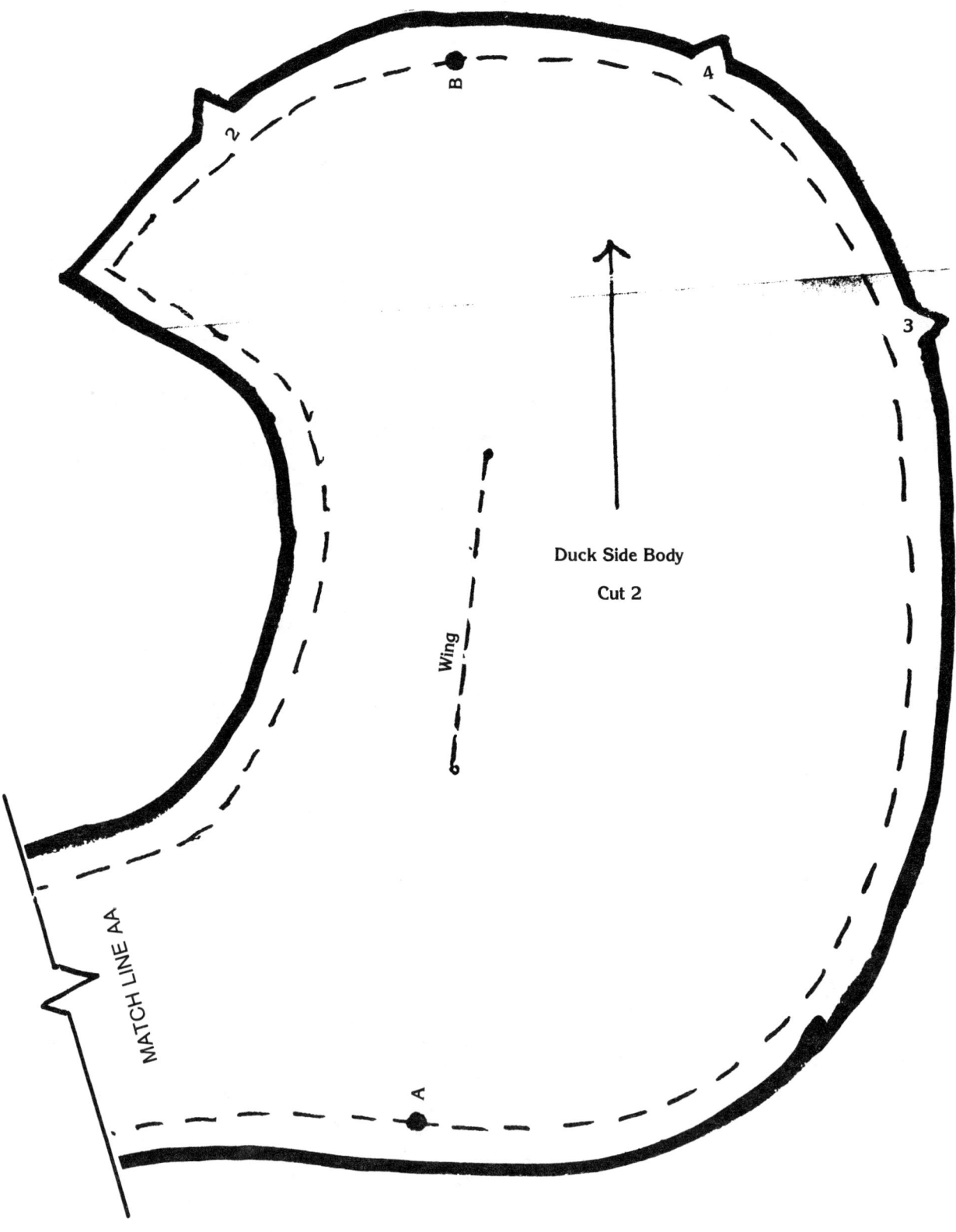

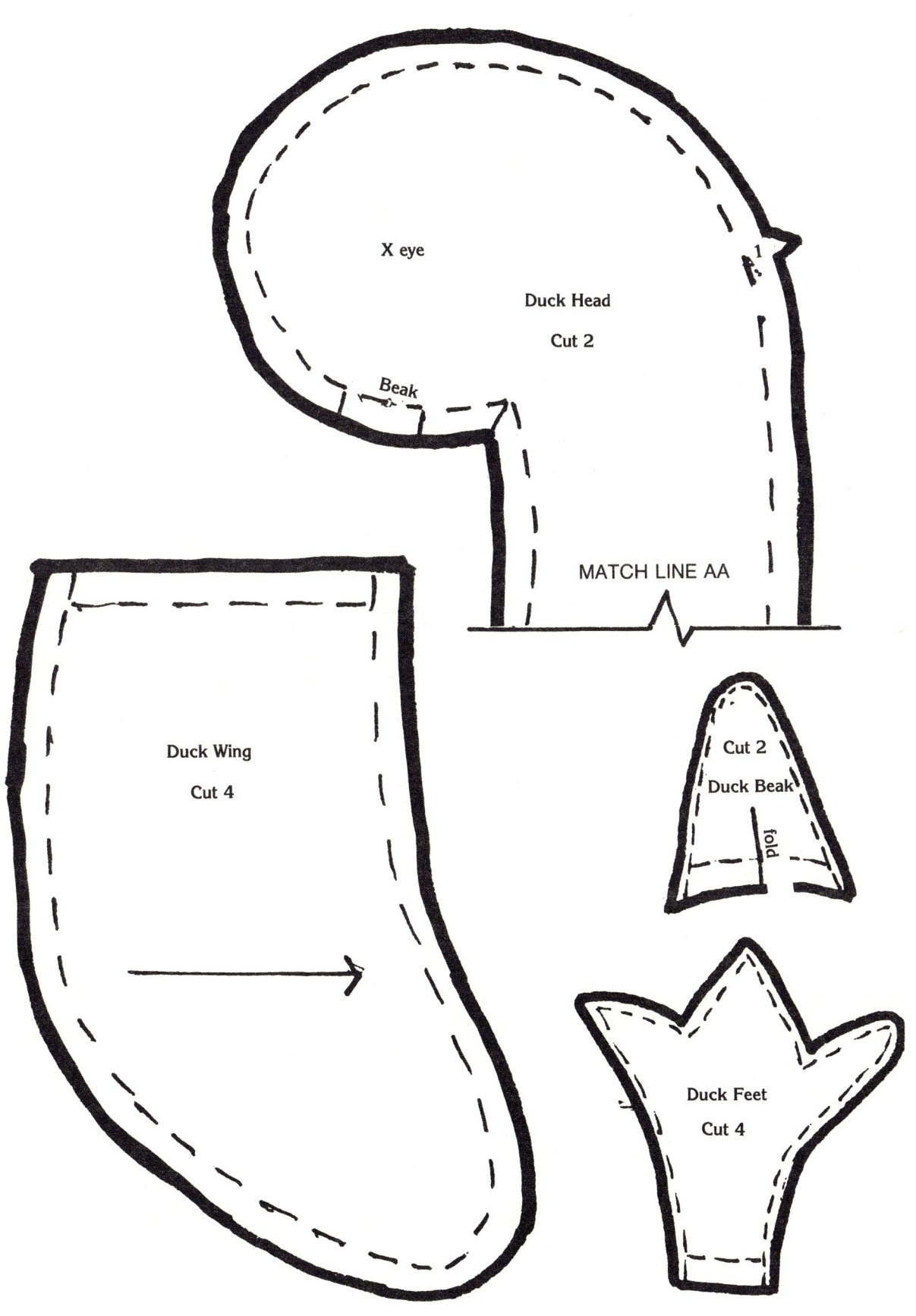

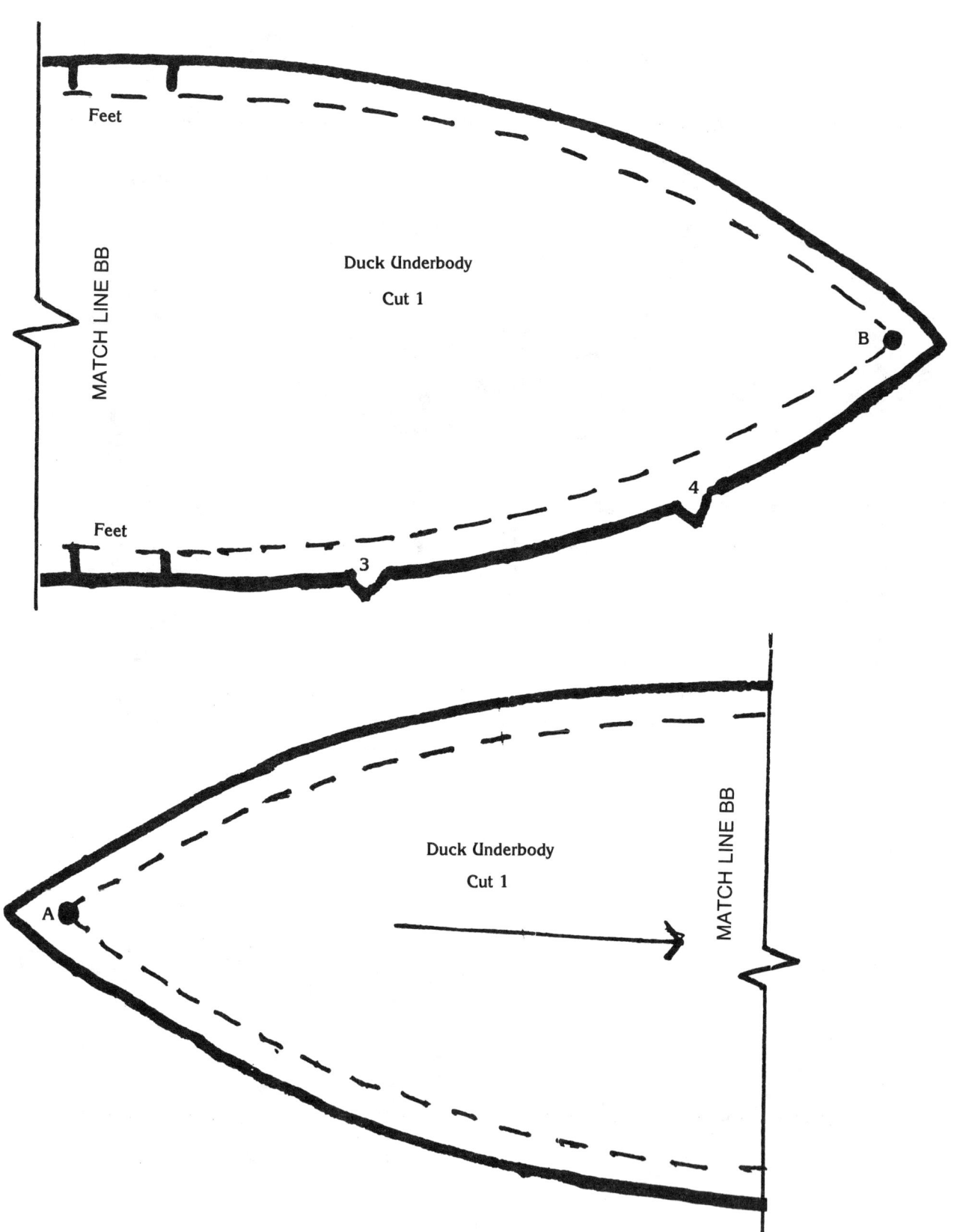

FOURTEEN PATTERN PIECES
15" (38 cm) LONG

Cutting Diagram

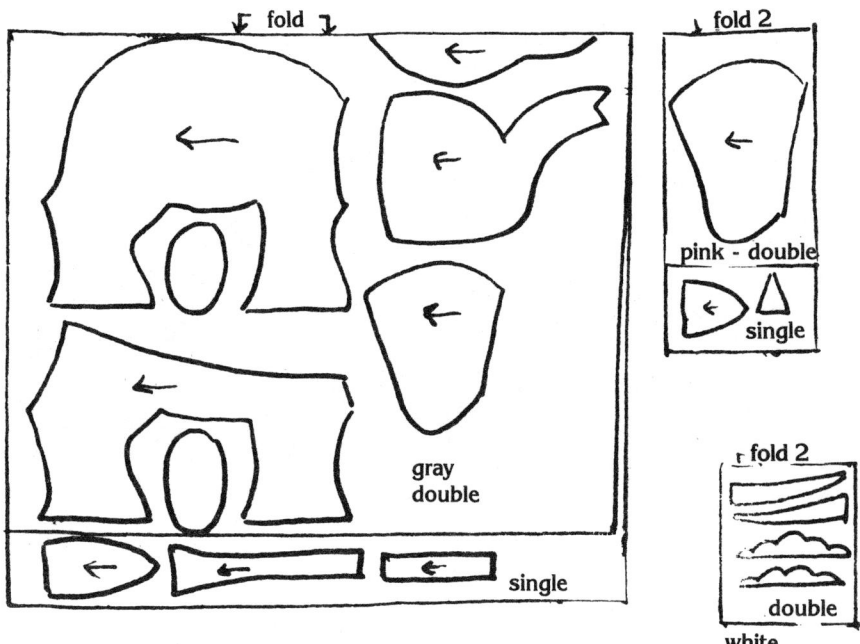

Materials Main color (gray): ½ yard of 45" material (½ m of 1 m 15 cm width fabric)
Pink or print fabric: 6" × 15" piece (15 cm × 38 cm)
White vinyl or felt: 6" × 8" piece (15 cm × 20 cm)
1½ lbs. (675 g) polyester fiberfill for stuffing
1 pair of safety eyes or 2 buttons or embroidery thread or felt scraps to appliqué eyes

6
Elephant

Materials are listed for a gray elephant with pink ears, trunk tip, and lip. You may, of course, choose any color you want, like a pink elephant with polka-dot ears. Elephants aren't shaggy, so the body should be made of a short pile or napped fabric like nonwale corduroy or velour, or a sturdy, nonstretch, plain-weave fabric.

Cutting Instructions

If using napped fabric, be sure to lay the pieces so all the arrows are in the same direction.

Of main color, cut two side bodies, two underbodies, two side heads, one head center, one undertrunk, two ears, one chin, one tail, and four soles.

Of pink fabric, cut two ear facings, one trunk tip, and one lower lip.

Of white vinyl or felt, cut two front toes and two back toes. See step 1 under sewing instructions before cutting tusks.

Sewing Instructions

All seams are ¼" (⅗ cm) unless otherwise stated.

1. *Tusks.* Fold vinyl or felt in half, wrong sides together. Draw the outline of the tusk pattern on the right side. Stitch just inside the outline (still folded), then cut out close to stitching. *Note:* If vinyl sticks under the presser foot, rub a thin film of sewing machine oil over the top surface. Wipe off after stitching. Stuff the tusks lightly.

On side heads, slit the tusk dart to the square. Sew the tusks into these darts in the side head at the base of the trunk. See Figure 1.

2. *Ears.* Sew ear facings to ears, right sides together, leaving straight edge open. Clip curves, turn right side out. Pleat where indicated on

the pattern, bringing the upper line to the lower line on the pink side of the ear. Machine baste the ears to the side heads between lines shown on pattern, having the pink side of the ear to the right side of the head and matching notches 1. See Figure 1.

3. *Head.* Sew darts in side bodies. Sew side heads to side bodies, from top edge to dot A, matching notches 1 and catching in ears. See Figure 2.

Sew head center to head/body sides, from dot B to dot C, matching and clipping at the square, also matching line to seam and notches 2.

4. *Trunk.* Sew top trunk seam, from dot B to the front end of the trunk. See Figure 2. Sew the undertrunk piece to each side of the side heads from the trunk tip to dot D, matching notches 3. Be sure tusks are facing forward. Sew trunk tip into the triangular opening. This is easiest if the pink triangle is laid on the bottom and the gray trunk is spread around it. Sew, with the gray side up, on each side of the triangle, breaking the stitching at the seams. See Figure 3.

5. *Lip and chin.* Stitch the lower lip across the bottom of the undertrunk, between dots D, matching notches 4. Stitch chin around the lower lip and along the bottom of the head on each side, matching notches 5 and 6 and dot D. End the stitching at dot A on each side. Be sure the tusks are facing forward. See Figure 4.

6. *Toes.* Sew darts in underbody pieces. Clip across the center of each dart as indicated on the pattern and Figure 7. Stitch the underbodies to the side bodies along the front of each leg, from the square to the bottom of the foot. See Figure 5. Open the front leg seam out flat, right side up. With white thread, top stitch the toes across the leg seam just above the seam allowance. (If using vinyl for toes, you want to oil the surface, as with the tusks.) See Figure 6. The front feet have five toes; the back feet have four.

7. *Feet.* Stitch the remaining part of the underbody seam, right sides together, from dot E to dot A, leaving the bottoms of the feet open. See Figure 7. Clip along the bottom edge of the feet inside the seam allowance, as shown on the pattern and Figure 8. Matching centers, right sides together, pin the sole of the foot into the opening, spreading the clips to Vs so the edges match. See Figure 9. With the sole down, stitch around the foot just above the clips. Repeat for the other three feet.

8. *Body.* Fold tail lengthwise and stitch, leaving both short ends open. Turn right side out, using a bodkin or safety pin. If your fabric ravels, you may want to turn in the ends and stitch. Or let it fringe a bit, as elephants may have some tuft on the ends of their tails. Or tie a tight knot at the end. Sew tail to the side body where indicated on the pattern and Figure 7.

Sew the center back seam from dot E to dot C, enclosing the tail. Sew the center underbody seam, from dot E to the neck edge, leaving open between notches 7 and 8 for stuffing. Sew the underpart of the neck seam, between dots A, matching notches 9.

9. Clip curves and turn right side out. Insert safety eyes, if you are using them. Stuff the elephant firmly. Begin with the trunk, using small wads of fiberfill in the tip. Dimple in the sides of the pink triangle, so it folds like a prehensile trunk. Use a dowel or a chopstick to pack the stuffing in tightly. You may want to use a 6" (15 cm) piece of ¼" (⅗ cm) diameter doweling in the center of each leg to keep them from breaking as the elephant ages. Pad the bottom of the feet and stuff firmly all around the dowel, so it stays centered in the leg. Stuff the body last. Sew up the opening. Sew buttons for eyes, or embroider or use felt appliqué if you didn't use safety eyes.

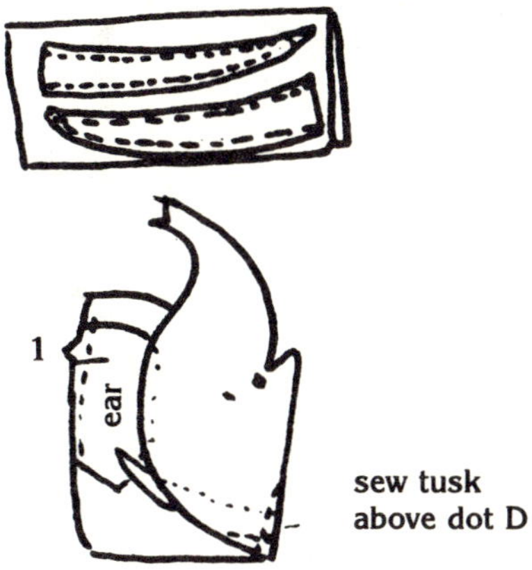

Figure 1

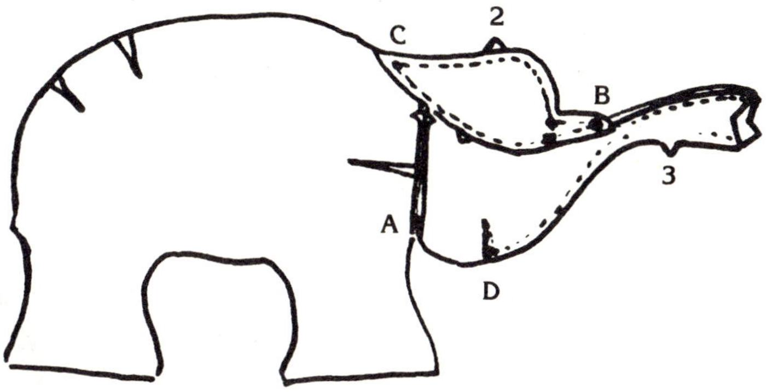

fold

1
ear
sew tusk above dot D

Figure 2

Figure 3

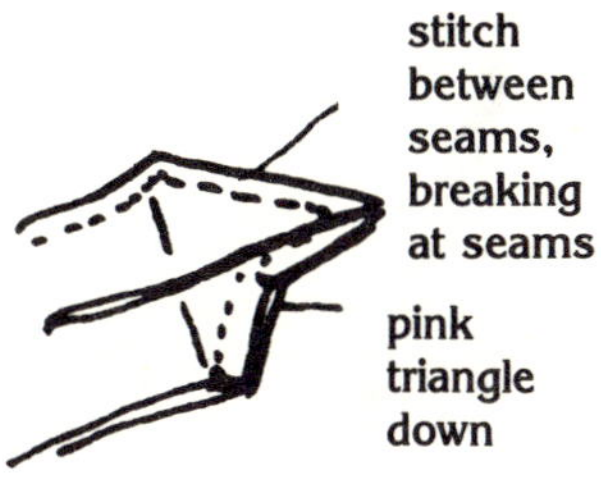

stitch between seams, breaking at seams

pink triangle down

Figure 4

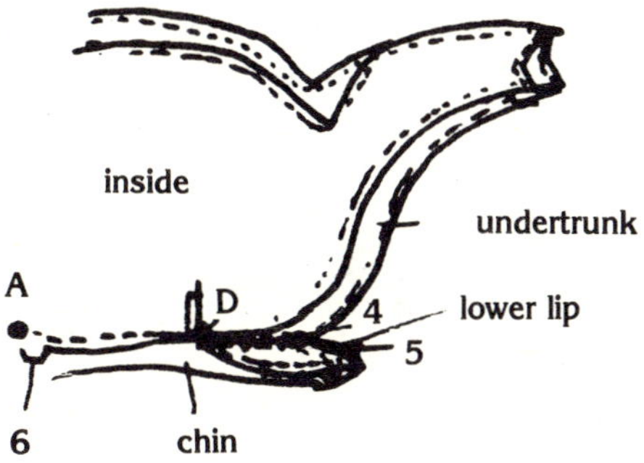

inside
undertrunk
A D 4 lower lip
5
6 chin

Figure 5

Figure 6

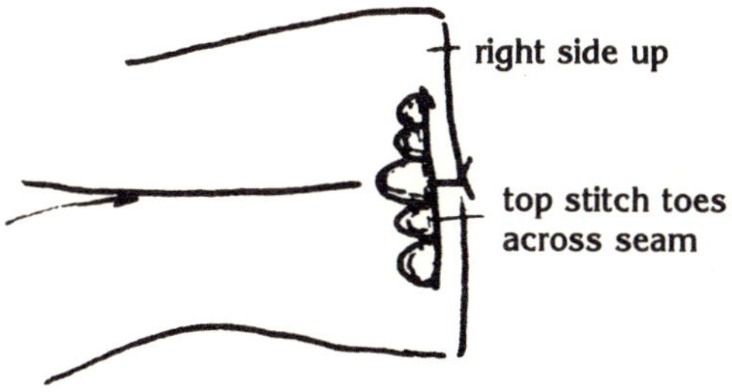

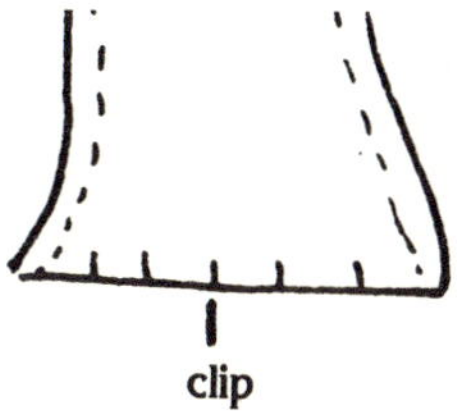

right side up
top stitch toes across seam

Figure 8

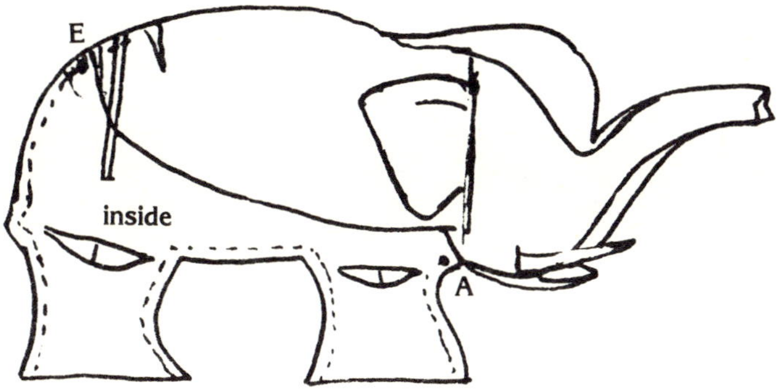

clip

Figure 7

E
inside
A

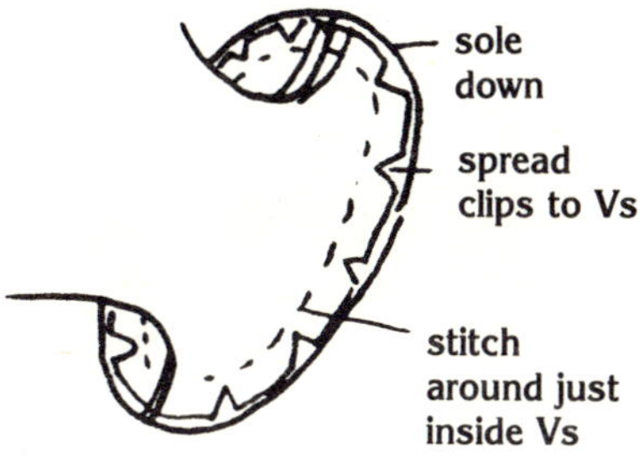

Figure 9

sole down
spread clips to Vs
stitch around just inside Vs

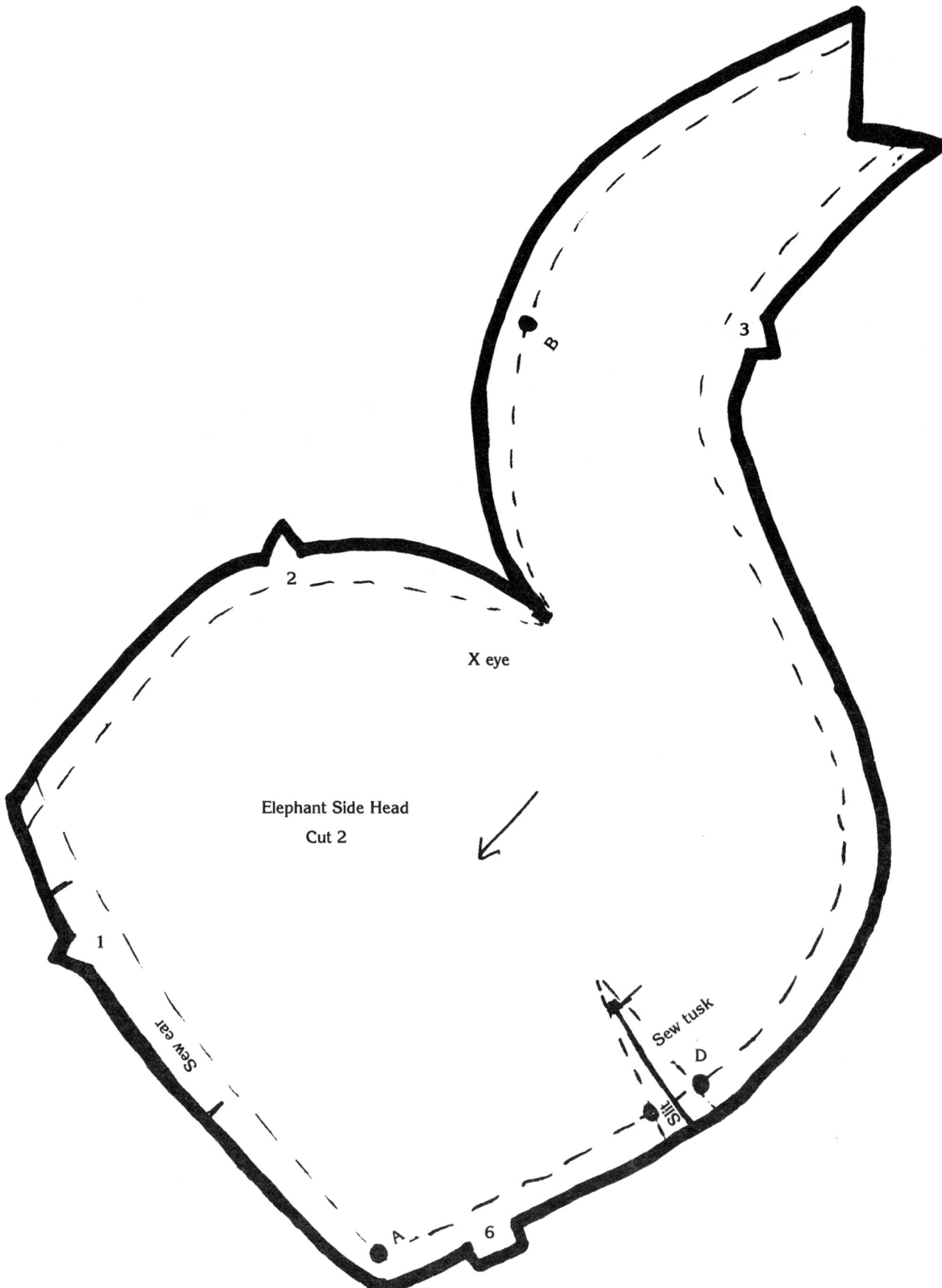

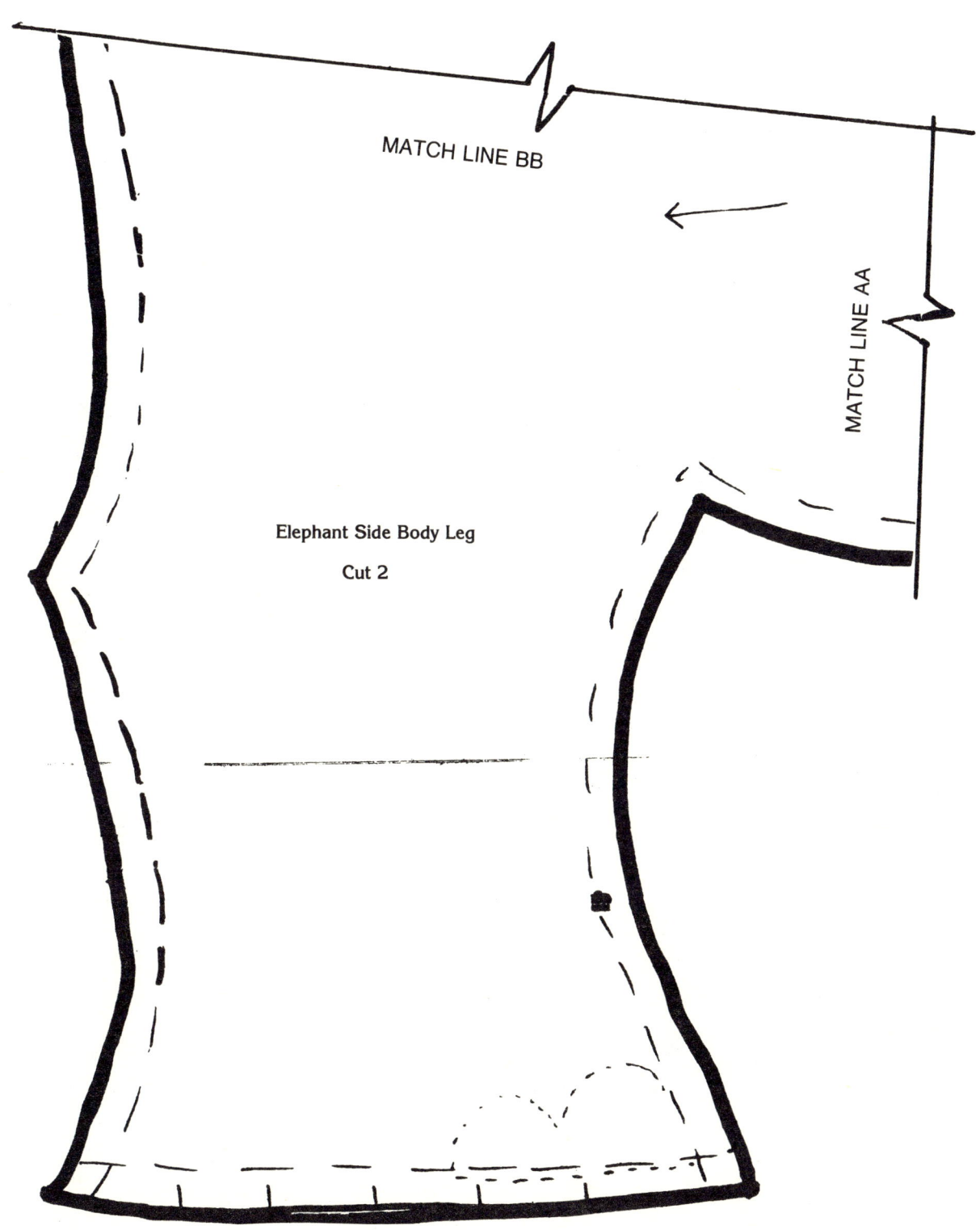

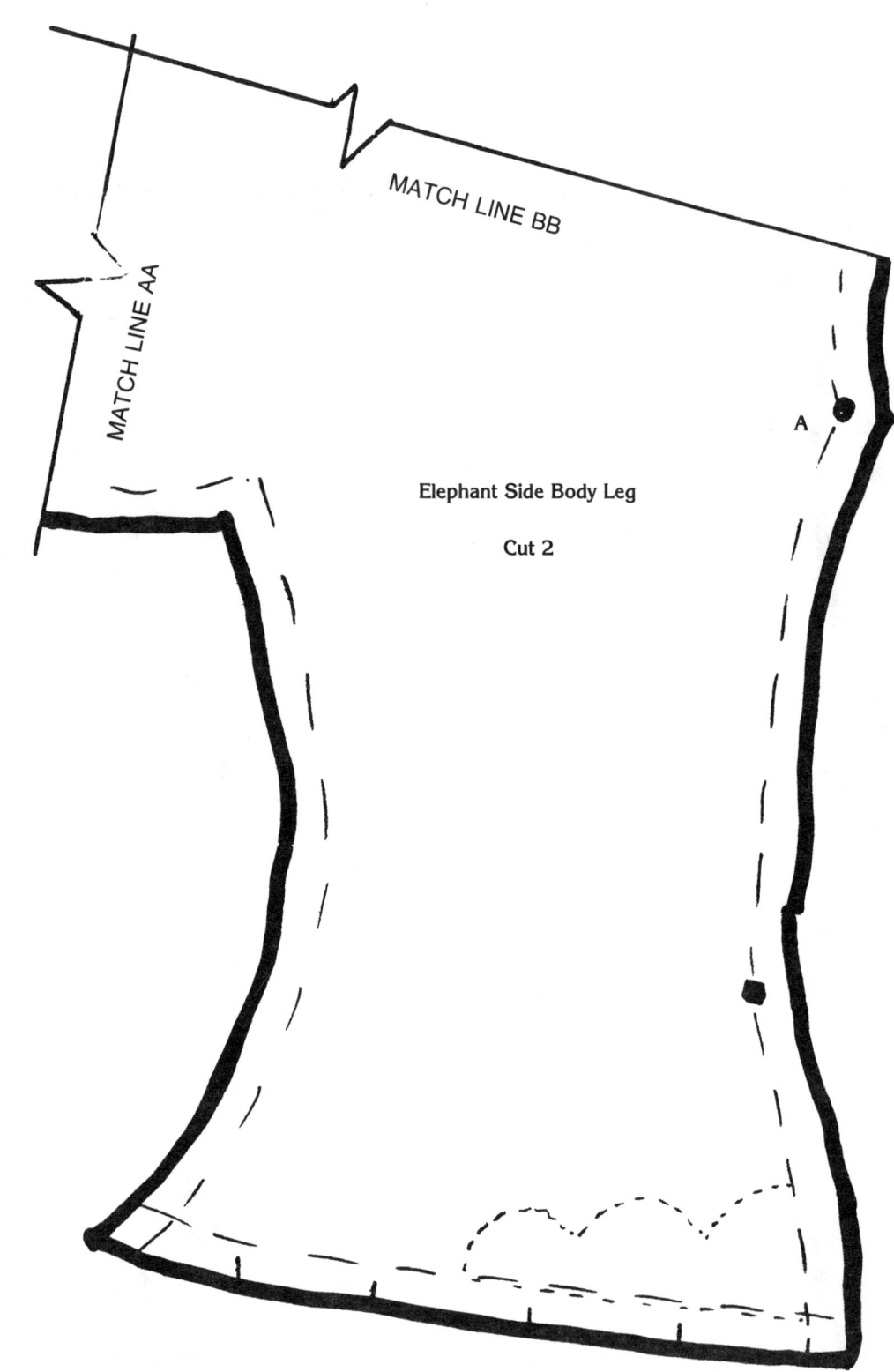

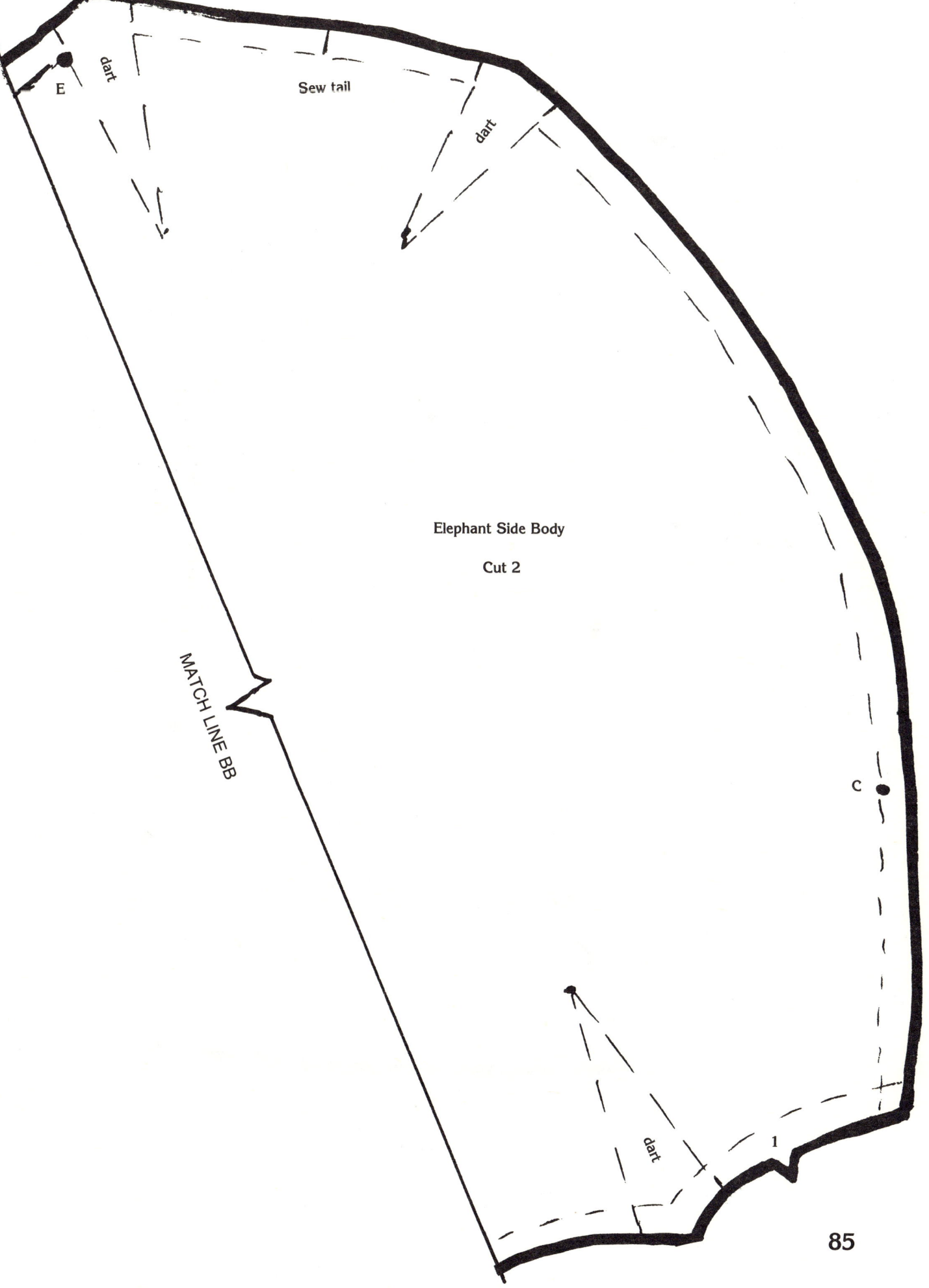

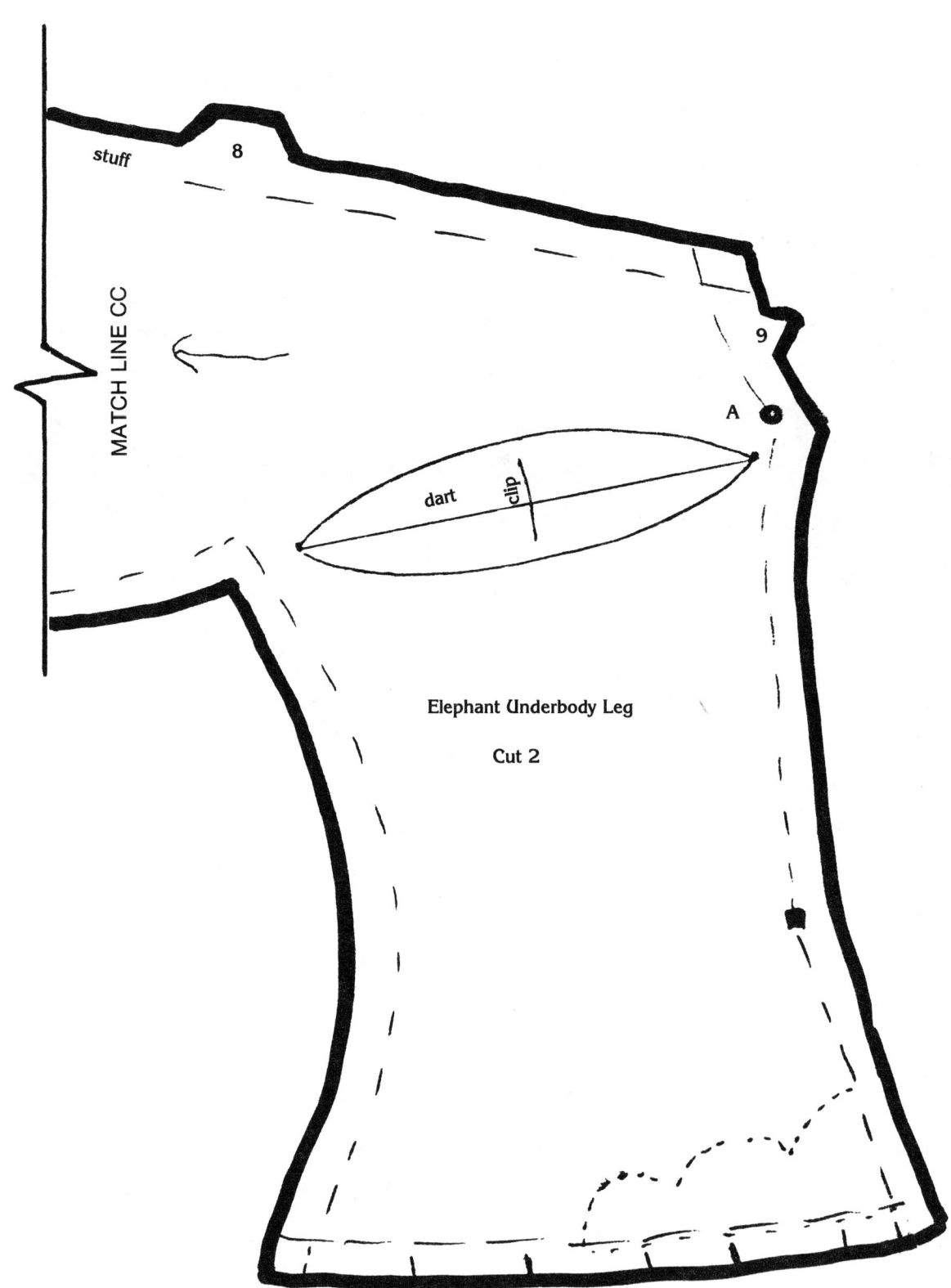

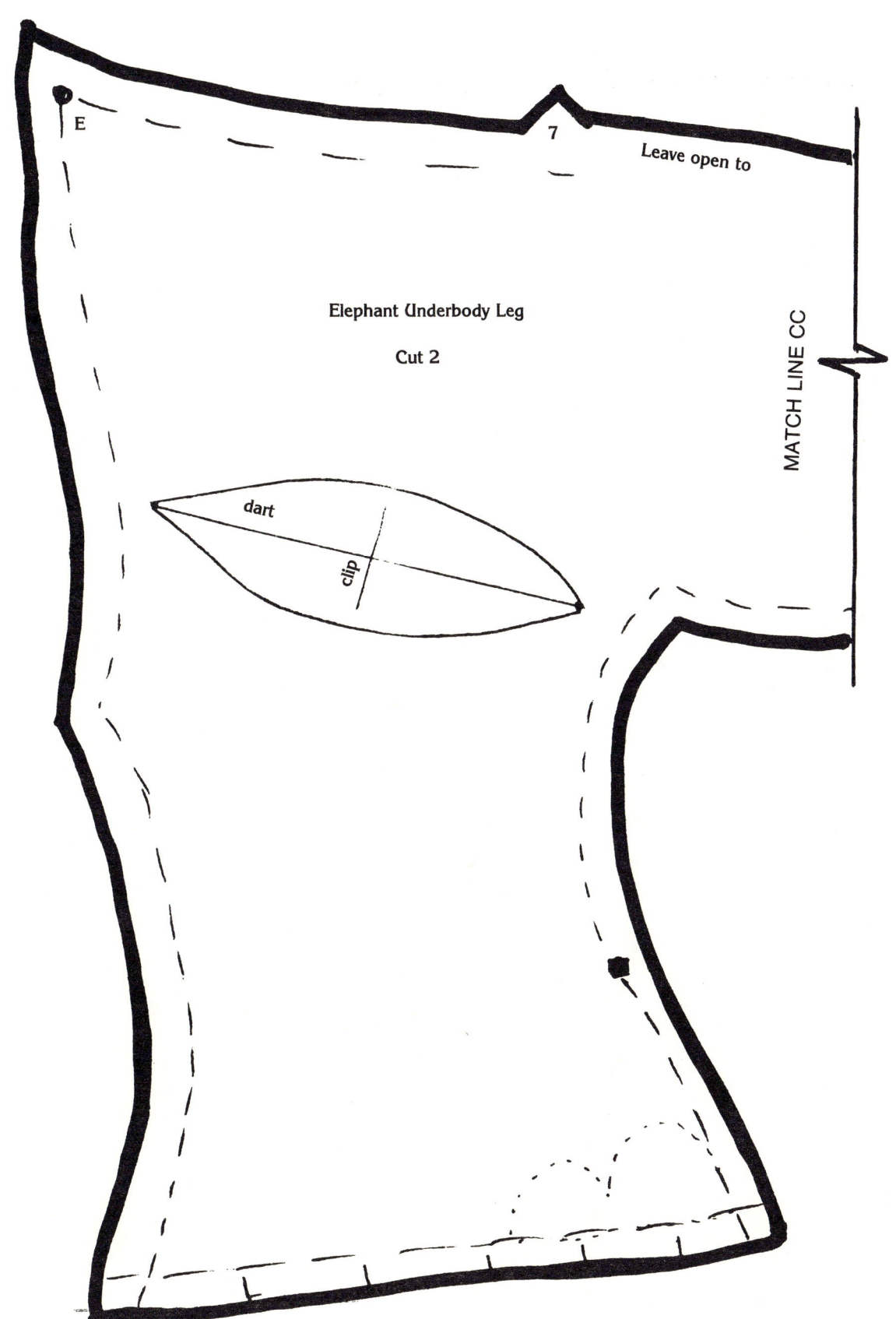

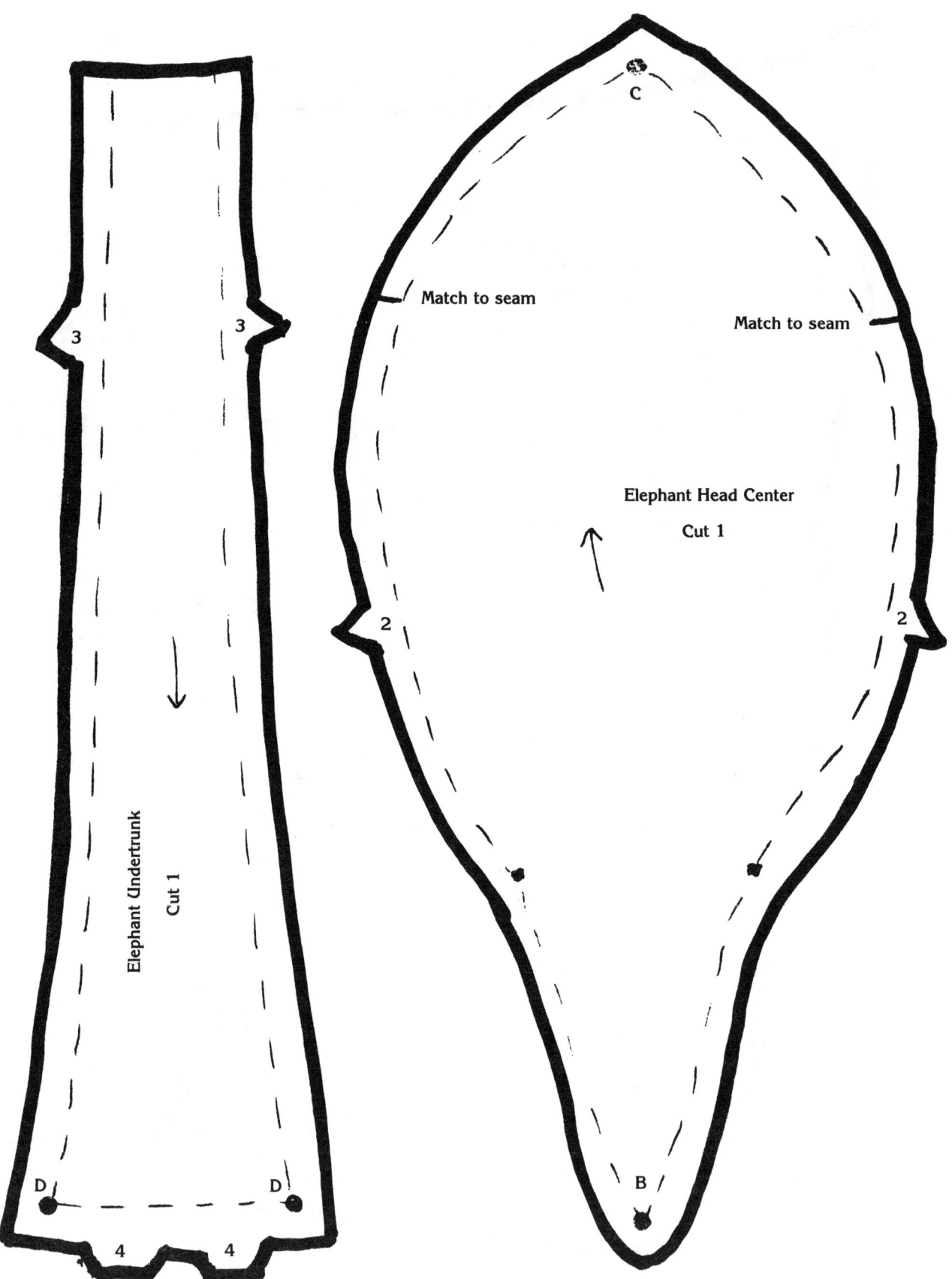

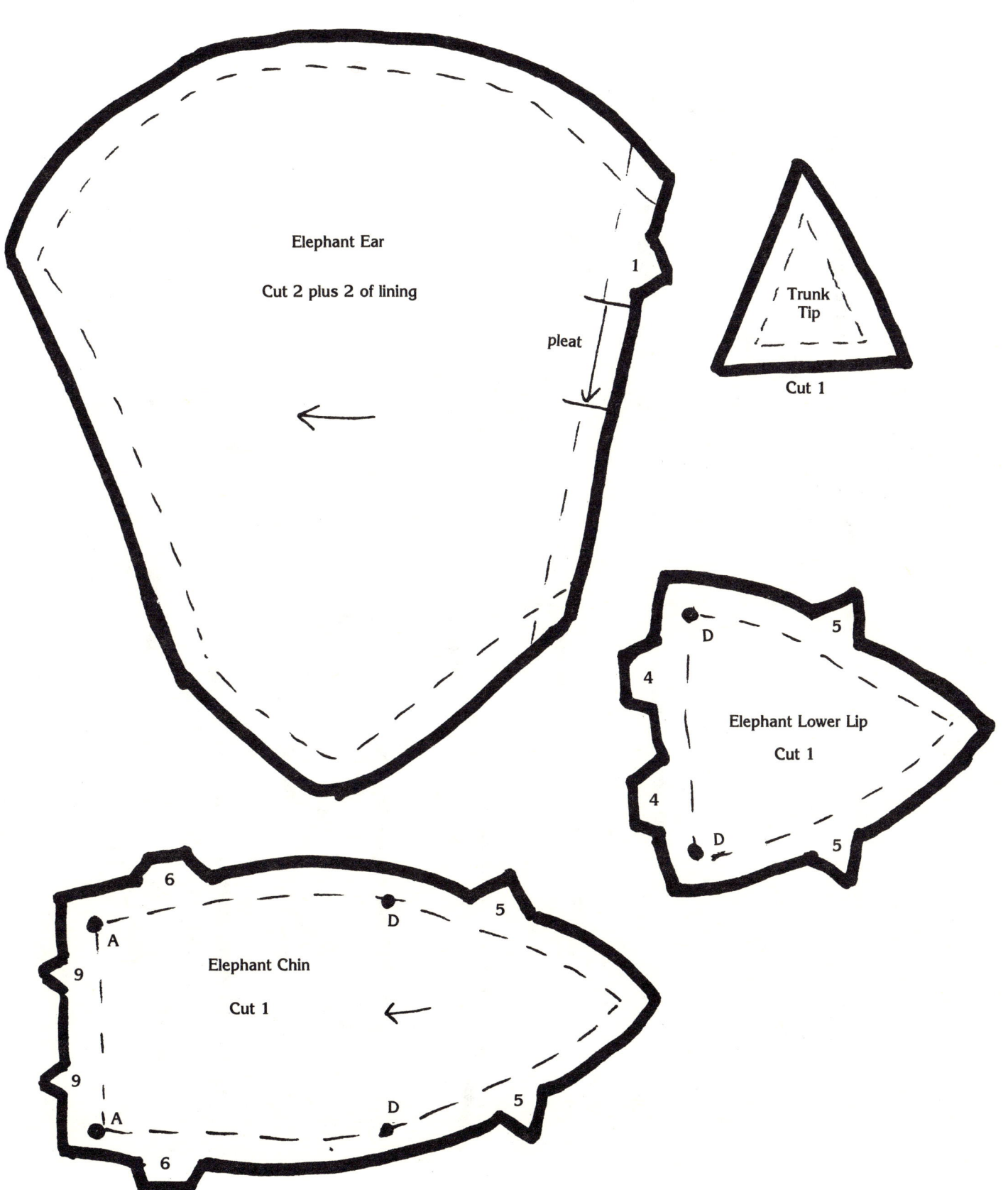

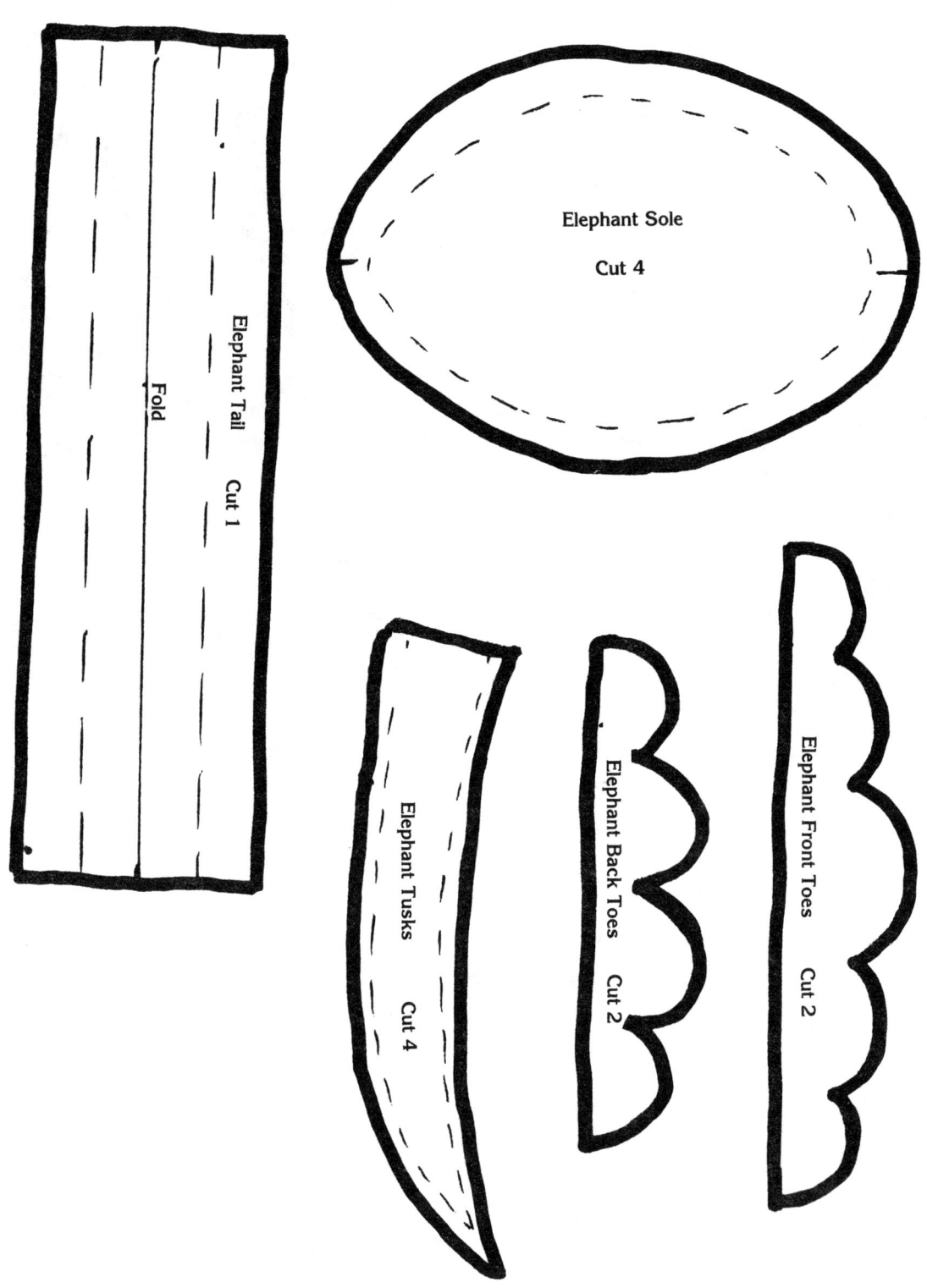

TWELVE PATTERN PIECES
LARGE 15" (38 cm) TALL
SMALL 10" (25 cm) TALL

Cutting Diagram

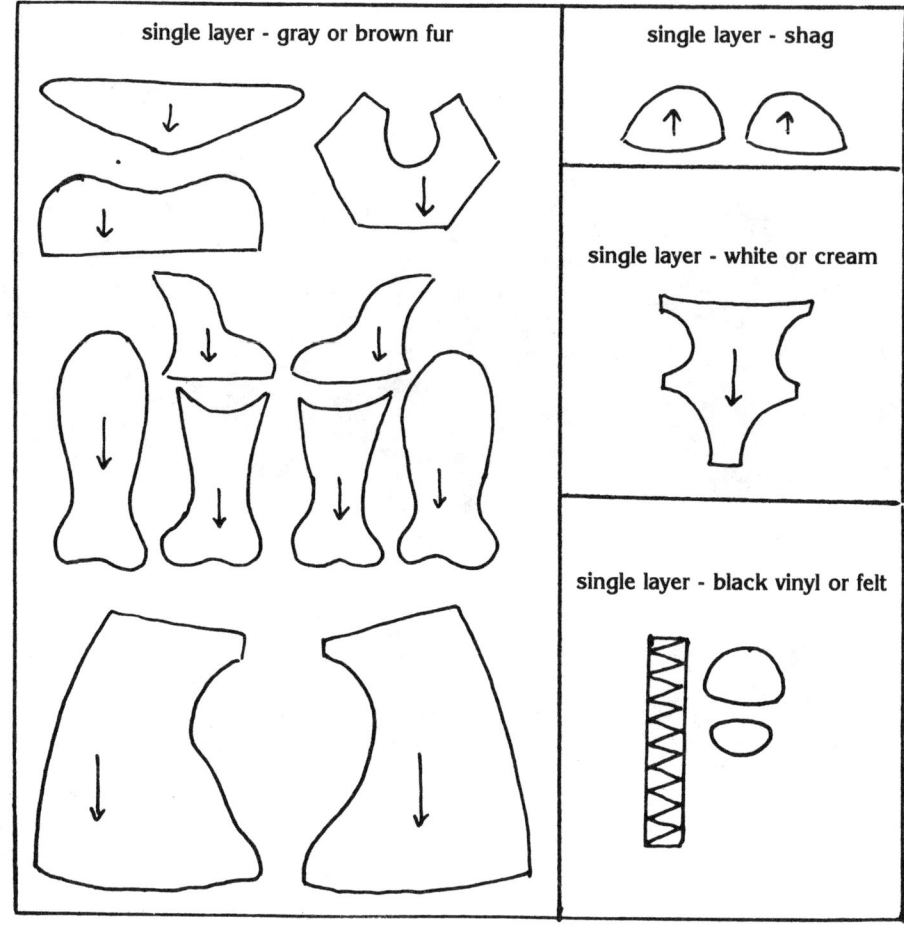

	Large	Small
Materials Gray or brown fur fabric:	¾ yard of 36" or ½ yard of 40" (68 cm of 1 m width fabric)	½ yard of 36" (½ m of 1 m width fabric)
White fur fabric:	9" x 11" piece (23 cm x 28 cm)	8" x 9" piece (20 cm x 23 cm)
Shag fur fabric:	6" x 8½" piece (15 cm x 22 cm)	3½" x 10" piece (9 cm x 25 cm)
Black vinyl or firm fabric:	2½" x 15" piece (6 cm x 38 cm)	2½" x 12" piece (6 cm x 30 cm)
Polyester fiberfill:	2 lbs. (1 kg)	1½ lbs. (675 g)

1 pair safety eyes or 2 buttons

7
Koala

Koalas are very popular animals. They look so furry, so cute and cuddly. This koala is designed to sit, but it also nestles nicely in your arms so it's very hugable. Koalas have two thumbs and three fingers on their forepaws, so the claws are divided like that. The claws are optional, of course. Koalas have large noses and shaggy ears.

Cutting Instructions

See the Introduction for working with fur fabrics.

Of gray or brown fur, cut one head front, one head back, one underbody, two body backs, two inner legs, two outer arms, two underarms.

Of white fur, cut one body front.

Of shag fur, cut two ear linings.

Of black vinyl, or fabric, cut one nose, one nose tip and 16 claws (claws optional).

Sewing Instructions

Use ¼" (⅗ cm) seam allowance unless otherwise indicated.

1. *Claws (optional)*. Fold each of the 16 claws on the center fold, wrong sides together, and top stitch ⅛" (³⁄₁₀ cm) from the edge. (If using vinyl and it sticks under the presser foot, rub a thin film of sewing machine oil on the tip surface before stitching. Wipe off after stitching.) Trim close to stitching. Set aside. (You might want to hold the edges together with a bit of masking tape while stitching. Tear away after stitching.)

2. *Nose*. Sew nose to nose tip along curved seam shown on pattern,

stitching to edges, and curving pieces to fit. See Figure 1. Fold nose tip along center line, wrong sides together, top stitch on stitching line. See Figure 2. On outside, form a box pleat by bringing center to stitching line, and baste across bottom to hold. See Figure 3.

3. *Head.* Sew darts in head front. Sew center front seam, matching notches 1. Stitch nose into center hole in face, matching centers and notches 2. Pleat ear linings and stitch to head front, matching notches 3. Stitch head back to head front/ears, matching notches 4 and 5, and center. Clip curves and turn head right side out. See Figure 4.

If using safety eyes, insert at x in pattern. If using buttons for eyes, sew on after the animal is stuffed. Set head aside.

4. *Body.* Stitch inner legs to body backs from dot A to lower edge, matching notches 6. Sew center back seam, leaving open between notches 7 and 8 for stuffing. Stitch front to inner legs from dot A to bottom edge, matching notches 9. Matching notches 10, sew the front to the back at the shoulder seam. See Figure 5.

Fold six claws so the seam is centered underneath. Stitch to the right side of the bottom, seam side down, as indicated on the pattern and Figure 6. Sew bottom into koala body, matching center front and back and notches 11, and catching in claws.

5. *Arms.* Fold ten claws so seams are centered underneath. Stitch, seam side down, to the right side of the underarms, as shown on the pattern and Figure 7.

Sew wrist and shoulder darts in the outer arms. Clip shoulder darts down center and open flat. Clip across center of wrist dart as indicated on pattern. Stitch underarms to outer arms between dots B and C, right sides together catching in claws. Clip curves, turn right side out. Insert arms into armholes, matching notches 12. (Thumbs are facing inward in finished animal.) Match the shoulder dart in the outer arm to the shoulder seam, and dot A on the underarm to dot A where the back, front, and inner leg meet. Ease to fit if necessary. If there are too many thicknesses to go under your presser foot, you may have to trim some tips or even do some hand sewing in that area.

6. Sew head into neck opening of body, matching centers and notches 13. Clip curves, turn koala right side out through center back opening. Stuff firmly. Sew up center back opening. Sew on buttons for eyes, if you did not use safety eyes.

Figure 1

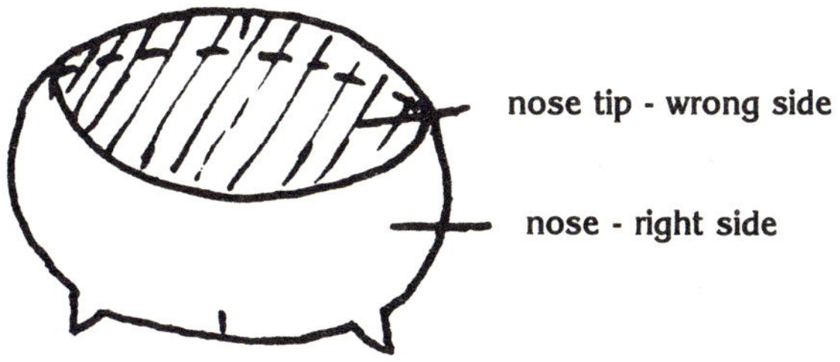

nose tip - wrong side
nose - right side

Figure 2

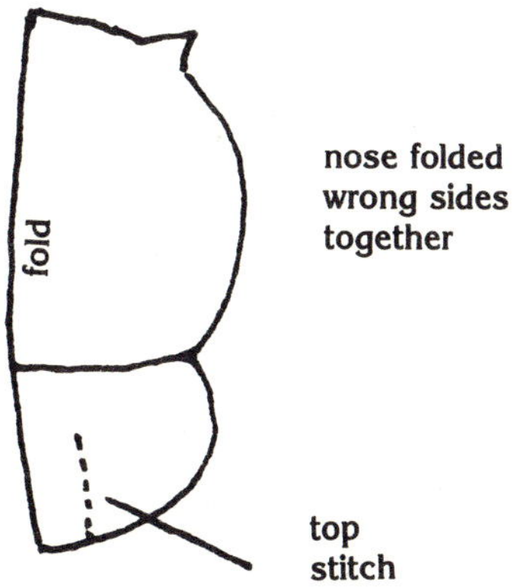

fold

nose folded wrong sides together

top stitch

Figure 3

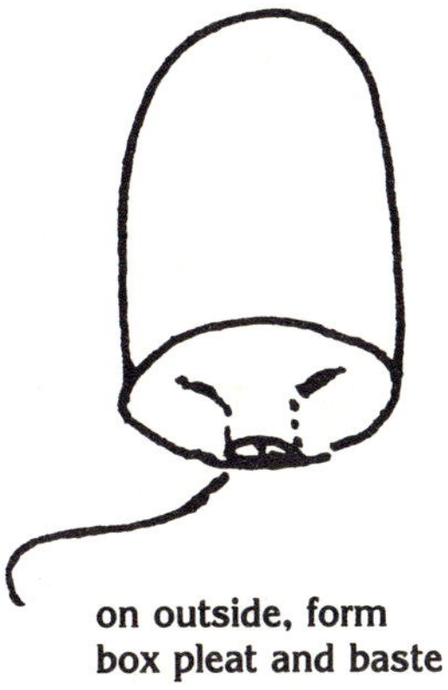

on outside, form box pleat and baste

Figure 4

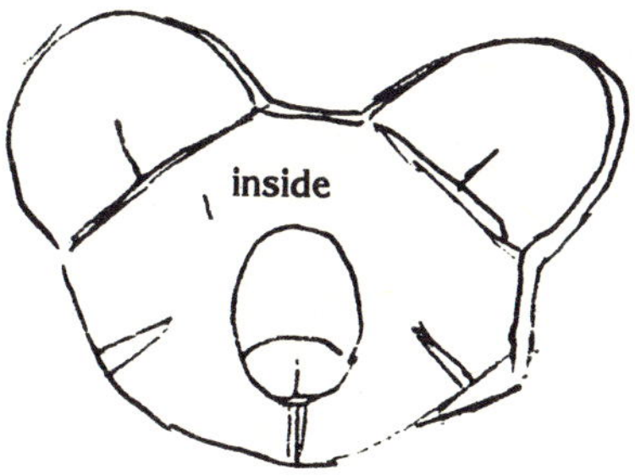

inside

Figure 5

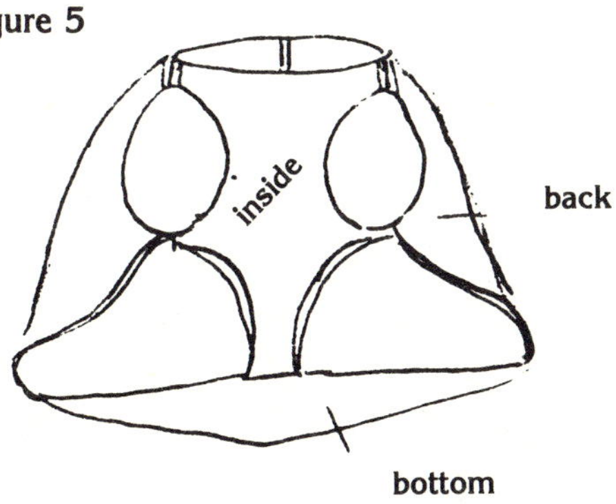

inside

back

bottom

Figure 6

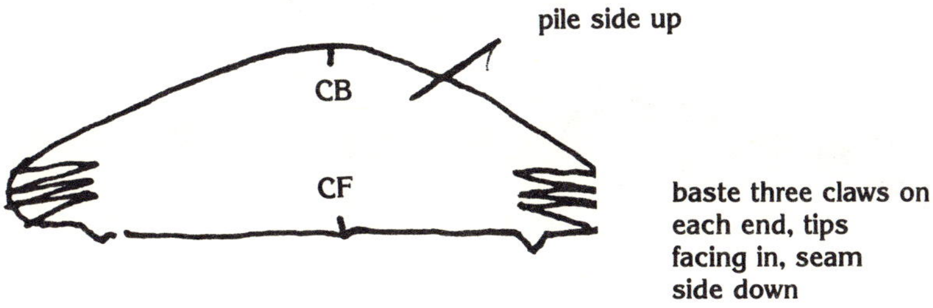

pile side up

CB
CF

baste three claws on each end, tips facing in, seam side down

Figure 7

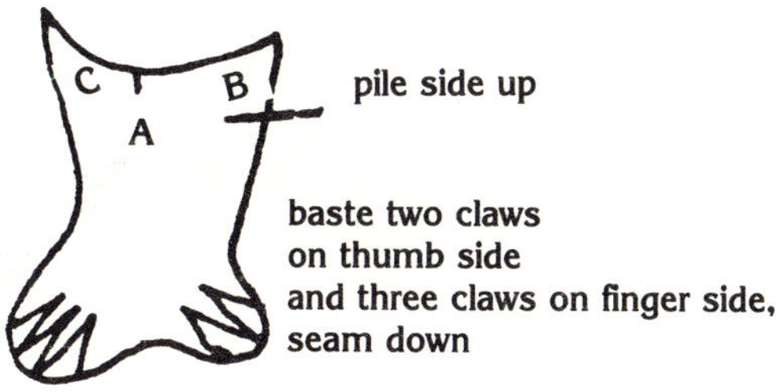

C B
 A

pile side up

baste two claws on thumb side and three claws on finger side, seam down

95

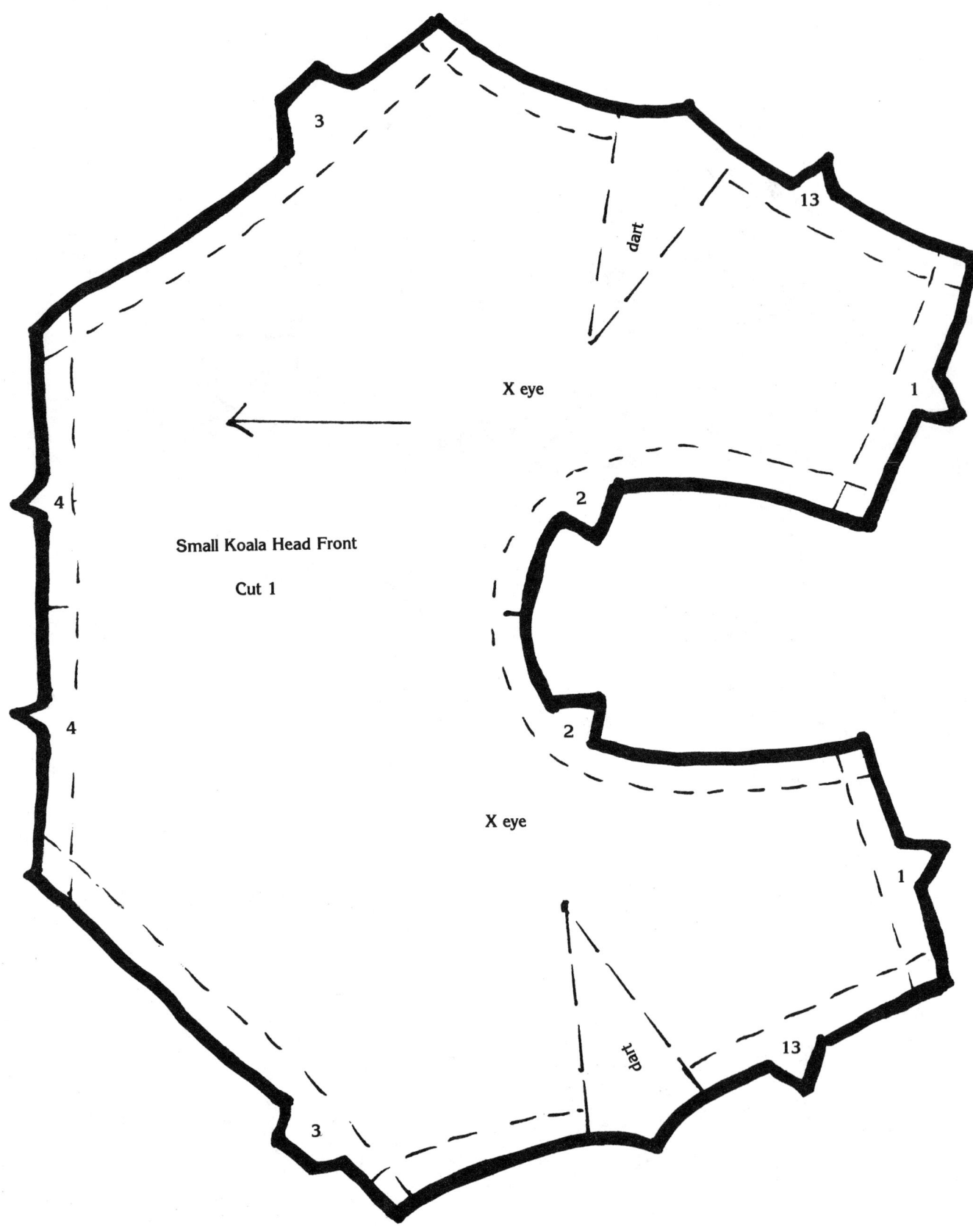

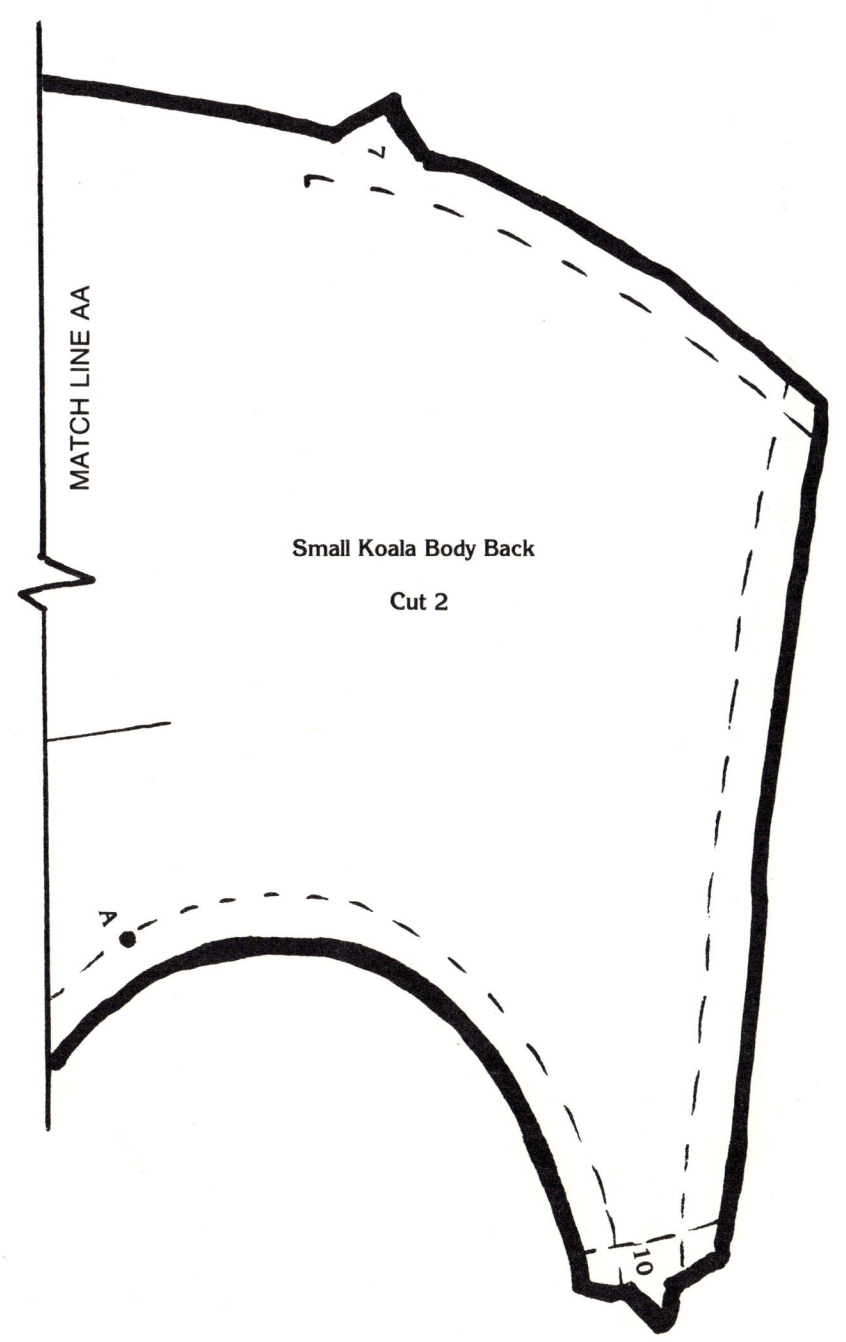

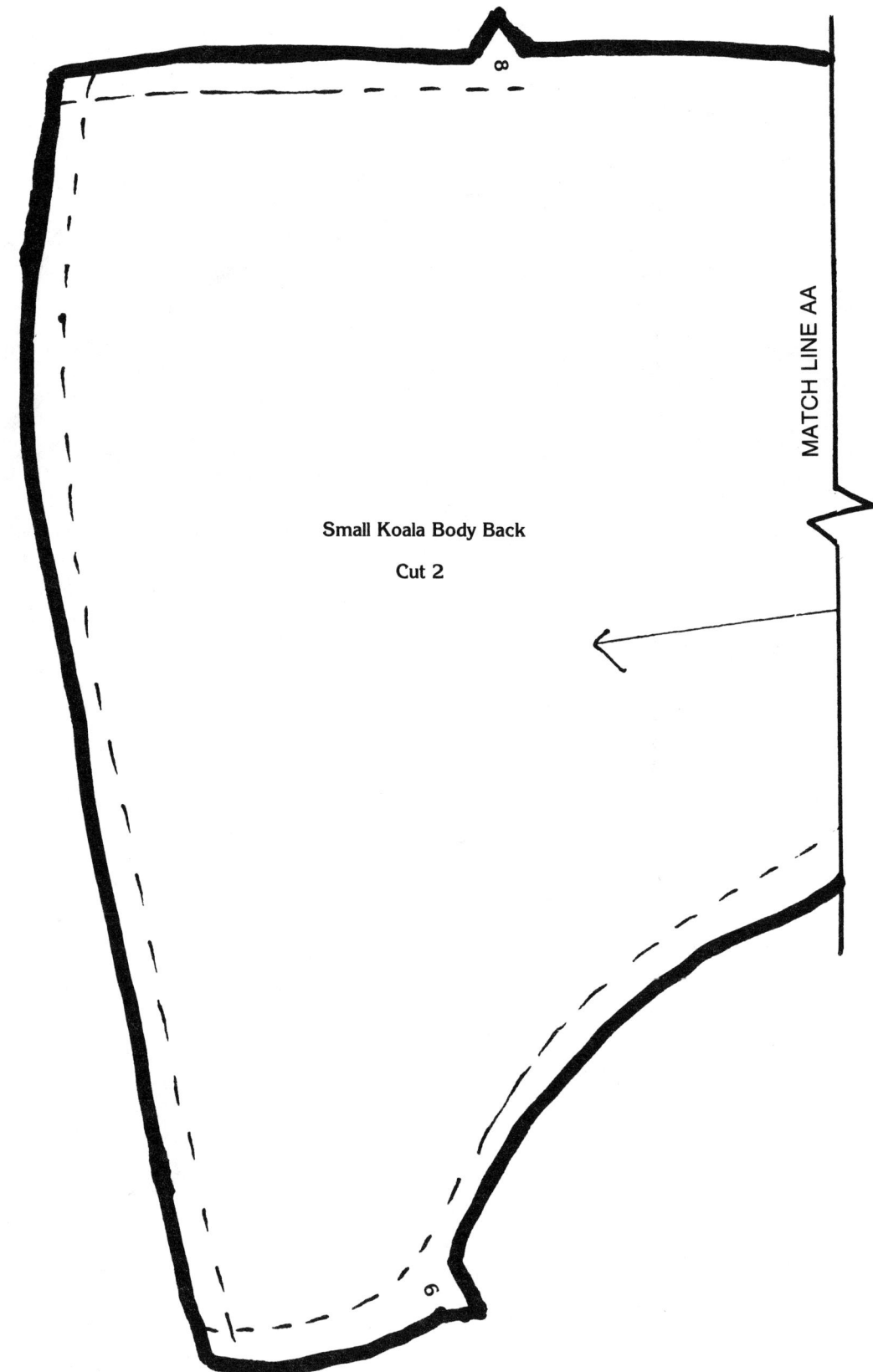

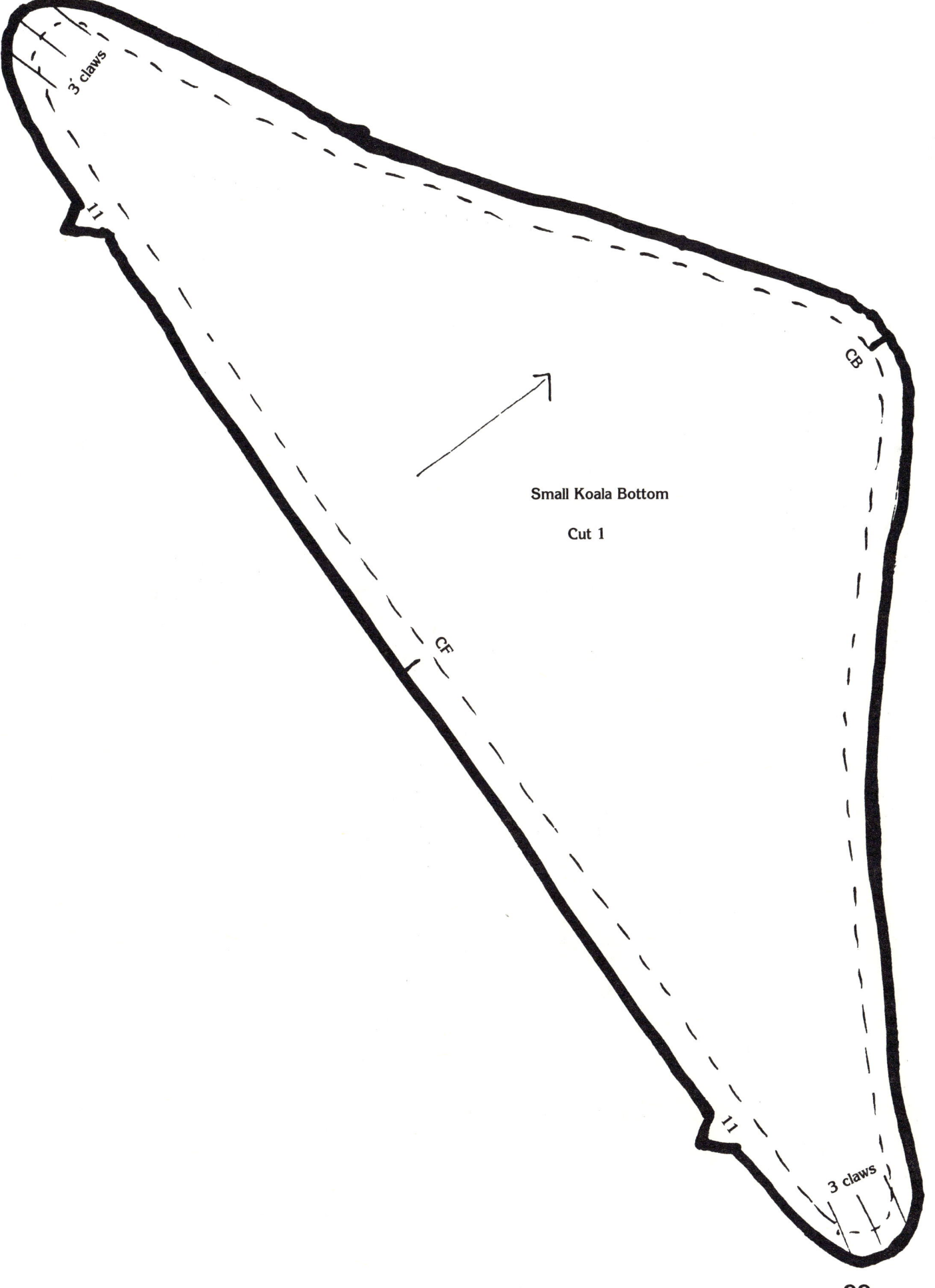

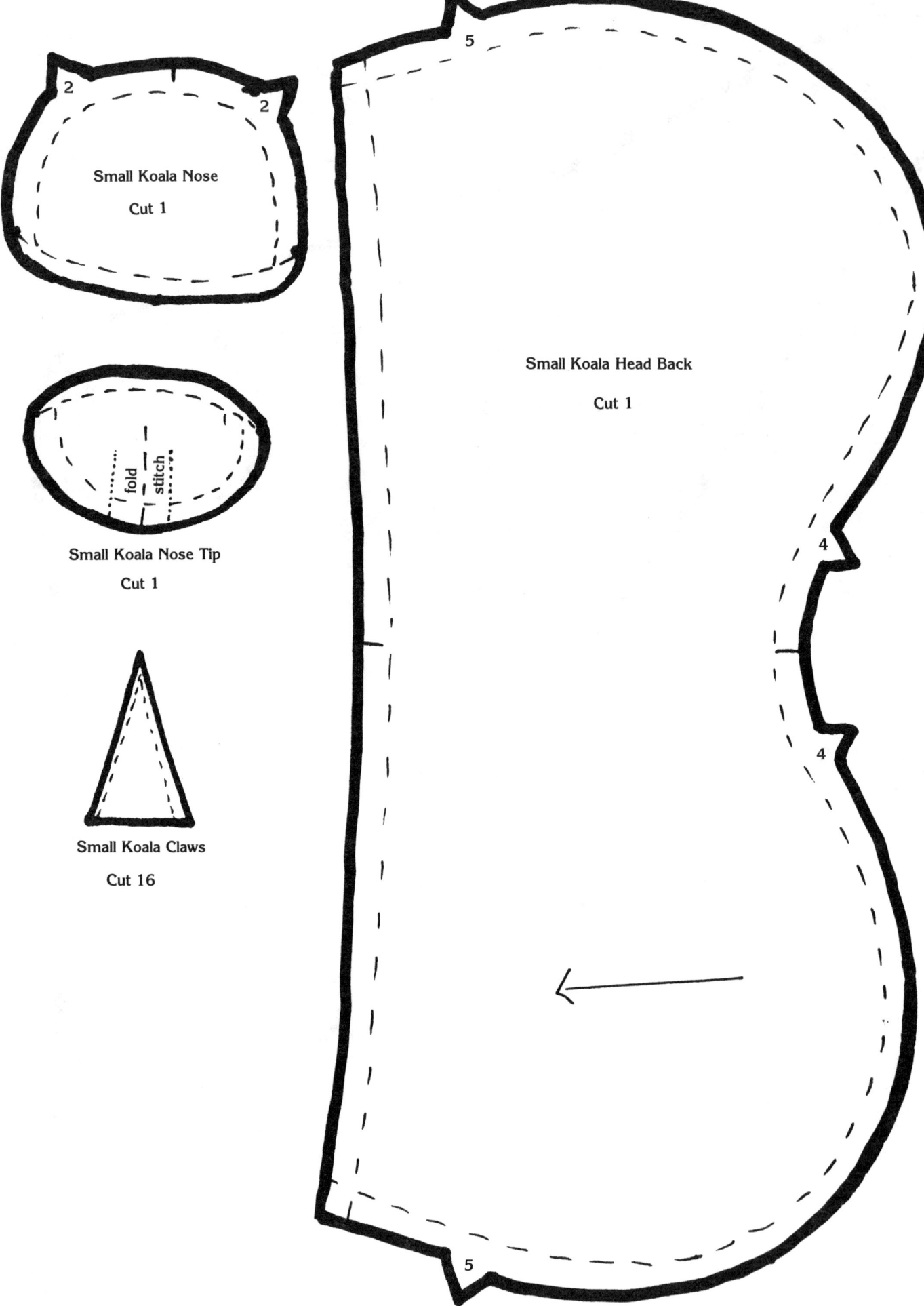

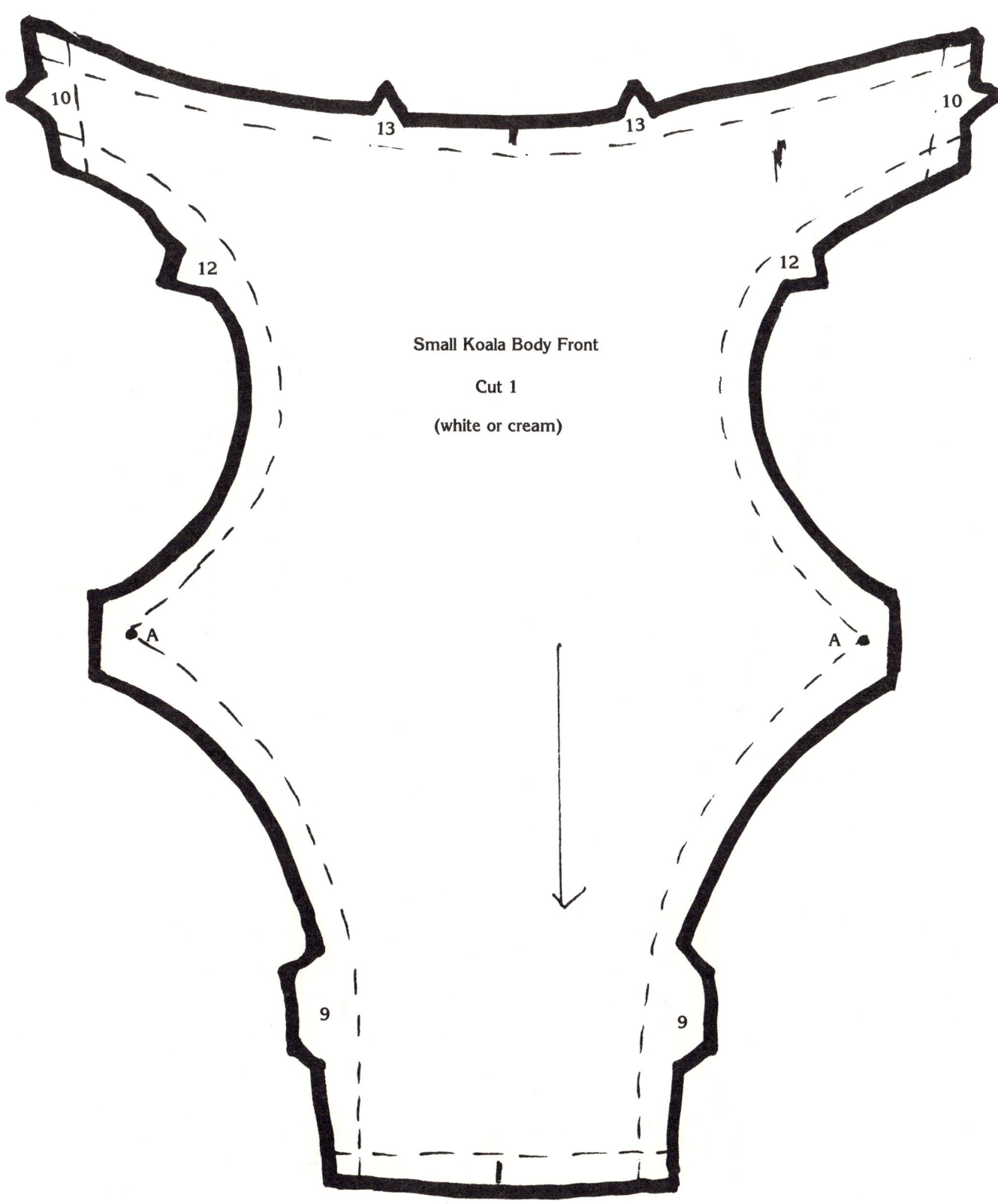

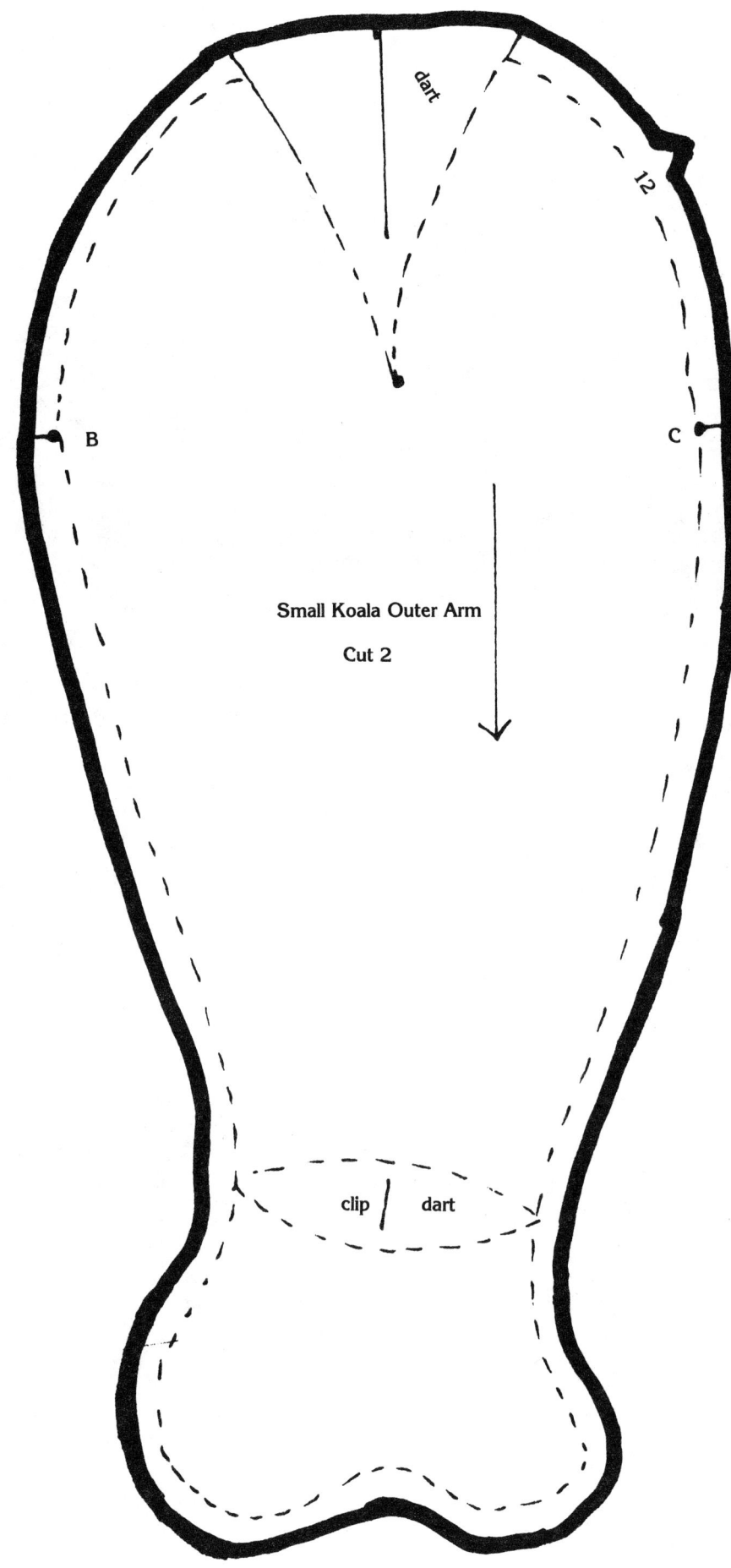

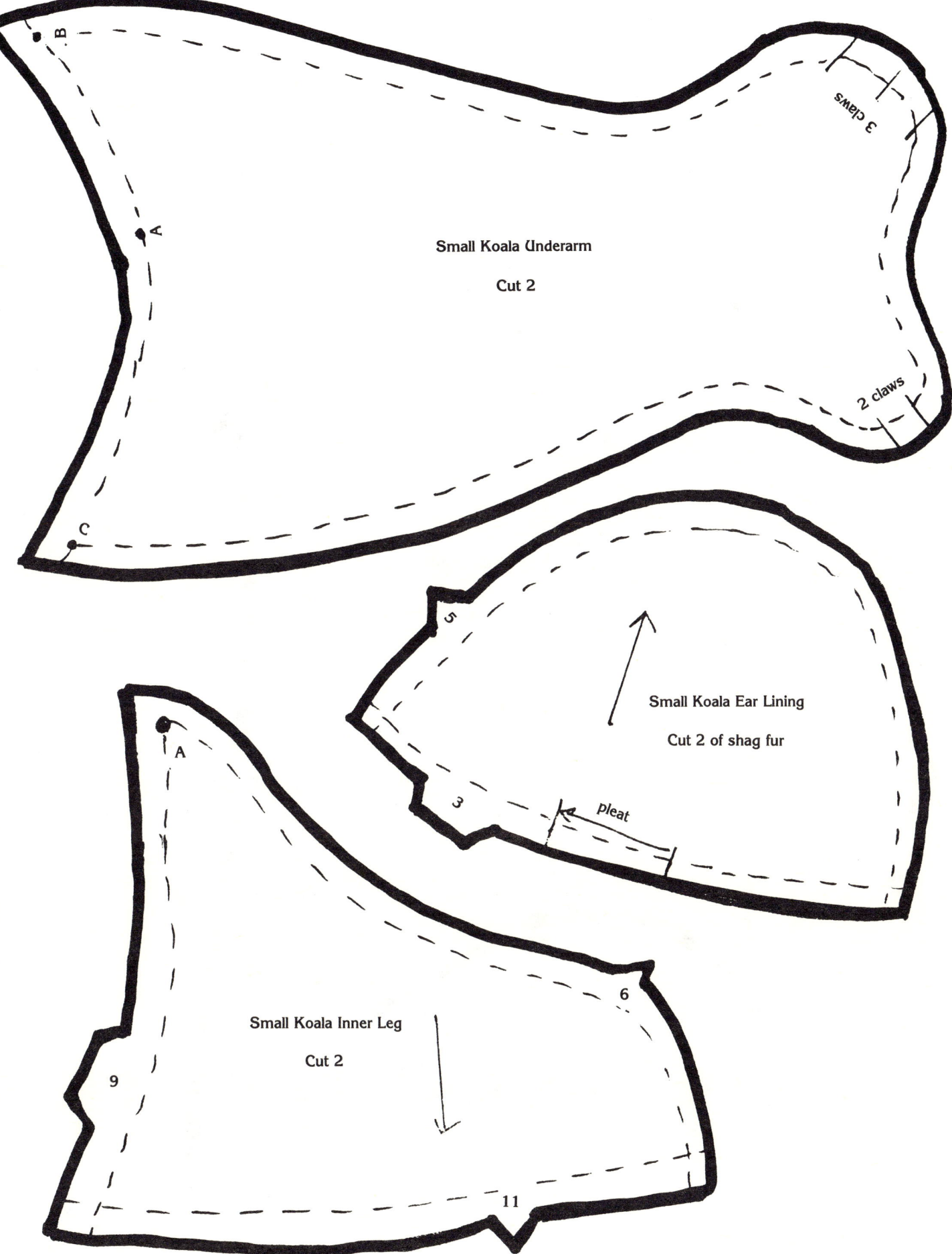

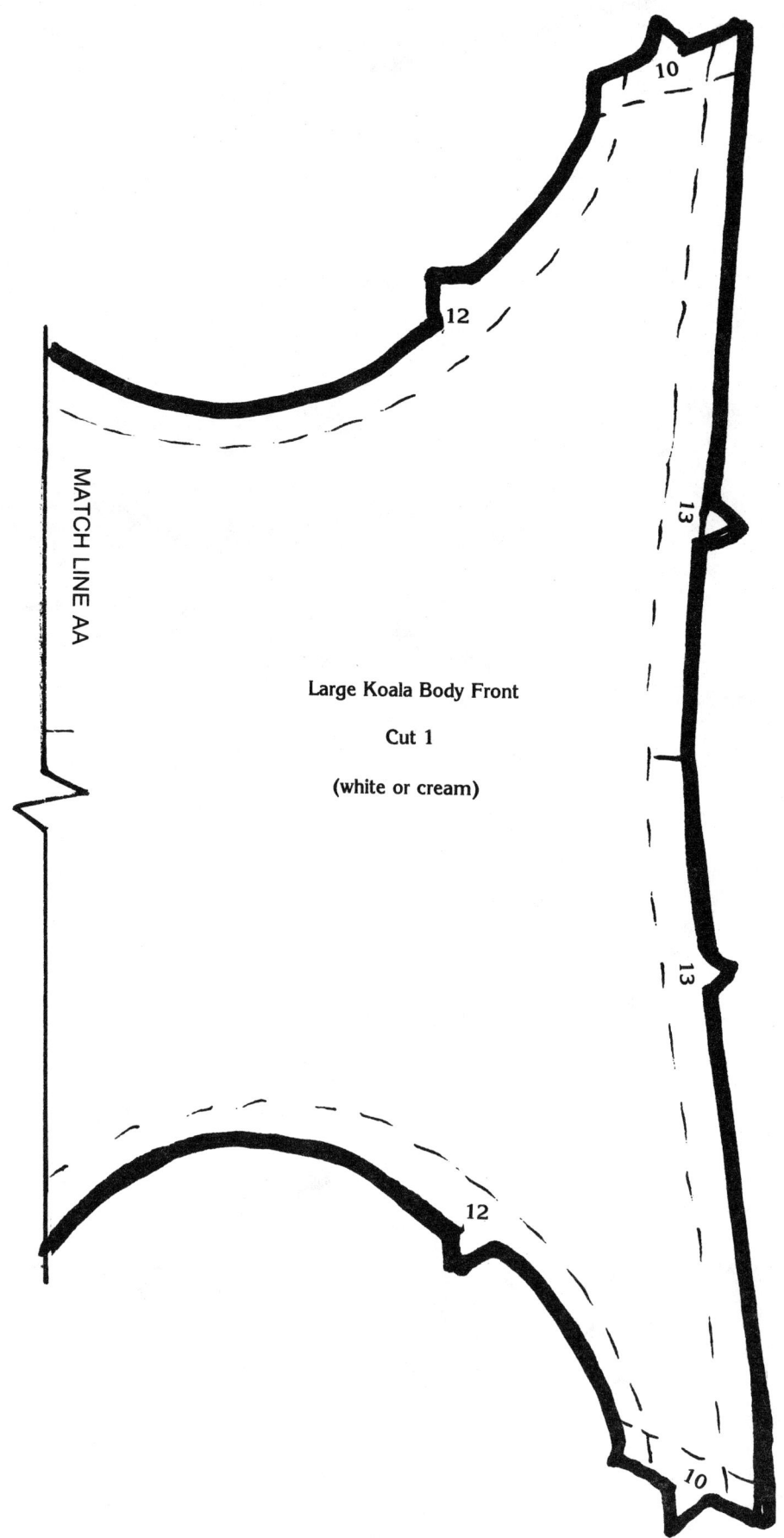

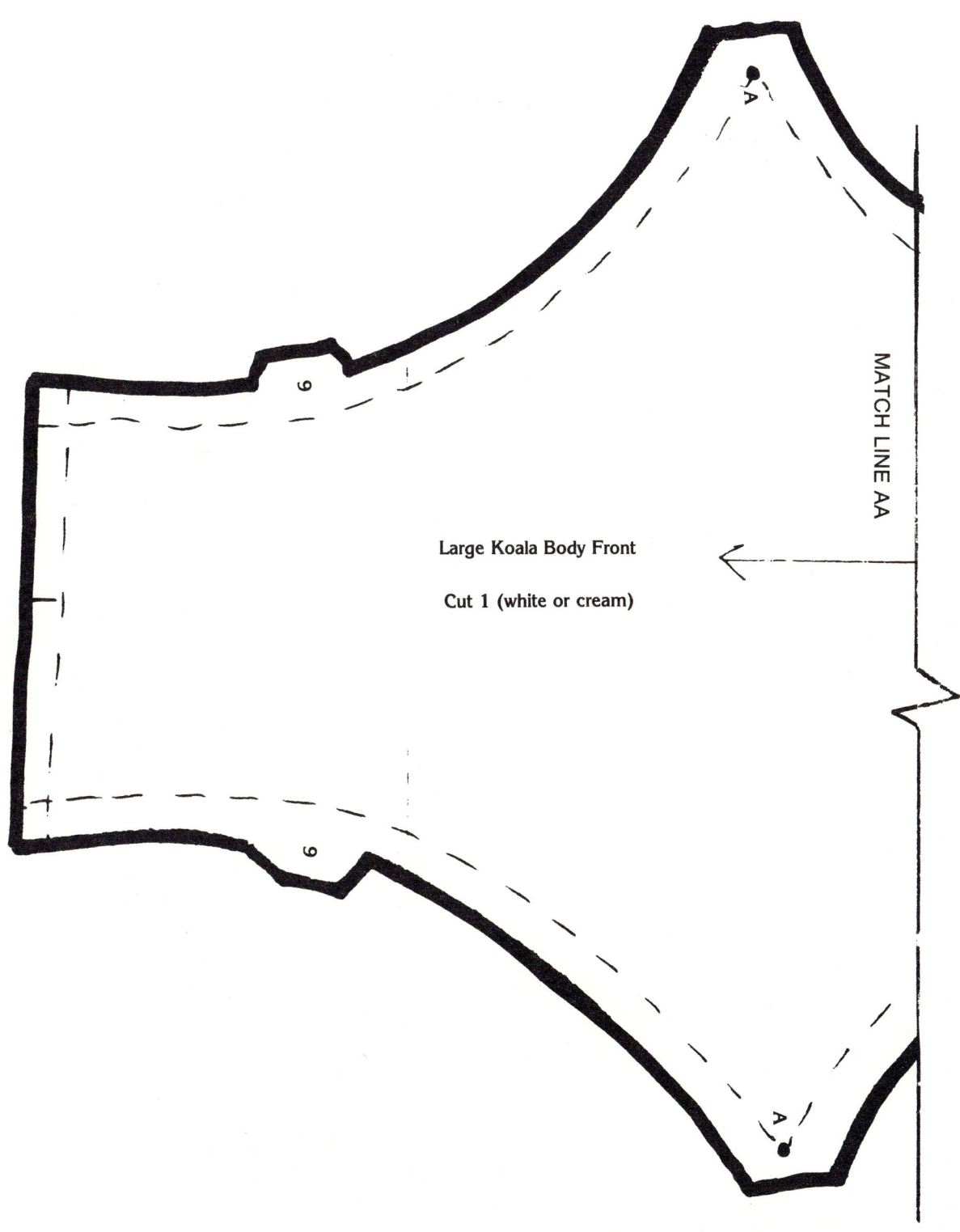

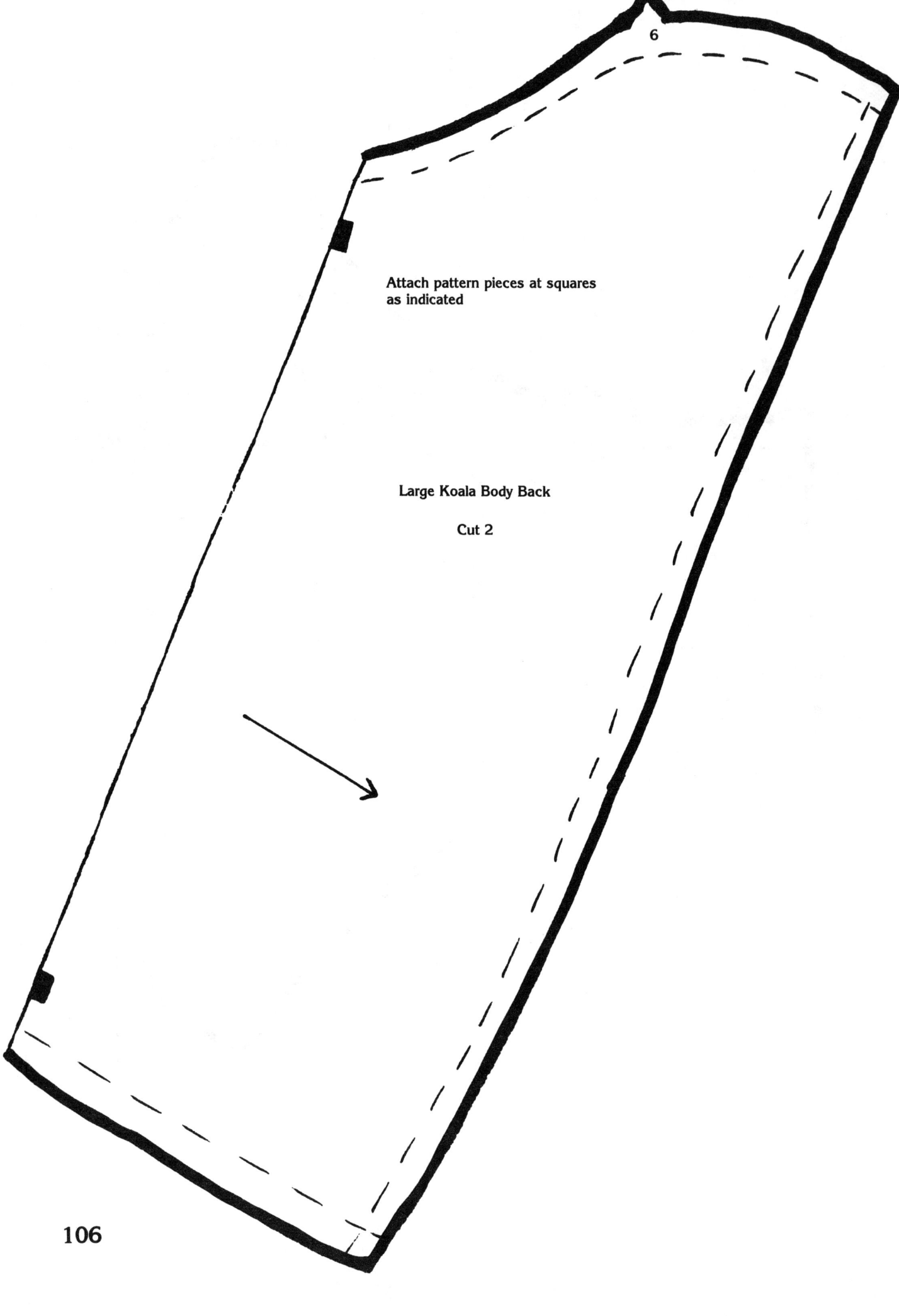

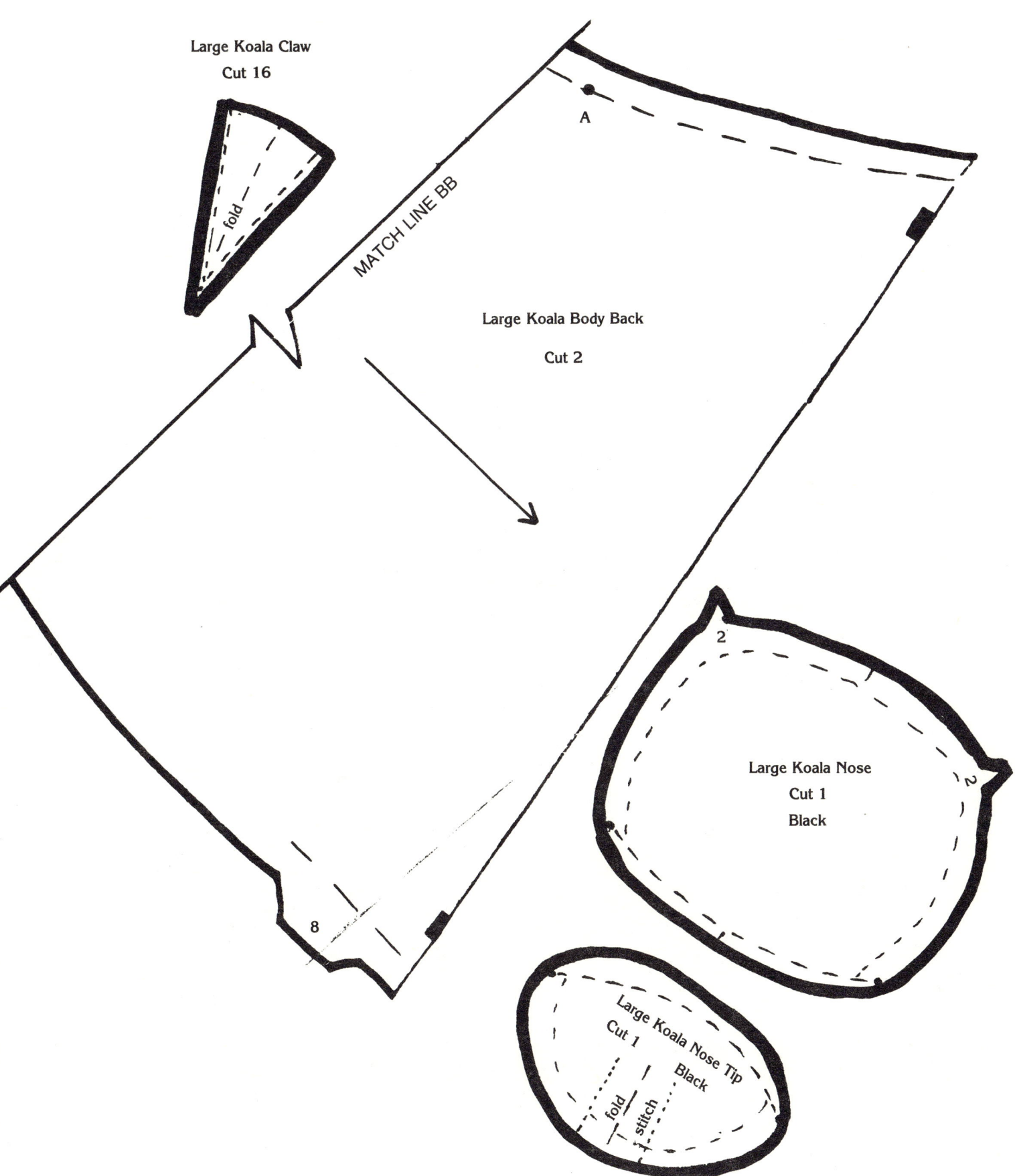

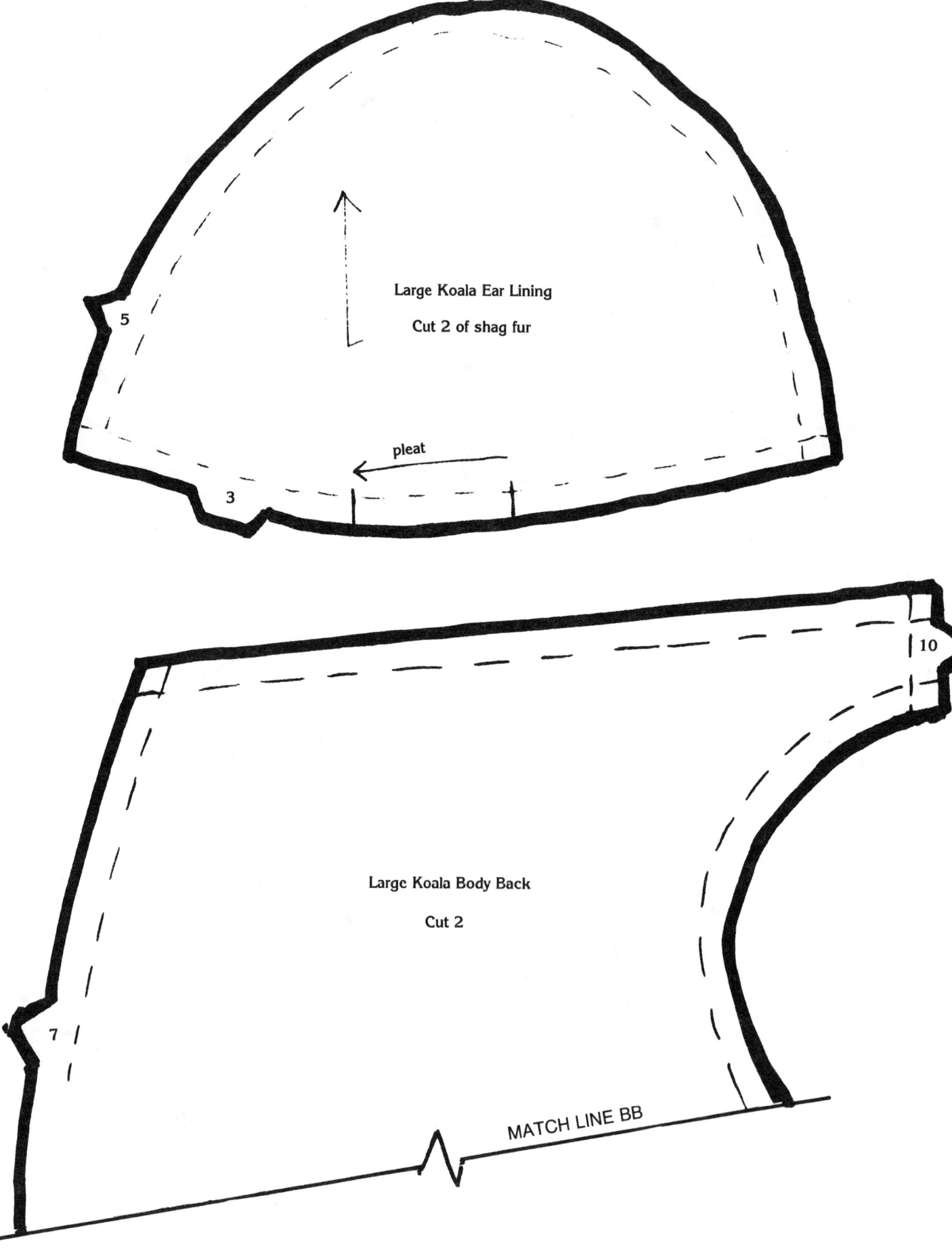

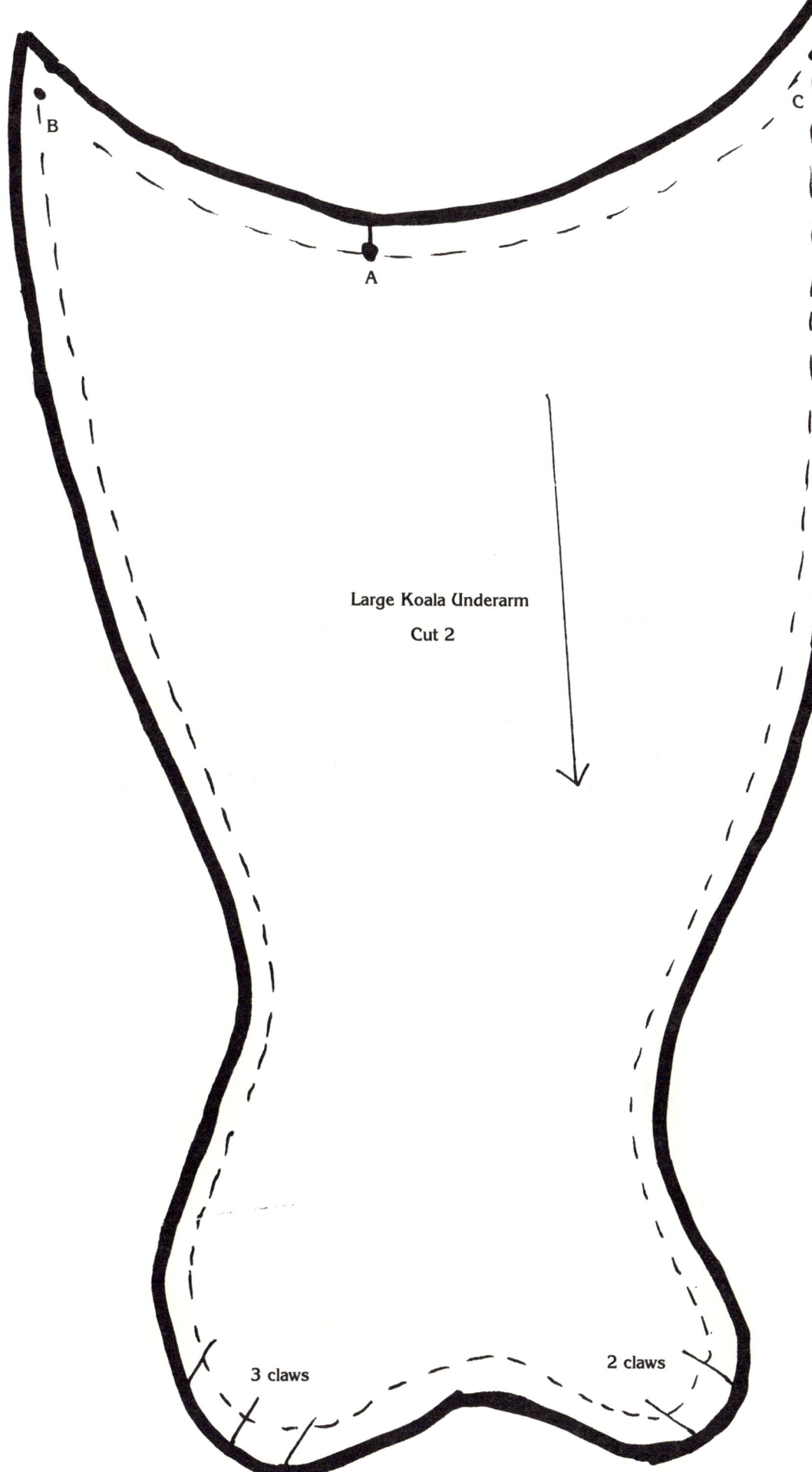

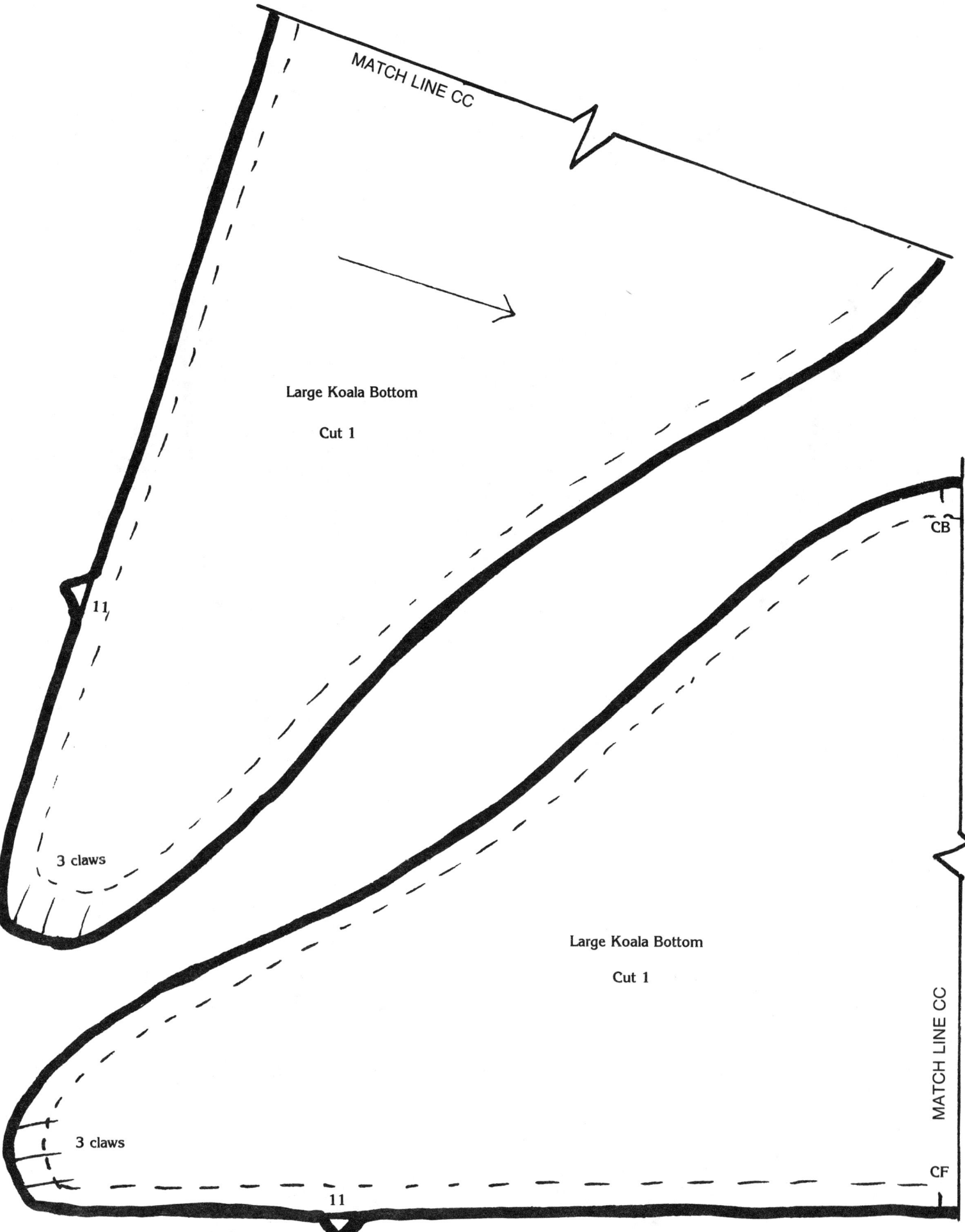

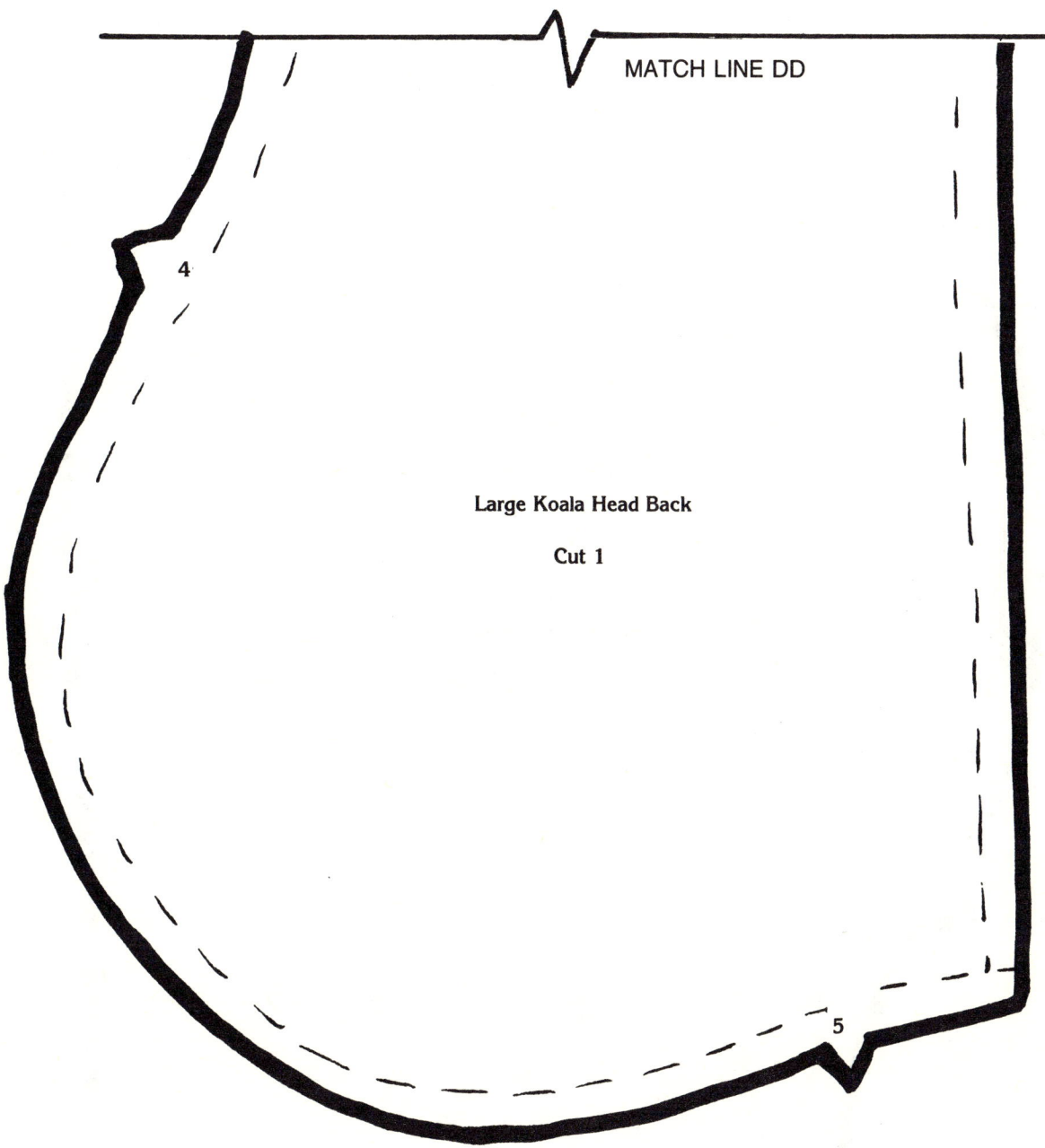

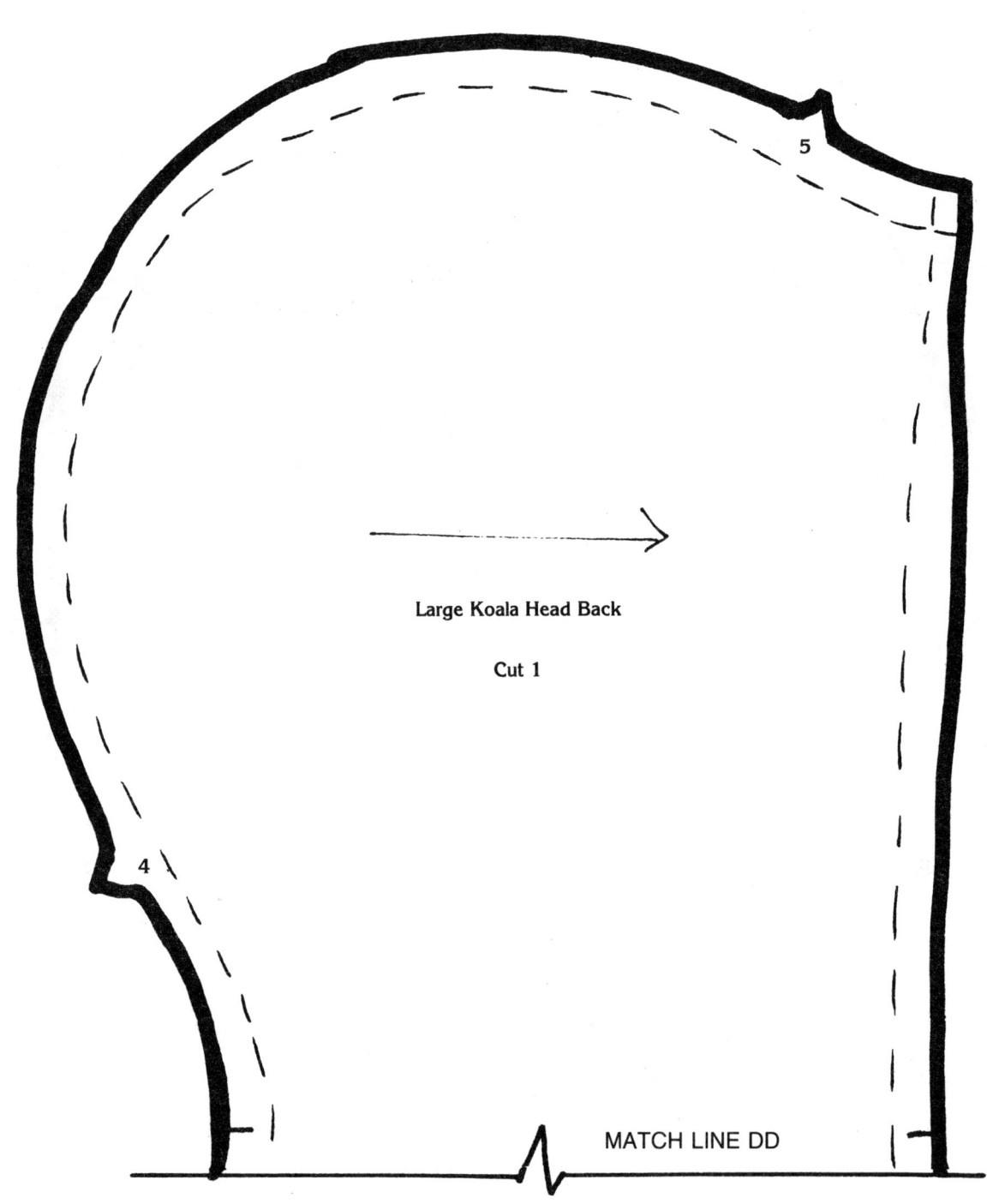

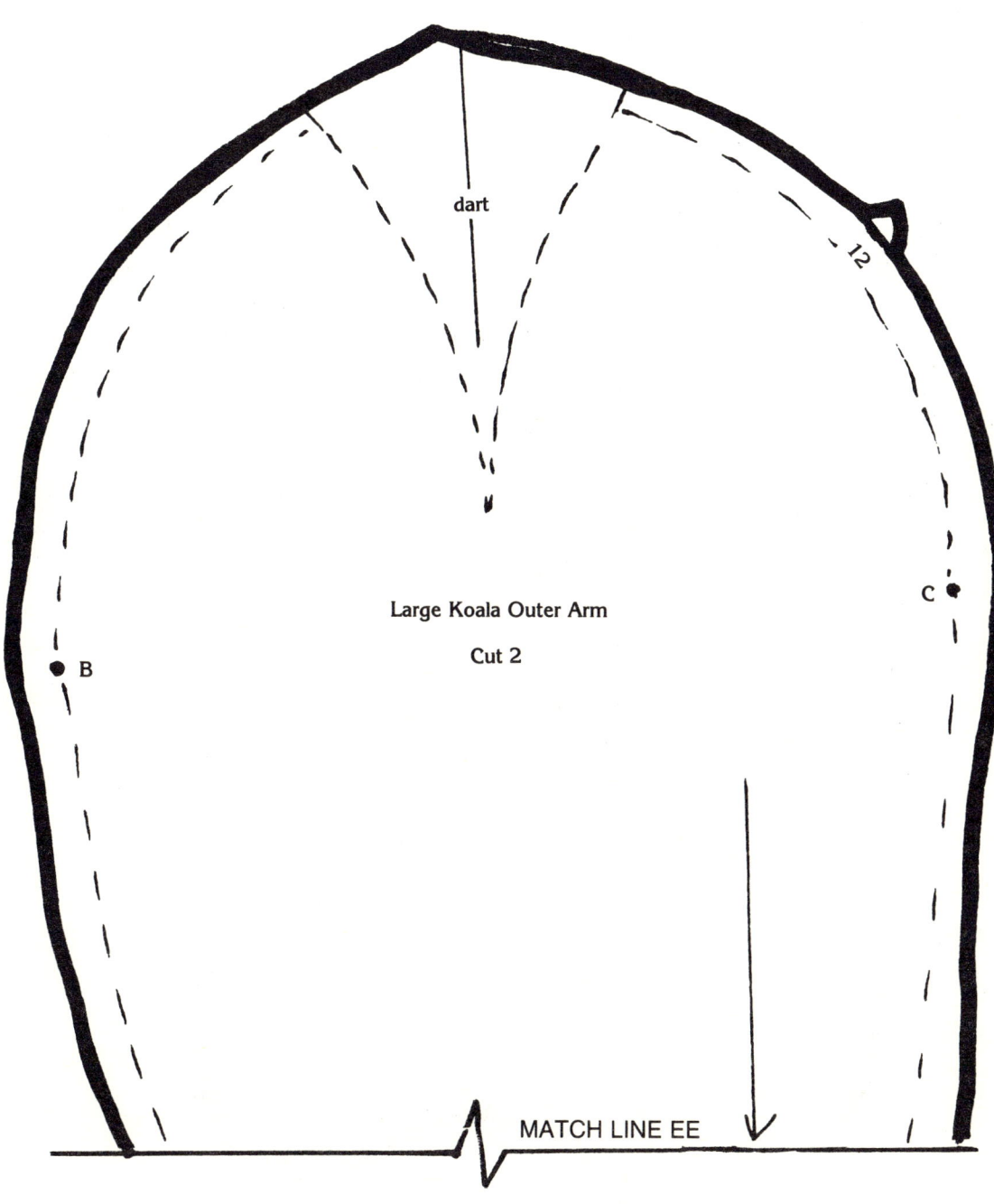

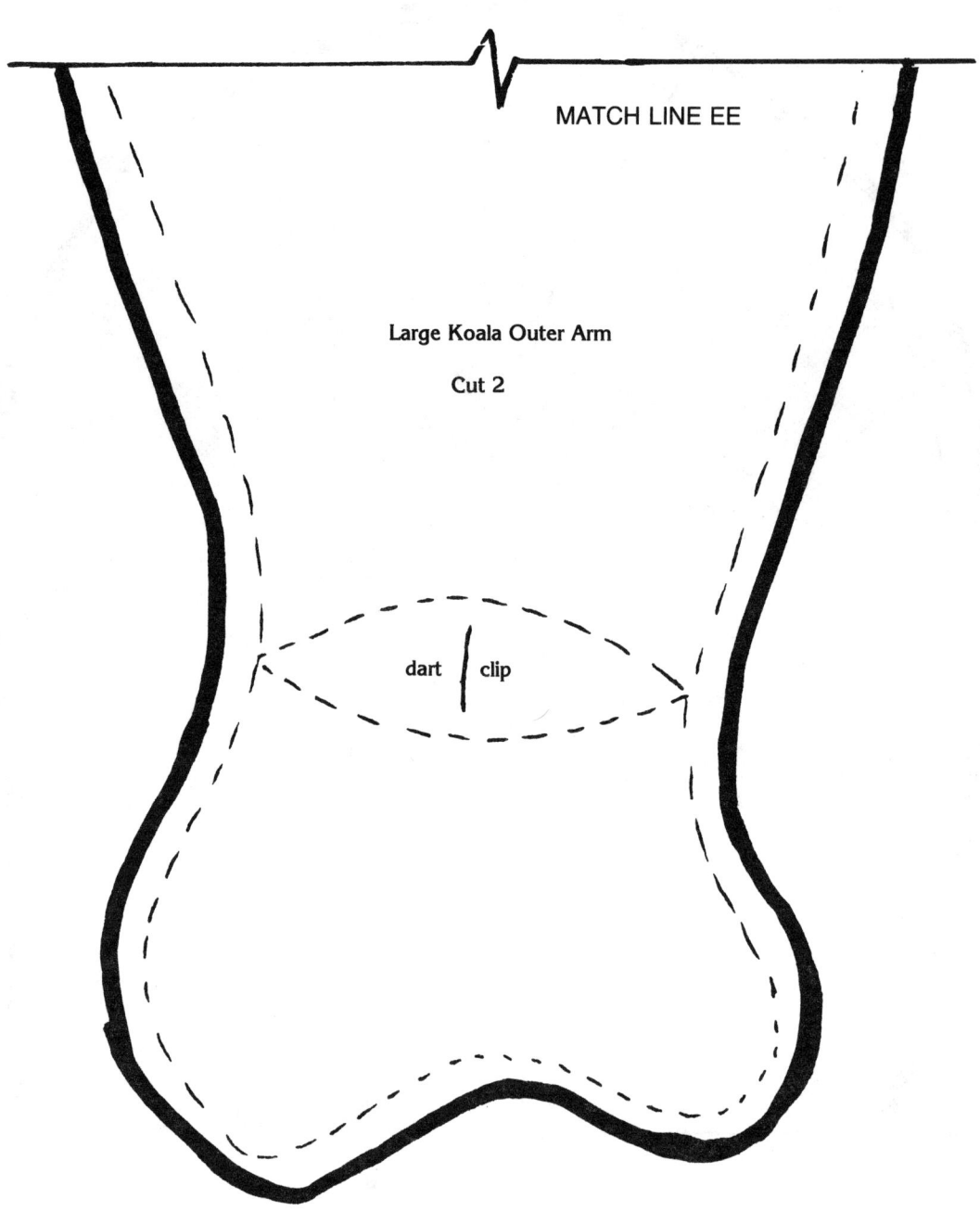

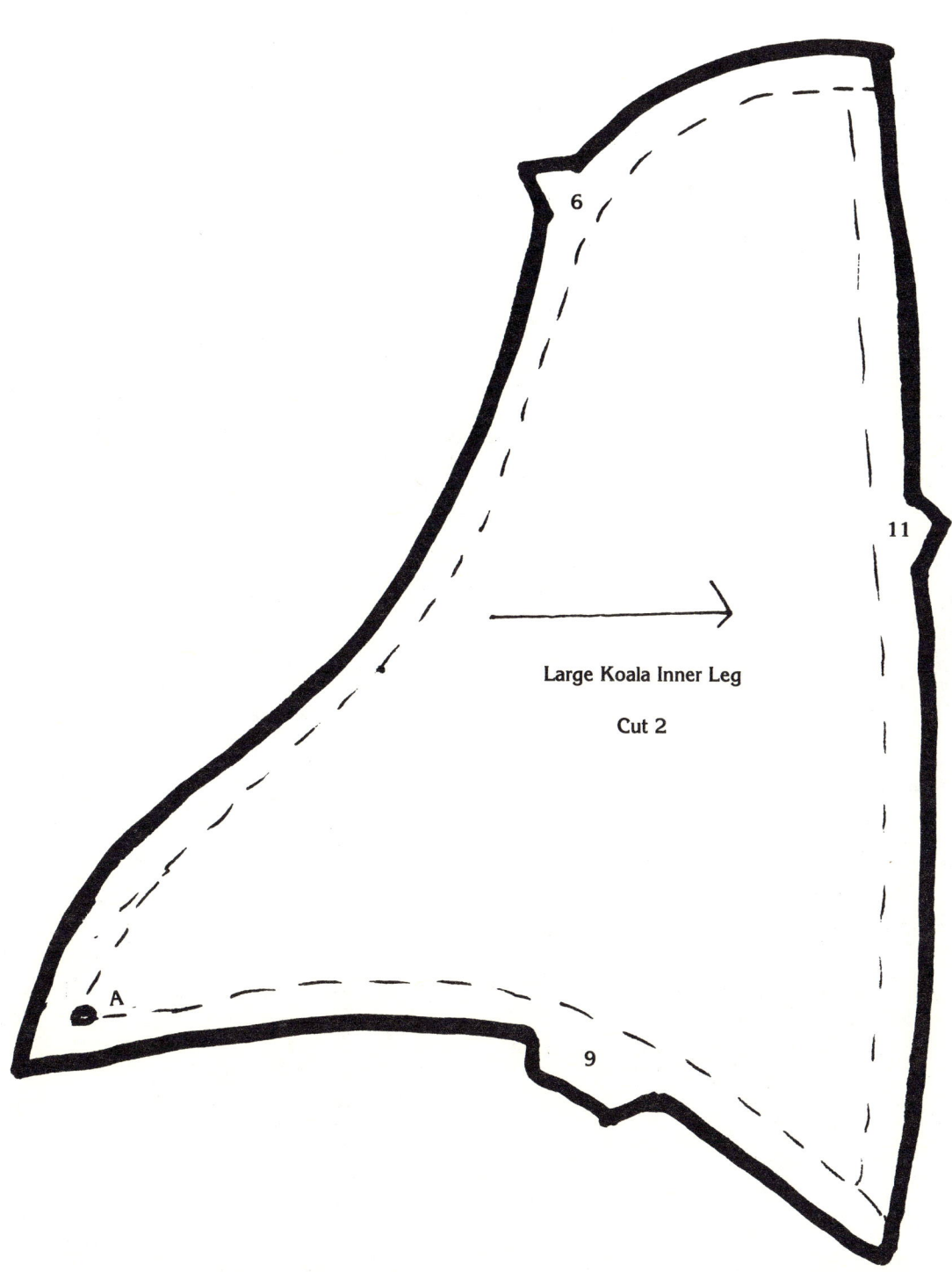

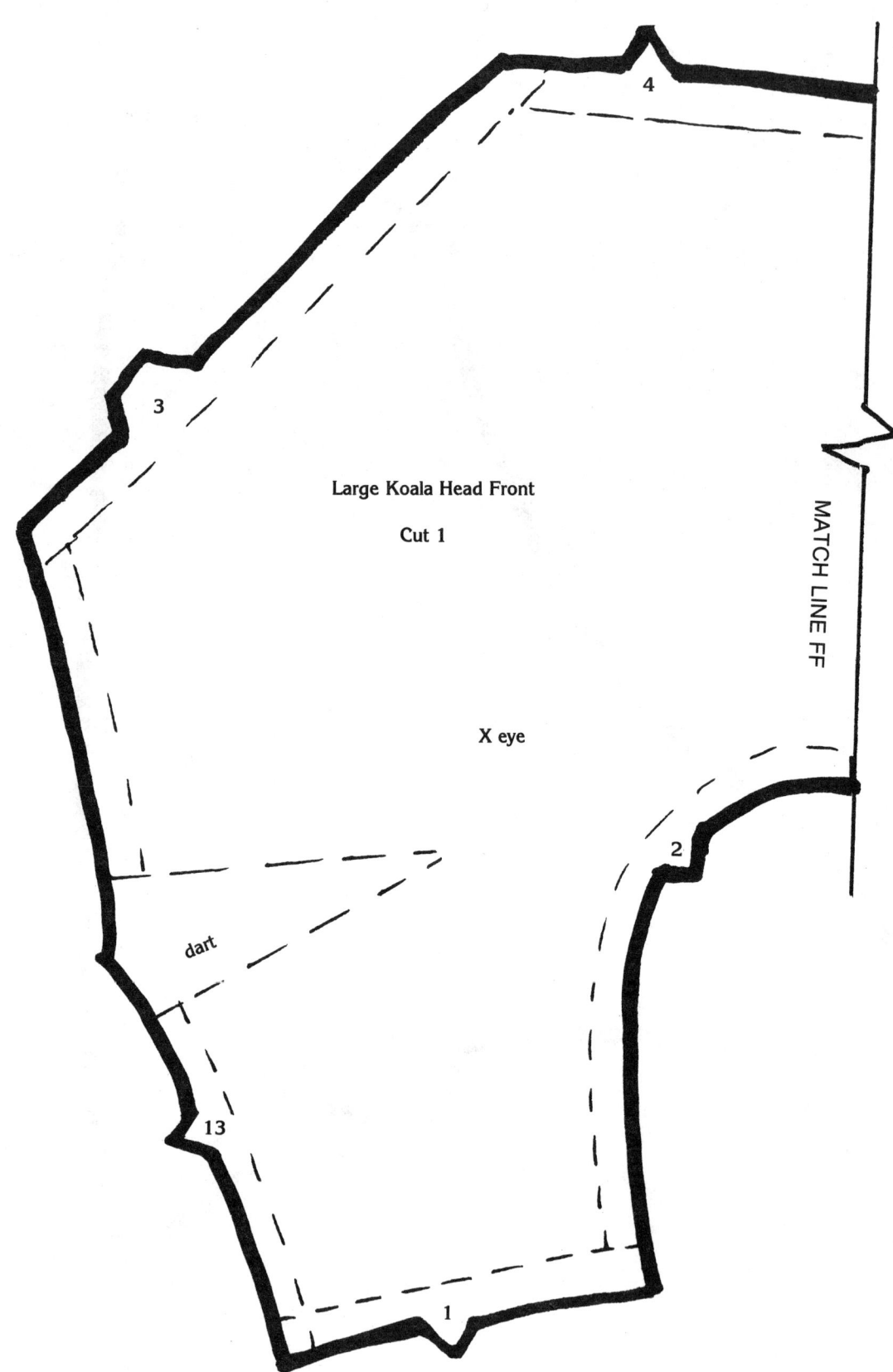

AARDVARK

ANTEATER

BISON

DODOS

DUCK

ELEPHANT

KOALAS

MOOSE

PIG

PETER RABBIT FAMILY

SLOTH

SNAKE

SPIDER

UNICORN

ZEBRA/DONKEY

HOBBY CAMEL

HOBBY HORSE

HOBBY UNICORN

HOBBY RABBIT

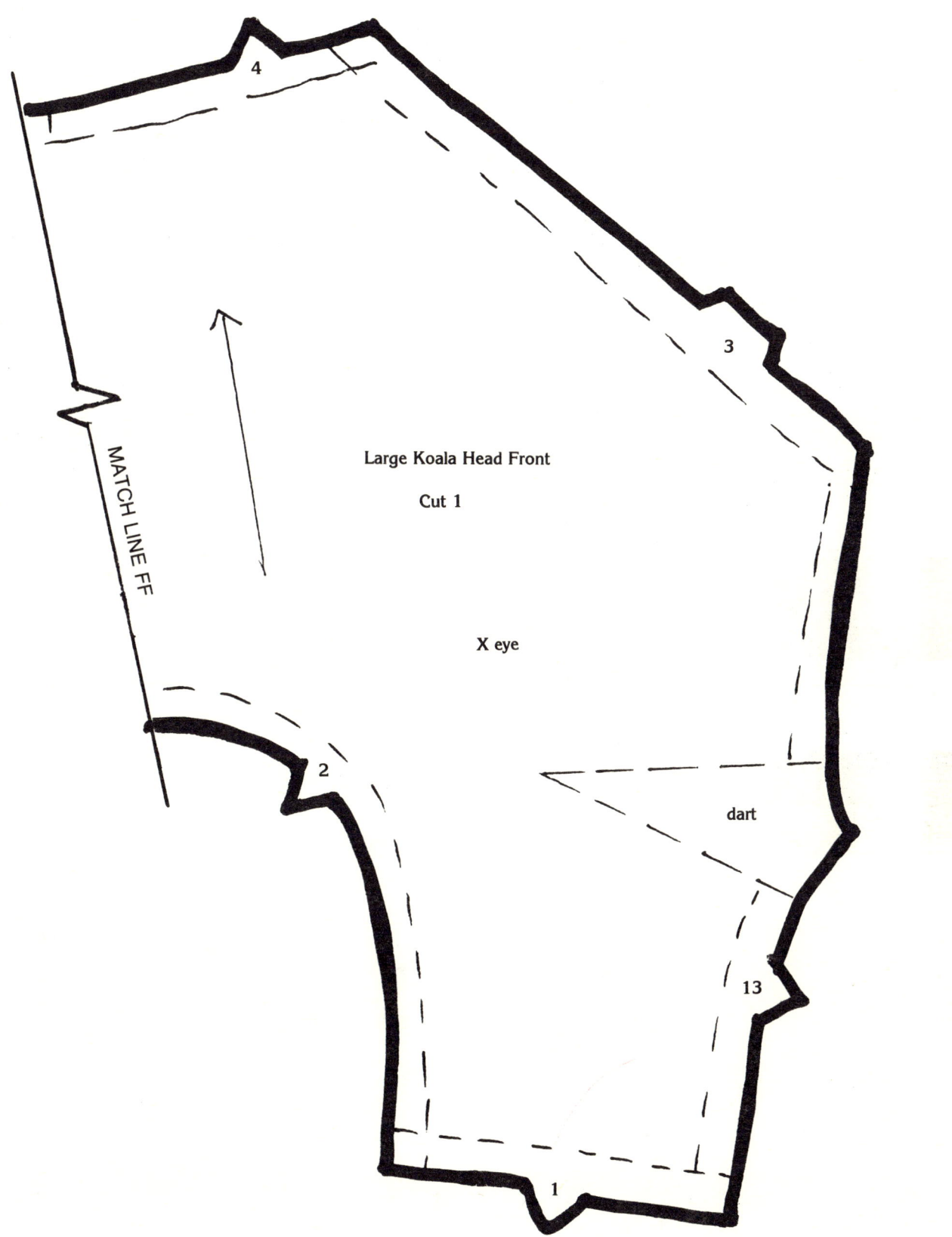

EIGHT PATTERN PIECES
16" (41 cm) LONG

Cutting Diagram

Materials   Fur fabric, or fabric of choice: ½ yard of 60" (½ m of 1 m 53 cm width fabric)
Tan suedecloth or velour: of 36" or 45", ¼ yard for antler covering (¼ m of tan suedecloth, 1 m or 1 m 15 cm width fabric)
Black vinyl or felt, for hooves (optional): 4" x 6" piece (10 cm × 15 cm)
42" of ¼" diameter dowel (1 m 8 cm of ⅗ cm diameter dowel)
1 pair of safety eyes or 2 buttons
3½ yards (3½ m) of yarn to match fabric for tail and beard
1 gal. (4 l) plastic bottle, empty
1½ lbs. (675 g) polyester fiberfill

8
Moose

A refugee from the North Woods, the moose makes a lovable and safe toy. The antlers are stiffened with pieces cut from plastic milk or bleach bottles. The curved shape is already molded in, but the plastic is soft enough to bend on contact without breaking. A wooden dowel through the head gives further support. This allows a more realistic representation of moose antlers without stuffing them. Yarn tufts form the tail and beard. Vinyl hooves are more realistic, but felt is easier to handle.

Cutting Instructions

See the cutting diagrams. Also see instructions for cutting fur fabrics in the Introduction if you are using this material.

Of main fabric, cut two side bodies, two underbodies, one head center, two ears, and four soles of feet.

Of suede or velour, cut four antler covers and two ear linings.

Of black vinyl or felt, cut four hooves (optional).

Sewing Instructions

Use ¼" (⅗ cm) seams throughout unless otherwise instructed.

1. Sew ears to ear linings, right sides together, leaving bottom open. Trim tip and turn right side out. Fold on line and sew to side body between lines indicated on pattern.

Sew lower antler cover to side body between lines, right sides together, as shown in Figure 1. Pleat the nostril by folding on the outer lines and bringing these to meet at the center line, on the outside. See Figure 1.

2. Sew darts in the underbodies. Clip dart where shown on pattern and Figure 4.

3. The hooves may be appliquéd by machine at this point, or they may be hand sewn on after the moose is stuffed and finished. Or, of course, they may be omitted. To machine appliqué them, stitch the underbodies to the side bodies along the front of each foot, from the dot to the bottom of the feet. See Figure 2. Open the foot flat, right side up. Top stitch the hoof across the seam, as shown in Figure 3. (Note: If using vinyl, a thin coat of sewing machine oil rubbed on the right side can prevent the presser foot from sticking.) Repeat for the other three feet.

4. Sew the rest of the underbody seam, from dot A to dot B, matching notches 1, 2, and 3, leaving the bottoms of the feet open. See Figure 4.

5. Clip along the bottom of the feet inside the seam line as shown on the pattern and Figure 5. Matching center front and back seams to centers on the sole of the foot, spread the clips to Vs around the edges of the foot. With the sole down, stitch around the foot, just inside the clips. See Figure 6.

6. Sew upper antler covers to head center, right sides together. See Figure 7. Sew dart in head center. Sew head center to side heads, leaving open where the antlers are attached. Match line to nostrils and stitch from dot C to dot D. See Figure 8.

7. Sew center front seam between dots D and A. Sew center back seam between dot C and dot B. Sew center underbody seam from dot B to dot A, leaving open between notches 4 and 5 for stuffing. Clip curves, turn right side out.

8. Cut antler supports from a gallon plastic bottle, as shown in Figure 9. Be sure to reverse the pattern for a right and left side. It is easier to stitch the antler covers together partway around, insert the plastic supports, and then finish stitching; stitch with a close zigzag satin stitch from the front edge around to dot E. Slip the plastic form inside the antler, working the stem inside the head through the opening in the seam. Finish zigzagging the antler covers together. See Figure 10.

9. To keep the antlers from flopping, a wooden support is needed. Cut a 6" piece of ¼" diameter dowel and sand ends smooth. Slip your hand inside the body through the stuffing opening, and insert the dowel across the top of the head, through the seam openings on each side, into each antler under the plastic. See Figure 10. On the outside, to keep the support from shifting, top stitch along the dotted line, through both cover layers and the plastic. See Figure 10.

10. If using safety eyes, cut a small hole at the x on the pattern. Insert the shank of the eye from the right side; push the washer onto the shank inside the head. If using buttons for eyes, sew on after the moose is stuffed.

11. Stuff the moose firmly, using a dowel or chopstick to push the fiberfill into the far corners. For extra support in the legs, cut four 9" (23 cm) lengths of ¼" (⅗ cm) dowel, and sand the ends. Insert one dowel in each leg, being sure the stuffing is well packed beneath and all around the dowels so they cannot be felt from the outside. Stuff the center of the body last and sew up the opening.

12. For tail and beard, wrap yarn around your fingers ten to fifteen times, depending on the thickness of the yarn. Sew the strands together at the top and cut across the bottom. Brush to frizz. Sew onto the moose where indicated on the pattern and shown on the cover illustration. Sew buttons on for eyes, if you did not use safety eyes. Or embroider or appliqué eyes, if you wish. Sew hooves onto the feet, if you didn't machine appliqué them in step 3.

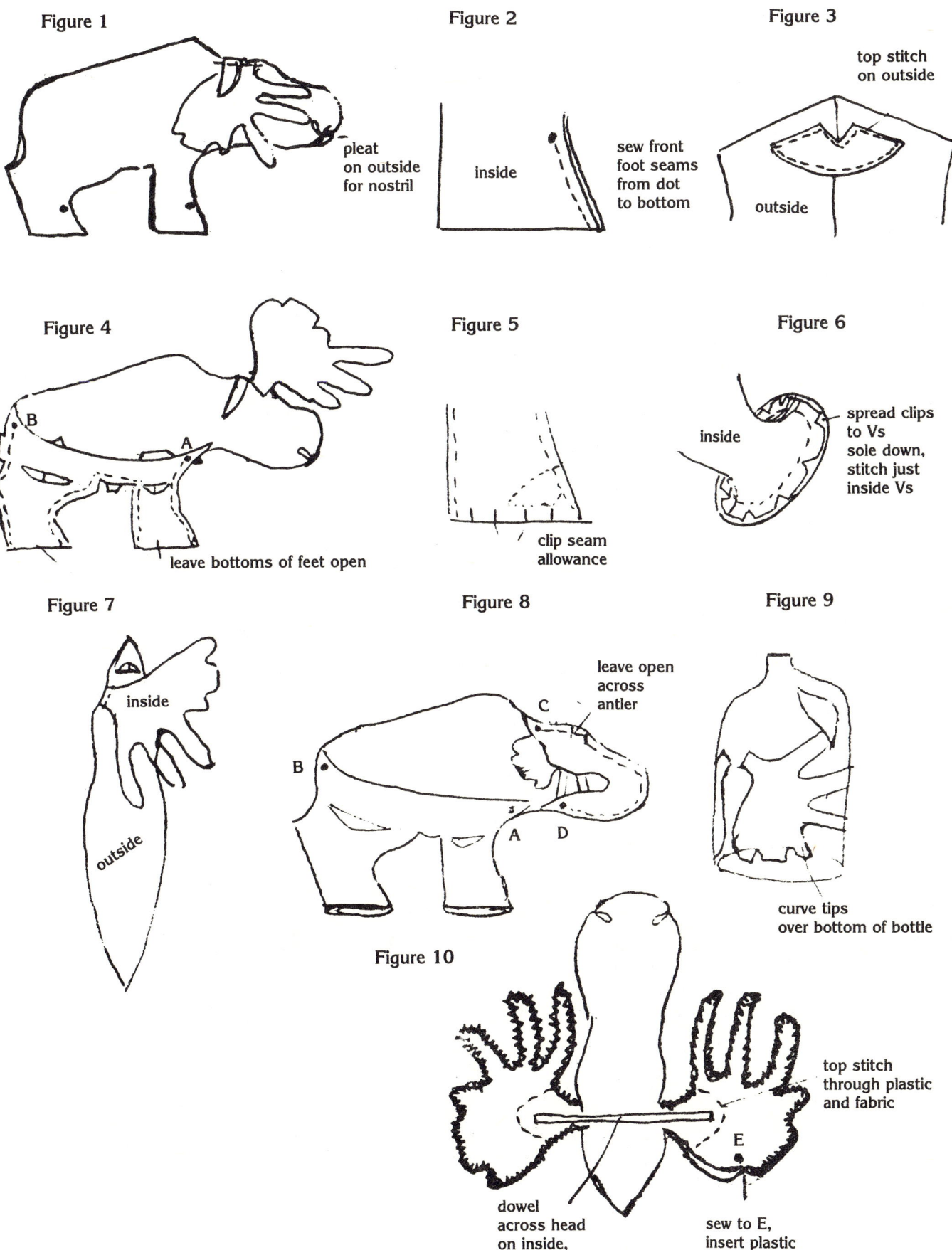

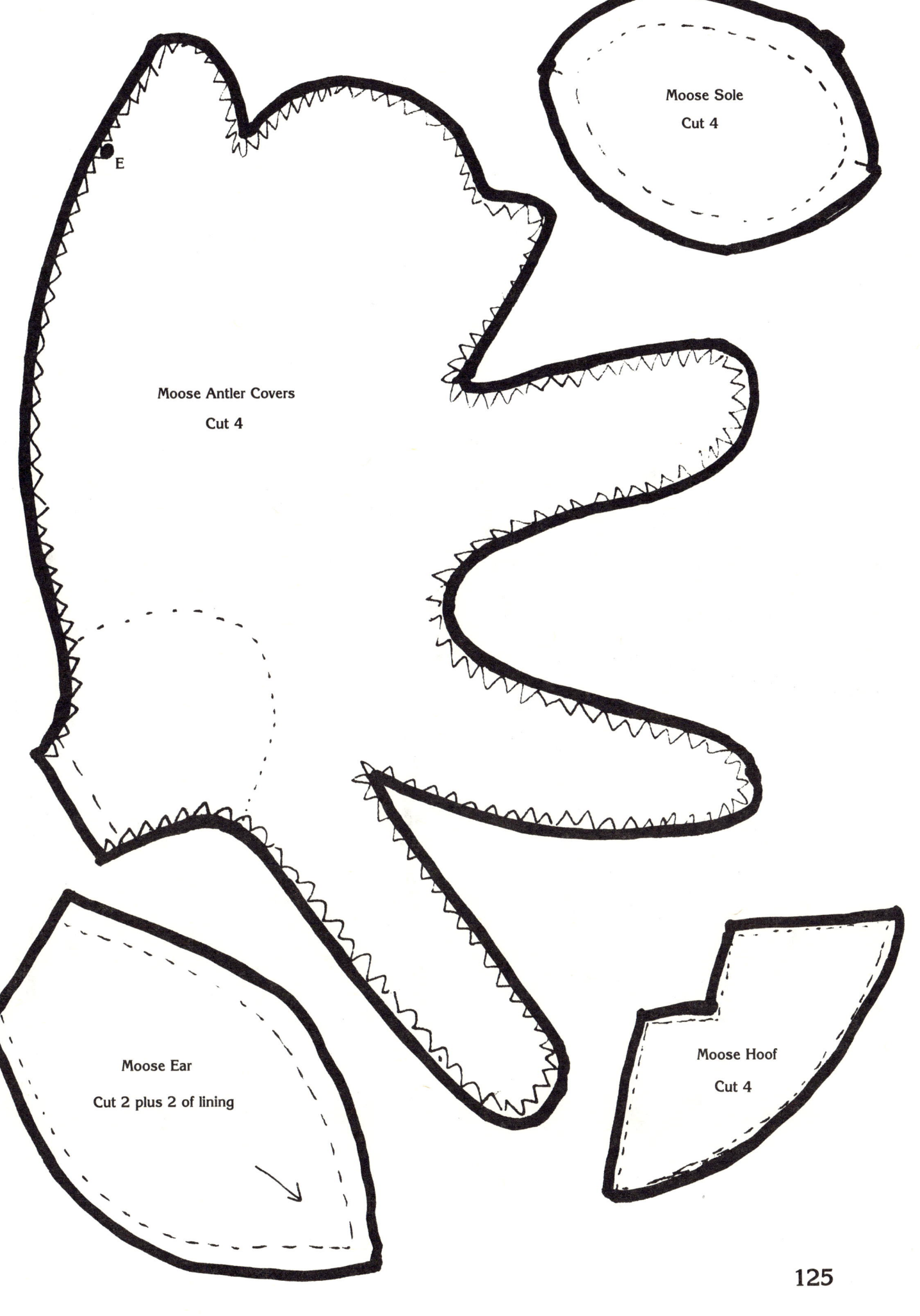

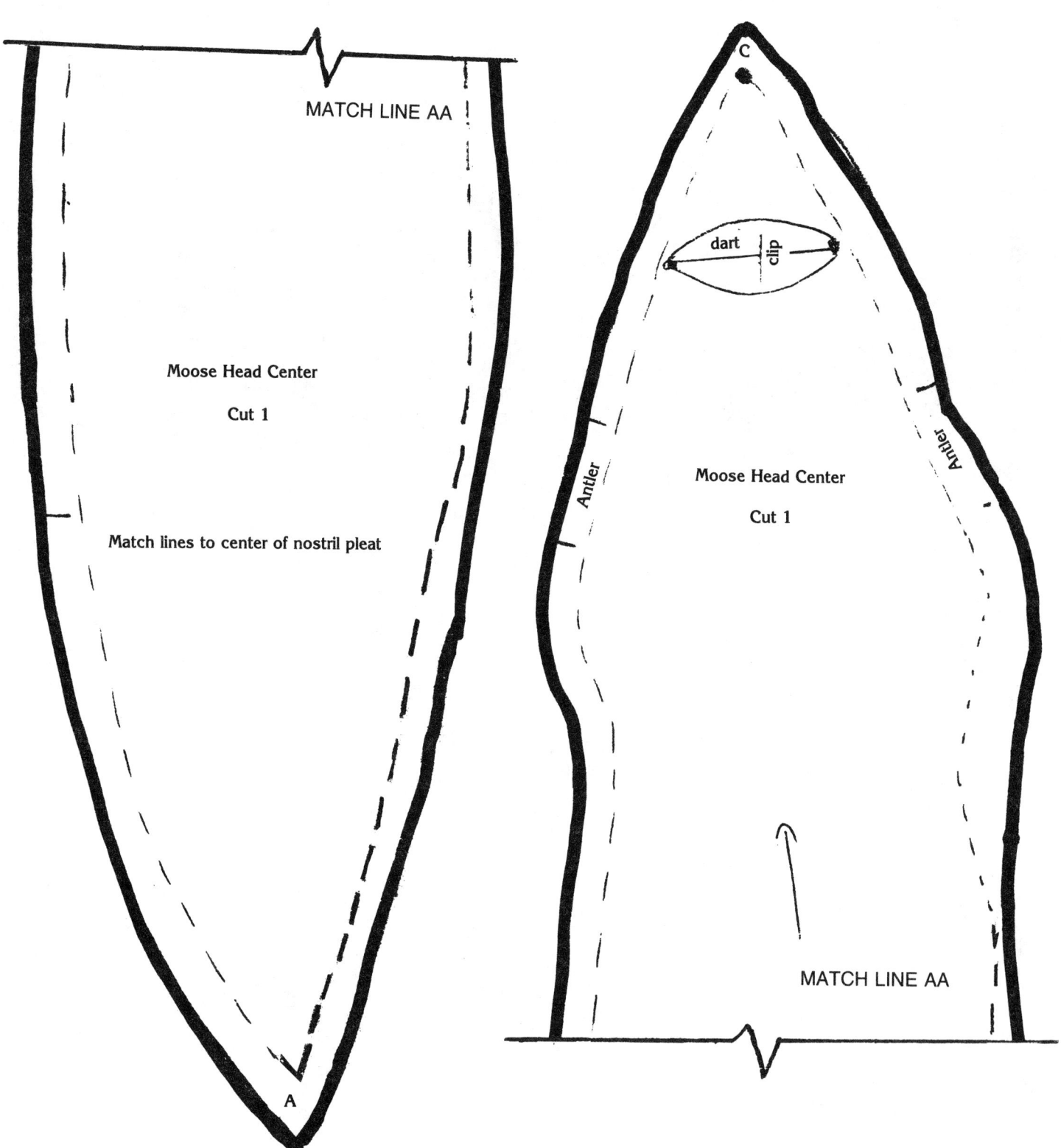

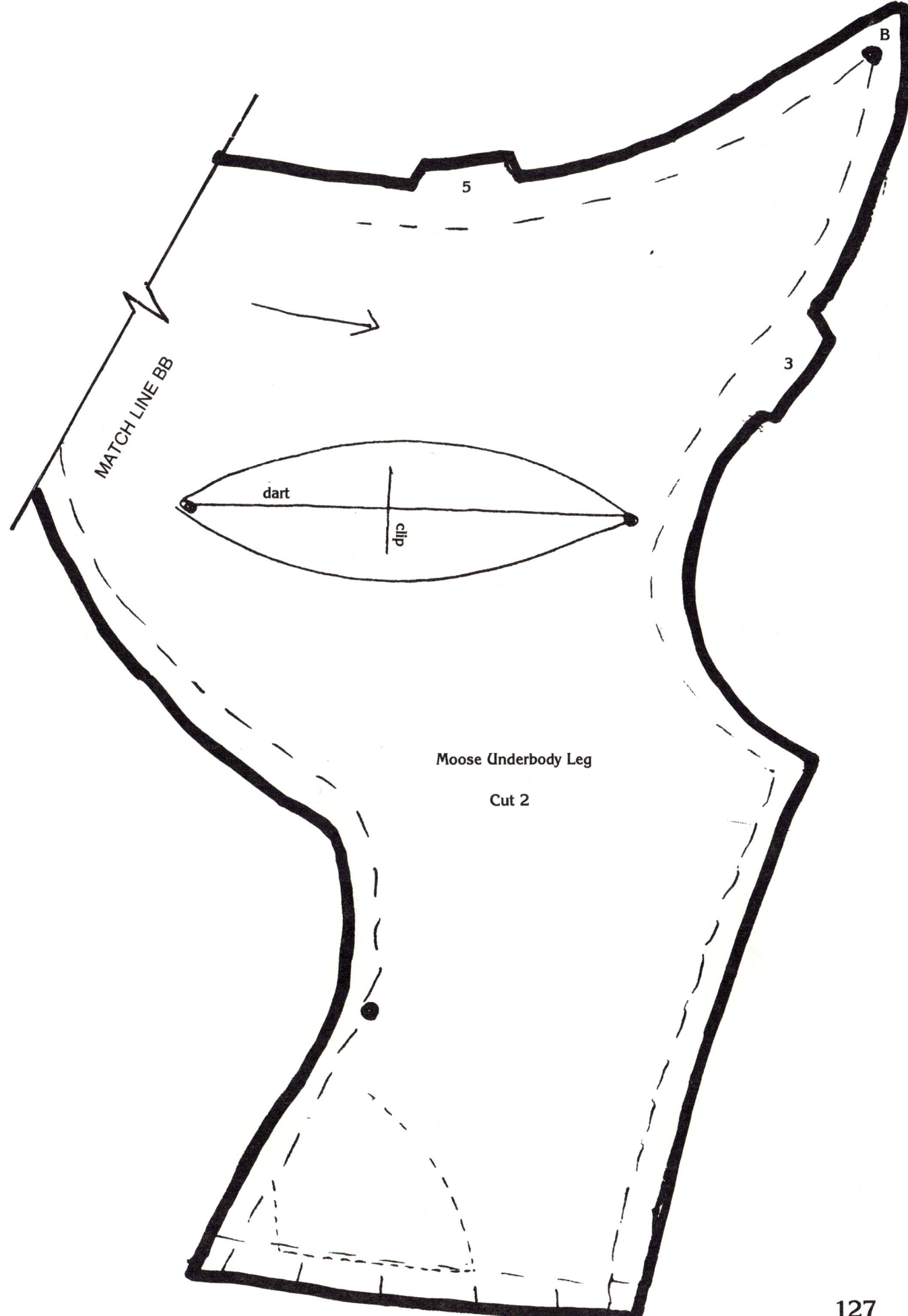

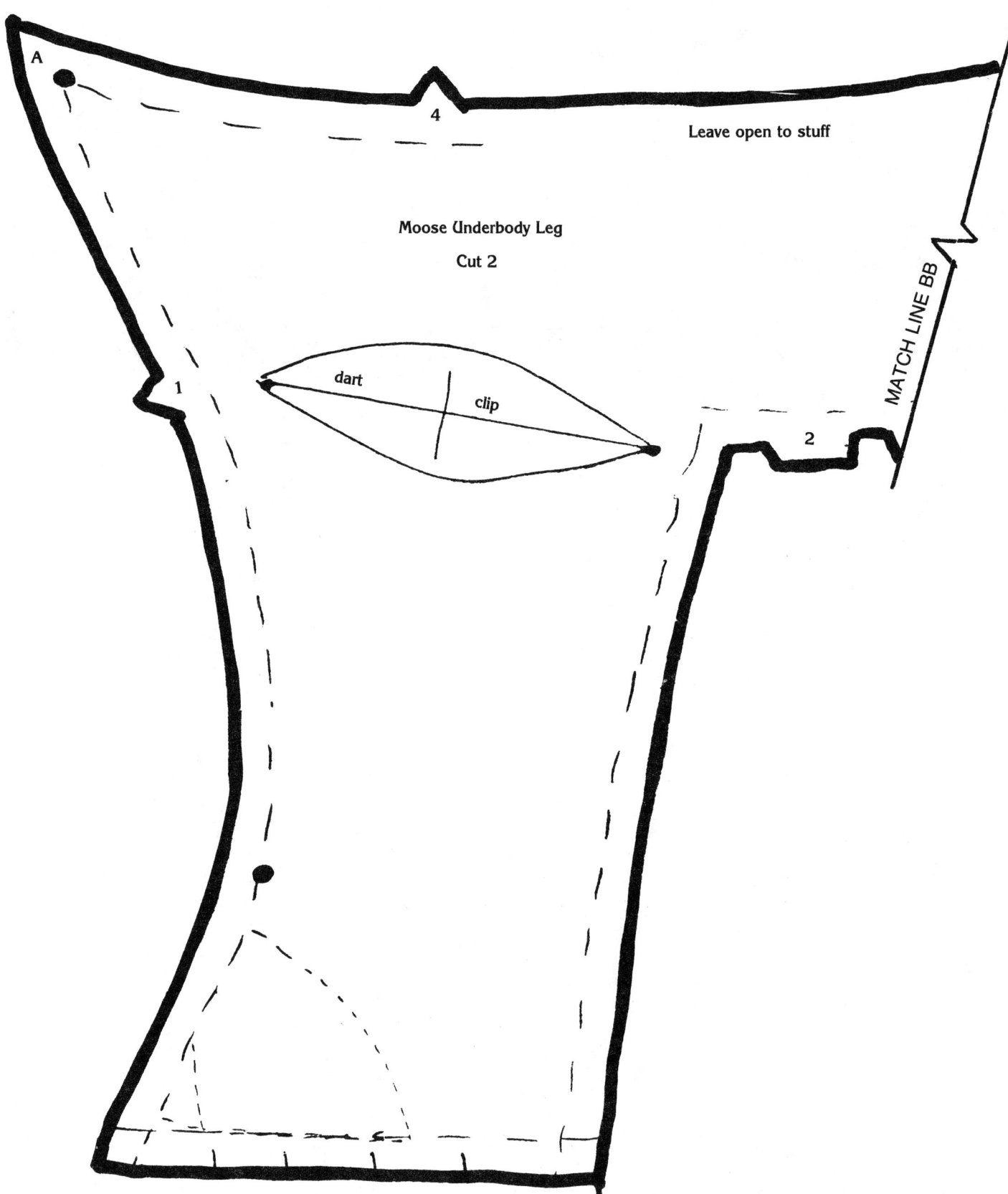

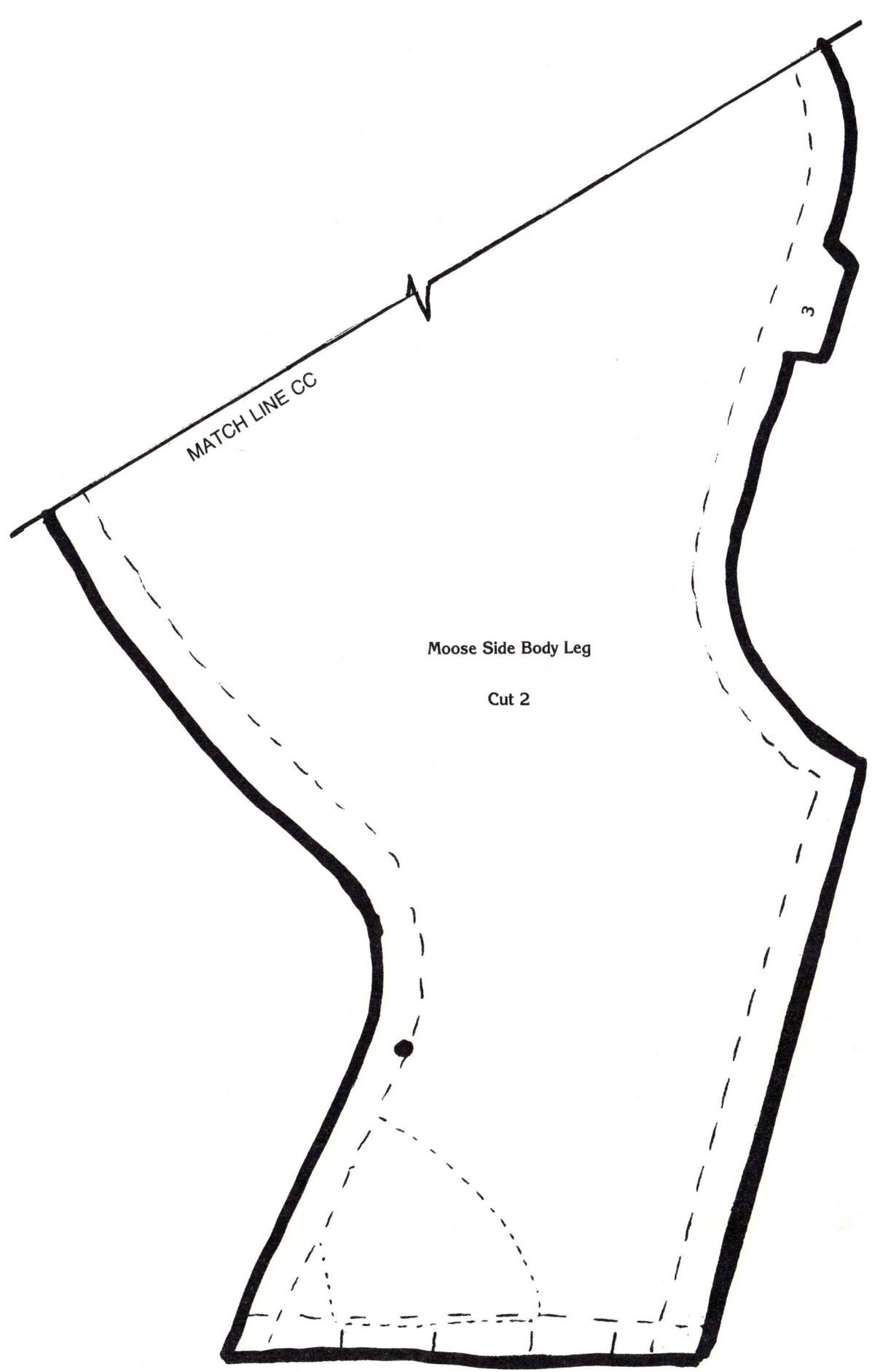

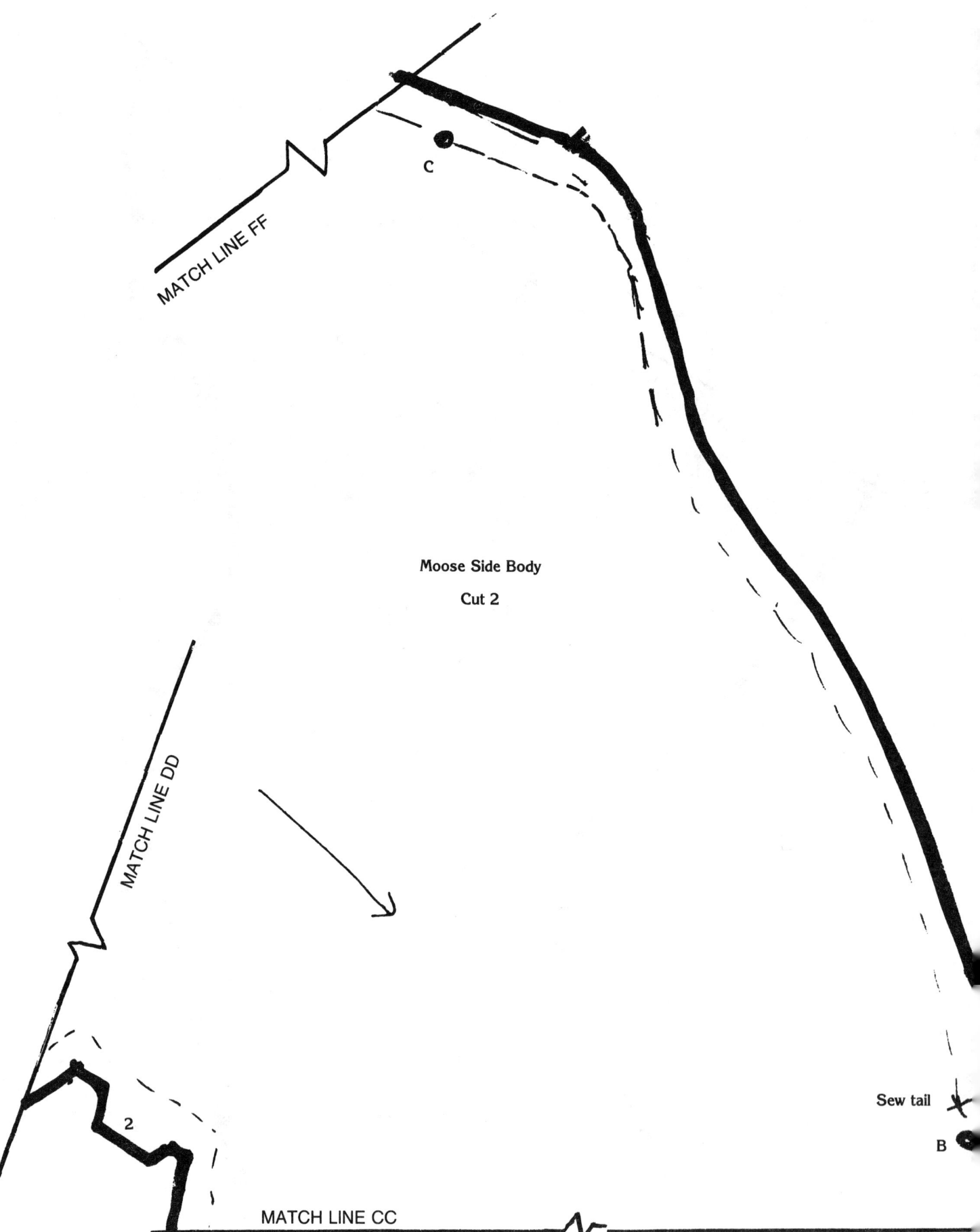

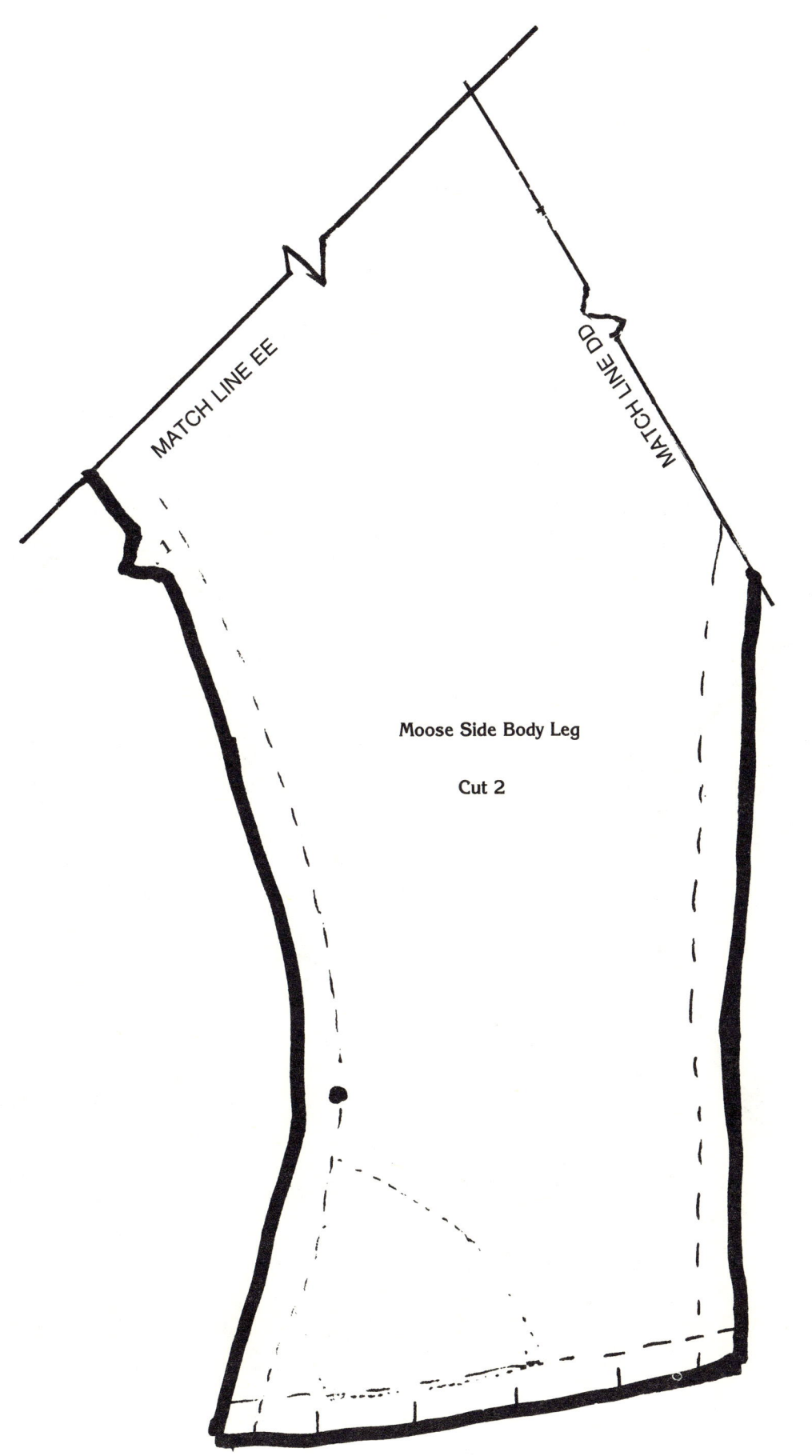

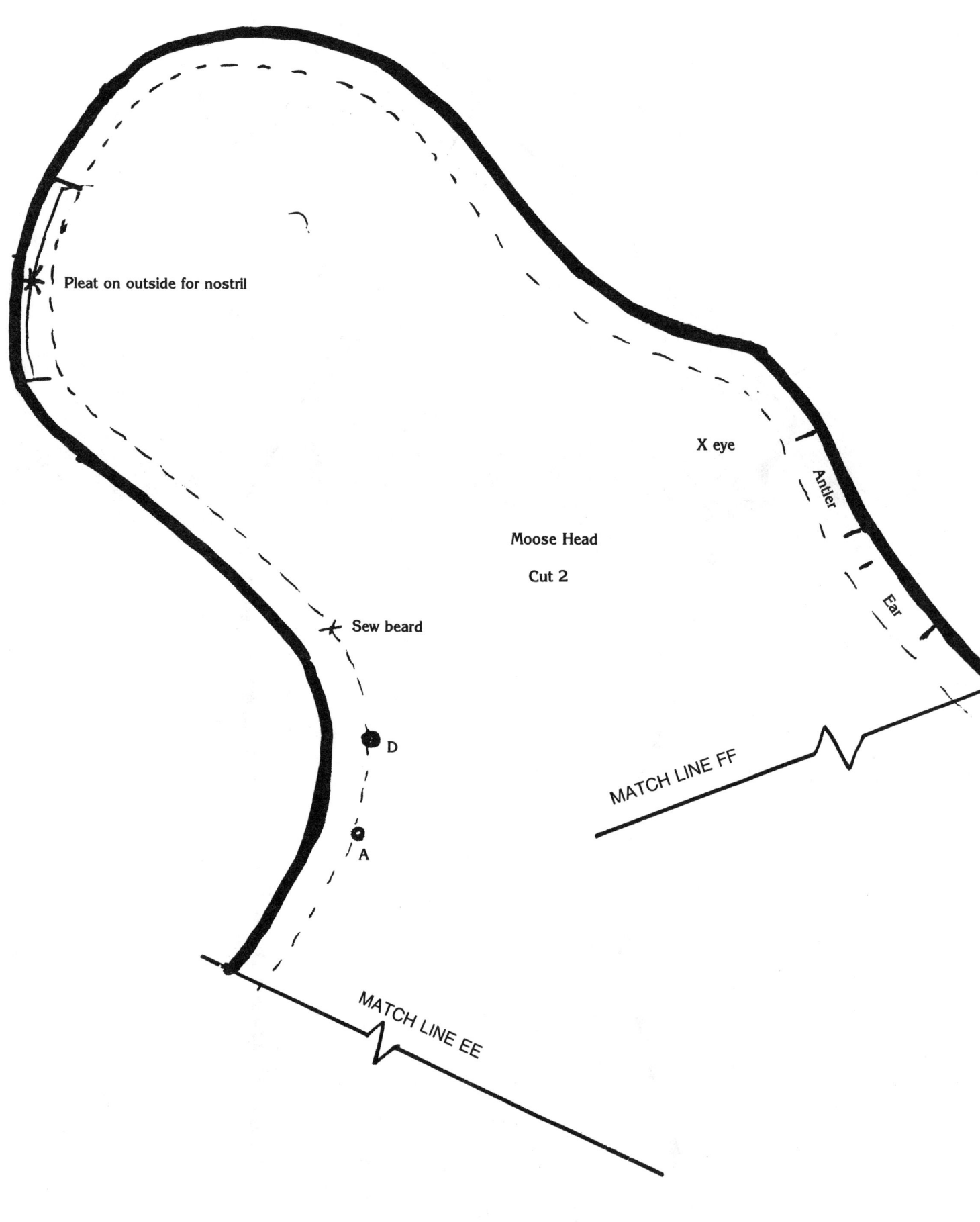

EIGHT PATTERN PIECES
13" (33 cm) LONG

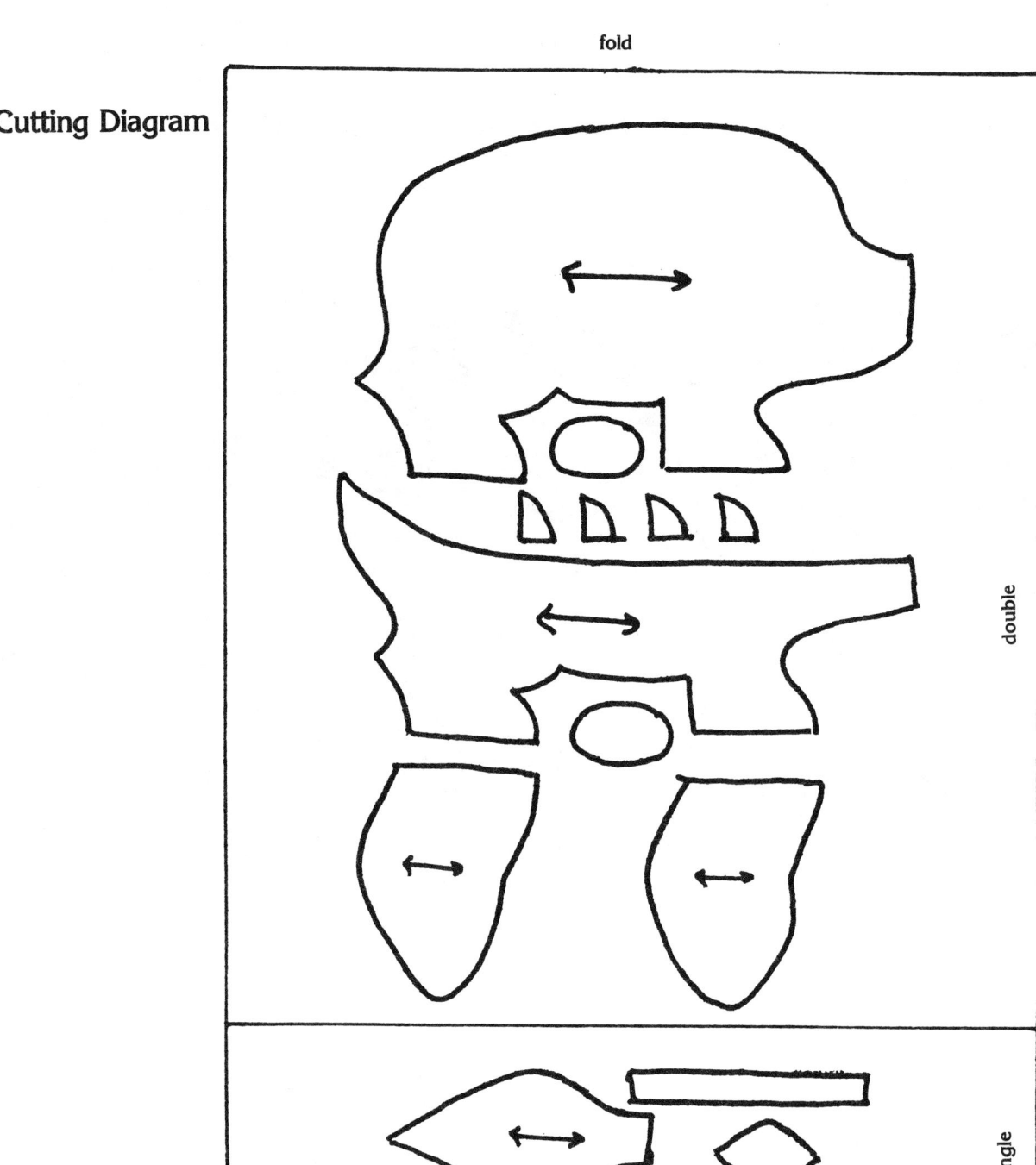

Cutting Diagram

Materials Pink velour, suedecloth, thin fur, etc: ⅔ yard of 54" fabric (⅔ m of 1 m 38 cm width material)
1¼ lbs. (560 g) polyester fiberfill (for stuffing)
4 popsicle or craft sticks (optional)
Black embroidery thread
Buttonhole twist or carpet thread to match fabric

9
Pig

This is a cute little pig with a wrinkled nose and a smug smile. It has split hooves, but these can be eliminated if you wish to simplify the pattern. The pig is nice when made up in a soft, light pink velour or a lightweight fur. Do not use stretch material unless you line it with a firm fabric, as it won't hold its shape when stuffed.

Cutting Instructions

Cut two side body/heads, one tail, two underbodies, four ears, one head center, four soles of feet, one snout, and eight inner toes (optional).

Do not cut the front slit in the soles of the feet unless you are making the split feet.

Sewing Instructions

Use ¼" (⅗ cm) seams throughout unless otherwise directed.

1. *Head.* Sew ear facings to ears, right sides together, leaving notched edge open. Turn right side out. Fold on the line indicated and sew to the side head between the lines, matching the square and notch 1. See Figure 1.

Sew head center to side bodies from nose opening to dot A, matching notches 1 and 2.

2. *Tail.* Fold tail lengthwise, right sides together, and stitch. Turn right side out to make a tube. Either tuck the tail tip inside and hand sew closed, or tie a tight knot at the tip of the tail. Stitch the tail to one side body where indicated on the pattern. (You could make a yarn tail, braided or twisted, or crochet a curly tail if you'd rather. See directions below for crocheting a tail.)

3. *Feet.* Sew darts in underbodies, clipping the center of each dart.

To make split feet, stitch underbodies to side bodies from dot B to nose opening, matching notches 3, 4, and 5. Leave open below small dots and along bottom of the feet. See Figure 1. Clip along the bottom of the feet inside the seam allowance, as indicated on the pattern and in Figure 2. Sew inner toes to feet from small dot to bottom, along unnotched edge. Sew inner toes together along the inner edge, matching notches 6. See Figure 3. Cut the front slit in the soles of the feet. Stitch bottom of inner toes into the V, from dot to dot, matching notches 7, and tapering at the inner corner. Back stitch at the inner corner to secure. See Figure 4. Matching center back and notches 8, spread clips so edges of foot match the soles. With sole down, stitch around the back of the feet just inside the clips. See Figure 4.

For plain feet, stitch underbodies to side bodies from dot B to nose opening, matching notches 3, 4, and 5, leaving open along the bottoms of the feet. Clip the bottom edges of the feet inside seam line as shown on the pattern and Figure 5. Do not cut soles of feet along the front slit; leave them whole. Matching center front and back and notches 8, pin soles to feet, spreading clips to Vs so edges match. Stitch around foot, with sole down, just inside the Vs. See Figure 6.

4. *Body.* Sew side bodies together along center back seam, from dot A to dot B. Sew center underbody seam from nose opening to dot B, leaving open between notches 9 and 10 for stuffing.

Sew snout into nose opening, matching centers and notches 11.

5. Clip curves and turn right side out. Stuff firmly, using small wads of stuffing. A dowel or chopstick is handy to push the stuffing into corners. A popsicle or craft stick may be inserted in each leg to keep the legs from breaking as the animal gets older. If you use sticks, be sure to stuff under and around them firmly, so they don't protrude to touch the outer fabric. (Never use wire or pointed sticks, as these are not safe.)

When the pig is well stuffed, sew up the opening by hand, using the ladder stitch.

On outside, pinch up the wrinkles across the nose, stab stitch across the wrinkle with matching heavy-duty thread, catching in some stuffing under the wrinkle. Make three wrinkles across the nose, one over each eye, and one at each corner of the mouth, as shown on the illustration. With black thread, embroider the eyes, nostrils, and mouth. Use outline and blanket stitches for the eyes, outline for the mouth, and satin stitch for the nostrils. See Figure 7.

You might want to tack the ears at the xs so they fall forward. The tail may be tacked into a curl also.

To crochet a curly tail, using yarn that matches your fabric, make a chain twice as long as you want the tail to be when curled. In the second chain from the hook, work two single crochet. Continue working two single crochet in each chain to the end. It will curl automatically. Sew to the body of the pig.

Figure 1

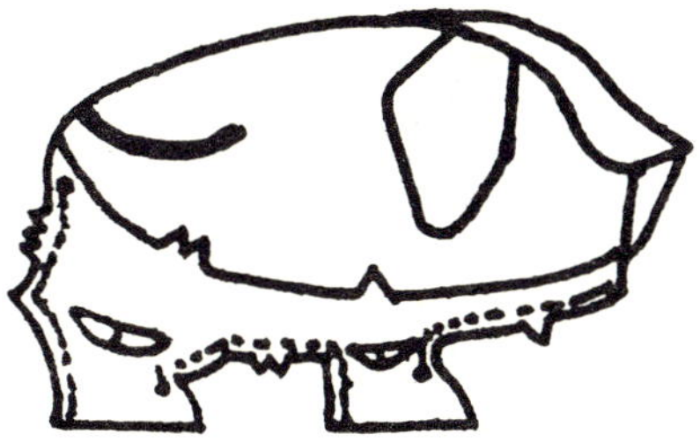

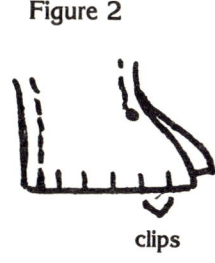

Figure 2

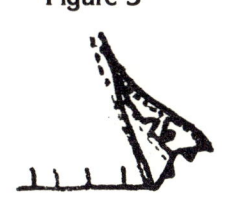
clips

Figure 3

Figure 4

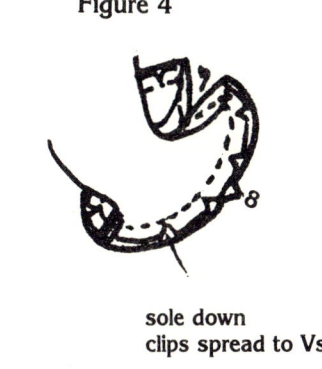

sole down
clips spread to Vs

Figure 5

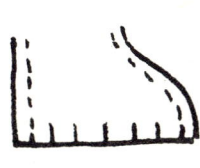

Figure 6

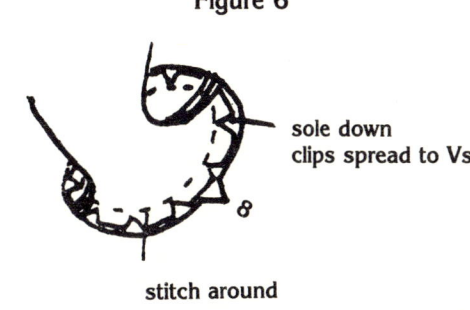

sole down
clips spread to Vs

stitch around

Figure 7

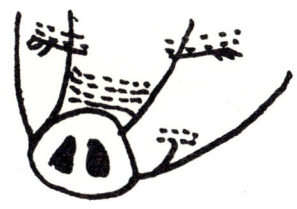

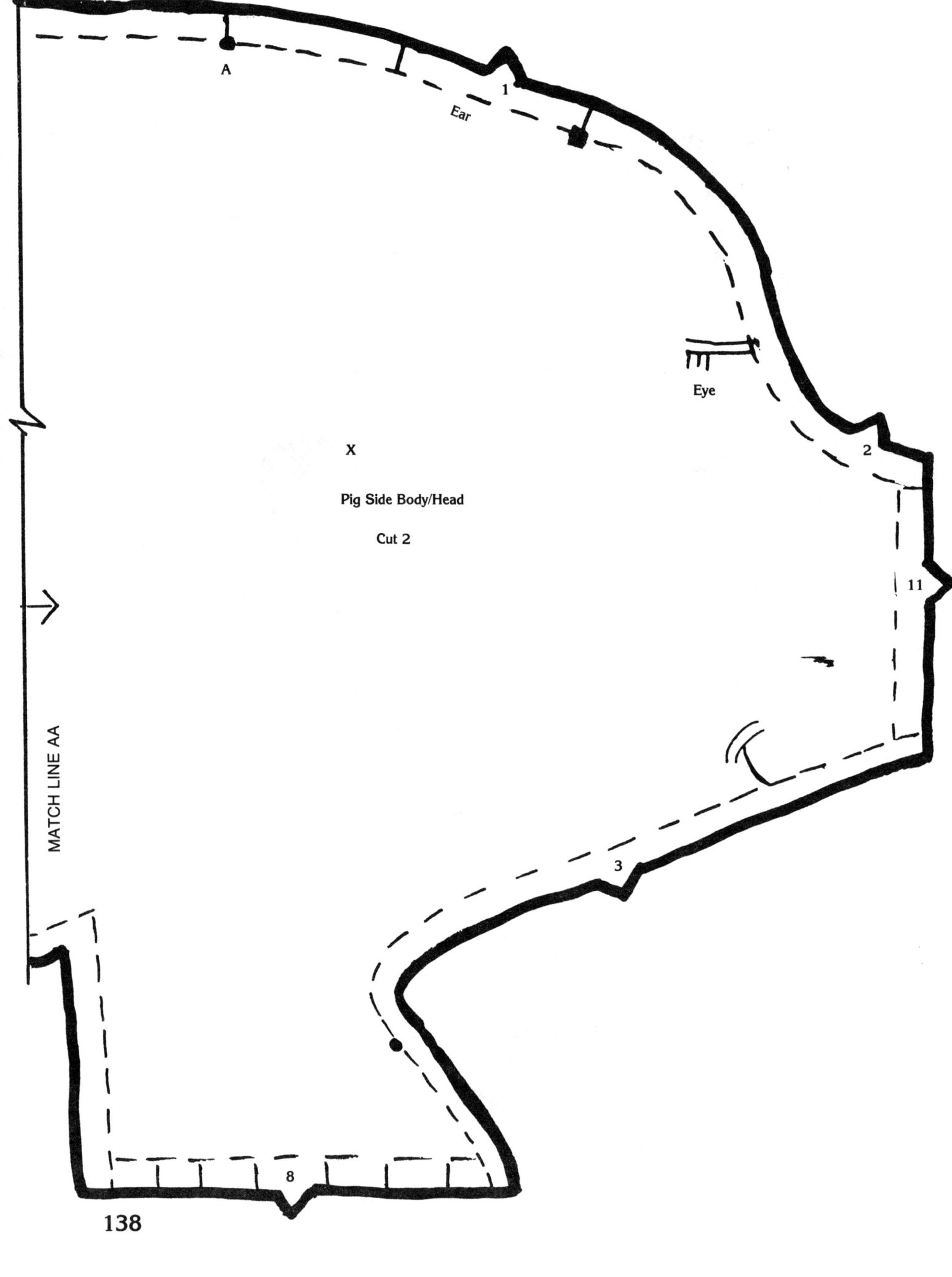

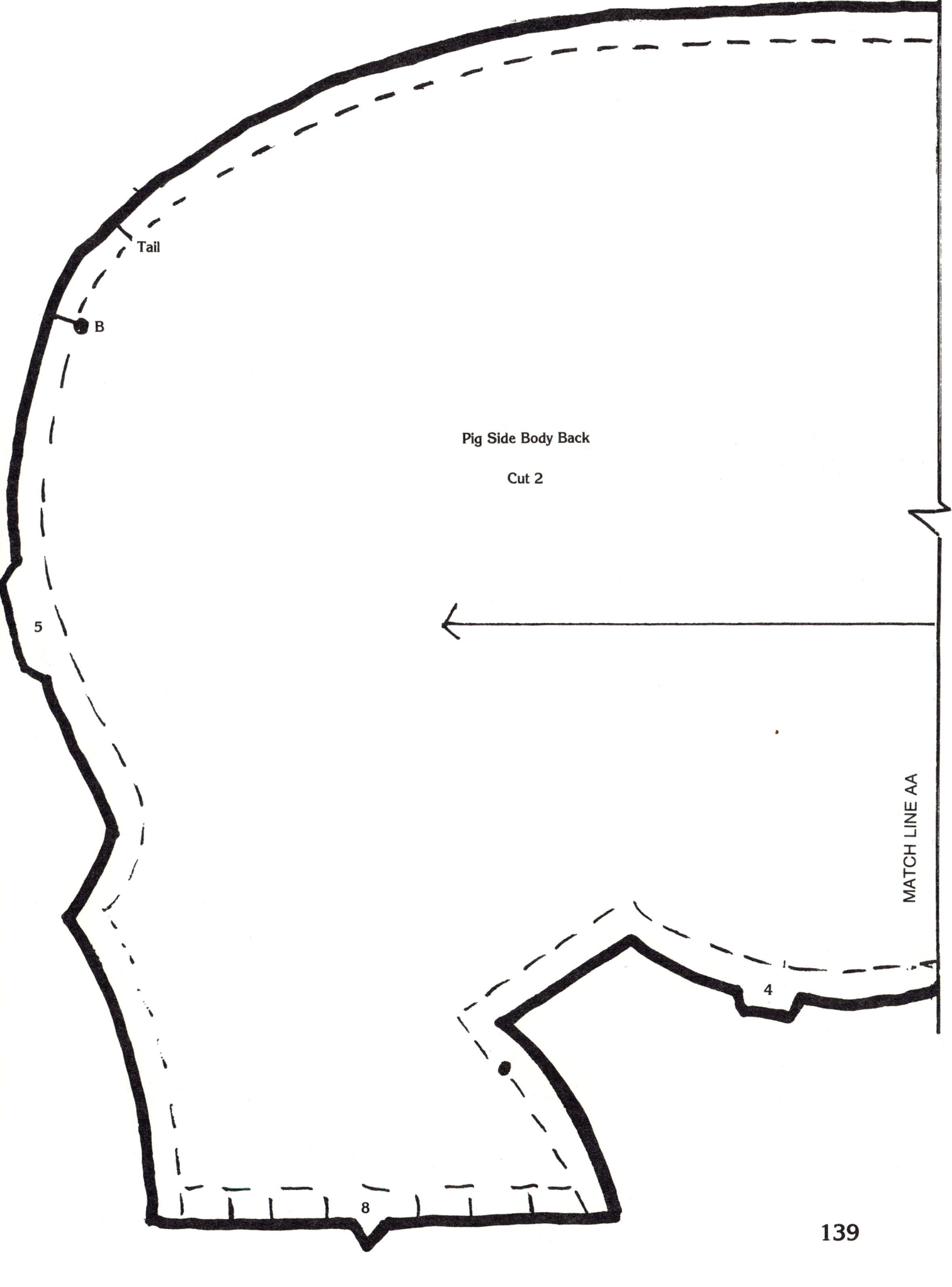

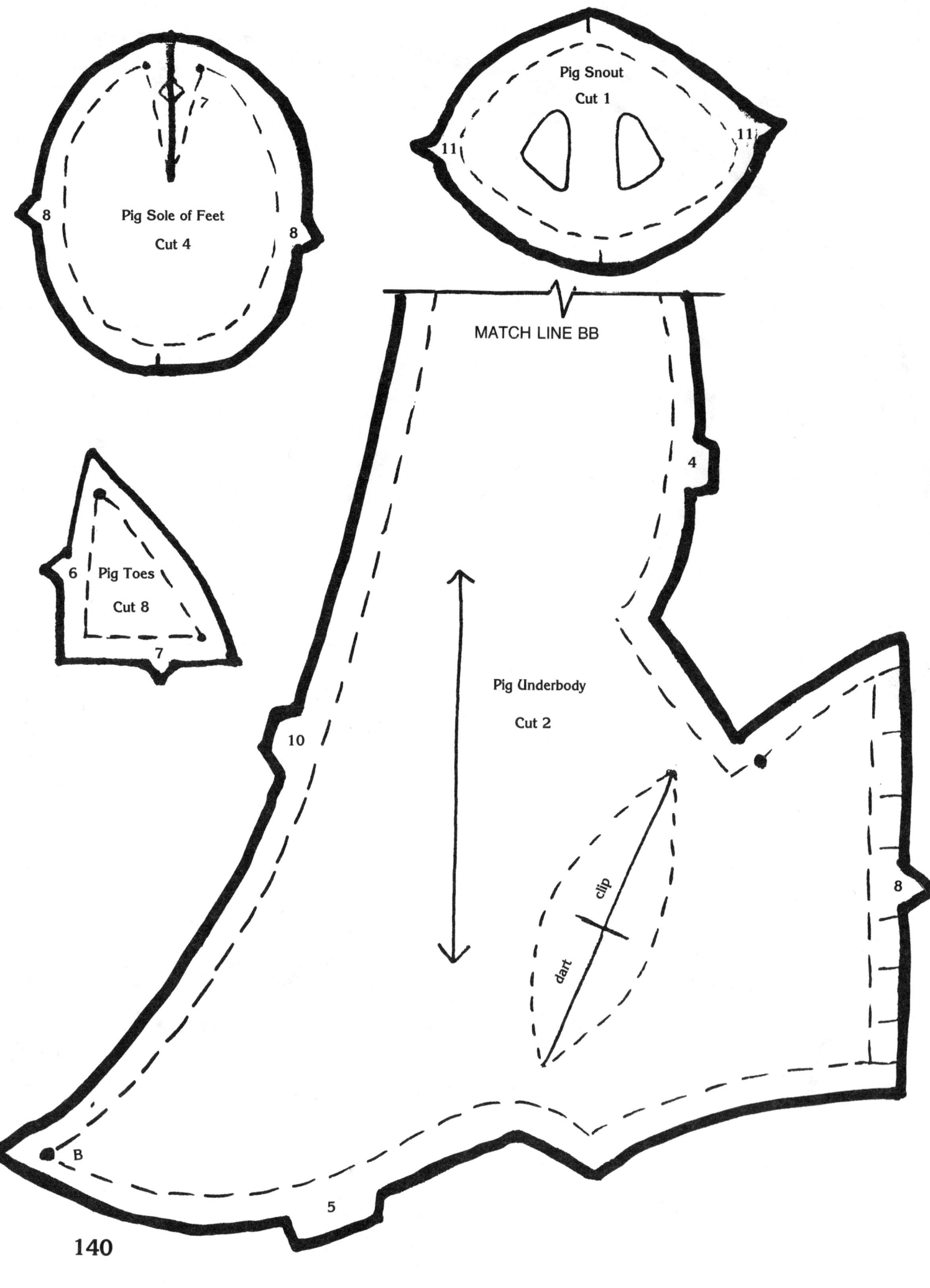

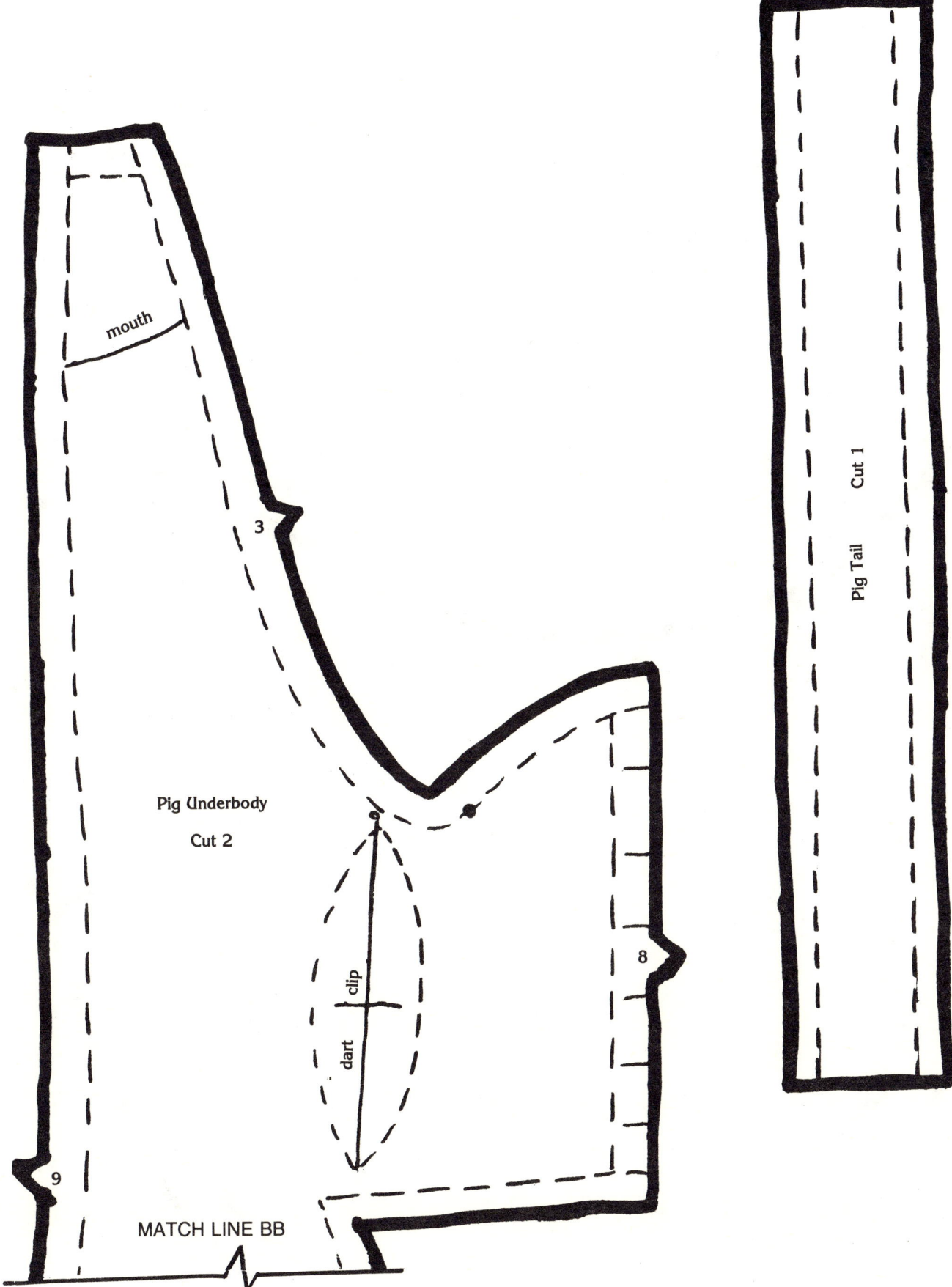

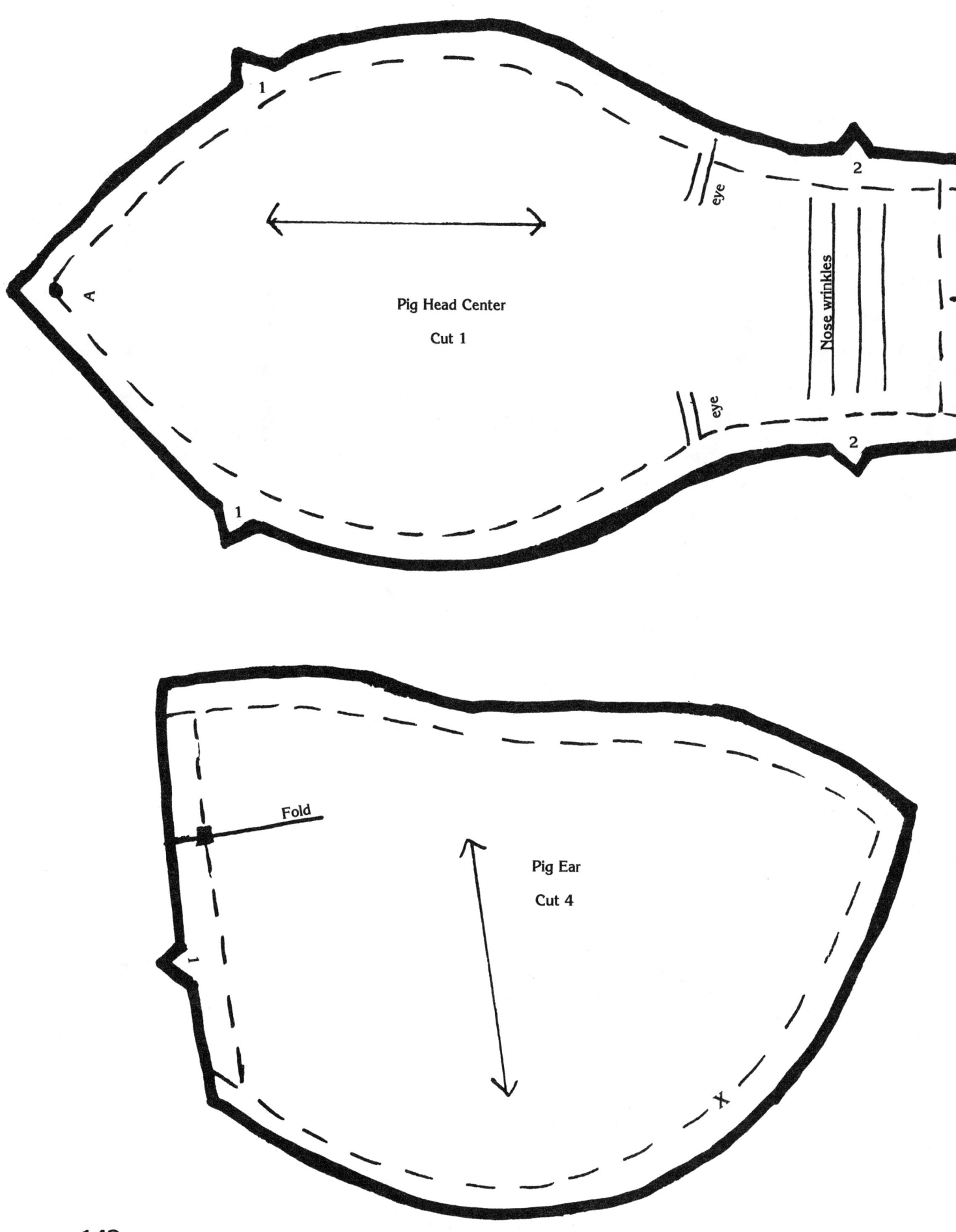

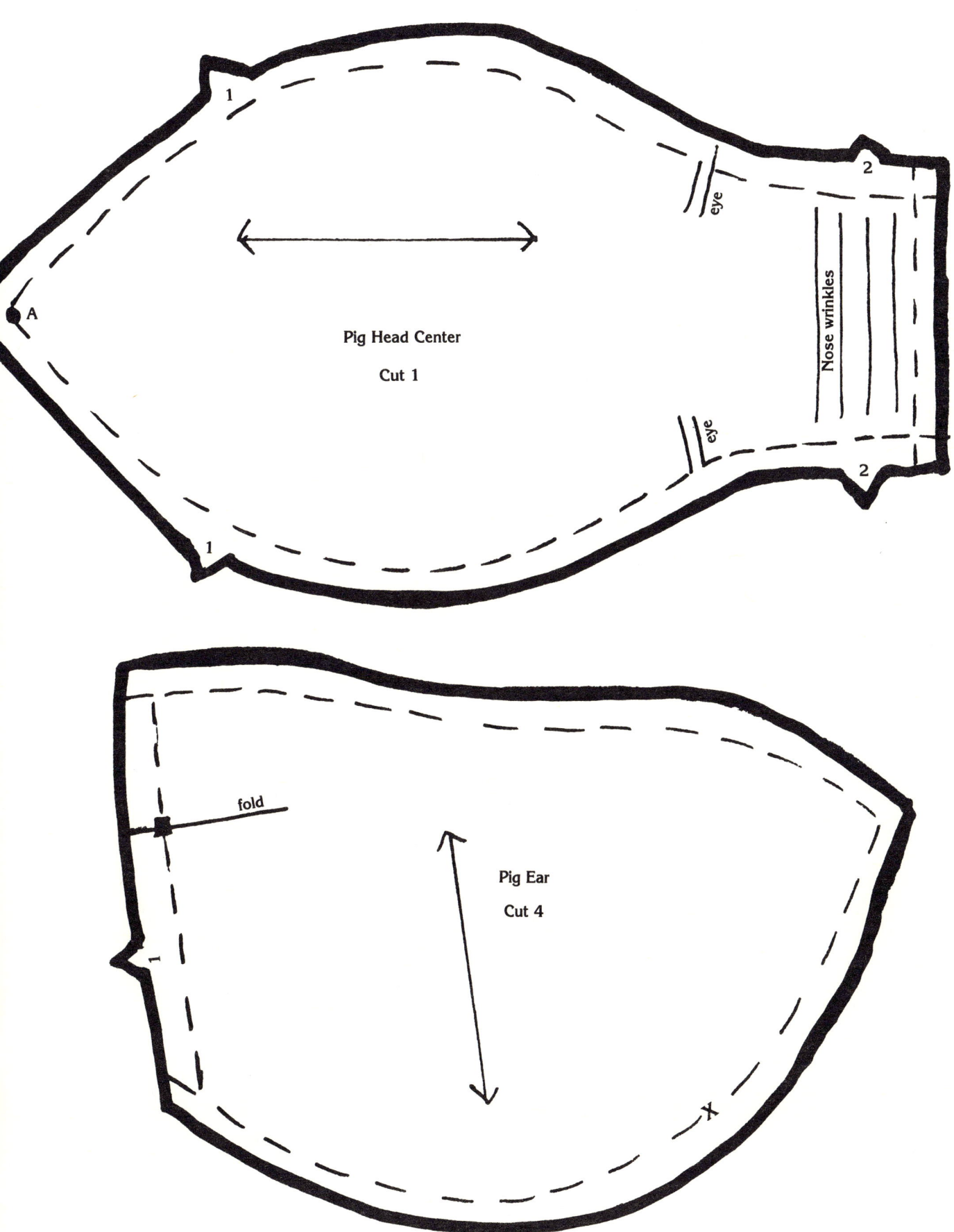

TEN PATTERN PIECES
15" (38 cm) TALL
24" (60 cm) TALL

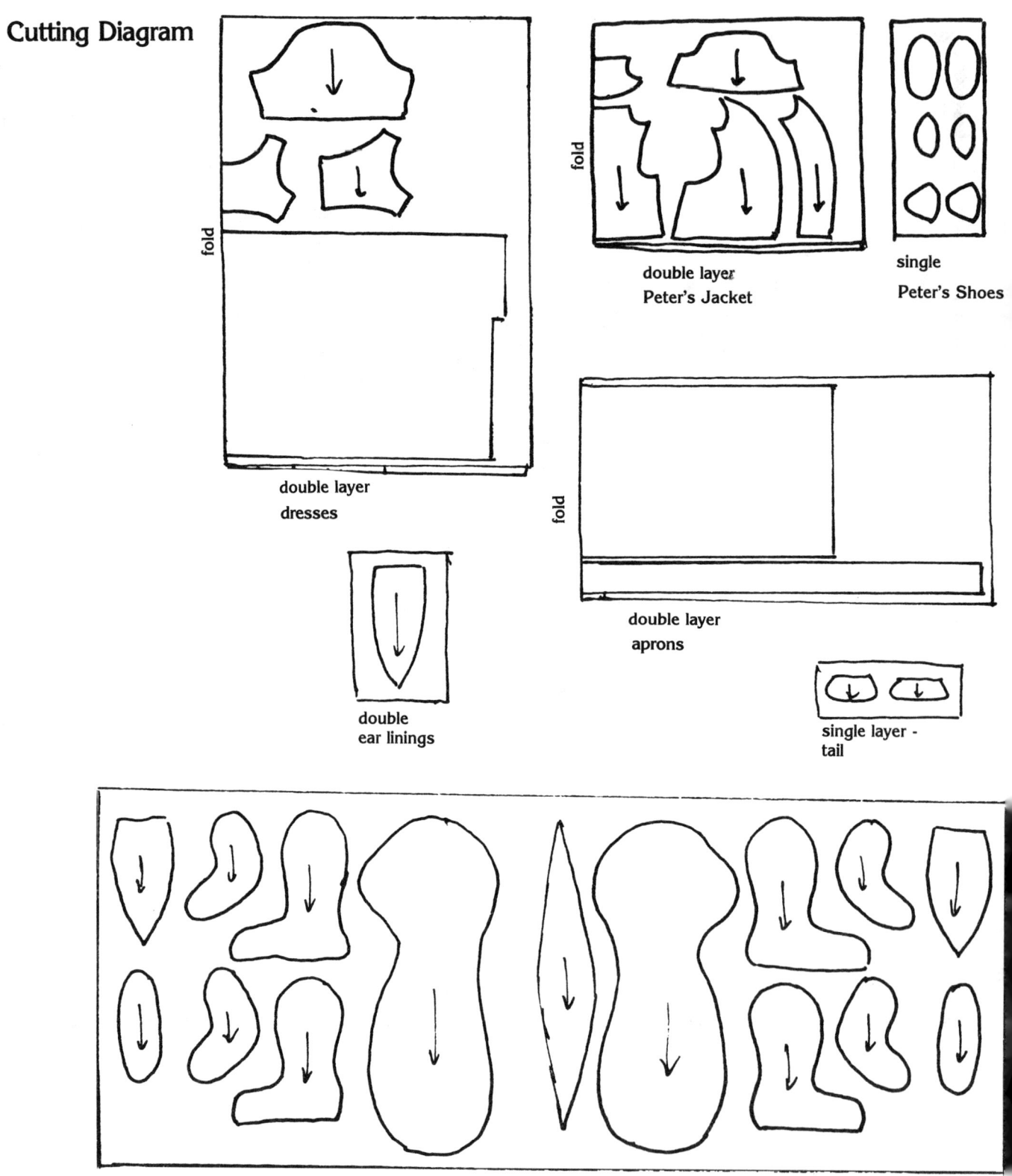

Cutting Diagram

Materials—Rabbits

	Large	*Small*
Tan, white, or gray fur fabric:	½ yard of 45" (½ m of 1 m 15 cm width fabric)	⅓ yard of 36" (⅓ m of 1 m width fabric)
Pink satin or velour for ear linings:	8" square (20 cm square)	4½" square (11½ cm square)
White shag for tails:	6" square (15 cm square)	3" square (8 cm square)

Scrap of cardboard, heavy-duty thread, four buttons with large holes, 4" to 6" (10 cm to 15 cm) upholsterer's needle, scraps for feet, and embroidery thread for features.

Fiberfill:	2 lbs. (1 kg)	12 ozs. (340 g)

Materials — Clothes

Peter's jacket: 20" × 11" piece (51 cm × 28 cm) (traditionally blue fabric), 2 gold buttons, 2 snaps

Peter's shoes: 5" × 10" piece (13 cm × 25 cm) felt, vinyl, or leather

Mama's dress: ½ yard of 36" material, 1⅔ yard trim (½ m of 1 m width fabric, 1⅔ m trim), 3 snaps

Girls' dresses: 18" × 16" piece for each, 1¼ yard trim (46 cm × 41 cm piece for each, 1¼ meter trim), 3 snaps for each

Mama's apron: 32" × 11" piece (81 cm × 28 cm)

Girls' aprons: 24" × 8" piece (60 cm × 20 cm) for each

Turtleneck sweater: one pair of socks

10
Peter Rabbit Family

This is a delightful version of the characters from a favorite children's story. They all have movable arms and legs, attached by a method where the buttons do not show at all. Peter wears a jacket and shoes; Mama and the girls wear dresses and aprons. Gingham is traditional for the dresses, but you may disregard tradition if you wish. Included are directions for making a turtleneck sweater out of a pair of socks to fit the small rabbit.

Cutting Instructions

See the Introduction for working with fur fabrics.
 Cut two bodies, one head center, four arms, four legs, two soles of feet, and two ears of the fur fabric
 Cut two ear linings of pink fabric.
 Cut two tails of white shag fabric.

Sewing Instructions

Use ¼" (⅗ cm) seams unless otherwise stated.
 1. *Head.* Sew ears to ear linings, leaving bottom open. Turn right side out, fold in half lengthwise. Insert the folded end of ears into the slits in the head and stitch the dart, as shown in Figure 1. Stitch head center from dot A to dot B, to each side of the head. See Figure 2.
 2. *Body.* Sew two tail pieces together, leaving open along the flat side. Turn, stuff lightly, and sew to one body between lines as indicated on the pattern.
 Sew body seam from dot A around the bottom (enclosing tail) to dot B, leaving open between notches 1 and 2 for stuffing. See Figure 3. Clip

curves, turn right side out. Stuff firmly and sew up opening, using ladder stitch. Set aside.

3. *Arms.* Sew arm pieces together, leaving open between notches 3 and 4 for stuffing. See Figure 3. Clip curves, turn right side out. Set aside. (Stuff after attaching to body.)

4. *Legs.* Stitch around legs, leaving bottoms open and leaving open between notches 5 and 6 for stuffing. See Figure 4. Clip inside seam allowance along bottom edge of foot, as shown in Figure 4 and on pattern. Matching center front and back, pin foot to sole, spreading clips to Vs so edges match. See Figure 4. With sole down, stitch around the foot, just inside Vs. Clip curves on legs and turn right side out. (Stuff after attaching to body.)

5. *To attach movable arms and legs to body.* Cut four circles of cardboard, ¾" (1.88 cm) diameter for small rabbit or 1¼" (3.13 cm) diameter for large rabbit. String 8 strands of heavy-duty thread or carpet cord through the eye of a long needle, 4" to 6" (10 cm to 15 cm) long. String through one button, one cardboard circle, the inner side of one arm, the body, the inner side of the other arm, a second cardboard circle, and a second button. Come back through, reversing the order, to the first button. See Figure 5. Tie strands tightly, making sure the cardboard circles and buttons are flat inside the arms, using a tight double knot. Trim ends of thread. Repeat for legs, using the other two circles and two buttons.

6. Stuff arms and legs firmly and sew up openings.

Go over the seams with a strong needle, pulling out any pile that is caught in the seams.

Appliqué eyes and nose to head, where shown in the pattern and the illustration. Embroider mouth. Make thread whiskers as shown in Figure 6.

Clothes

1. *Peter's jacket.* Cut one back on fold, two fronts, one back facing on fold, two front facings, and two sleeves.

Sew fronts to back at shoulder seams. Clip curve, open seams flat.

Hem lower edge of sleeves. Sew into armhole, matching notches 1 and 2. Stitch underarm and side jacket seams in one.

Sew front facings to back facing at shoulder seam. Sew facing to jacket around neck and down front edges. Turn under and stitch inner edge of facing. Turn facings to inside and tack down. Hem bottom of jacket. Turn collar back shawl-style. Sew two gold buttons where indicated on the pattern, and sew two snaps under the buttons.

2. *Peter's shoes.* The shoes may be stitched right sides together and turned right side out or they may be top stitched wrong sides together and trimmed close to the stitching to make a small ridge. If you are top stitching vinyl, it may stick under the presser foot. A light rubbing of sewing machine oil along the seam line will prevent this. Wipe oil off after stitching.

Cut two soles, two toes, and two heels.

Clip toes and heels inside seam allowance as shown in Figure 7 and on pattern. Pin toe and heel to sole, so edges meet at the dots. Spread clips to Vs so edges match. Stitch ¼" (⅗ cm) seam around (sole down) just inside the Vs. Trim close to the stitching.

3. *Dresses.* Cut one skirt on fold, one bodice front on fold, two bodice backs, and two sleeves.

Sew shoulder seams. Hem neck edge and trim as desired. Hem bottoms of sleeves and trim to match neck edge. Sew ¼" (⅗ cm) elastic across on line shown on pattern, 4" (10 cm) long for large rabbit and 3" (8 cm) long for small rabbit, stretching as you stitch. Run gathering stitches between notches on sleeve caps, and pull up gathers to fit between notches on the bodice. Matching dot to shoulder seam, and notches 1 and 2, sew sleeve into armhole. Sew underarm/side bodice seam in one.

Gather top of skirt to fit the bodice. Stitch. Sew center back seam as far as the dot. Hem raw edges of the back opening. Hem bottom of skirt. Sew three snaps along the back opening, as shown on pattern.

4. *Aprons.* Cut one apron on fold and one waistband/ties on fold.

Narrow-hem the sides of the apron. Turn up the bottom and hem. Run gathering threads along the top and draw up to fit between the dots on the waistband/ties. Stitch between dots. Fold waistband over top and turn ¼" (⅗ cm) under. Turn long edges and ends under ¼" (⅗ cm) on each side of ties and press. Top stitch the length of the waistband/ties. See Figure 8.

5. *Turtleneck sweater.* An old pair of socks with holes in the toes or heels is fine; you only use the tops. If you do not have a pair of matching socks, make a sleeveless vest, or use a contrasting sock for the sleeves and collar.

Use zigzag stitch to sew edges of pieces together. If you do not have a zigzag sewing machine, straight stitch two rows close together.

Body: Cut one sock 5" (13 cm) down from the top. Invert so the ribbing forms the waistband. If the sock has a design, fold so the design is centered in the front and back. Cut down from the raw edge 2¾" (6.88 cm) on each side to make armholes. Turn inside out and stitch ½" (1¼ cm) in from each edge for shoulder seams. See Figure 9.

Sleeves: Cut other sock 4" (10 cm) down from top. Invert. Center any design and cut all the way down sides to make two sleeves. Shape the caps of each sleeve as shown in Figure 10. Turn inside out and sew side seams of each sleeve. Turn right side out and sew sleeves into armholes.

Collar: Cut 3" (8 cm) section from the sock for the collar. Fold so raw edges meet. See Figure 11. Sew both raw edges to neck opening, stretching to fit. Turn sweater right side out. See Figure 12.

It is easier to pull the sweater on over the feet than over the head.

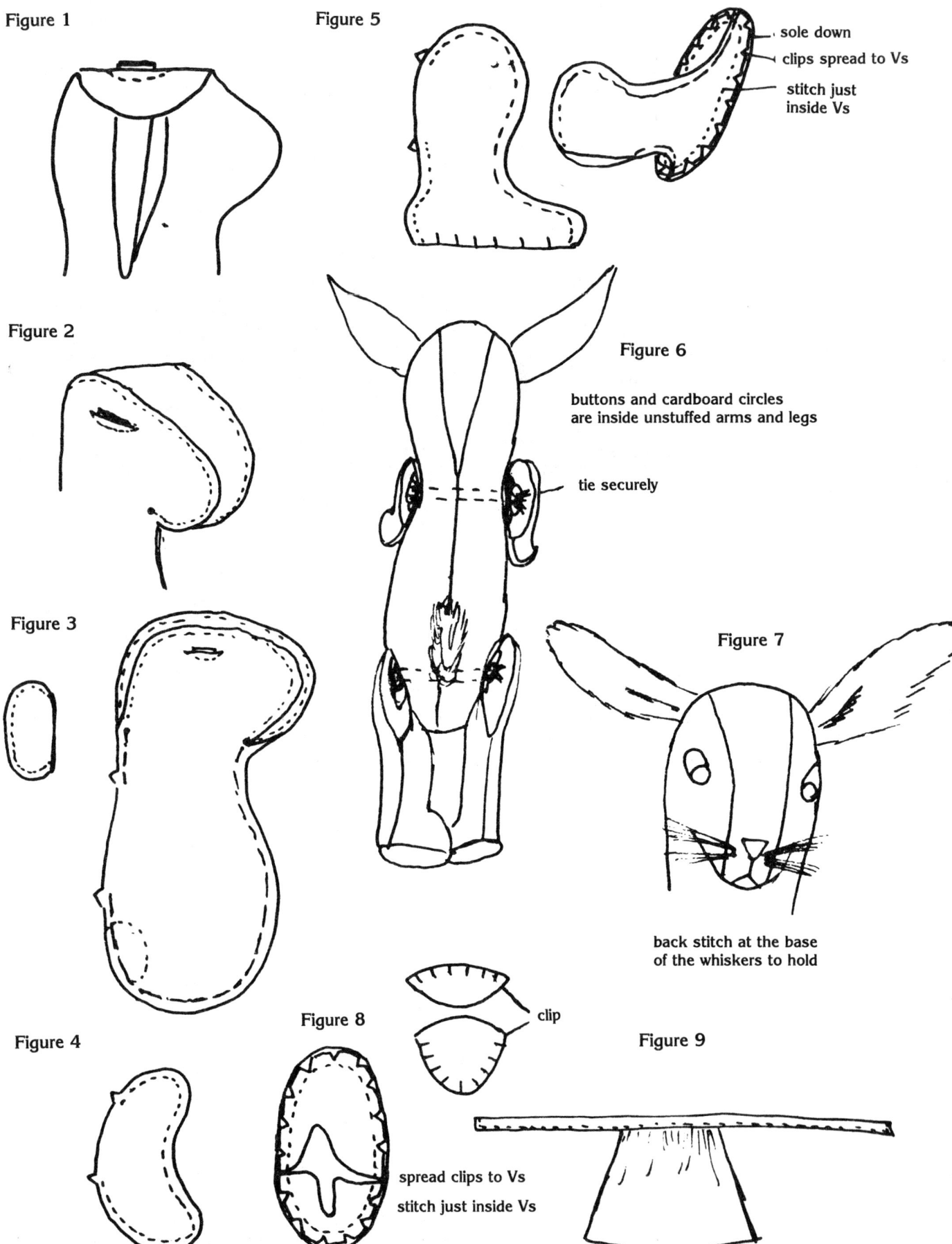

Figure 10

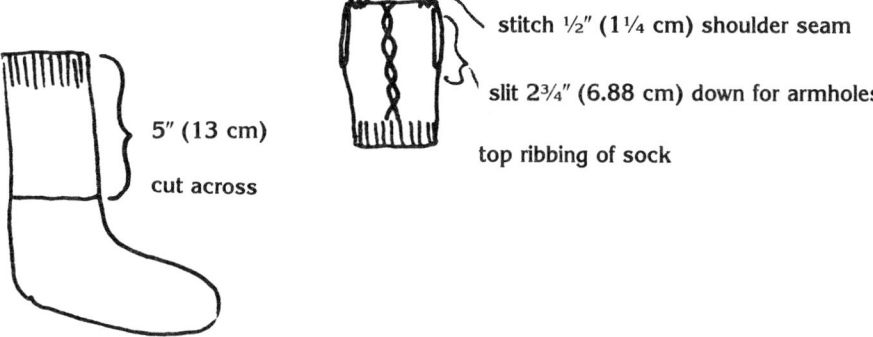

5" (13 cm)
cut across

stitch ½" (1¼ cm) shoulder seam

slit 2¾" (6.88 cm) down for armholes

top ribbing of sock

Figure 11

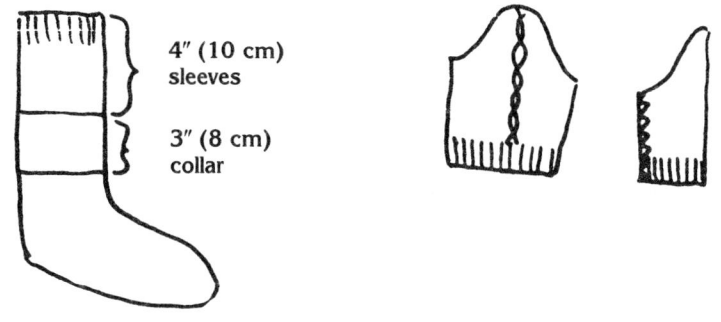

4" (10 cm) sleeves

3" (8 cm) collar

Figure 13

Figure 12

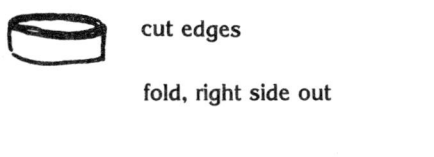

cut edges

fold, right side out

153

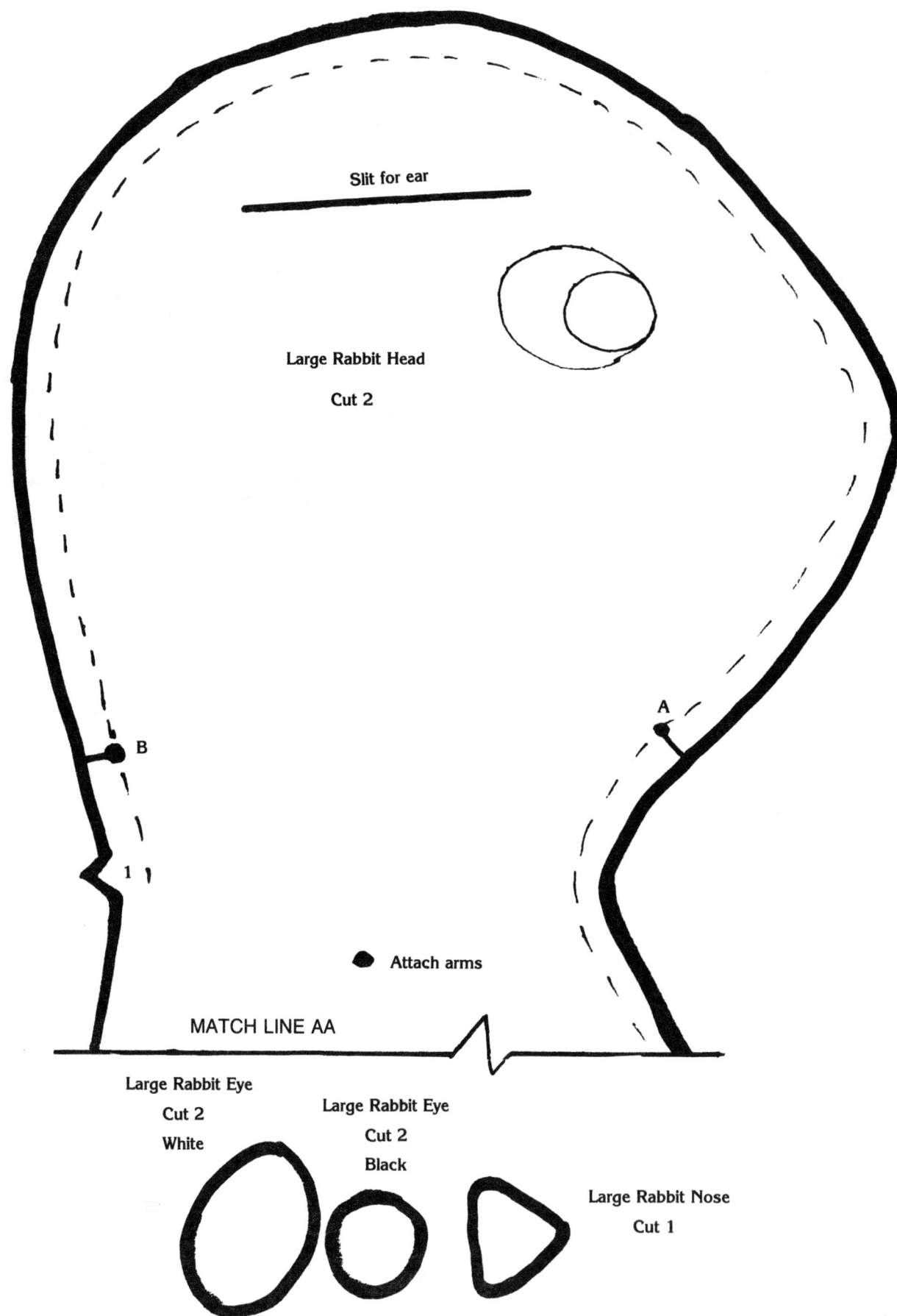

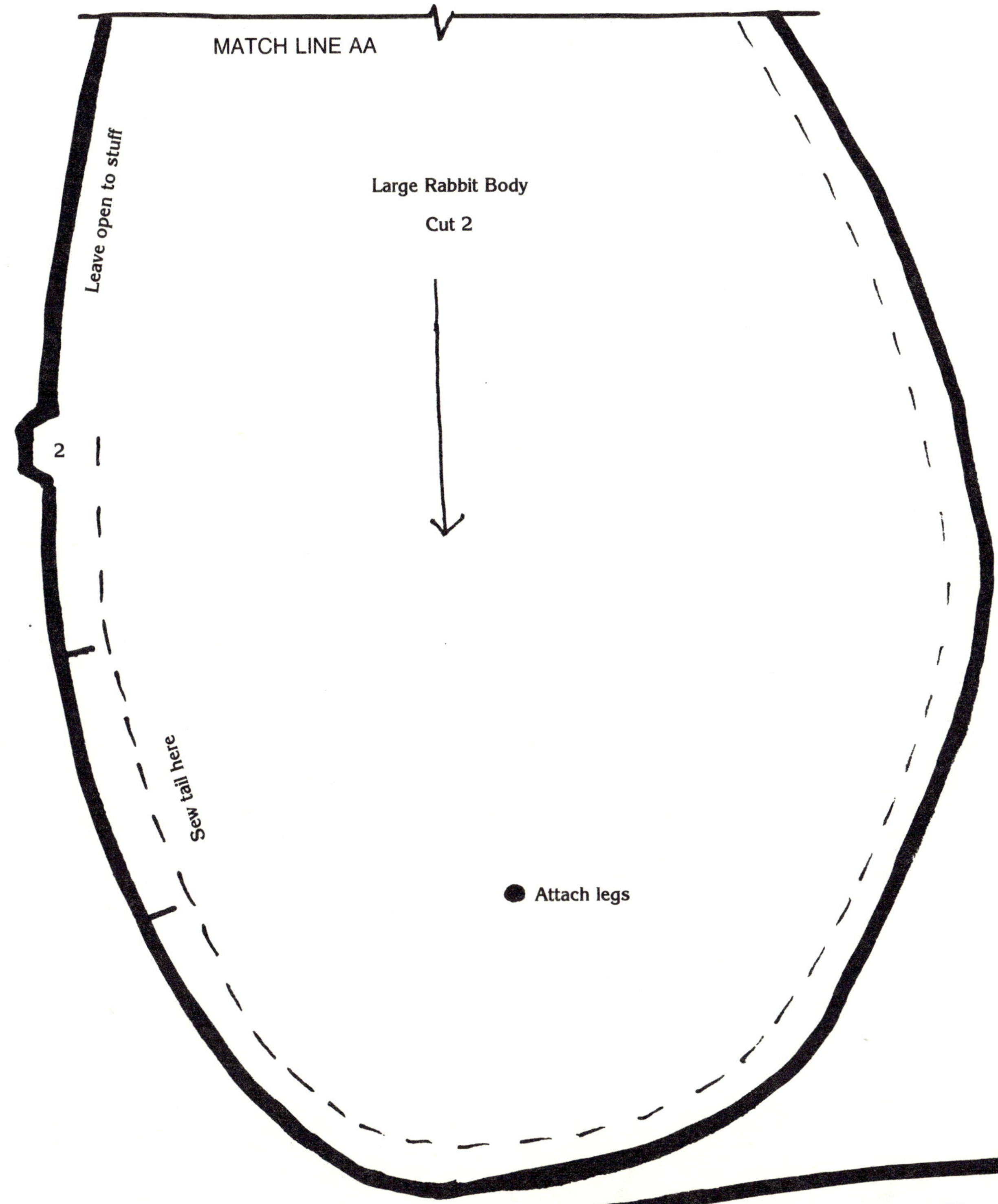

MATCH LINE AA

Leave open to stuff

2

Large Rabbit Body

Cut 2

Sew tail here

● Attach legs

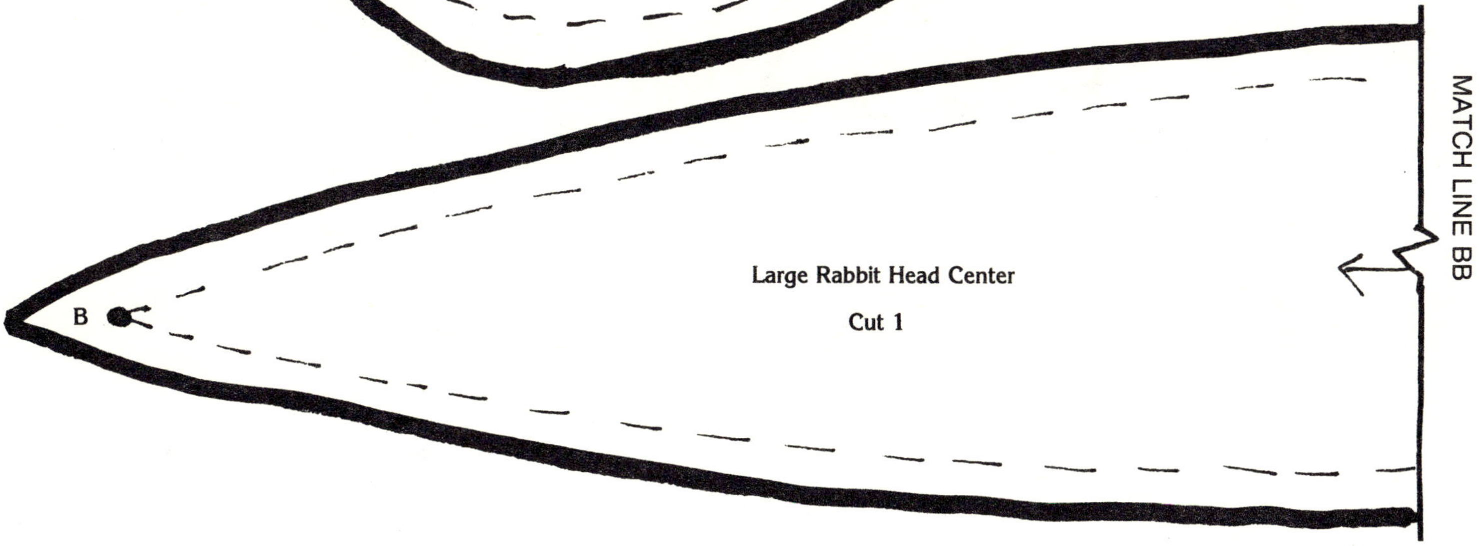

B ●

Large Rabbit Head Center

Cut 1

MATCH LINE BB

155

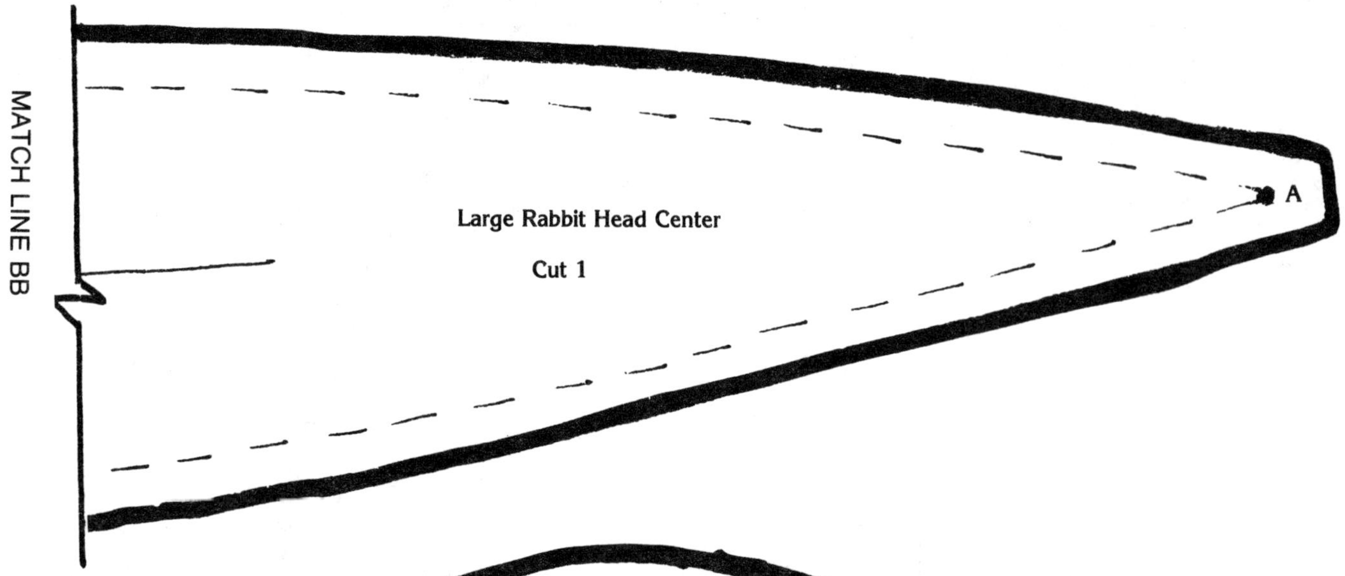

MATCH LINE BB

Large Rabbit Head Center

Cut 1

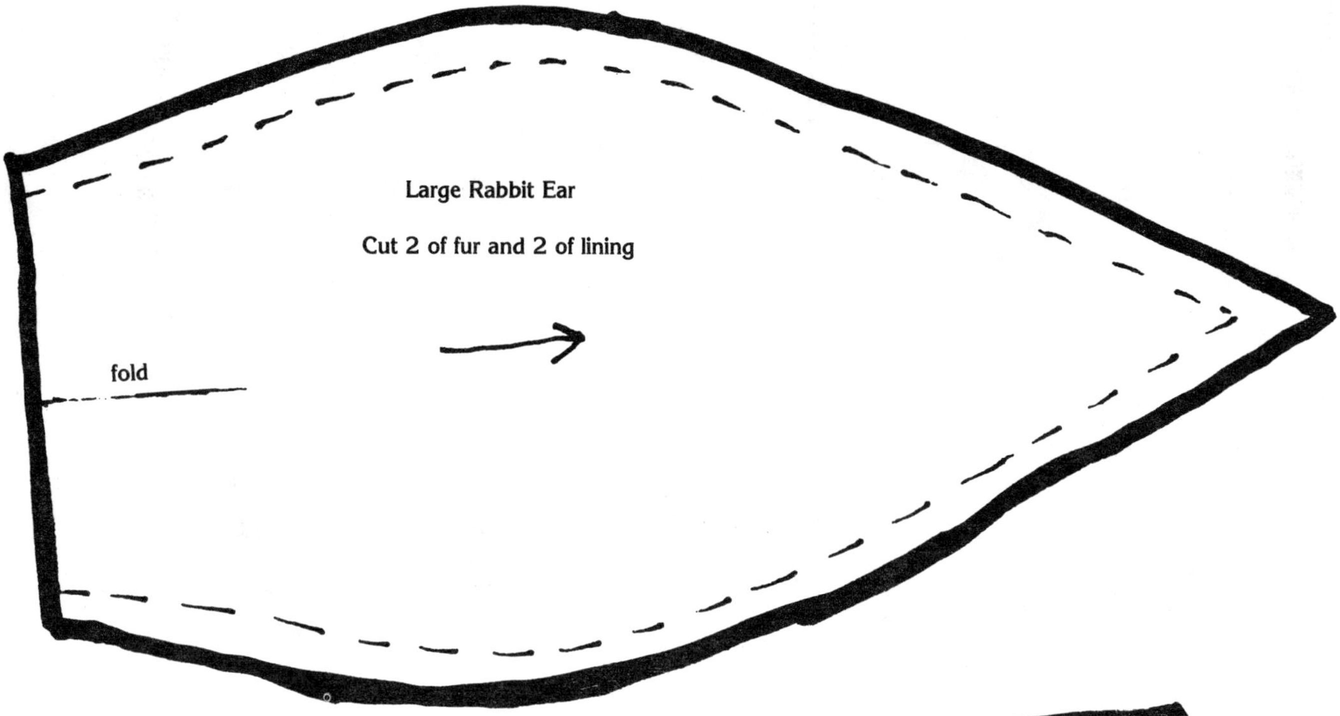

A

Large Rabbit Ear

Cut 2 of fur and 2 of lining

fold

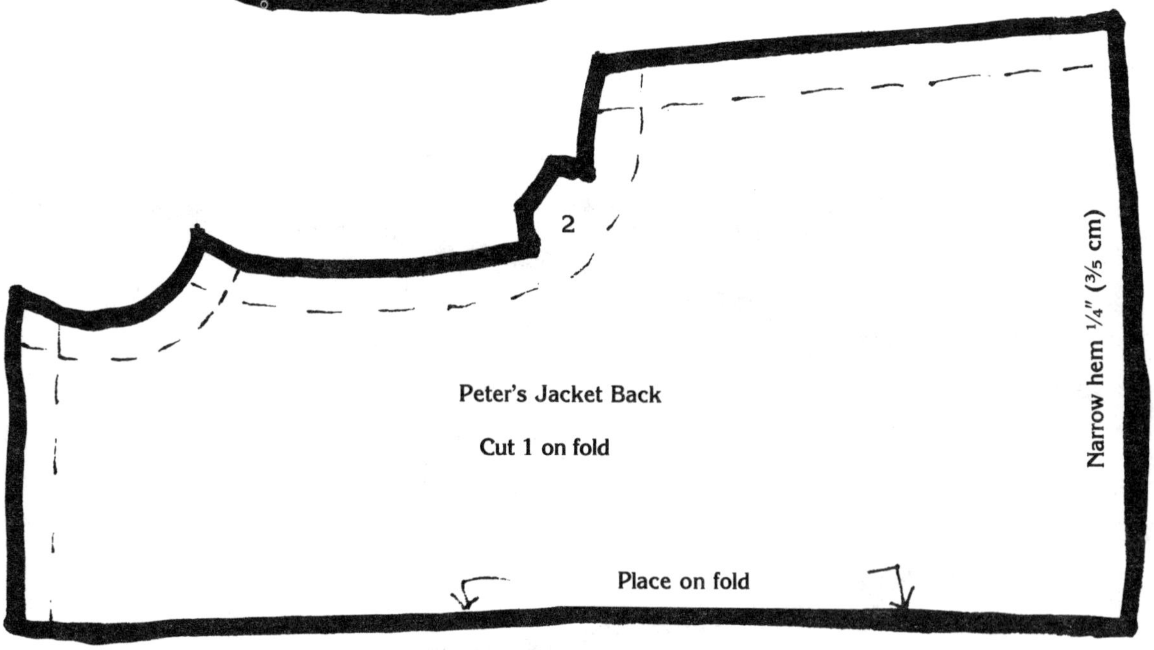

Peter's Jacket Back

Cut 1 on fold

Place on fold

Narrow hem 1/4" (3/5 cm)

156

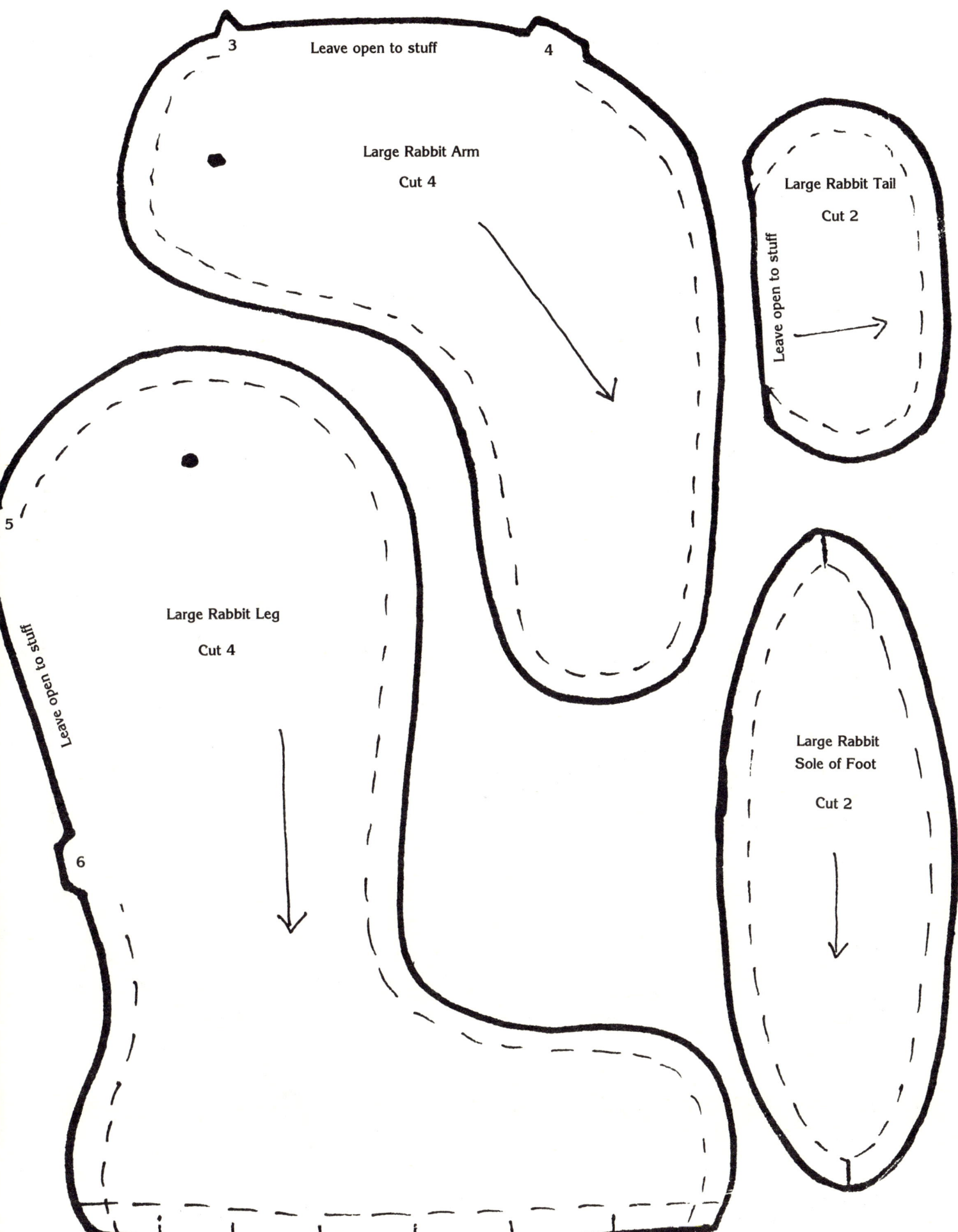

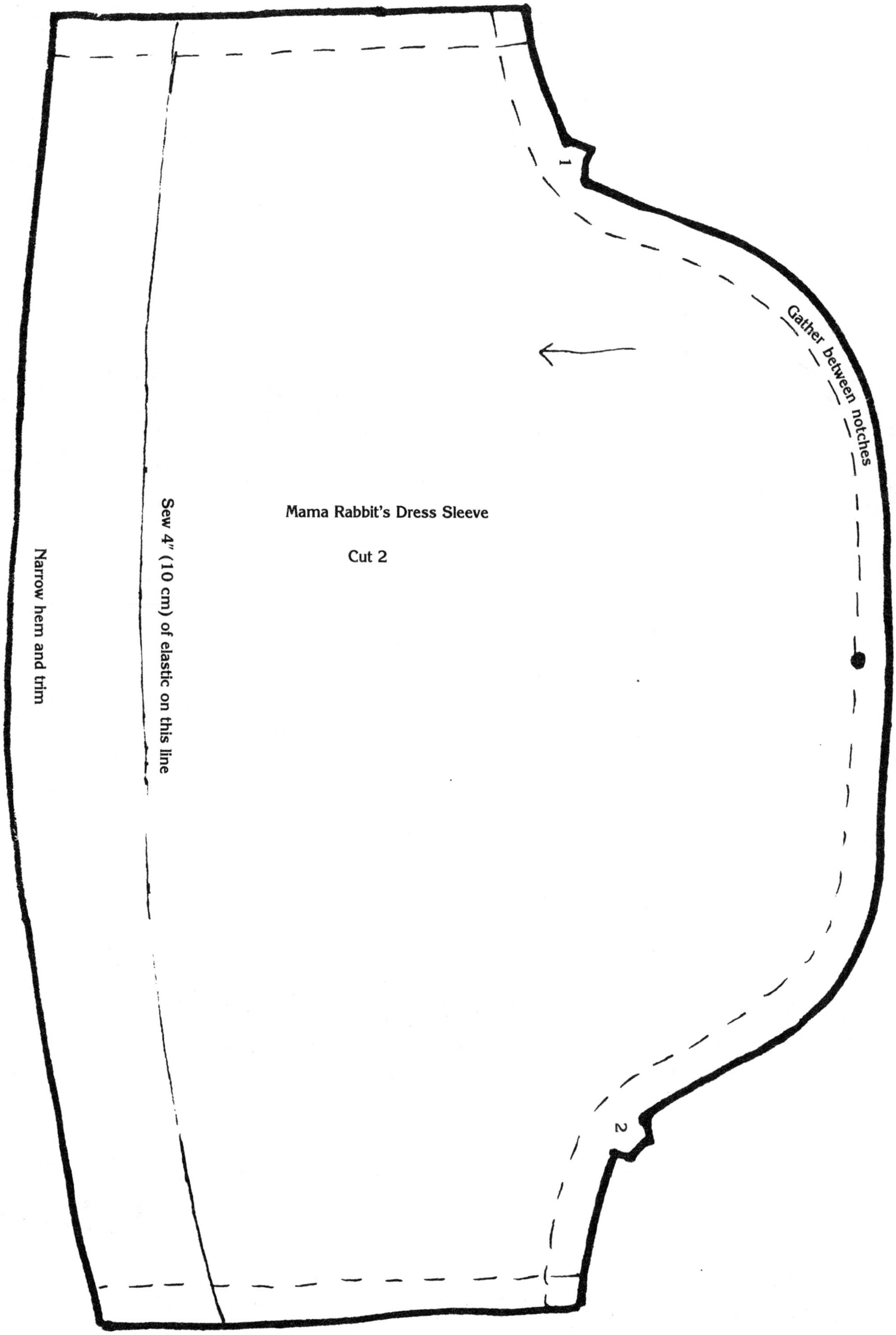

Mama Rabbit's Dress Sleeve

Cut 2

Gather between notches

Sew 4" (10 cm) of elastic on this line

Narrow hem and trim

Gather to fit bodice

Mama Rabbit's Dress Skirt

Cut 1 on fold

MATCH LINE CC

Narrow hem and trim with 1½" (3¾ cm) wide lace or eyelet or add 3" (8 cm) along bottom and turn up 1½" (3¾ cm) hem

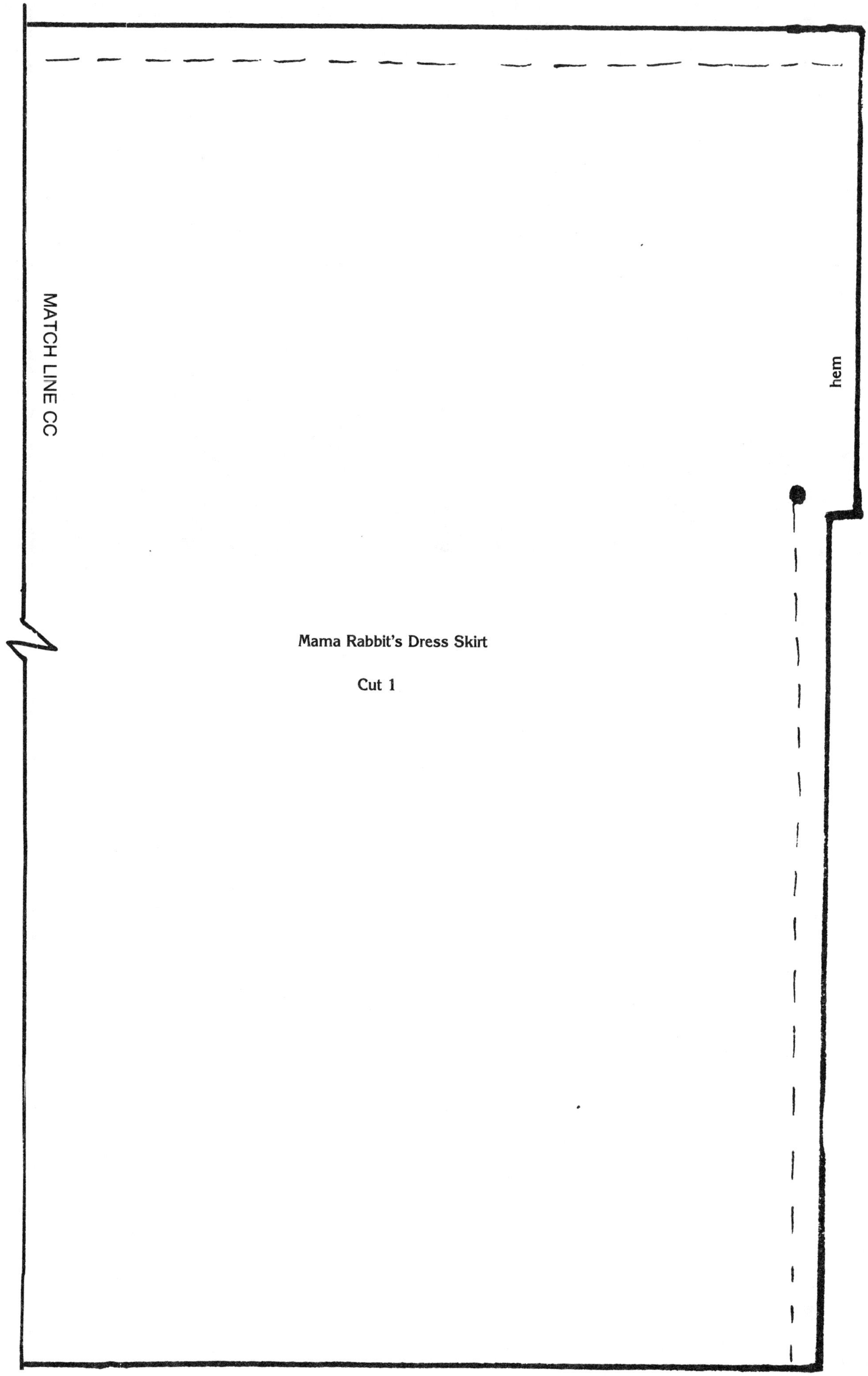

MATCH LINE CC

Mama Rabbit's Dress Skirt

Cut 1

hem

Place on fold

Mama Rabbit's Apron

Cut 1 on fold

Narrow hem sides

Gather to fit between dots on waistband

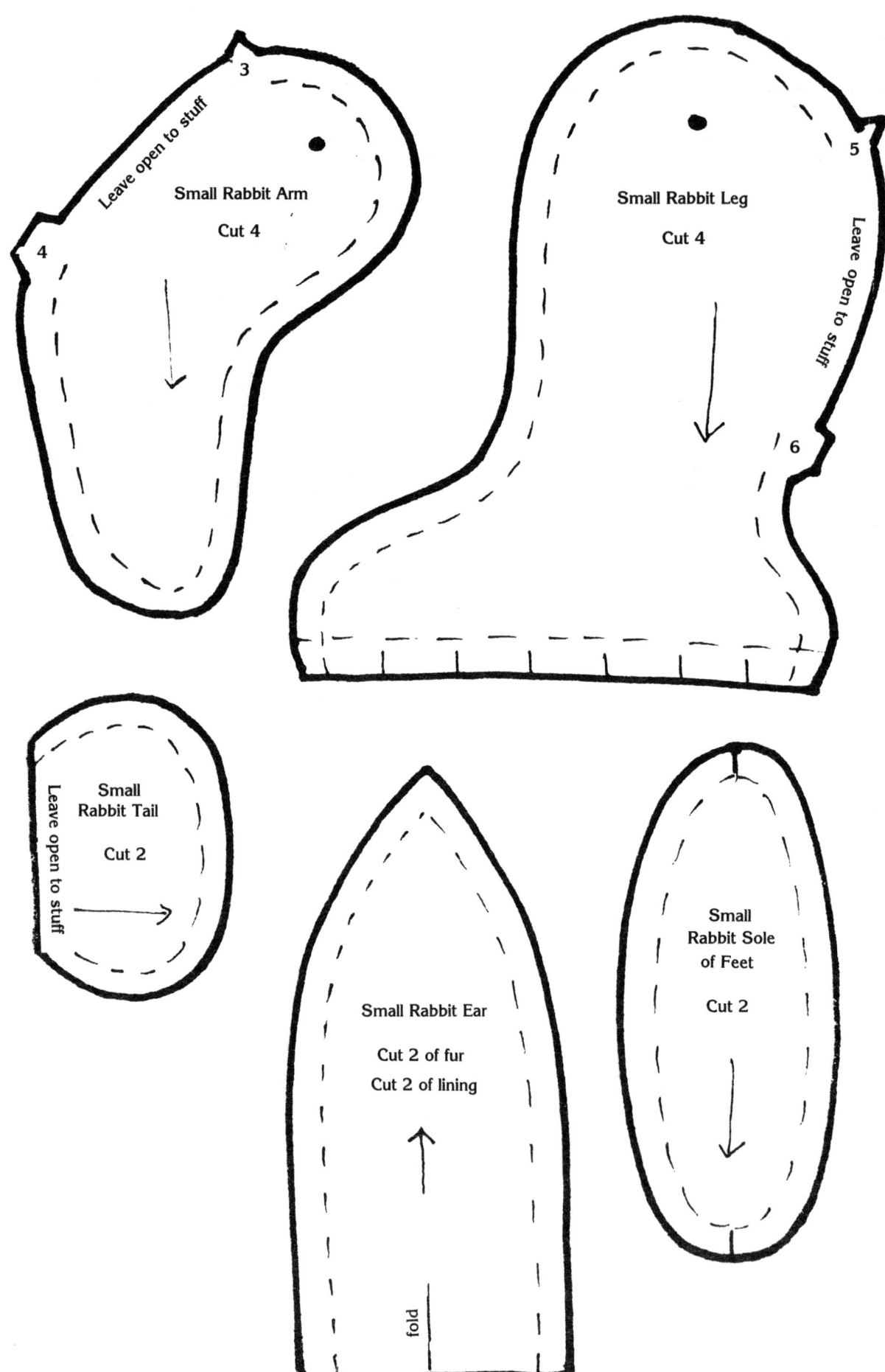

162

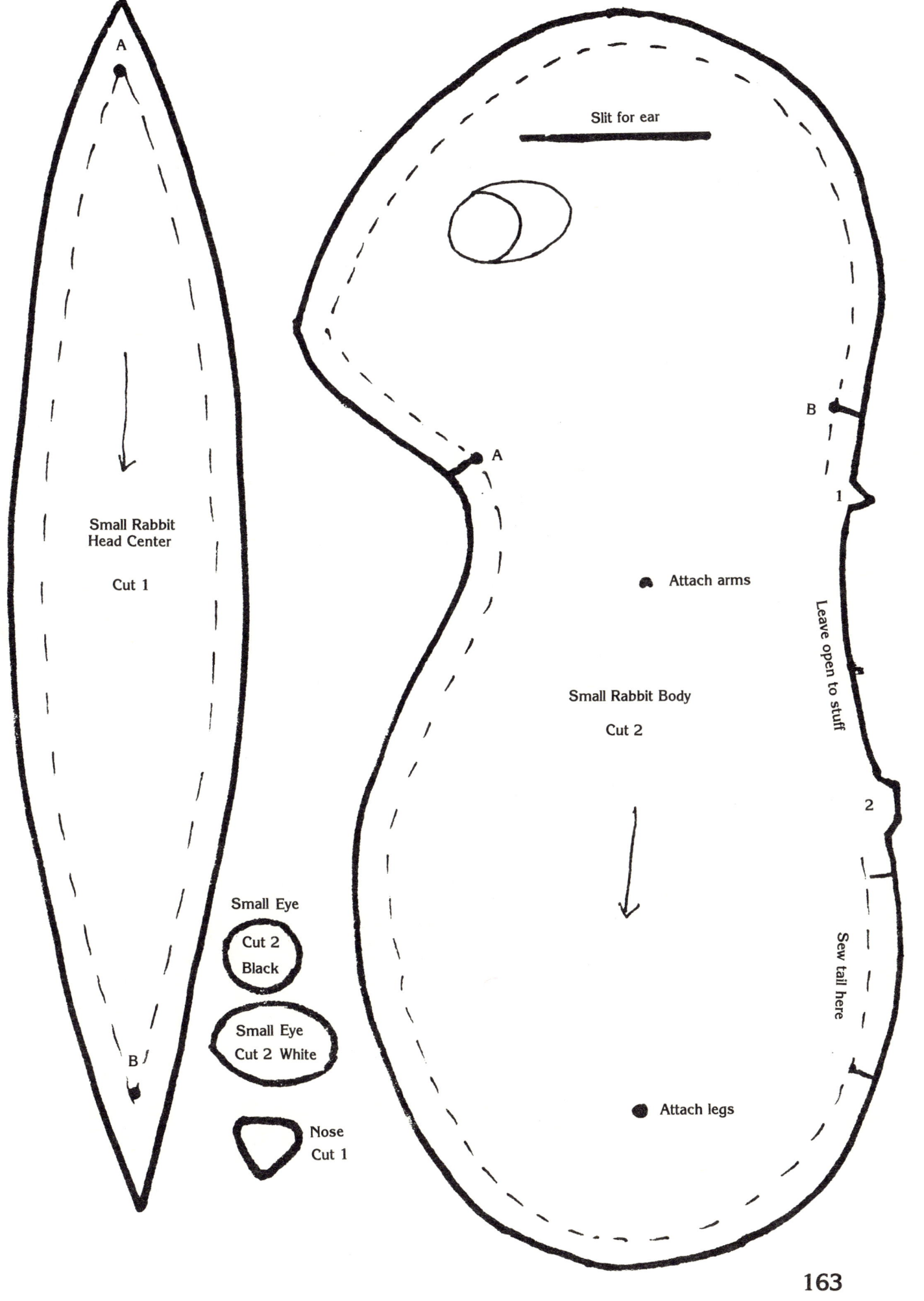

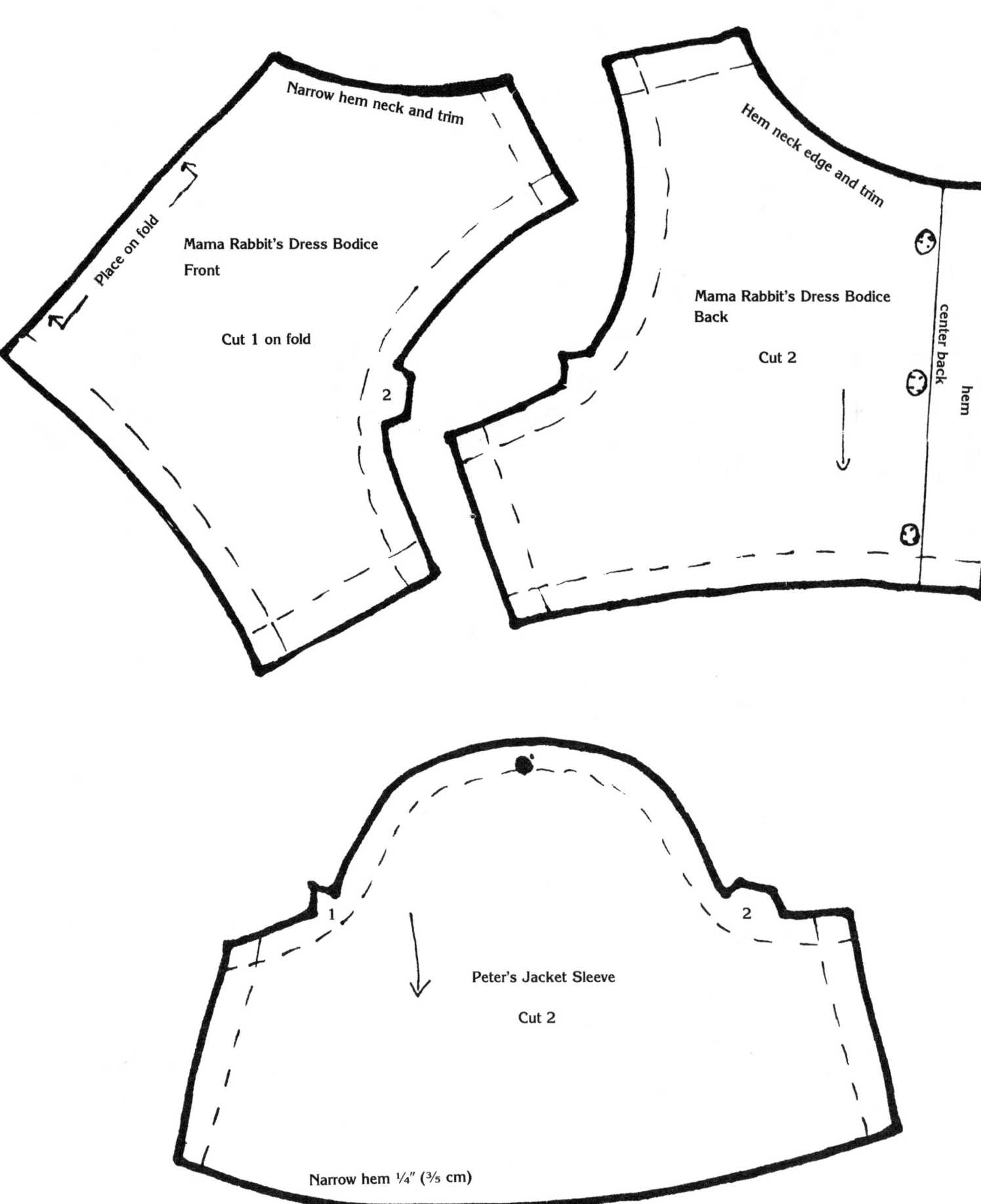

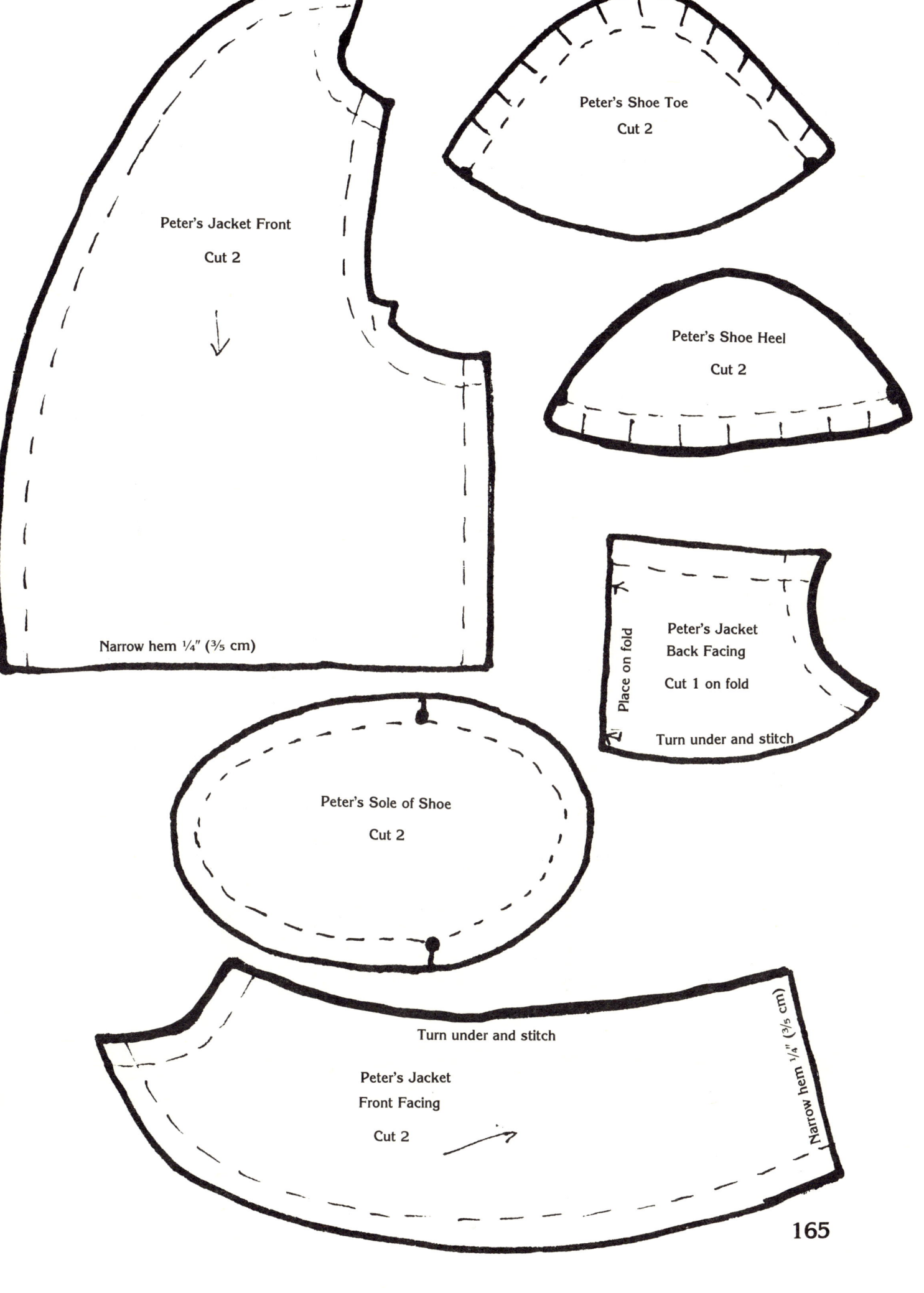

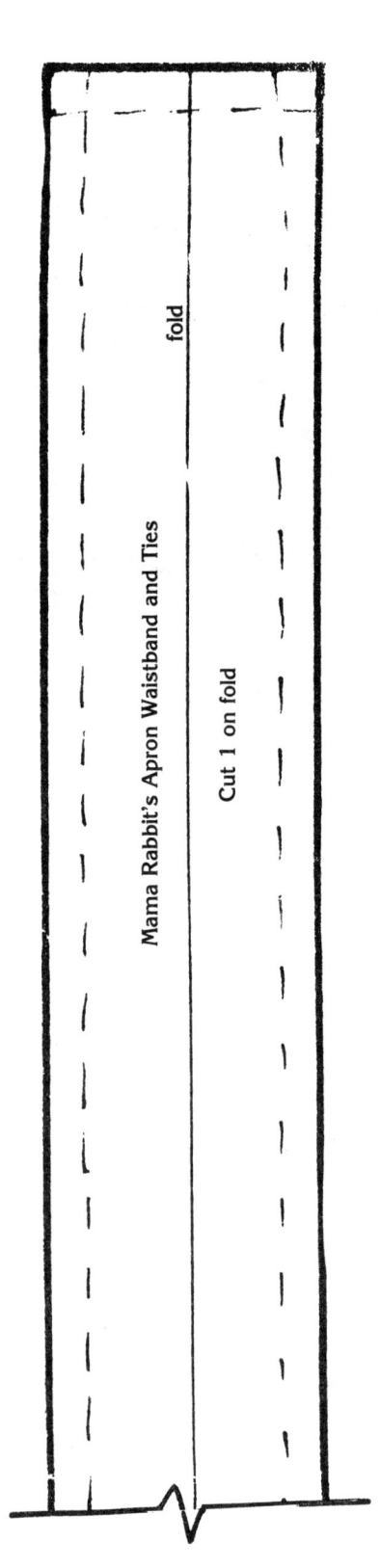
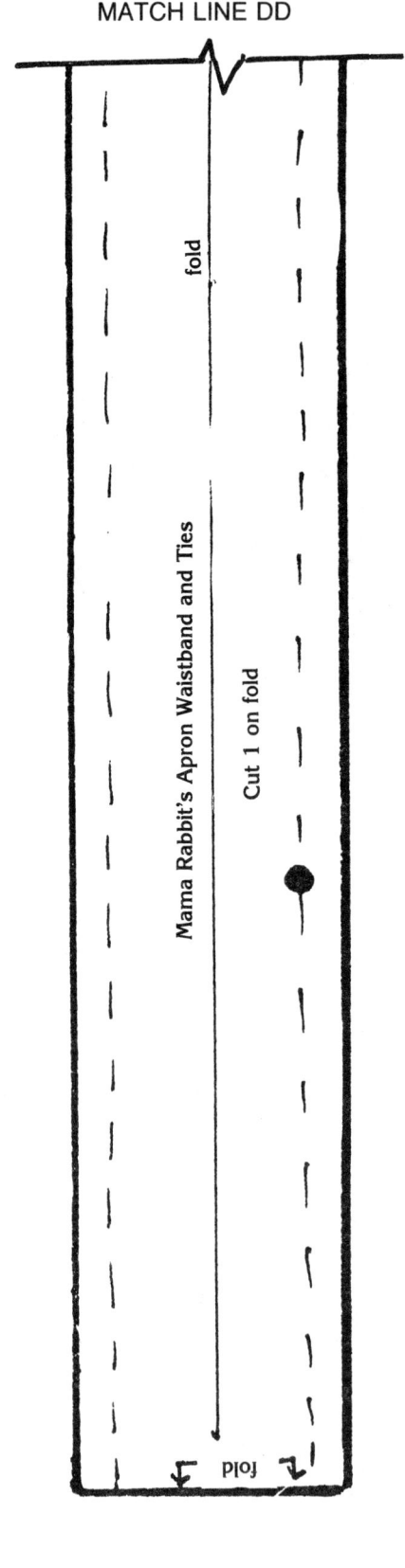

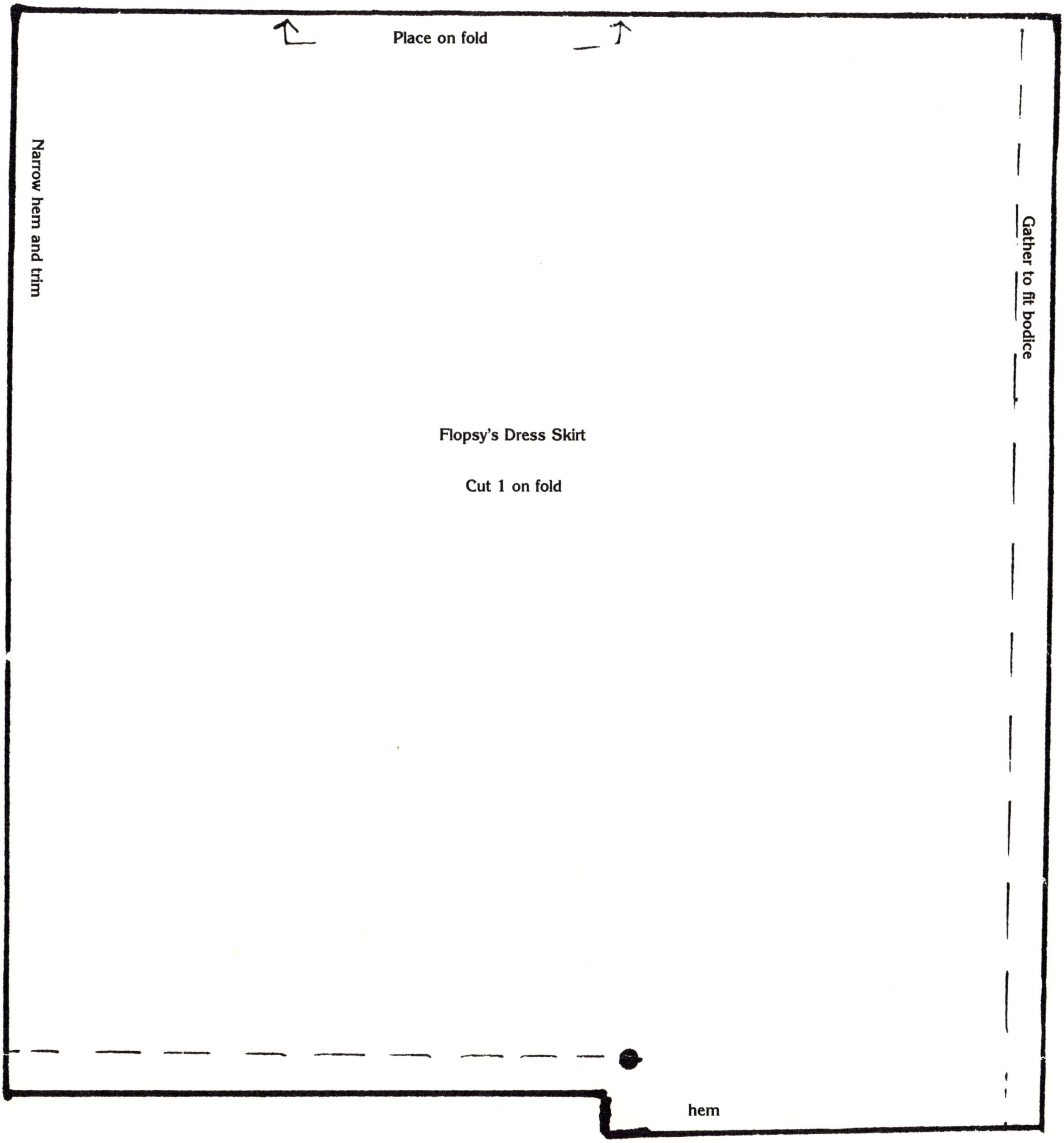

Place on fold

Narrow hem and trim

Gather to fit bodice

Flopsy's Dress Skirt

Cut 1 on fold

hem

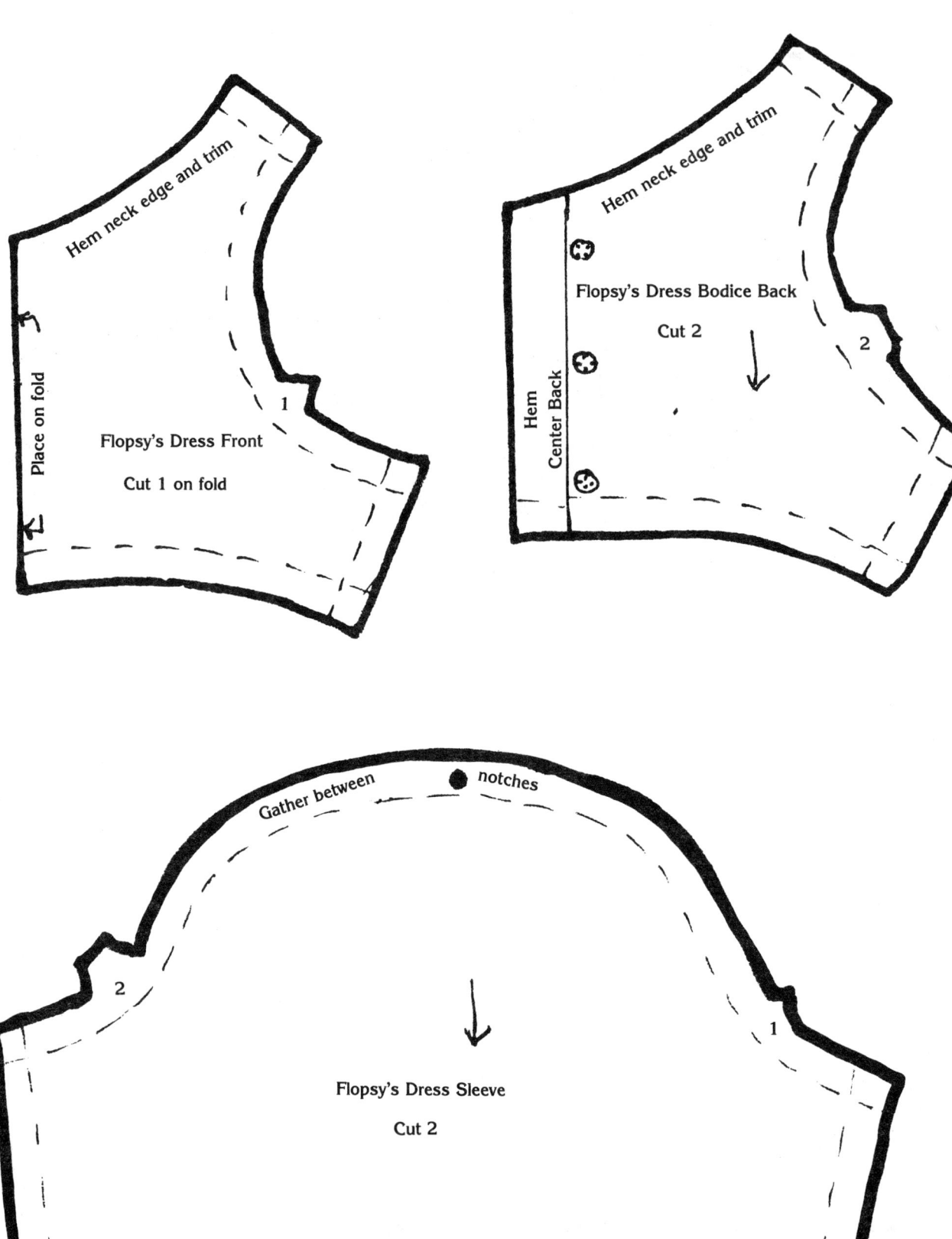

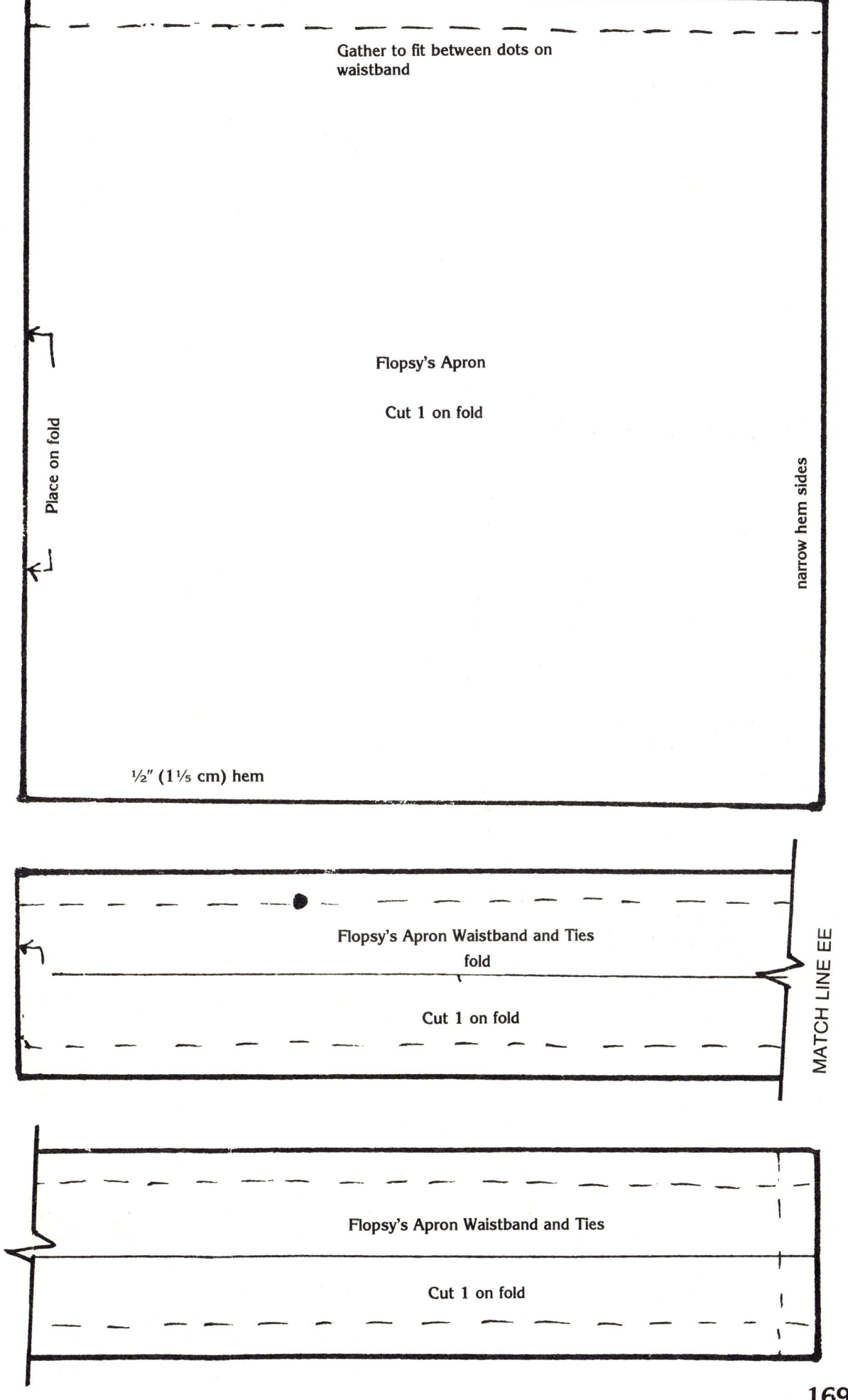

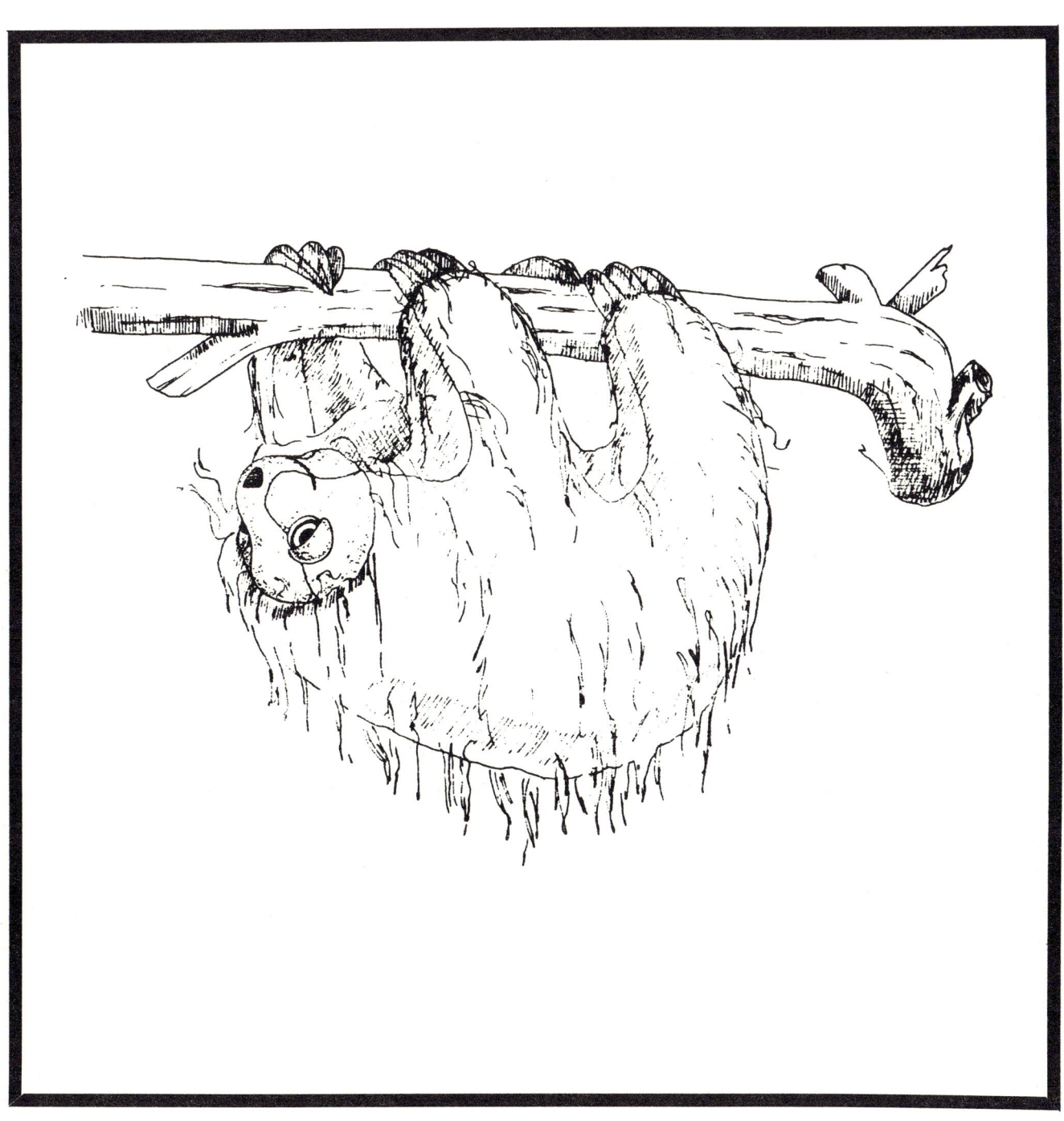

SIX PATTERN PIECES
14" (36 cm) LONG

Cutting Diagram

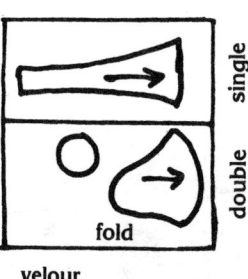

velour

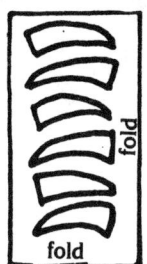

felt or vinyl
4 layers thick

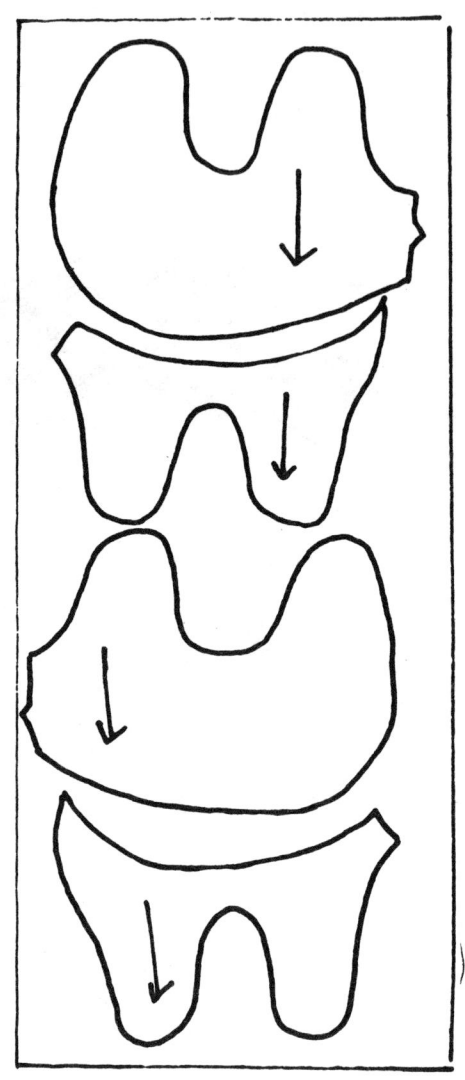

shag fur - single layer

Materials Gray or tan shag fur fabric: ½ yard of 46" material or ⅔ yard of 36" (½ m of 1 m 18 cm width fabric or ⅔ m of 1 m width fabric)
Gray or tan velour: 7" × 7" piece (18 cm × 18 cm)
Black vinyl or felt: 7" × 18" piece (18 cm × 46 cm)
2 buttons for eyes or 1 pair safety eyes: ⅝" or ¾" diameter (1¾ cm or 2 cm)
2 lbs. (1 kg) polyester fiberfill
1 dowel or tree branch about 18" (46 cm) long
Nylon fishline or black or clear heavy carpet cord
Black embroidery thread

11
Sloth

Three-toed sloths are slower than two-toed sloths, I am told. They differ in the number of toes on the front feet; both have three toes on the back feet. Since sloths spend their lives hanging upside down in a tree, the fur lies from toes to back so rain will run off. A light brown or gray shag fur is most suitable, with a smooth fabric like velour for the face. Vinyl claws look most realistic, but felt is easier to sew. The eyelids are optional but make the animal look sleepy.

Cutting Instructions

See the Introduction for working with fur fabrics.
 Of shag fur, cut two side bodies and two underbodies.
 Of velour, cut two side heads, one center head, and two eyelids.
 Of felt or vinyl, cut 24 claws for a three-toed sloth or cut 20 claws for a two-toed sloth.

Sewing Instructions

Use ¼" (⅗ cm) seams throughout unless otherwise stated.
 1. *Claws.* If you are using vinyl for the claws and it sticks under the presser foot, a light rubbing of sewing machine oil on the seamline will prevent this. Wipe oil off after stitching. If you do not want pinholes in the vinyl, the pieces may be held together with masking tape while stitching.
 With right sides together, sew notched edge seam (outer curve). See Figure 1. Trim close to stitching. Fold on seam so wrong sides are together and top stitch inner curve. Trim close to stitching. Stuff lightly. Make twelve claws for three-toed or ten for two-toed.

Fold the claws so the seams meet and baste across the open end. Stitch three claws to each foot of the underbody (only two on each front foot for a two-toed sloth). The inner curve (the top-stitched seam) should be down, the pile side up on the underbody. See Figure 2.

2. *Body.* Stitch darts in the underbodies. Clip center of each dart as shown on the pattern.

Sew darts in the neck edge of the side bodies. Cut along fold of these darts and open flat.

Stitch underbodies to side bodies from neck edge around legs to dot A catching in claws. Match notches 1, 2, and 3. (Stitch slowly across claws to avoid breaking the needle. You may have to hand sew if your machine will not sew over these thicknesses.)

Stitch center back seam from neck edge to dot A. Stitch underbody center seam from neck edge to dot A, leaving open between notches 6 and 7 for stuffing. See Figure 3.

3. *Face.* Clip seam allowance along sides of center head piece, as shown on pattern and Figure 4. Sew center head to side head pieces, spreading clips to Vs so edges match. Match notches 4 and 5. Sew face into neck opening, matching centers. (Seams will not match.)

4. Clip curves and turn right side out. If using safety eyes, cut small xs where indicated on pattern. Insert the shank of the eye from the outside and push the washer onto the shank on the inside. If using buttons, sew on after the animal is stuffed.

Stuff the sloth firmly, using a dowel or chopstick to pack the fiberfill in tightly. Sew up the opening. Sew on button eyes, if you did not use safety eyes. Embroider the nose and mouth as indicated on the pattern and Figure 5. Fold eyelids on the line, right sides together. Stitch 3/16" (2/5 cm) from the edge to the dot. Turn right side out, sew opening shut. Sew over the eyes to make eyelids half-closed.

5. *To mount on a stick or branch.* With clear nylon fishline or heavy carpet cord, sew through the tips of the claws of one foot and pull them close together. Wrap the line around the branch and sew through the foot again. Fasten thread firmly. Repeat with each foot in order, so sloth appears to be walking under the branch. Use clear fishline or cord to make a hanging loop at each end of the branch. See Figure 6.

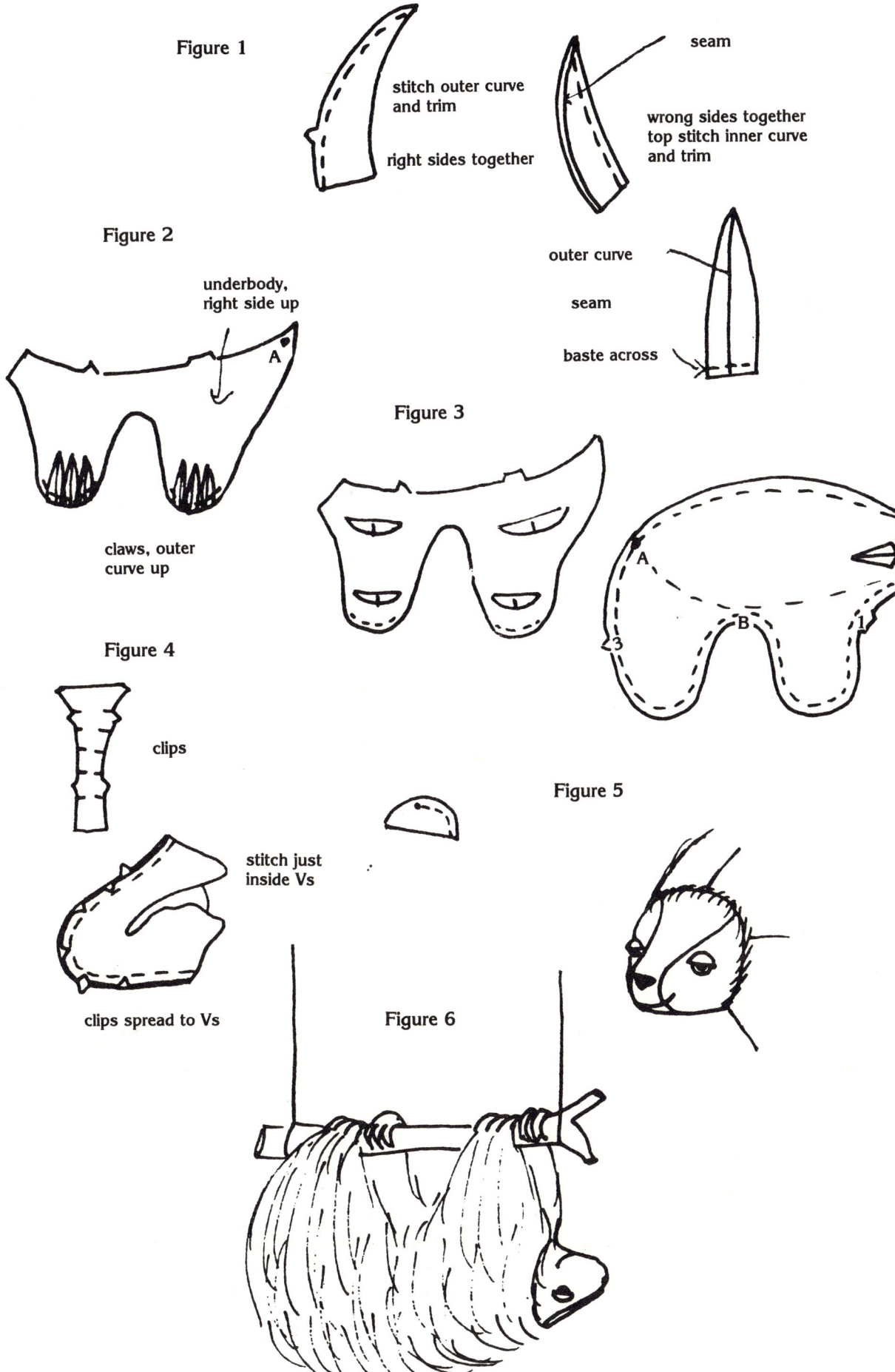

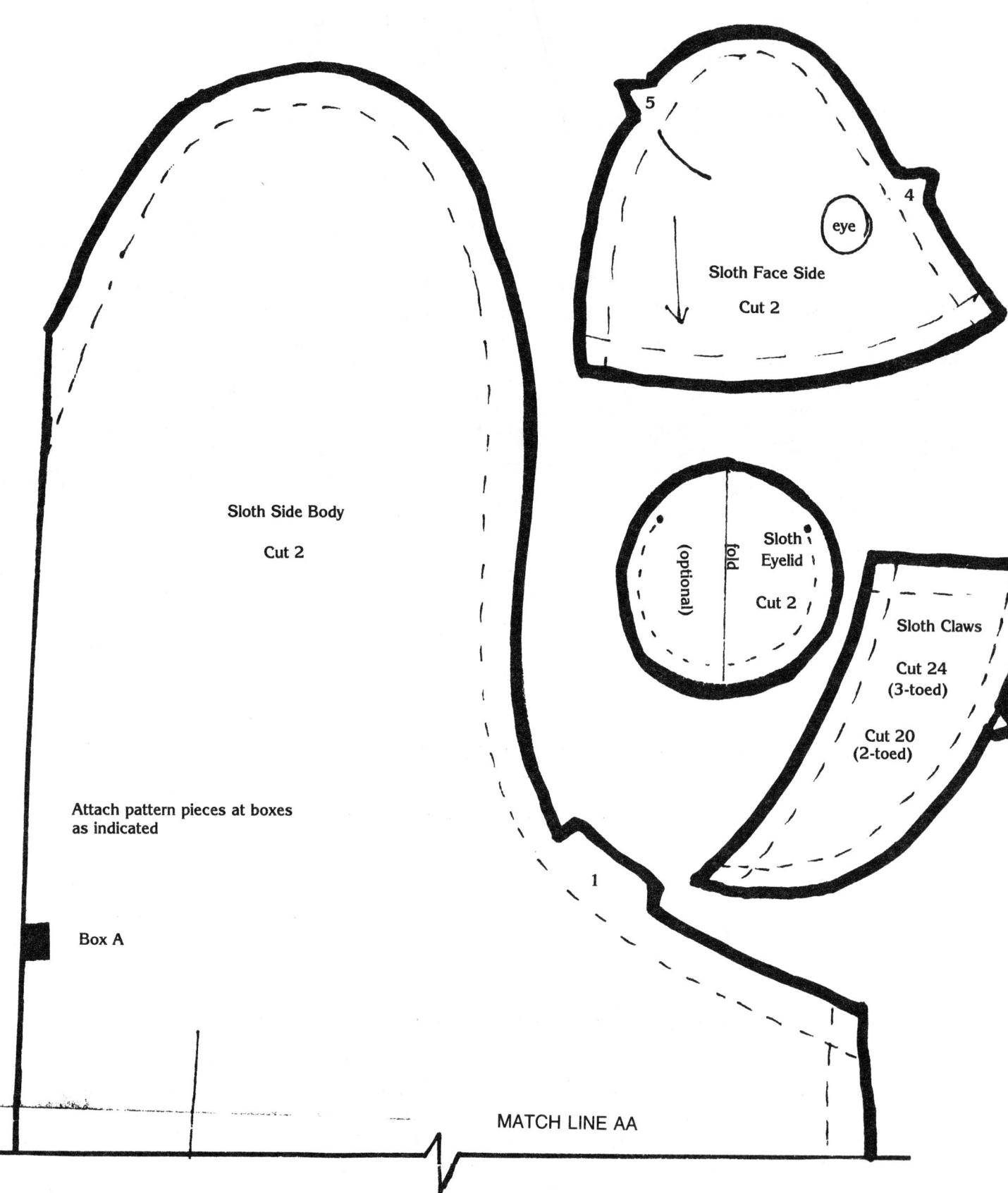

176

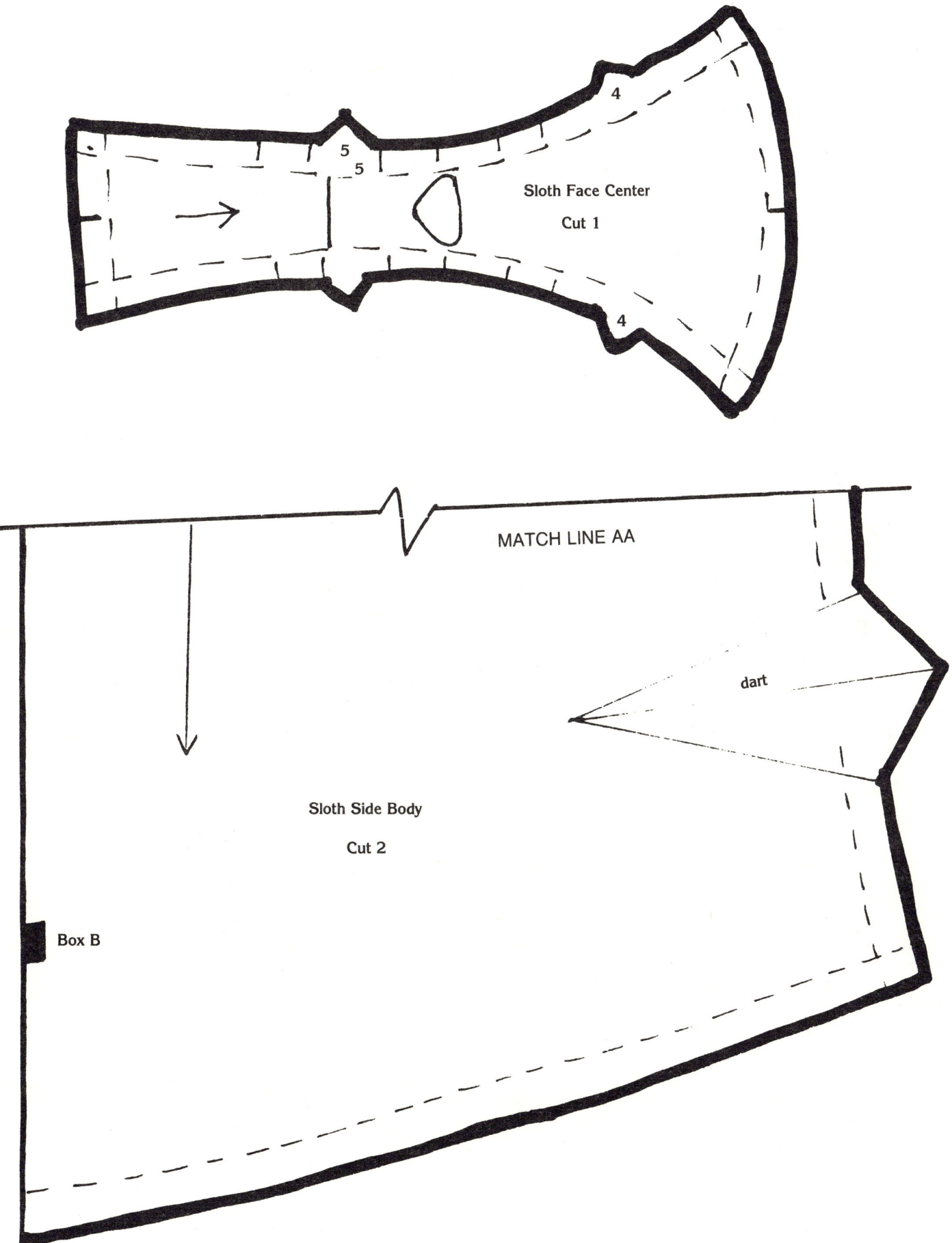

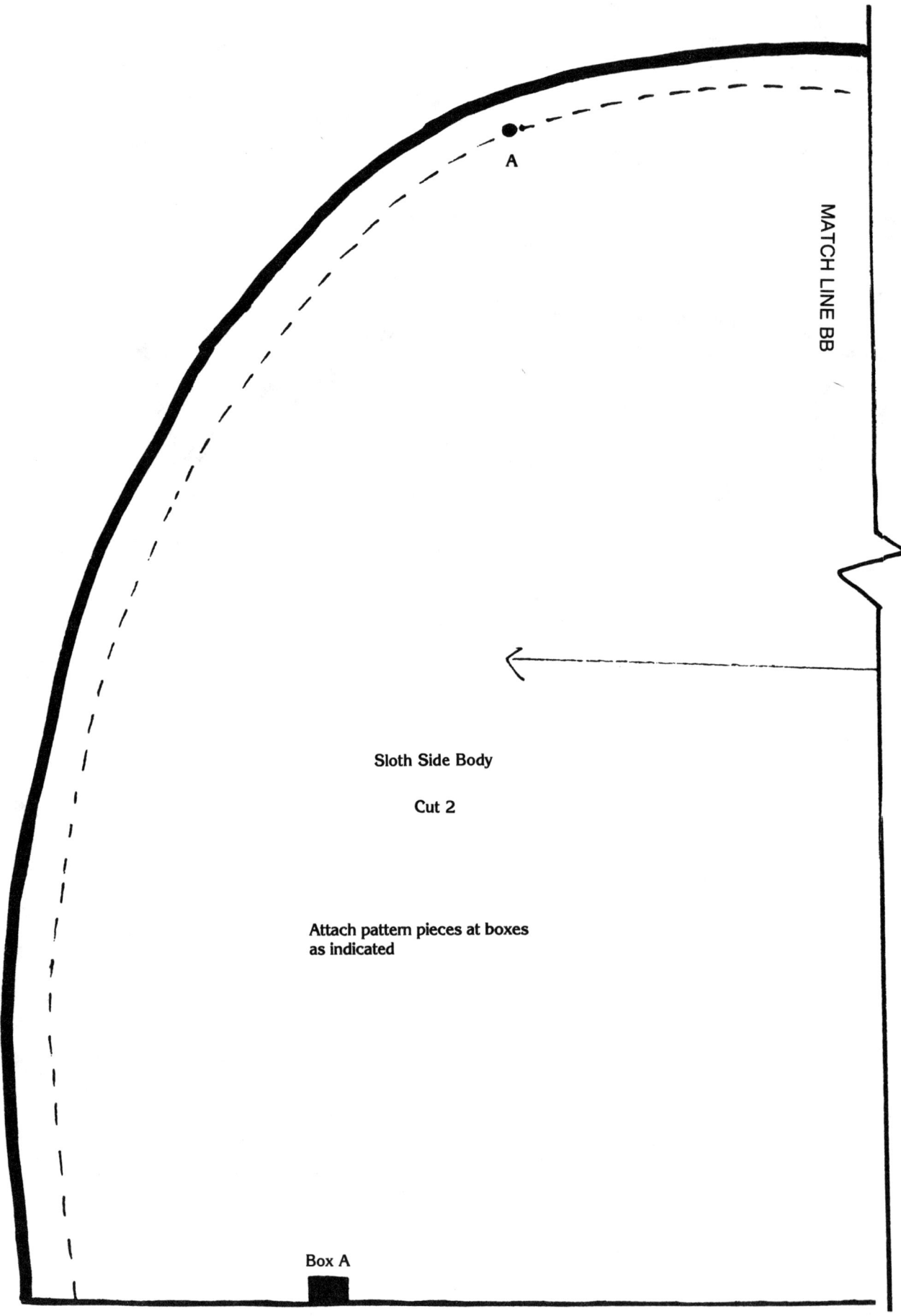

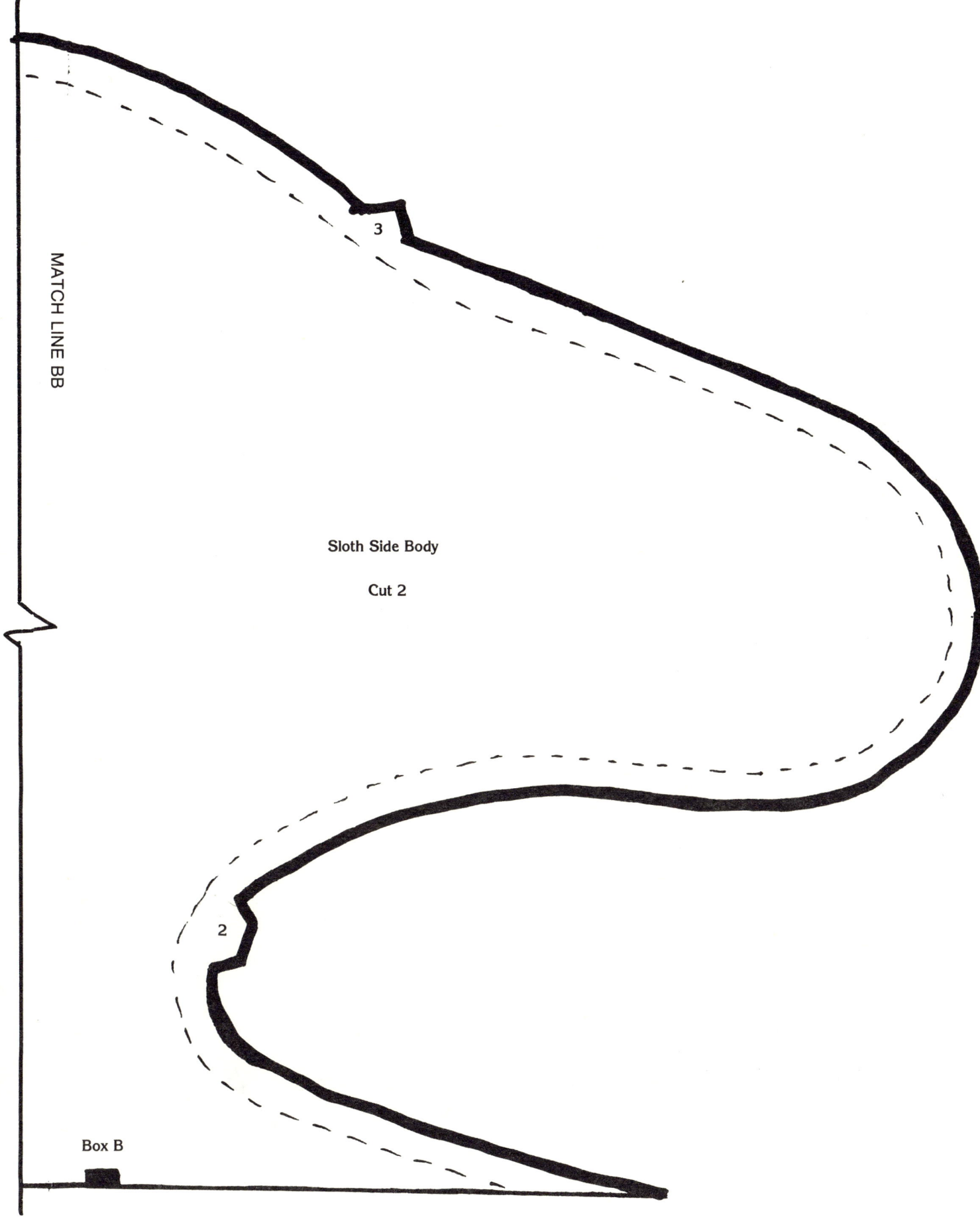

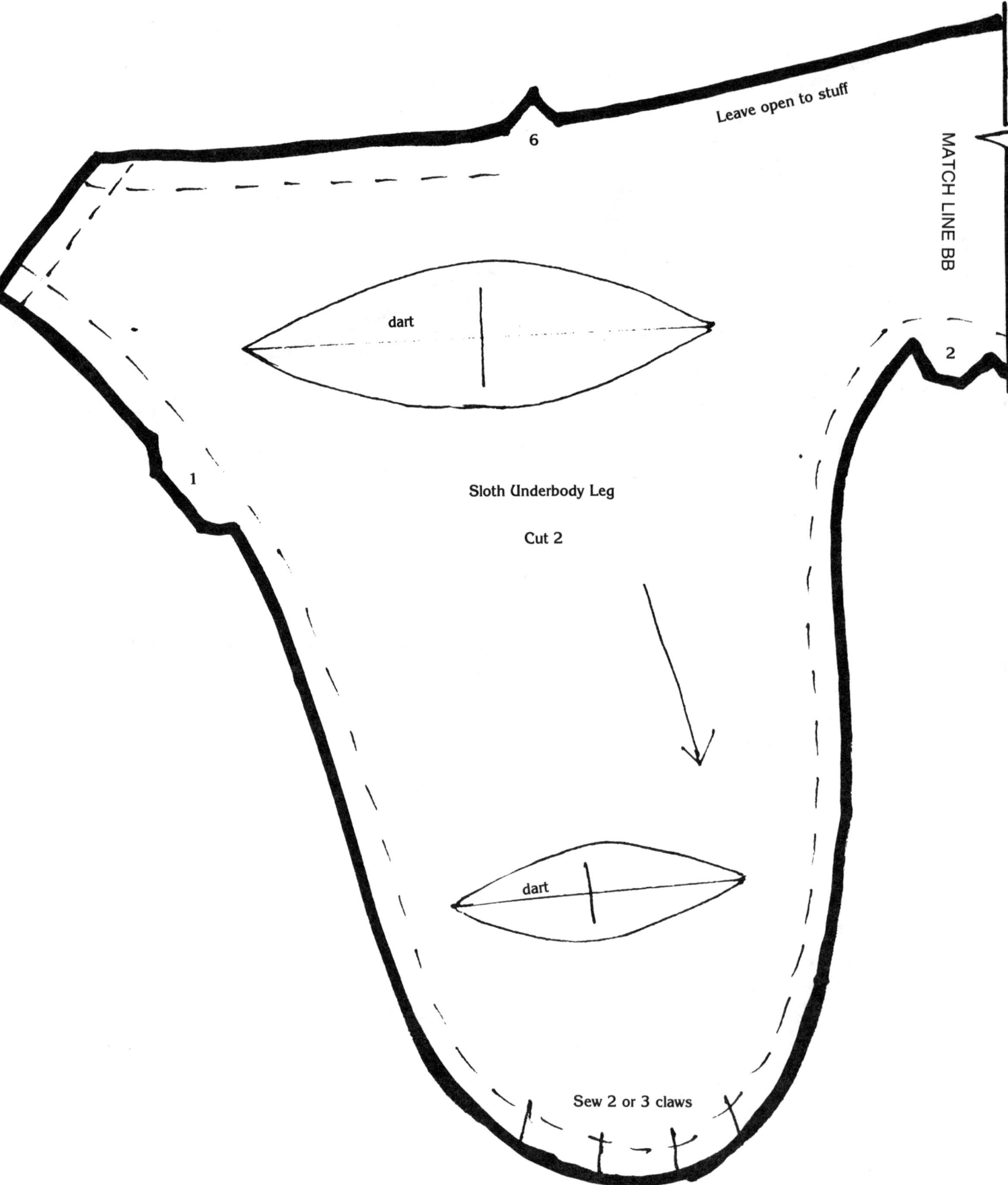

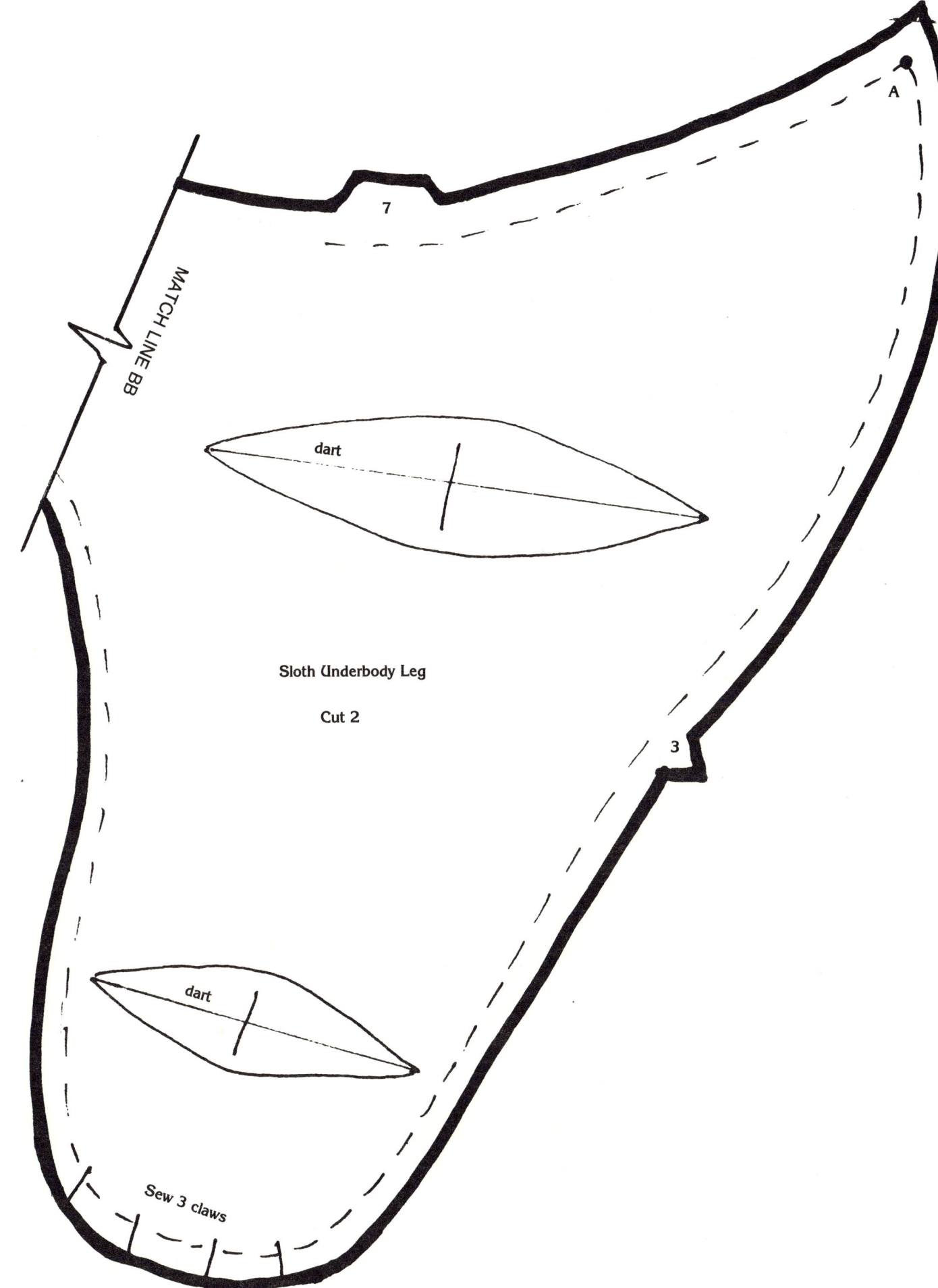

183

TWELVE PATTERN PIECES (SNAKE)
4" DIAMETER (10 cm) LENGTH VARIABLE

EIGHT PATTERN PIECES (MOUSE)
4" DIAMETER (10 cm) 5" LONG (12.5 cm)

Cutting Diagram

Snake

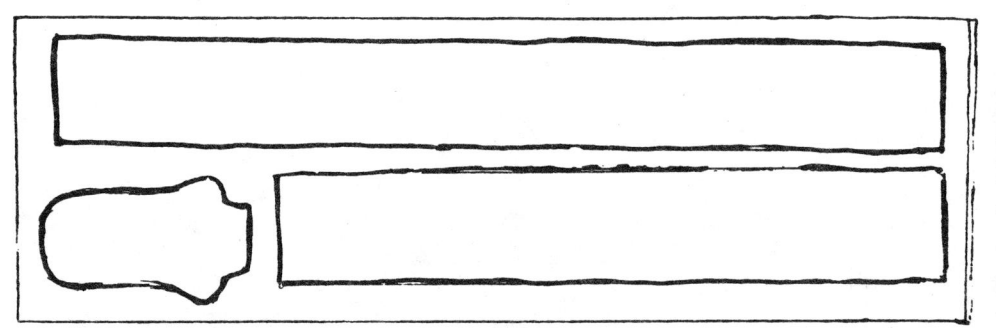

Mouse

single double layer

double single

Materials—Snake Fabric: ⅔ to ¾ yard (⅔ to ¾ m), depending on how long you want your snake to be
1½ to 2 lbs. (675 to 900 g) fiberfill
Scraps of felt in different colors for the features
Trims, as desired

Materials—Mouse Scraps of felt or lightweight fur: 8" × 11" (20 cm × 28 cm)
Scraps of pink felt for ears, paws, and tail
Stuffing

12
Snake

This is a simple pattern that allows as much creativity as you can muster. It is a fun project. It may be made of a plain fabric, left plain, or decorated any way you wish. Choose snakeskin print or use fabrics from your scrapbag to make a striped or patchwork design. Any firm fabric is good, such as corduroy, velour, short-pile fur, double-knit, or heavy satin—in plain, print, or stripe. Avoid heavy fur or shag fabrics, or the snake will look more like a caterpillar. Do not use stretch fabrics because they will expand as you stuff to make a very chubby snake.

First we have directions for a plain snake; then come suggestions for some fancy ones.

Cutting Instructions—Snake

Cut one strip for the body, 9" (23 cm) wide and as long as you like. It should be at least 6' (2 m). Most likely, you will have to piece the strip. If you are using a patterned fabric, be sure to match it at the seams. Use tail pattern to taper the end of the body strip.

Cut two head pieces (one upper and one lower).

Cut one tongue of red or pink felt and two fangs of white felt (optional).

Cut two nostrils, and two of each of the three eye pieces, also of felt. Each eye piece should be a different color, coordinating with your body fabric. See Figure 1.

Sewing Instructions—Snake

Use ¼" (⅗ cm) seam allowance.

Using matching thread, appliqué the eye pieces and nostrils to upper head where indicated on pattern. Stitch tongue and fangs between marks, inside seam allowance. See Figure 2.

Stitch upper head to lower head, right sides together, from neck around to dot A. See Figure 3. Open neck so sewn seam is centered across the straight 9" (23 cm) end of the body and stitch body to head, right sides together. (Body has only one side seam.) Sew side seam from dot A to and around tail, matching any seams where the body was pieced. Leave at least two openings for stuffing. Clip curves at the back of the head and turn the snake right side out. Stuff firmly, using a dowel to push the fiberfill to ends. Sew up openings.

Suggestions for fancy snakes

1. Make your snake of a floral, polka-dot, print, or stripe material. It does not have to look natural; it can be whimsical. Or use velvets or brocades, as long as the fabric is strong. A fabric that is thin, stretchy, or ravels easily may be lined.

2. Use a diamond-patterned or embossed fabric. Sew sequins or beads on all or some of the points of the diamonds.

3. Use several compatible colors of the same type of fabric (maybe from your scrapbag) to make stripes all down the body. Cut each stripe 9" (23 cm) long. Stripes can be even or uneven in width, symmetrical or unsymmetrical in spacing, or random. See Figure 4 for possible arrangements. Be sure to match the seams of the stripes carefully as you sew up the side seam.

4. Trim with lace or braid. A wide, solid lace or braid can be used as a stripe, while narrow trim or rickrack is better appliquéd to a stripe.

5. Use quilt pattern to make a patchwork design all down the body strip.

6. Appliqué diamonds along the body. It is easier to do this by machine before sewing the stripes or body pieces together. Several diamond patterns are given. These may be used inside each other or separately. Remember that the body has only one side seam, so the diamonds must be placed so they will be centered on the back and/or belly of the finished snake. See Figure 5.

7. Put a rattle on the end of the tail. This could be a jingle bell or a group of beads of decreasing size. Do not do this if there is a baby of button-swallowing age around.

8. Use Seminole Indian patchwork for some of the stripes. Sew strips together lengthwise. Cut into strips crosswise, of even widths. Sew these pieces together again, offsetting each strip the same amount to form a pattern. Cut off the pointed edges, allowing ¼" (⅗ cm) seam allowance. Sew into body as a stripe. Rickrack trim goes well with this. See Figure 6.

9. You may want to make the upper part of the snake of one fabric and the lower part of another plain or lighter color. In this case, cut an upper head and a lower head of the different fabrics. For the body, cut upper and lower strips 4¾" (12 cm) wide. The body will have two side seams.

10. If you are really ambitious, cut scales (hundreds of them) of felt or other nonraveling fabric and hand sew in overlapping patterns to the back of the stuffed snake. This will occupy many evenings before the TV.

11. Use one section toward the middle of the body, 12" to 18" (30 cm

to 46 cm) long, of stretch fabric. Stuff heavily in this place to make a bulge around the snake's "dinner." If the fabric stretches in one direction only, be sure the stretch is around the snake, not along the length. If the stretch material is different from the rest of the material, so it looks odd, you may want to cut several other stripes of the stretch material and insert them along the body, so the pattern looks planned. Each of these other stretch stripes must be lined with nonstretch fabric, however, to keep them from bulging when stuffed.

12. For a more elaborate version of the stomach bulge, use two layers of material, one stretch and one a firm nonstretch. Stuff between the layers to make a big bulge. Put a zipper in the side seam along this section. Inside the zippered stomach, place a mouse. To make a zippered stomach, first find a zipper to match the stretch fabric you are using. Cut both the stretch and lining pieces 9" (23 cm) wide and the length of the zipper tape. Lay the lining fabric right side up on the table, lay the closed zipper (the zipper stays closed throughout construction) right side up along the side edge, and lay the stretch fabric right side down on top, as illustrated in Figure 7. Pin or baste. Stitch halfway between the teeth and the edge of the tape, beginning and ending ⅝" (1.5 cm) from ends (stitch beside metal part of zipper only, not to ends of tape) enclosing zipper.

Fold back both layers on either side to expose zipper. See Figure 8. Fold stretch fabric up to edge of zipper tape along unsewn side of front zipper, and lining fabric up to same edge of the back of the zipper, as illustrated in Figure 9. Pin or baste and stitch the length of the metal part of the zipper, as before, enclosing zipper. Turn tube right side out, so lining is inside. See Figure 10. Fold back edges of stretch fabric and stitch across the ends of the lining, close to ends of zipper. See Figure 11. Set aside.

Sew up head and front of body according to general directions, including the side seam. Leave an opening for stuffing close to the end that will attach to the stomach. Slip the stomach section (which is right side out) inside the front body section (which is inside out), aligning zipper seam with side seam. Being careful not to catch in lining, stitch around the circular opening. Pull whole front of snake through stuffing opening so it is right side out.

Sew up tail section of body, including side seam. Leave a stuffing opening in side seam, close to end that attaches to stomach. Slip stomach (which is right side out) inside tail tube (which is inside out). Align side seam and zipper seam, and sew around circular seam. Turn snake right side out and stuff. The fiberfill will go between the lining and the stretch material in the stomach section. Sew up the openings. Unzip the stomach and insert the mouse.

13. Make the stomach compartment big enough to be a pajama bag.

Cutting Instructions— Mouse

Cut two side bodies, one bottom, four arms, and four legs of body fabric. Cut one tail, two ears, four paws, and two eyes of pink felt.

Sewing Instructions— Mouse

Baste tail to one side of mouse body between dots. Sew side bodies, right sides together, leaving unnotched edge open and leaving open between notches 2 and 3 for stuffing. Clip along bottom edge of side bodies as shown on pattern and Figure 11. Matching centers, pin bottom to side bodies, spreading clip to Vs so edges align. With bottom down, stitch around just inside the clips. See Figure 12. Clip curves, turn right side out, stuff, and sew up.

Baste paws to one side of arms between lines. Stitch arms, right sides together, enclosing paws, and leaving open between dots. See Figure 13. Turn right side out, stuff, and sew up. Sew legs the same as arms. Hand sew arms and legs to body. Fold ears and hand sew to sides of head. Sew eyes where indicated on pattern. Make whiskers with clumps of thread on each side of nose.

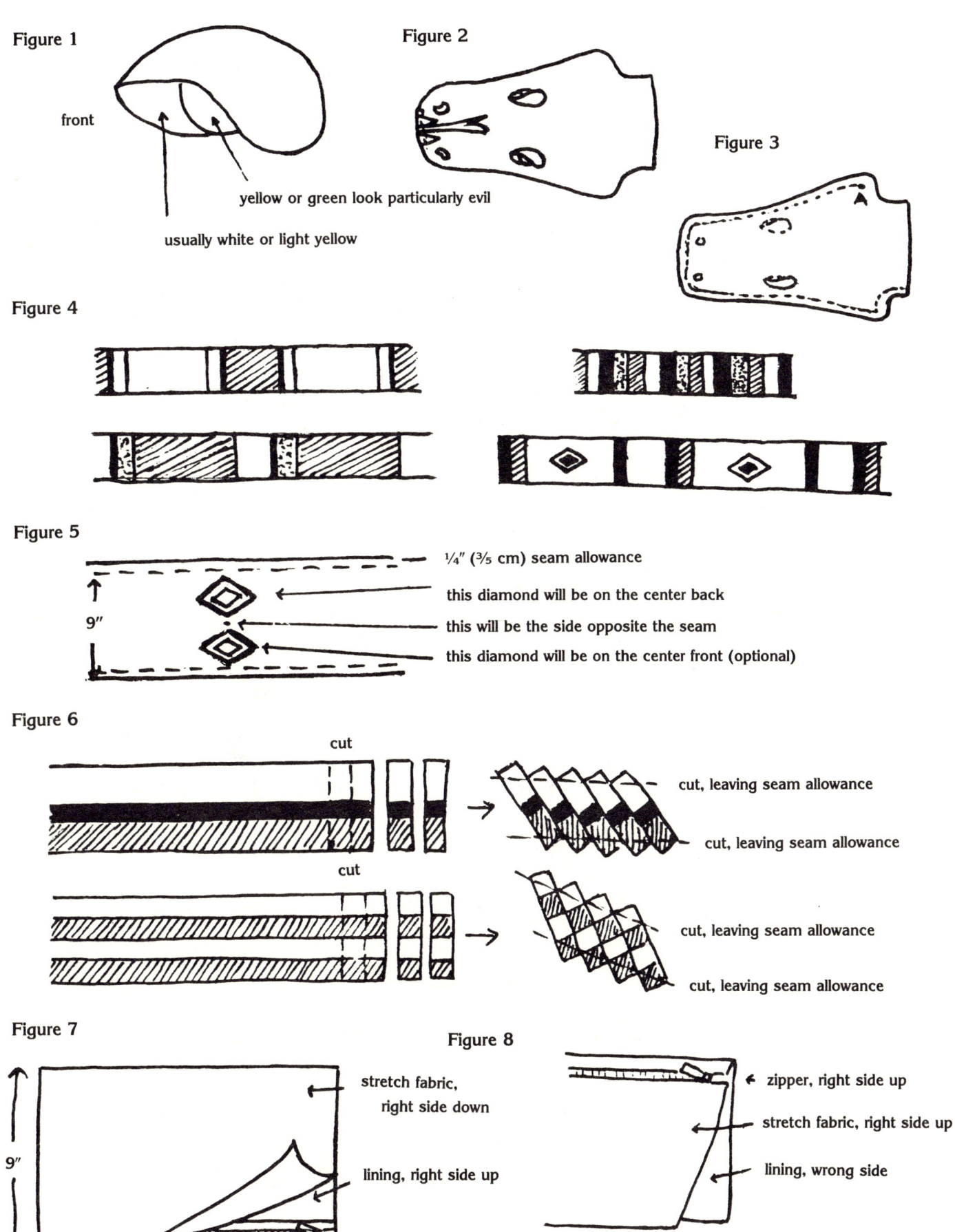

Figure 9

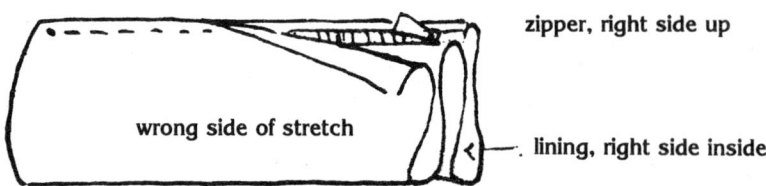

Figure 10

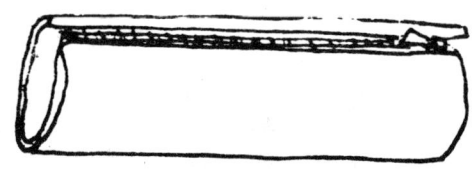

Figure 11

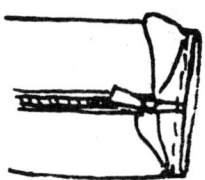

Figure 13

Figure 12

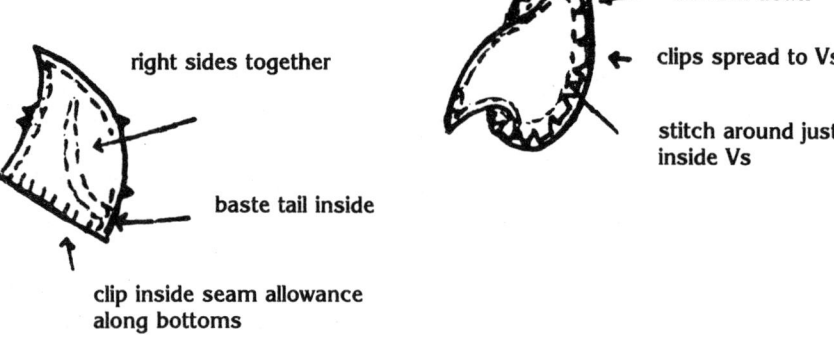

Figure 14

Figure 15

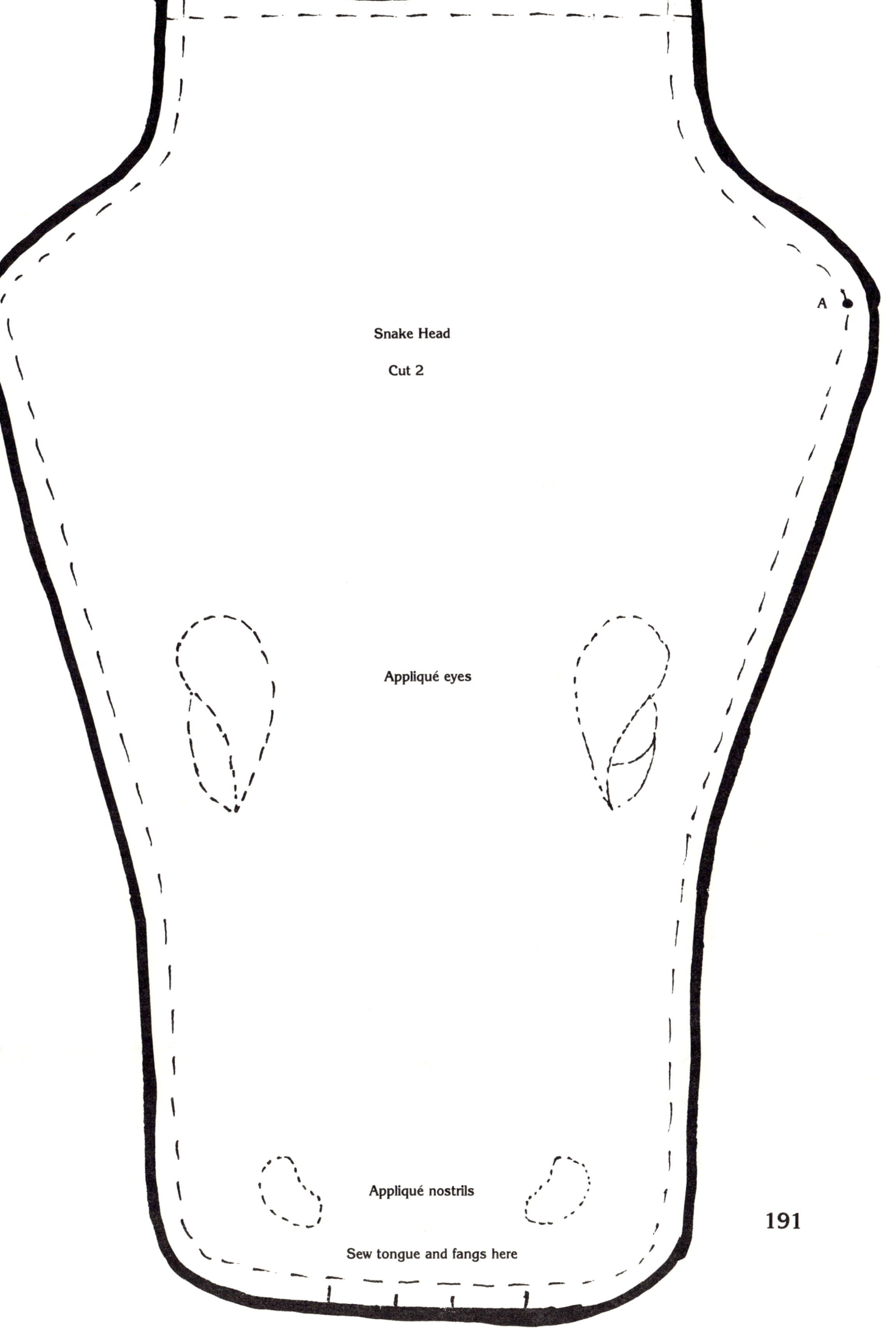

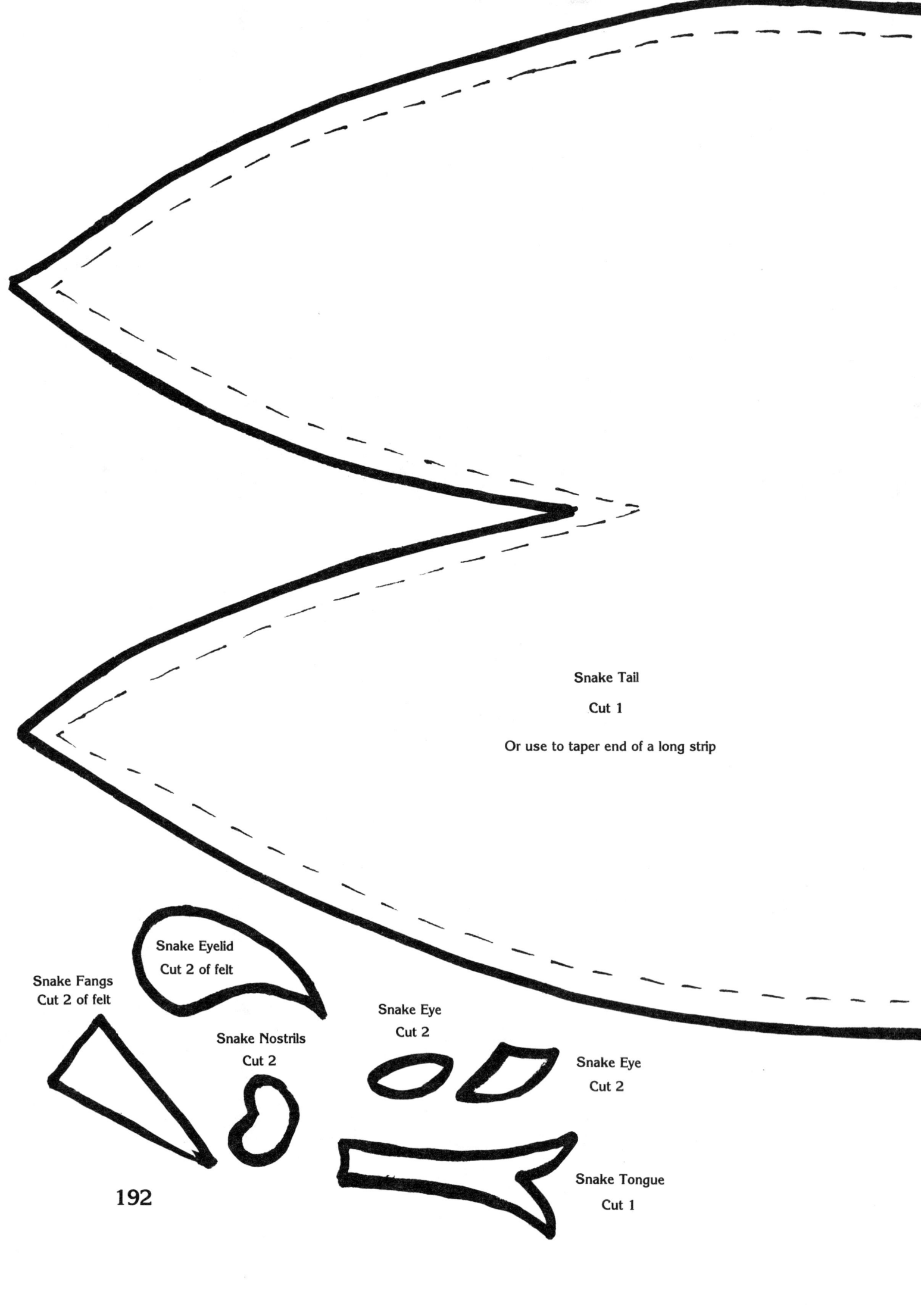

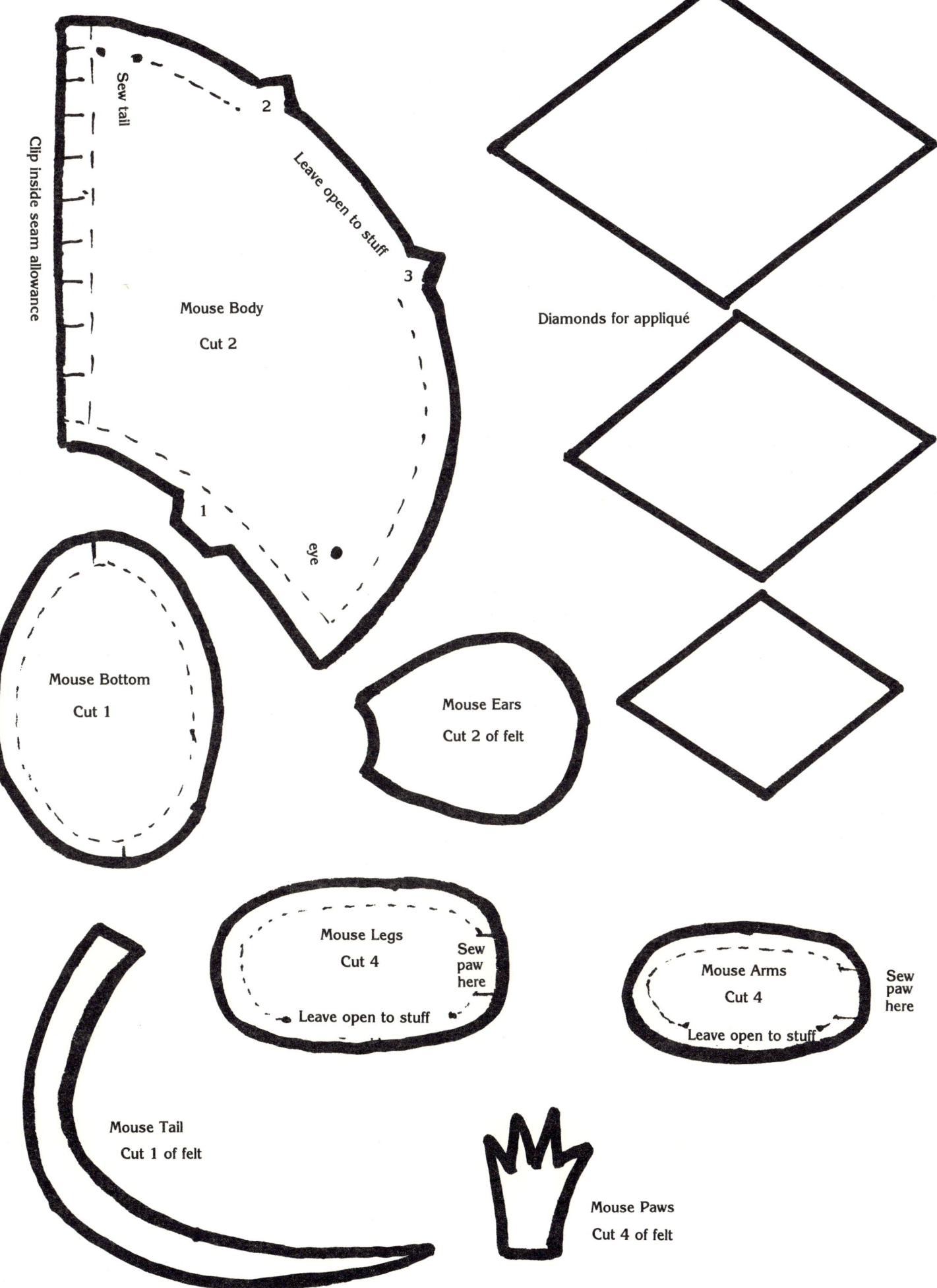

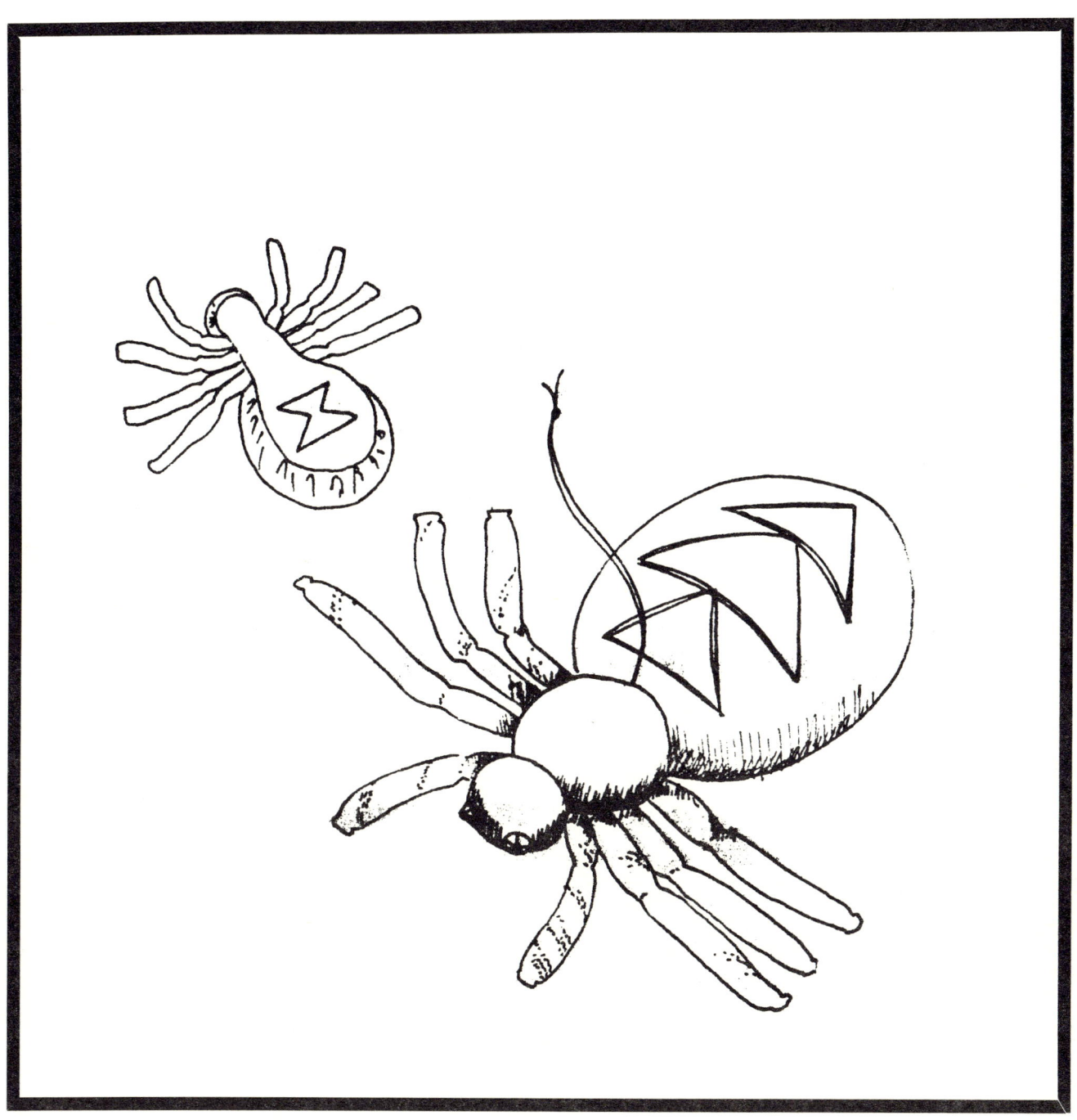

FOUR PATTERN PIECES
4" (10 cm) LONG

Cutting Diagram

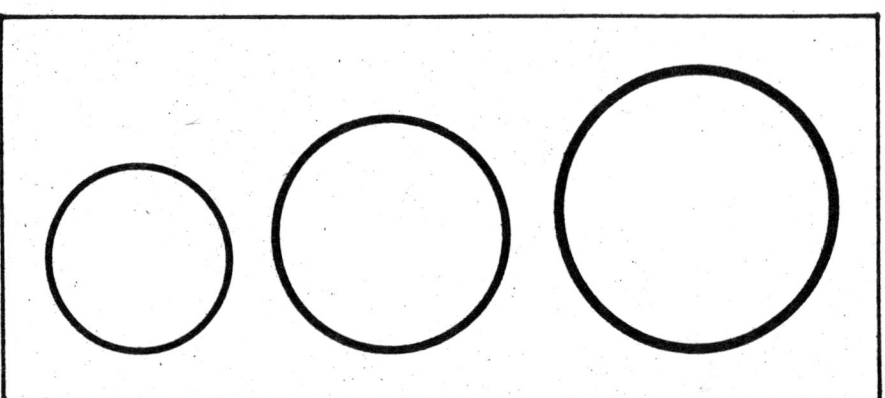

main fabric

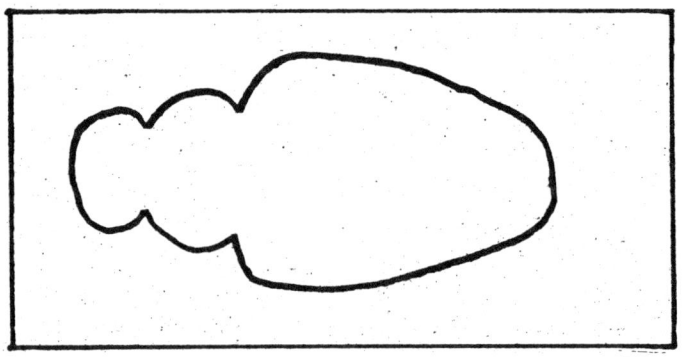

felt

Materials Velvet, velveteen, velour, or lightweight fur, calico, or fabric of your choice: 6" × 8" piece (15 cm × 20 cm)
Felt: 2" × 4½" piece (5 cm × 11 cm)
Velvet or satin tubing: 2' (61 cm)
2 ozs. (56 g) polyester fiberfill (for stuffing)
Buttonhole twist or carpet thread to match fabric
Red felt or red embroidery thread for hourglass (optional)
2 beads, preferably faceted, for eyes

13
Spider

Children have a wonderful time with this spider. It can be hung, dangled from a finger, or left to crawl on something. Mounted on a stick, it's a cute potted plant decoration. Hang it from a car mirror, give them out as Halloween favors, or use it as a pincushion. They can be made from scraps of any kind of fabric, any color or pattern or fuzziness you choose, and decorated with embroidery, beads, sequins, lace, and so on.

Cutting Instructions Cut one head, one thorax, and one abdomen of main fabric, and one underbody of matching or contrasting felt. Cut eight legs of tubing, each 3" (8 cm) long.

Sewing Instructions All sewing is done by hand. With buttonhole twist or other heavy-duty matching thread, make short running stitches around the circumference of the abdomen circle, close to the edge. Draw up around a wad of stuffing to shape so it's slightly pointed at one end. Pull the opening closed and fasten the thread securely. See Figure 1.

Repeat for the head and thorax circles, forming round shapes. Sew the thorax to the rounded end of the abdomen, and then the head to the thorax. See Figure 2.

For each leg, sew one end of a piece of tubing closed, then insert the needle in that end, and bring the thread through the inside of the tubing and out at the midpoint of the leg. Wrap the thread around the tubing tightly, and tack to form a joint in the middle of the leg. Bring the thread up inside the leg to the top, and sew to the underside of the thorax. Repeat for the other seven legs, sewing four on each side of the thorax.

Alternatively, legs can be knotted on the ends or at the joints. Legs can also be made of braided or twisted yarn or thread.

On the underside of the spider, slip stitch the felt underbody to cover the openings and ends of the legs. Sew a bead on each side of the head for eyes. See Figure 3.

To decorate your spider, you may either embroider the diamond pattern on the back with buttonhole twist, or make a red hourglass on the underside of the abdomen with felt or embroidery thread. See Figure 4.

If you want to hang your spider, make a thread loop with buttonhole twist, fastening about at the point of the largest triangle on the back, or wherever it balances well.

Figure 1

Figure 2

Figure 3

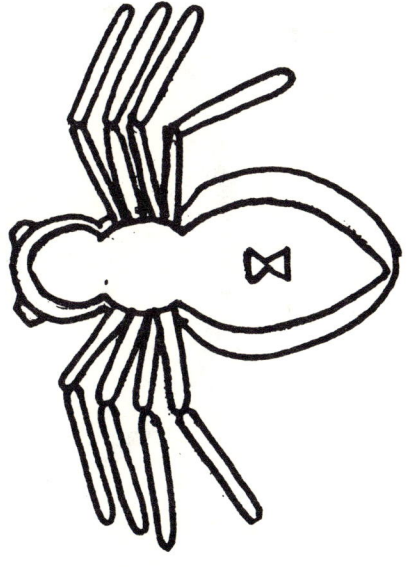

Figure 4

199

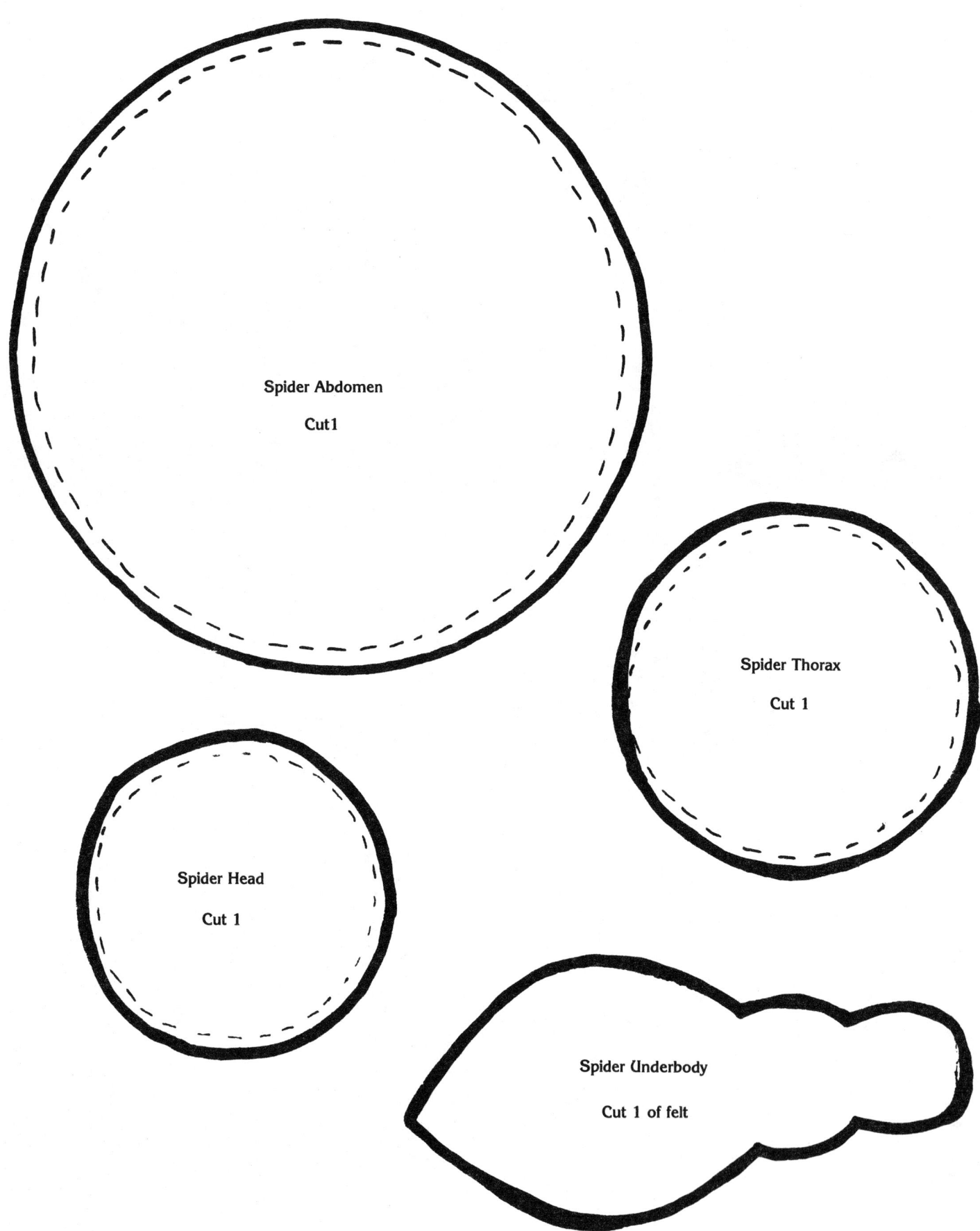

200

SEVEN PATTERN PIECES
13 inches (32.5 cm)
exclusive of the horn

Cutting Diagram

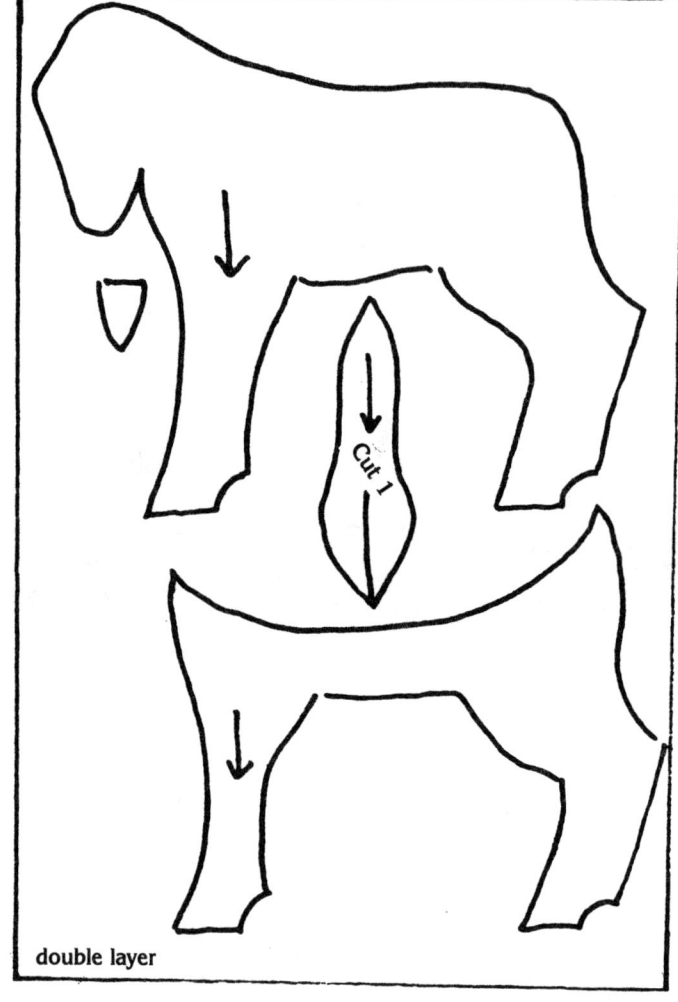

fabric with nap

double layer

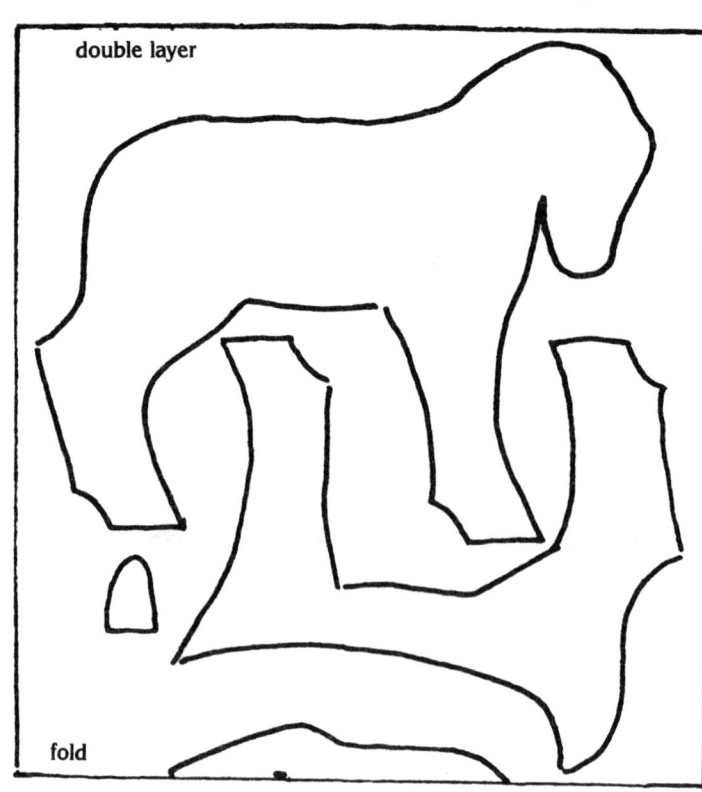

double layer

fabric without nap

fold

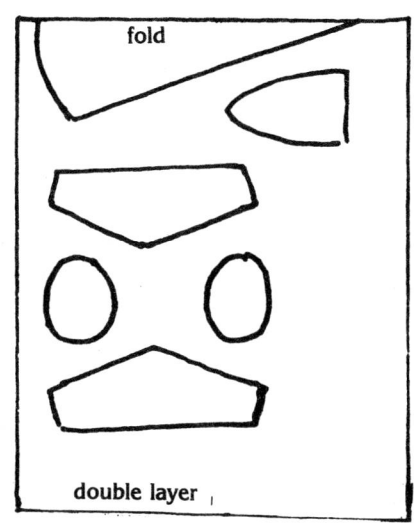

Materials ½ yard of 45" fabric, ⅔ yard of 36" fabric (½ m of 1 m 15 cm width fabric; ⅔ m of 1 m width fabric) (extra required if fabric has a nap)
½ yard (½ m) of muslin, if outer fabric requires strengthening
Contrasting fabric for horn and hooves: 4" × 20" piece (10 cm × 51 cm)
Yarn for mane, tail, beard: 1¼ ozs. or 10" of upholstery fringe at least 3" wide (35 g or 25 cm 8 cm wide)
1¼ lbs. (60 g) polyester fiberfill for stuffing
¼" (⅗ cm) dowel: 4 pieces 8½" (22 cm) long each (if you want a standing unicorn/horse)
Embroidery thread for eye, color of choice
Gold or silver thread if you choose one of these for horn and hooves

14
Unicorn/Horse

This unicorn will stand up on a table or shelf. It may also be hung, if you desire, or it may sit or lie if you soft stuff the legs. It may be made in any color, although white is traditional. Any smooth or slightly napped fabric may be used, but satin is particularly effective. Satin ravels easily, however, so it must be lined with muslin for strength. The mane may be made of yarn or brushed macrame cord or upholstery fringe, at least 3" (8 cm) wide. The horn and hooves are nice in gold or silver, but ivory or black is effective, too. Traditionally unicorns have a small beard like a goat.

Cutting Instructions

Of main fabric, cut two body sizes, two underbodies, one center head, and two ears. Of contrasting fabric, cut four hooves, four soles, one horn, and two ear linings.

If you use napped fabric, be sure all body pieces are laid with nap going in the same direction. If you use satin, cut linings of muslin: two side bodies, two underbodies, and one head center. Place linings on wrong side of satin pieces and treat as one.

Sewing Instructions

Use ¼" (⅗ cm) seams throughout unless otherwise stated.

1. *Hooves.* Make darts in underbodies. Clip across the center of each dart, as shown on pattern. Stitch underbody to side body along front of legs, from dot to bottom of foot. See Figure 1.

To apply hooves, open front leg seam flat, right side up. Lay hoof, right side down and facing toward the top of the leg, across the foot as shown in Figure 2. Stitch on the seam line. Fold the hoof down and machine baste across bottom of foot. Repeat with the other three feet.

2. *Soles.* Sew remaining underbody seams from dot A to dot B, leaving the bottoms of the feet open, matching notches 1, 2, and 3. See Figure 3. Sew soles in feet. Clip bottoms of feet, inside seam allowance, as shown on pattern and Figure 4. Matching center, right sides together, pin feet to soles, spreading clips into Vs so edges match. See Figure 5. With sole down, stitch around foot just inside clips. Repeat for other three feet.

3. *Ears and nostrils.* Sew ear linings to ears, right sides together, leaving bottom open. Trim tip and turn right side out. Fold on center line. Stitch ears to head between dots. Pleat nostrils on the right side of fabric and baste. See Figure 6.

4. *Head center.* Slit head center on line to square. Sew head center to side heads from dot C to dot D, matching dots to nostrils and tapering the seam at C to nothing. See Figure 7.

Sew center front seam on side bodies from dot D to dot A.

5. *Mane and tail.* If using upholstery fringe, sew 8" (20 cm) from square in head center to square at base of neck. Roll up 2" (5 cm) to make tail and sew to one side body.

To make yarn mane and tail, wrap yarn around a stiff piece of cardboard, 6" (15 cm) wide, 8" (20 cm) for the mane. See Figure 8. Cut along one 8" (20 cm) edge. Lay strands on a piece of tissue paper and cover with another sheet. Machine stitch down center. Tear away the tissue. Fold the mane on the stitching line and stitch folded edge to one side of the head/body between the square in the head center and the square at the base of the neck. For tail, wind 20 to 30 strands of yarn around the cardboard. Cut along one edge. Sew by one end to side body.

6. *Body.* Stitch center back seam from dot B along back and head, enclosing mane and tail and tapering to a point just below the square in the head center.

Sew center underbody seam from dot A to dot B, leaving open between notches 4 and 5 for stuffing. Overcast the edges of the opening between the notches if using satin to prevent raveling while stuffing.

7. Clip curves and turn right side out. Stuff the head and neck firmly, using a dowel or chopstick to push fiberfill compactly. For standing unicorn, stuff the bottom of the feet enough to pad. Insert an 8½" (22 cm) dowel in the center of the leg and stuff around it firmly. Be sure the dowel is well padded all around and doesn't rub or stick out against the outside fabric. Stuff all four legs, then the body. Sew up opening, using the ladder stitch.

If you are going to hang it or have it lie down, omit the dowels. Stuff legs lightly and bend at the joints if you want it to lie. You may want to tack the legs in place.

8. *Horn.* Fold horn, right sides together. Sew seam. Trim tip and turn right side out. Stuff, using very small pieces of fiberfill in the tip. Stuff firmly all the way down. Hand sew to the forehead, seam toward nose, covering the center head dart. See Figure 9. With thread that matches the horn, fasten at the base and wind the thread tightly around the horn in a spiral. Take a tiny stitch as you cross the seam each time to hold the spiral in place. Fasten the thread securely at the tip of the horn.

9. *Finishing.* Tack the ears to stand upright, if you wish. Pick up one strand of the tail and wind it around the rest at the base to make the

tail stand up. See Figure 10. Embroider eyes where indicated on the pattern, using satin stitch. Sew a few strands of yarn under the chin for a beard, if you want.

Horse The horse, too, may stand with dowels in the legs, may be hung, or may lie down. Any firm fabric may be used. There are nice pony furs available, some printed a piebald or pinto. The hooves are usually black, maybe in vinyl or felt.

Follow the directions for making the unicorn, omitting the horn and beard.

Figure 1

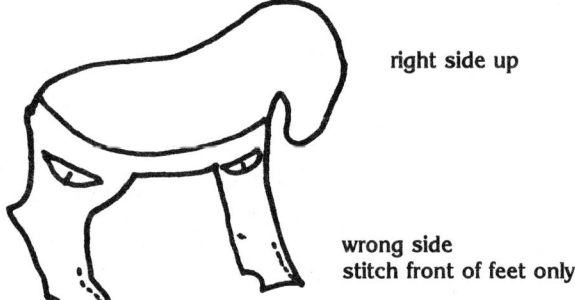

right side up

wrong side
stitch front of feet only

Figure 4

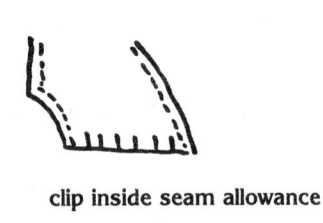

clip inside seam allowance

Figure 2

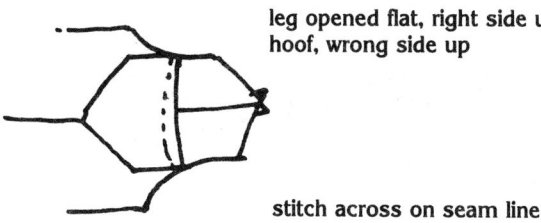

leg opened flat, right side up
hoof, wrong side up

stitch across on seam line

leg, right side up
hoof folded down

basted to bottom of foot

Figure 5

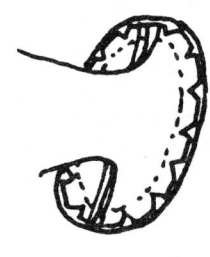

sole down
spread clips to Vs
stitch just inside Vs

Figure 6

right side up

Figure 3

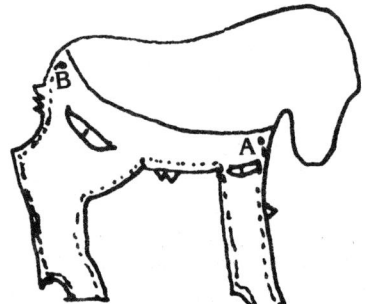

leave bottom of feet open

Figure 7

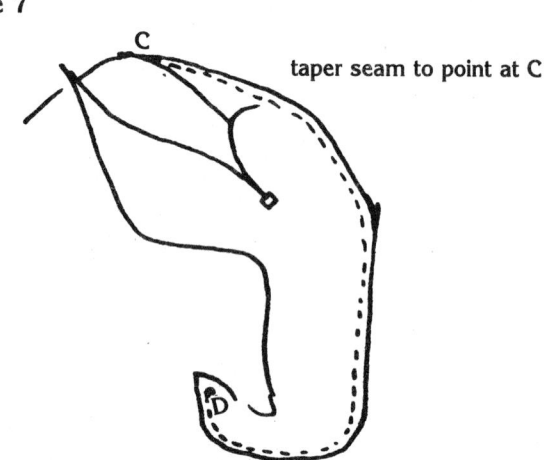

taper seam to point at C

Figure 8

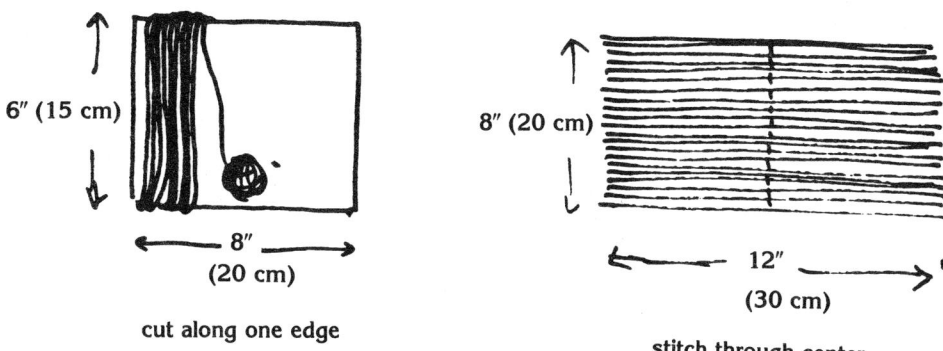

6" (15 cm)

8" (20 cm)

cut along one edge

8" (20 cm)

12" (30 cm)

stitch through center

Figure 9

Figure 10

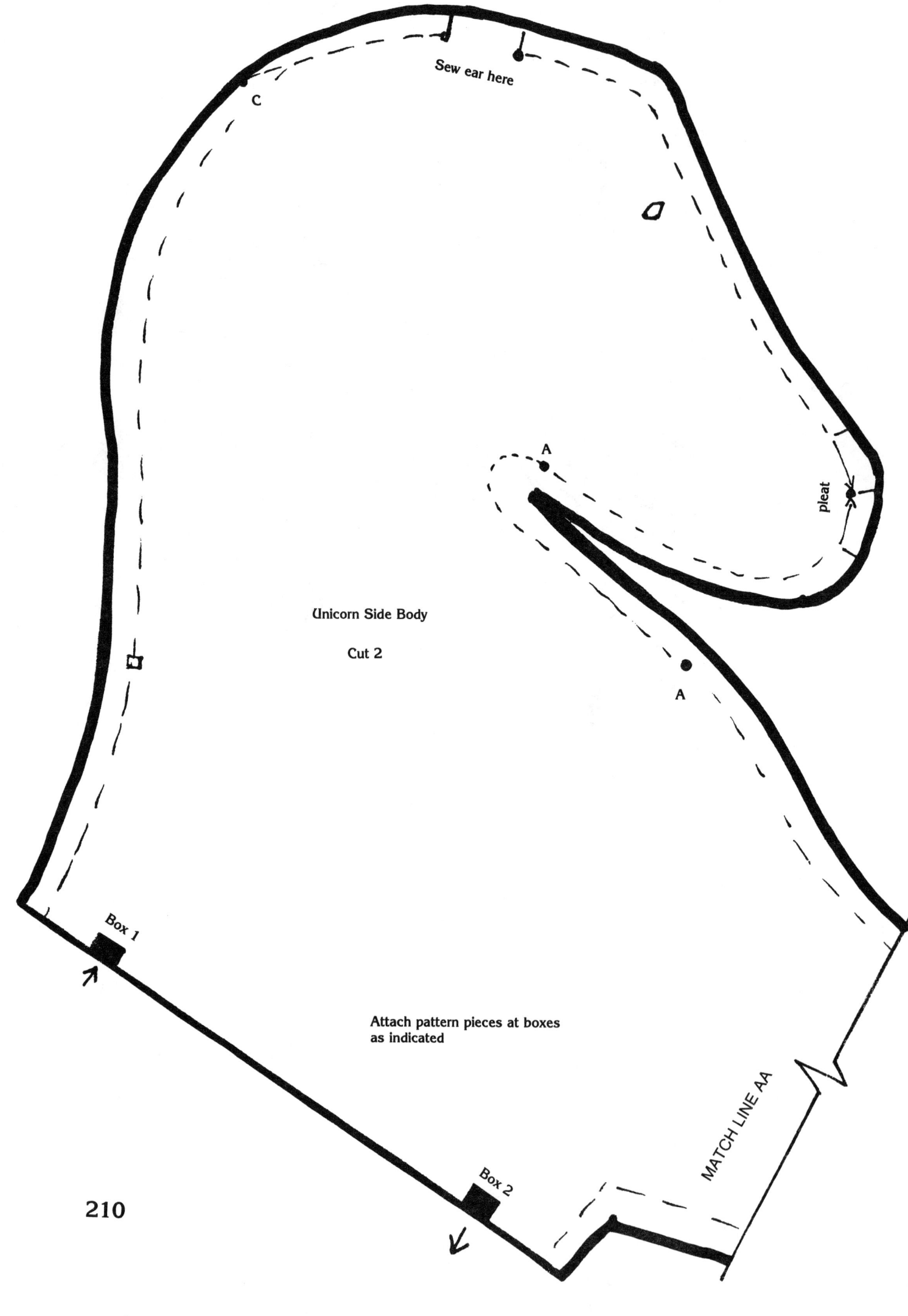

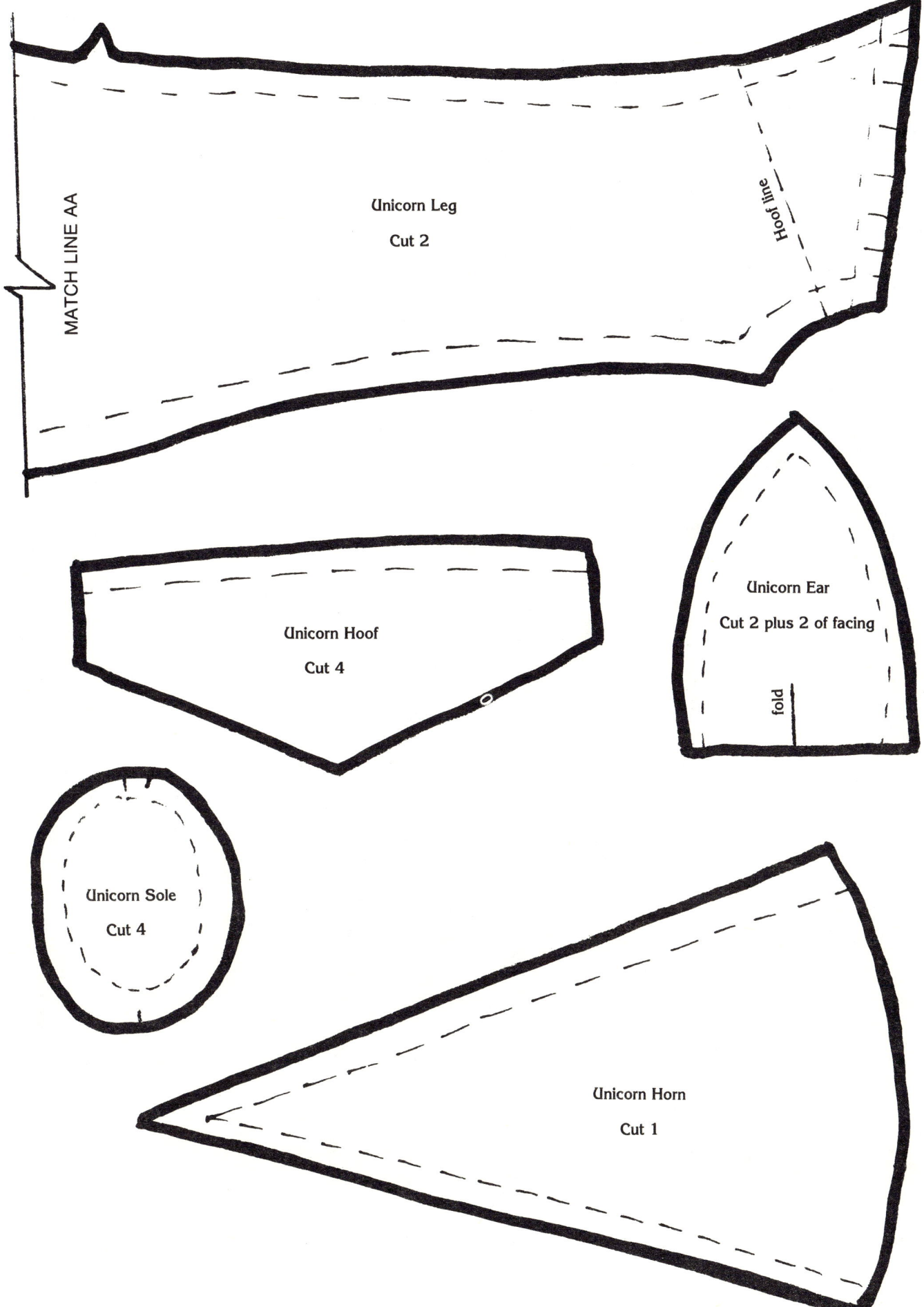

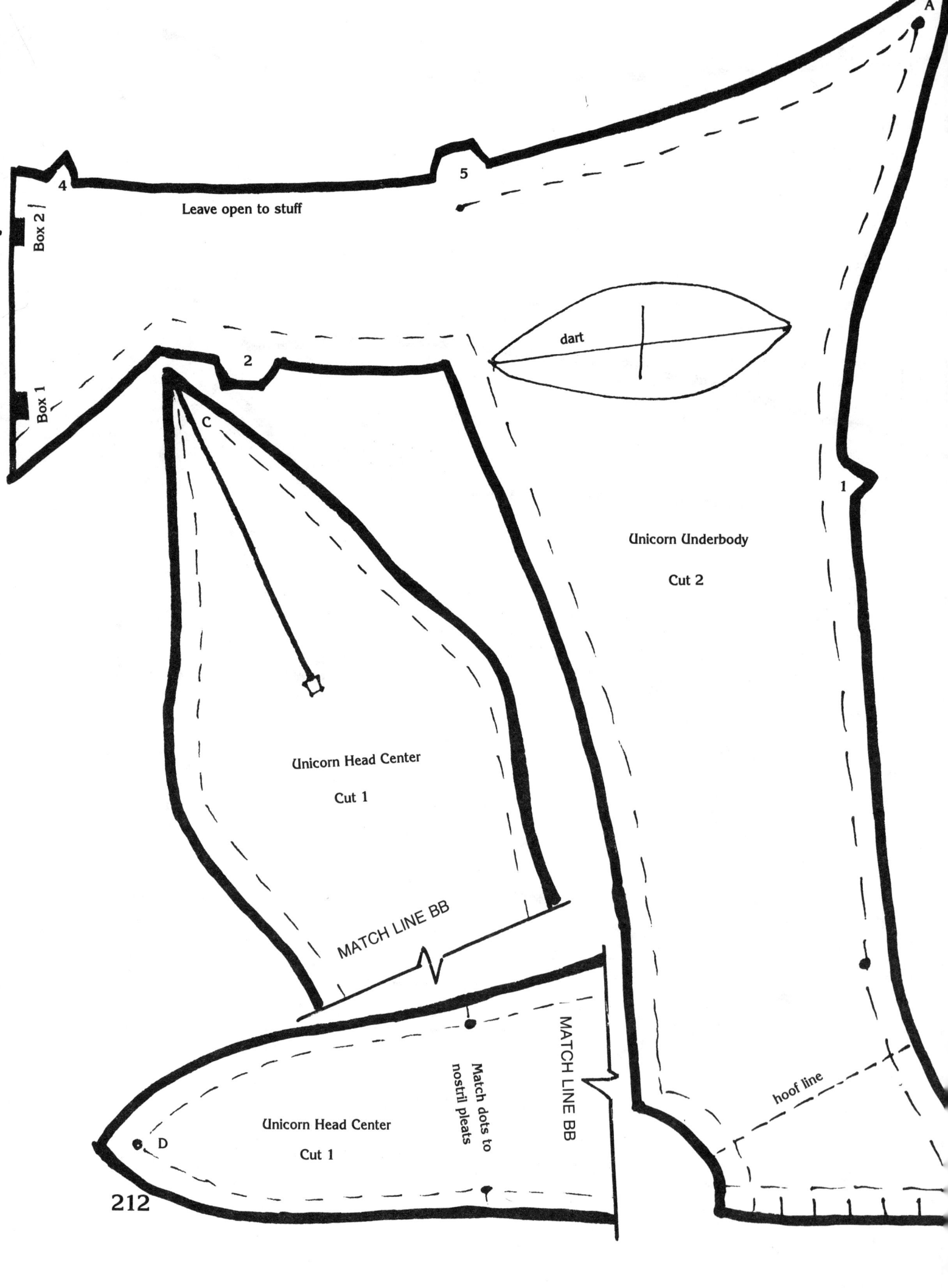

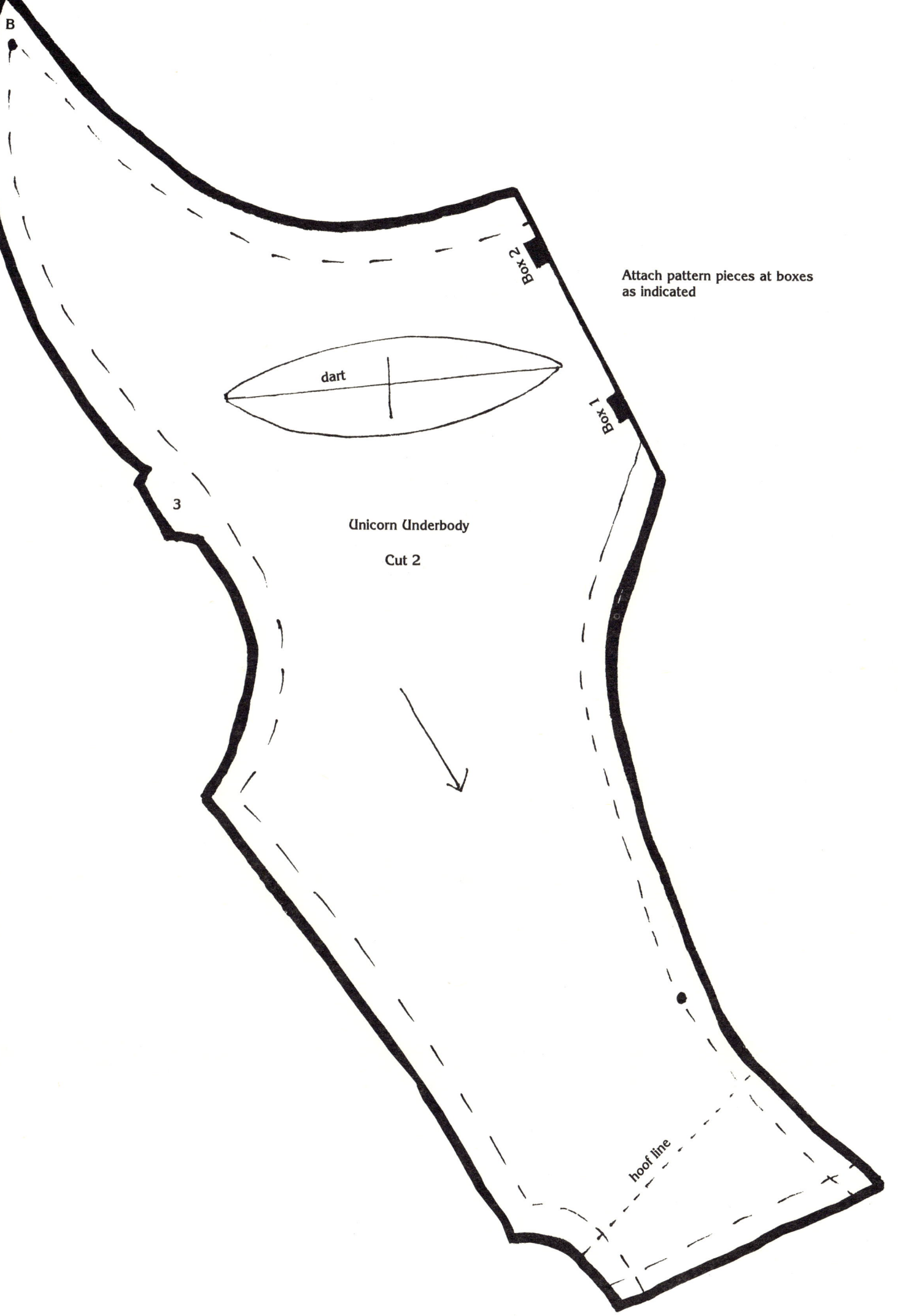

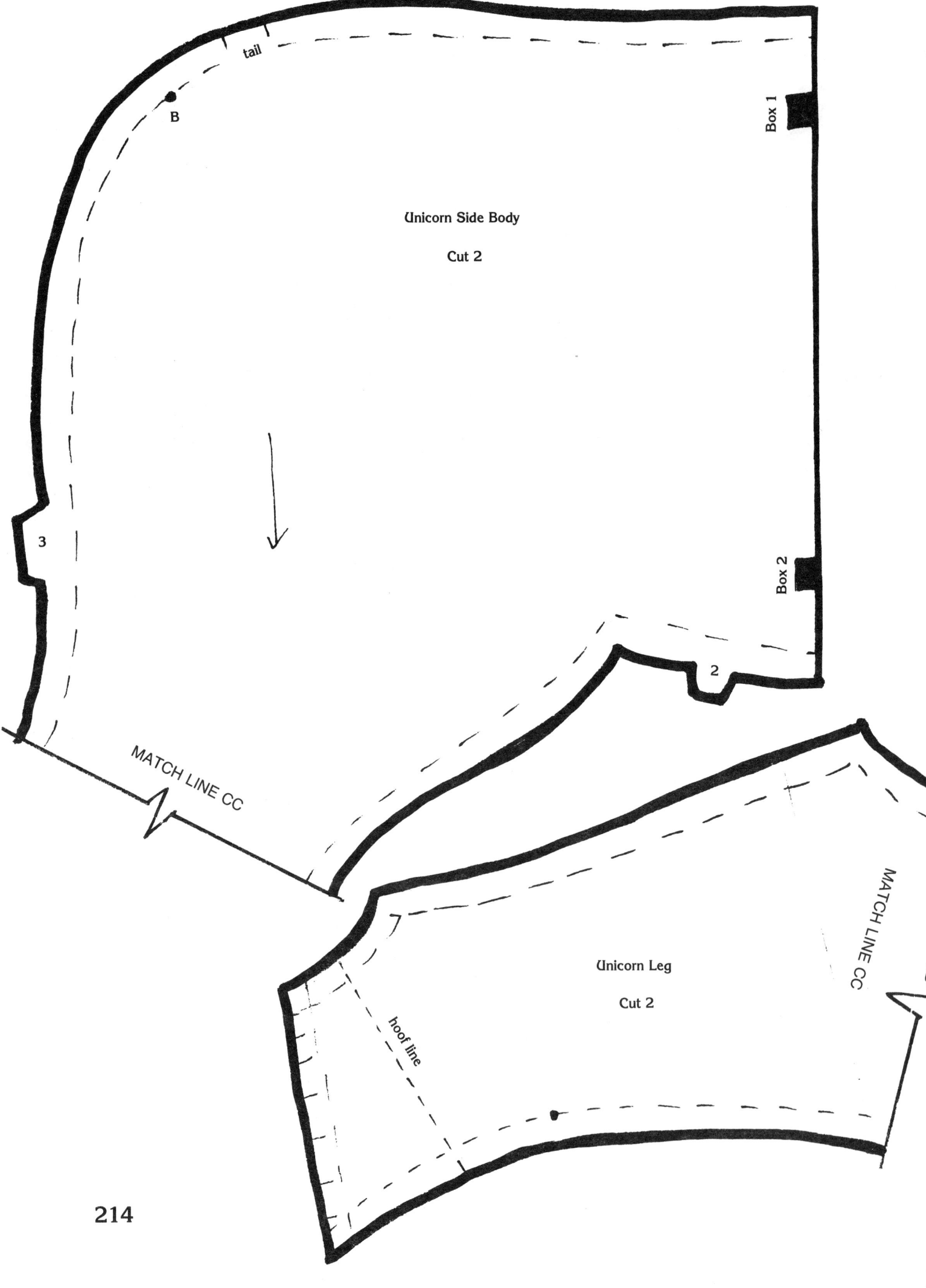

TEN PATTERN PIECES
13" (33 cm) LONG

Cutting Diagram

main color - single

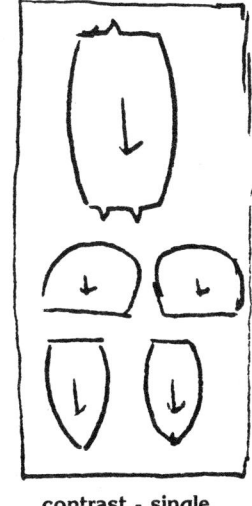

contrast - single

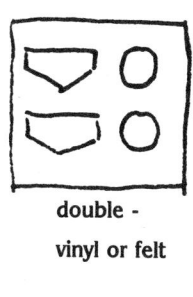

double - vinyl or felt

Materials for zebra (donkey in parentheses)

Zebra-printed fabric (gray or tan short fur) or fabric of choice: ½ yard (½ m)
6" × 10" piece (15 cm × 25 cm) of black (white) fabric for muzzle
Black (dark brown or black) felt or vinyl for hooves and soles: 4" × 12" (10 cm × 30 cm) piece
1 lb. (450 g) polyester fiberfill
4 popsicle sticks or ¼" (⅗ cm) dowels to support legs (optional)
½ oz. (14 g) each black and white yarn (black, gray, or brown, 1 oz. or 28 g) for mane
1 pair of safety eyes or 2 buttons

15
Zebra/Donkey

The zebra and the donkey are made exactly the same except that the donkey has longer ears. If you can't find zebra-printed fabric, you could draw the stripes with permanent black felt-marker pen, or embroider or appliqué them. Also, on either, if you don't want the contrasting muzzle, overlap the pattern pieces, matching seam lines, and cut as one piece. The donkey's baskets can be made of felt or a basket-weave fabric. The baskets in the photograph were cut from straw placemats.

Cutting Instructions

See the Introduction for working with fur fabrics.

Of main color, cut two side bodies, two underbodies, two outer ears, one head center, one chin, and one tail.

Of contrasting color, cut one center muzzle, two side muzzles, and two inner ears.

Of felt or vinyl, cut four hooves and four soles.

Sewing Instructions

Use ¼" (⅗ cm) seams throughout unless otherwise noted.

1. *Underbodies.* Sew darts in underbodies. Clip across the center of each dart, as shown in the pattern and Figure 1. Stitch the underbodies to the side bodies along the front of the legs from the dots to the bottom of the feet. See Figure 1.

2. *Hooves.* Open the front seam flat, right side up. Lay the hoof, right side down and facing toward the top of the leg, across the foot as shown in Figure 2. Stitch on the seam line. Fold the hoof down and machine baste across the bottom of the foot. See Figure 2. Repeat for the other three feet.

3. *Soles.* Sew the remaining underbody seams from dot A to dot B, leaving the bottoms of the feet open, matching notches 1, 2, and 3. See Figure 3. Clip the bottoms of the feet inside the seam allowance as shown on the pattern and Figure 4. With the sole down, matching centers and spreading the clips to Vs, stitch around the foot just inside the clips. Repeat for other three feet.

4. *Ears and nostrils.* Sew ear linings to ears, right sides together, leaving bottoms open. Trim tip and turn right side out. Fold on the center line. Stitch ears to head between lines. Sew the side muzzle to the side head, matching notches 4. Pleat the nostril on the right side of the fabric by bringing the outer lines to the center line. Baste. See Figure 5.

5. *Head center.* Slit the center head on the line to the square. Sew the center head to the center muzzle, matching notches 5. Sew the chin to the center muzzle, matching notches 6. See Figure 6. Stitch the whole center piece to the side heads, from dot C to dot D, matching seams and tapering the seam at dot C to nothing. See Figure 7.

Sew the center front seam on the side bodies from dot D to dot A. See Figure 7.

6. *Tail.* Fold the tail as shown in Figure 8, turning the long edges to the center, then folding again on the center line to enclose the raw edges. Top stitch close to the edge. Hand sew a tuft of yarn strands to the tip of the tail. Stitch the tail to the side body at the line indicated on the pattern.

7. *Mane.* Cut 4" (10 cm) strands of black and white yarn (all the same color for the donkey), sufficient to cover approximately 5" (13 cm) along the back neck seam. Fold the strands in half and stitch to one side body from the square at the end of the center head slit to the square at the base of the neck. In the zebra, match the pattern of the mane stripes to the pattern of the body stripes.

8. *Body.* Sew the center back seam, from dot B, along the back and neck, enclosing the tail and mane and tapering to a point just below the square in the center head. See Figure 9.

Sew the center underbody seam, from dot A to dot B, leaving open between notches 7 and 8 for stuffing. Clip curves, and turn right side out. To form the fold over the eyes (eyelids), top stitch on the outside, along the line shown on the center head and side head pattern pieces and Figure 10. Insert safety eyes, if using.

9. Stuff muzzle, then head and neck firmly. To help support legs, you may wish to insert a popsicle stick of ¼" (⅗ cm) dowel into each leg. Cut the dowels 5" (13 cm) long and sand smooth. Insert a wad of stuffing into each hoof and place the dowel into the center of each leg. Stuff around the dowels firmly so they can't shift. Be sure they are well padded on all sides so they don't rub against the inside of the fabric and can't be felt from the outside. Stuff the body firmly, then sew up the opening using the ladder stitch.

10. *Finishing.* Sew buttons on for eyes, if you didn't use safety eyes. Trim the mane evenly. Both donkey and zebra have short, upright manes.

11. *Donkey's blanket and baskets.* If you cut the baskets from felt, you need only overlap and sew the ends ¼" (⅗ cm), then fold the bottom of the basket up and stitch around it. The baskets can be tacked to braid or ribbon and wrapped around the donkey's body.

If you cut the baskets from a woven or knit fabric, you should overcast the seams, either by hand or using the zigzag on your machine. You may want to interface to stiffen the baskets.

If you cut the baskets from straw placemats, you will find the straw unraveling as soon as you cut. Try tracing around the basket pattern, drawing directly on the straw. Lay the straw over a stable fabric, like interfacing or nylon net. Zigzag around the drawn lines through both layers, just inside or on the lines. Cut out close to the zigzagged stitching, being careful not to cut the threads. Then sew the basket together as above.

The donkey's blanket is a rectangle, cut 7½" × 6½" (19 cm × 17 cm). Hem the edges, if necessary. Trim, if desired.

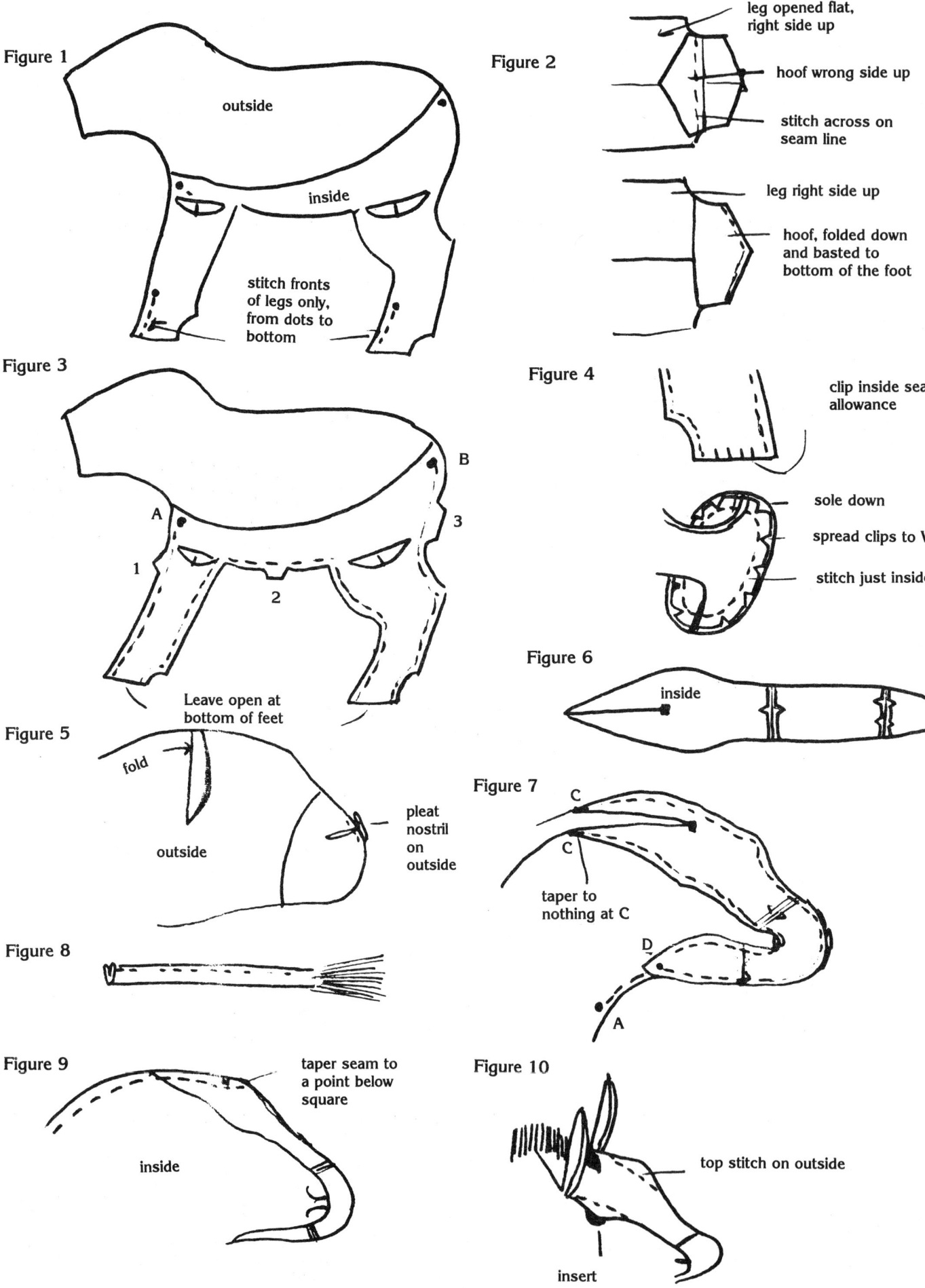

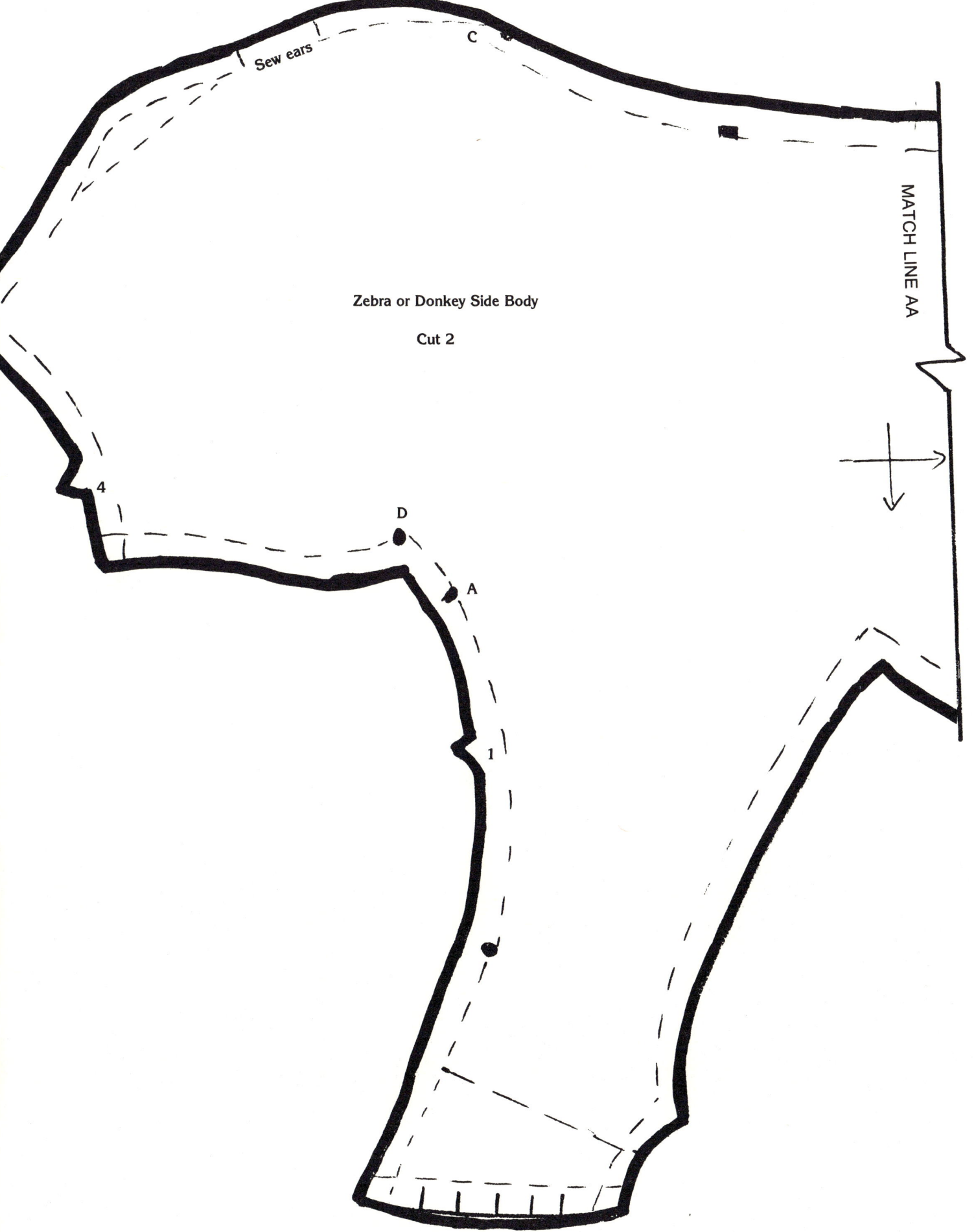

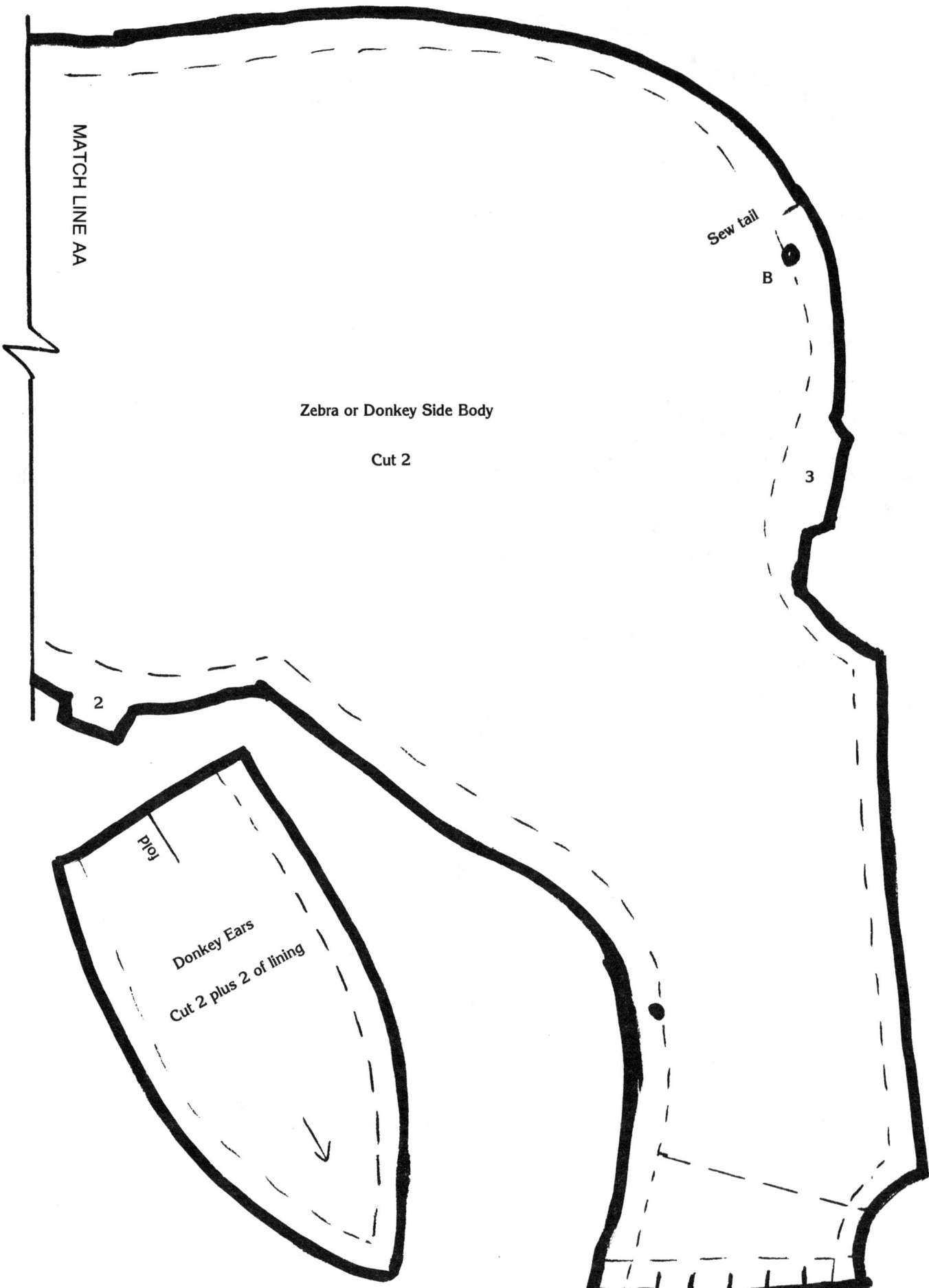

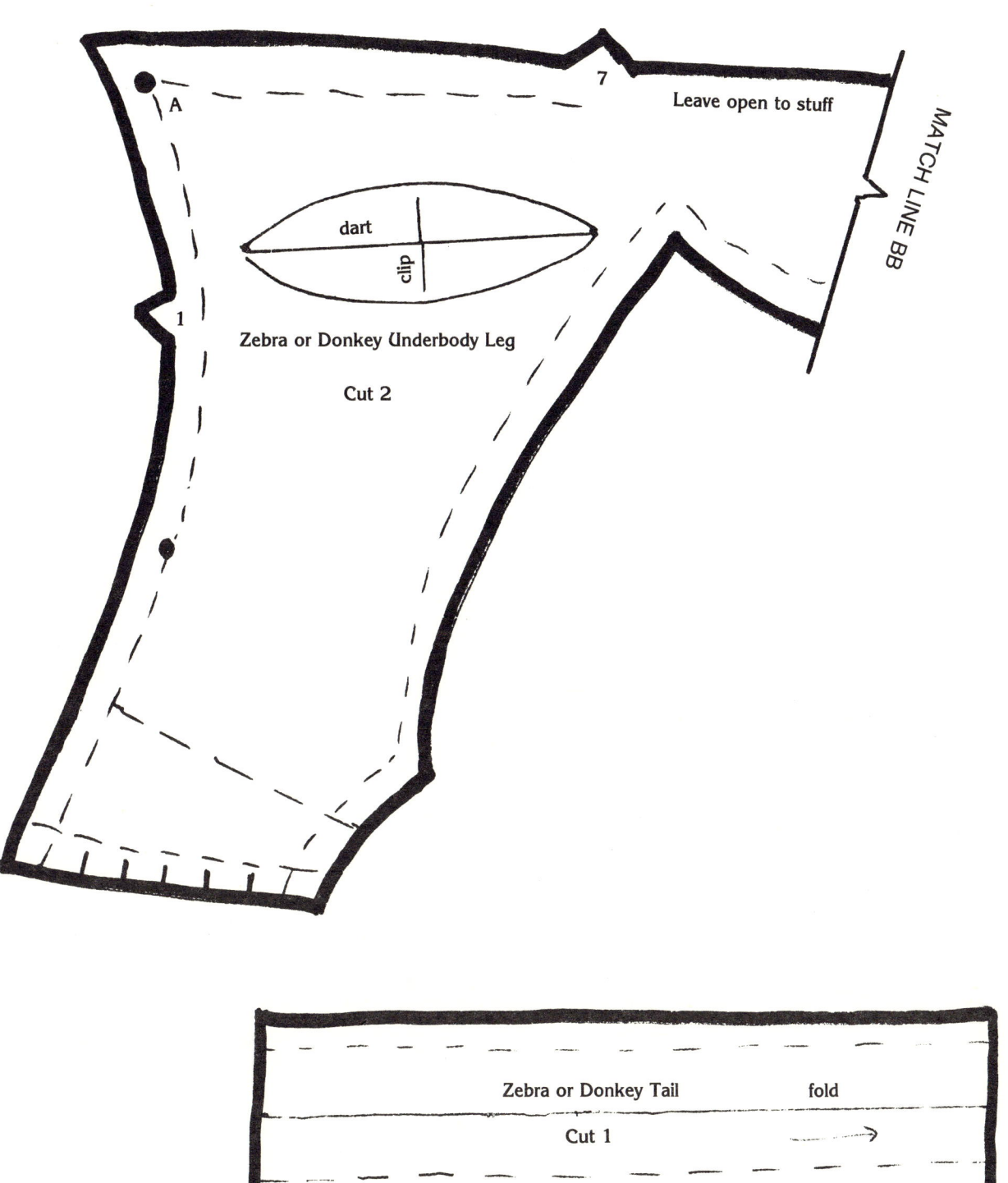

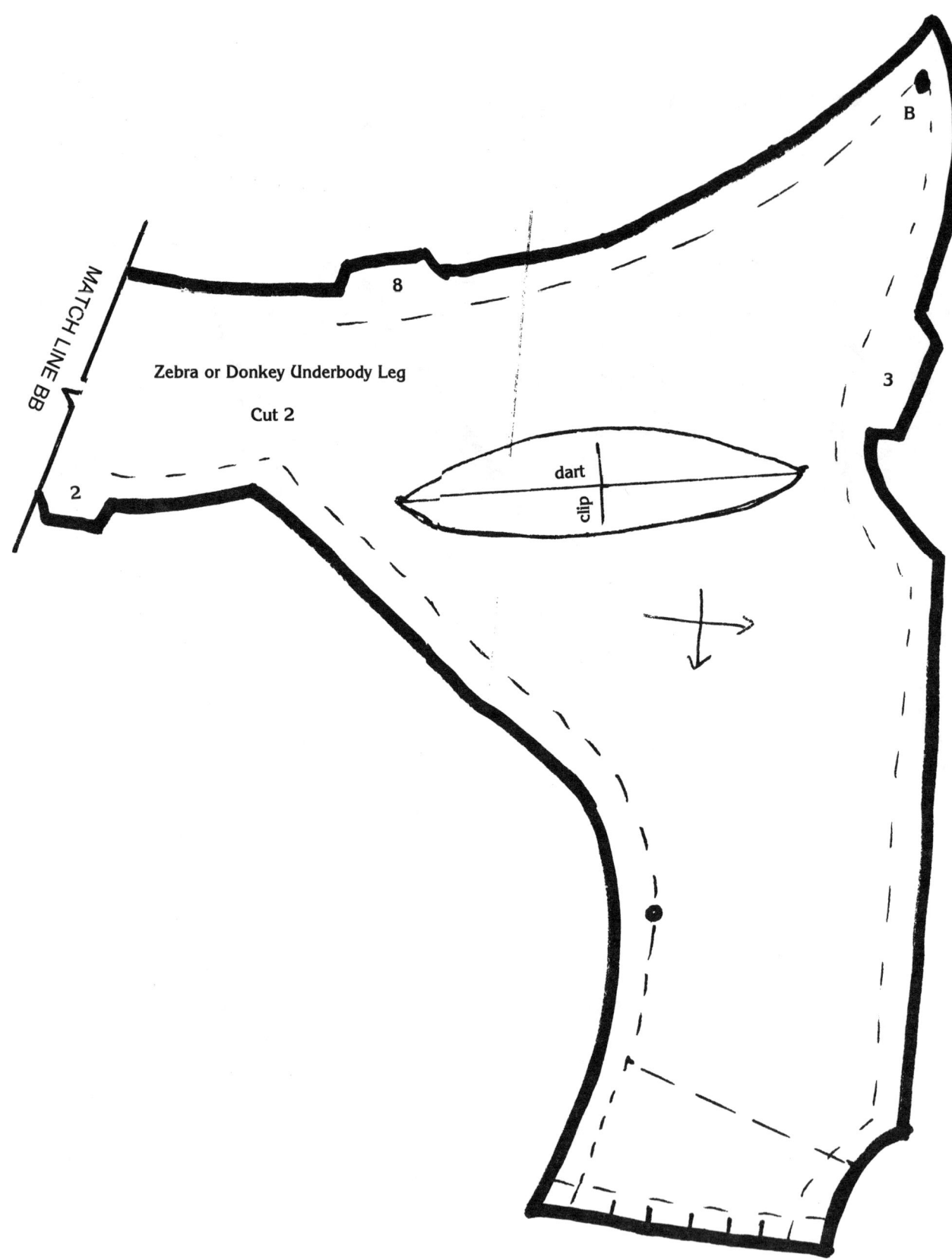

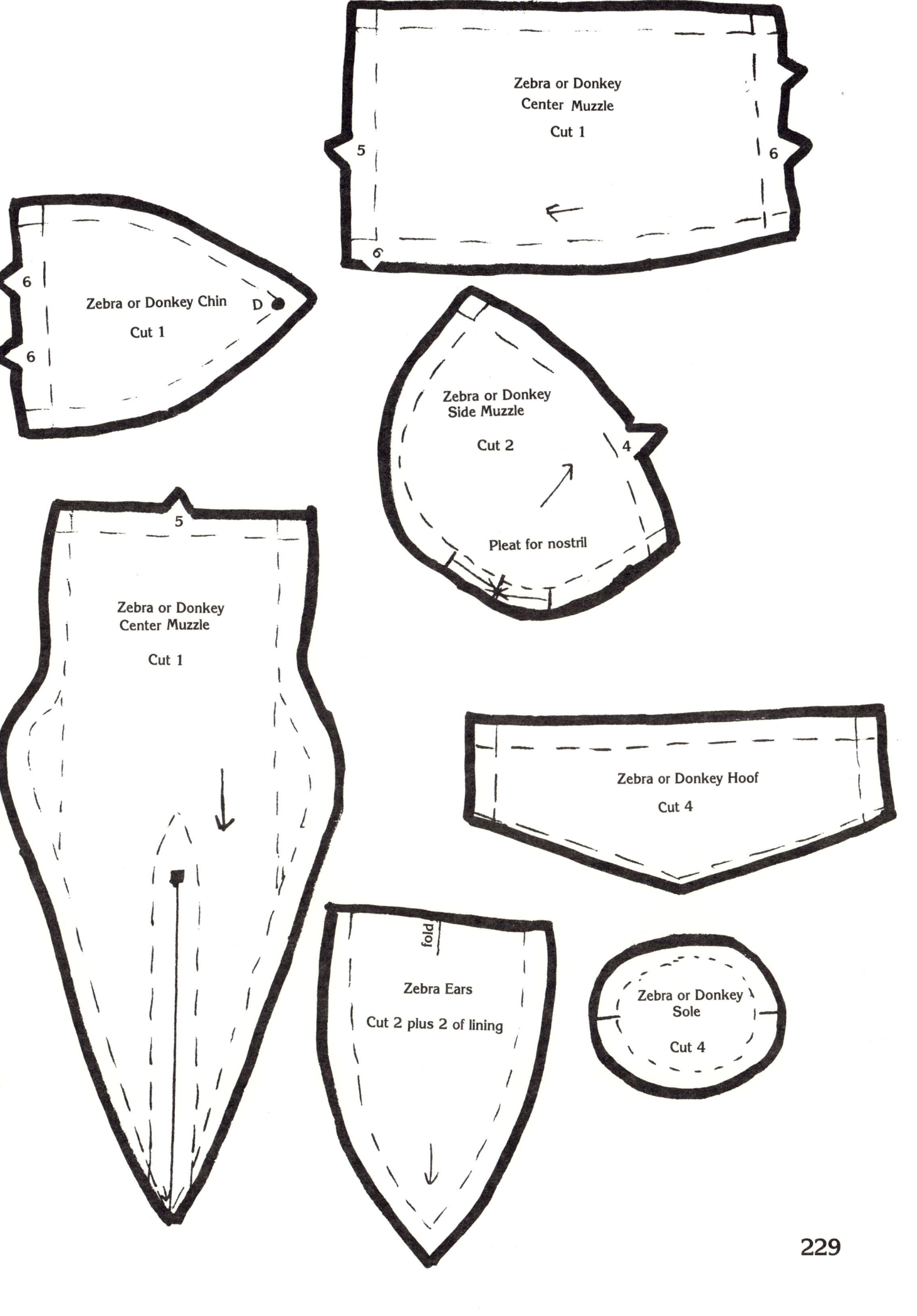

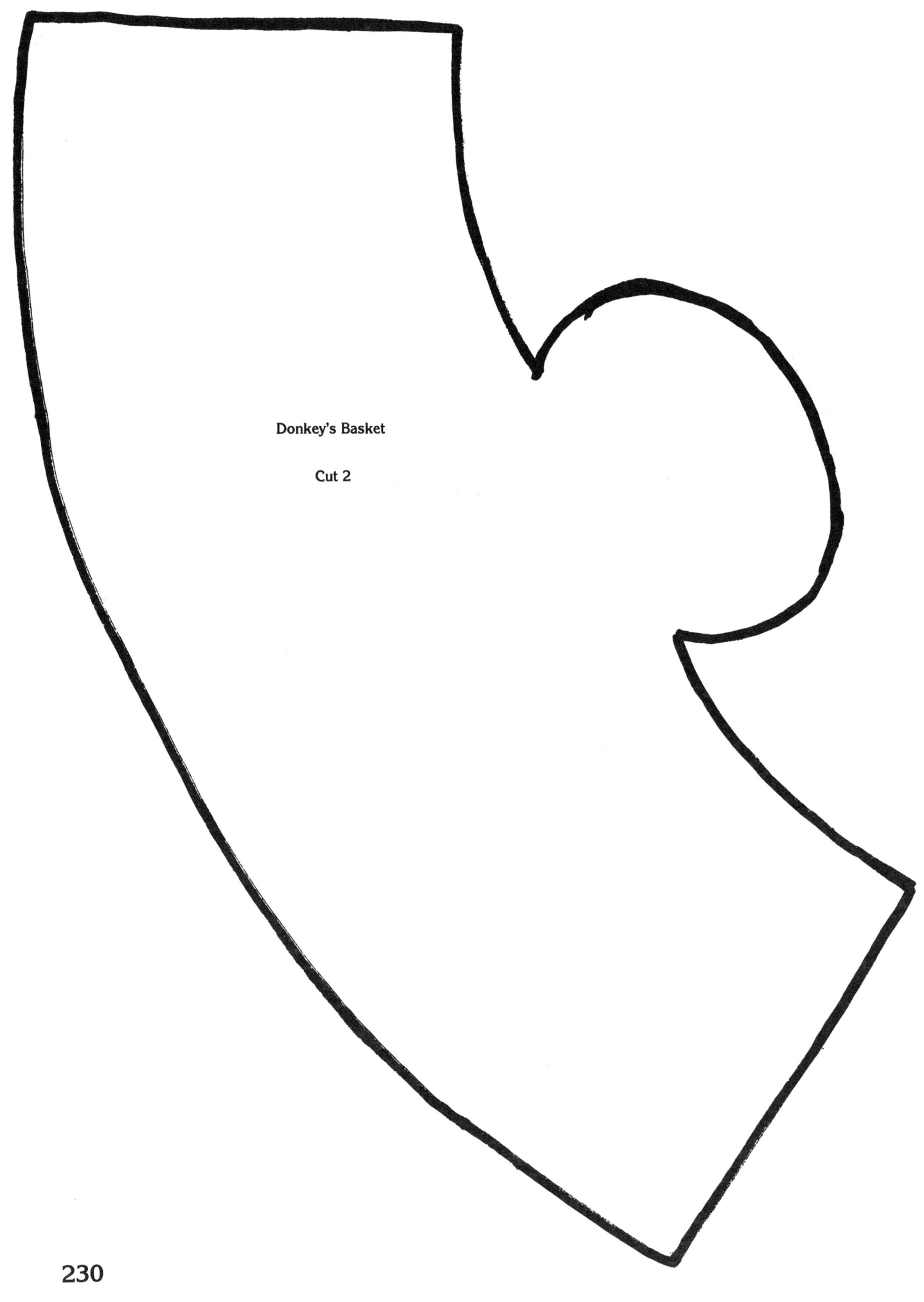

EIGHT PATTERN PIECES
11" (28 cm) LONG (HEAD)

Cutting Diagram

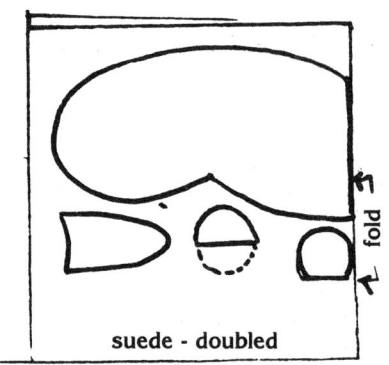

suede - doubled

fur - single layer

pink or red - single

Materials
⅓ yard of 45" or 60" fur fabric (⅓ m of 1 m 15 cm or 1 m 53 cm width)
¼ yard (¼ m) camel-colored suedecloth, velour, or fabric of choice
5" × 12" piece (13 cm × 30 cm) of red or pink fabric for mouth
1 pair of safety eyes, or 2 ball or half-ball buttons, 1½" (3¾ cm) in diameter
1 lb. (450 g) of polyester fiberfill for stuffing
1 dowel, ⅞" (2³⁄₁₆ cm) diameter, 3' (90 cm) in length
2 gold curtain rings, 1" (2½ cm) in diameter
1 yard (90 cm) ribbon or braid for reins

16
Hobby Camel

Who would want to ride an ordinary hobby horse when he or she could ride a camel? This one is shown with the shaggy head and neck of a Bactrian camel. If you choose, you can make it with a shorter fur, or all smooth. If you can't find the tufted shag fur for a Bactrian, try using a tan cotton bathmat. Sometimes a smooth fur fabric will become tufted after it is run through the washer and the dryer.

Preparation of stick: Round off one end of the dowel. Cut a groove 8½" (21 ¼ cm) from the other end, ¼" (⅗ cm) deep. Just below the groove, drill a hole through the dowel. See Figure 1. The groove allows you to gather the neck fabric in tightly and sew through the hole, to attach the head securely to the stick. You can, of course, simply tie and/or glue the head on, but it will come off more easily. Paint or stain the stick whatever color you choose.

Cutting Instructions

See the Introduction for working with fur fabrics.

Of fur fabric, cut two side heads, two ears, and one head center.

Of suedecloth, velour, or other smooth fabric, cut one muzzle on the fold, one chin, two ear linings, and two eyelids on the fold.

Of red or pink fabric, cut one upper mouth and one lower mouth.

Sewing Instructions

Use ¼" (⅗ cm) seams throughout unless otherwise instructed.

1. *Muzzle.* Fold muzzle on the center line. Stitch between dots A and B and from dot C to the lower edge. See Figure 2. Open the muzzle flat. On the inside, bring the center fold to lie directly over the stitching line, forming a box pleat. See Figure 3. Baste across the bottom edge and tack at A.

Stitch cheek darts in each side of the muzzle. Clip at the center of each dart, as shown on the pattern and Figure 3. Fold the muzzle on the center line again, and stitch the center top seam from dot D to dot E, matching notch 1. See Figure 4.

Turn muzzle right side out. On the outside, fold a deep pleat by bringing dot F on the center top seam to dot A on the center front seam, forming the nostrils. Tack securely on the outside. See Figure 5.

2. *Mouth.* With right sides together, insert the upper mouth, matching center fronts and notches 2. Stitch from dot G on one side to dot G on the other side. See Figure 6.

3. *Lower lip and chin.* Sew chin to lower mouth, matching center front and notches 3. Leave open across straight edge. (The mouth is narrower than the chin to allow the lips to curl over the edge.) Turn right side out. Stuff lightly. Baste across the straight edge.

With pink side of lower mouth against pink side of upper mouth (right sides together), stitch chin to upper mouth across the straight edge between dots G. See Figure 7.

4. *Side heads.* Sew the center front seam of side heads, matching notches 4 and 5. See Figure 8. Matching center front seam to center of chin, and matching dots G and notches 6 and 7, stitch muzzle to side heads, tapering the stitching to nothing at dot H. See Figure 9.

5. *Ears.* Sew ear linings to ears, right sides together, leaving straight edge open. Turn right side out. Fold on the center line and stitch to side heads between the lines, as shown on the pattern and Figure 9.

6. *Head center.* Sew head center to side heads on each side, from dot E to dot J, matching notches 8.

Sew center back seam from dot J to bottom edge. Leave neck edge open.

7. Clip curves. Turn the camel head right side out through the neck opening. If using safety eyes, insert at the xs on each side. Stuff the head firmly, starting with the nose area. When the front of the head is firmly stuffed, pad the top of the head with a good wad of fiberfill. Insert the stick so the groove is at the neck edge. Stuff around the stick very firmly so it stays centered in the neck and it is well padded all around.

Gather the neck edge into the groove of the stick. Wrap and tie the gathers tightly with heavy-duty thread, doubled. Sew the neck to the stick through the hole, passing doubled heavy-duty thread in a figure eight, catching the fabric on either side with each pass many times until the head is securely fastened to the stick.

Cut a strip of felt, vinyl, or leather about 1" (2.5 cm) in width and long enough to go around the stick and overlap slightly. Sew to the neck edge and along overlapping edges to cover the gathers and the threads.

8. *Finishing.* Sew on large ball or half-ball buttons at the xs, if you did not use safety eyes. Fold the eyelids in half, stitch around, leaving open between dots for turning. Turn right side out and hand sew the opening closed. Fold up a cuff as shown on the illustration, along folded edge. (The depth depends on the size of the eye.) Hand sew the eyelids over the eyes.

Pinch up a fold along the upper lip, keeping the stuffing up in the fold. Stab stitch across the fold, underneath the stuffing, to form a lip all around the mouth. See Figure 10. Do the same for the lower lip.

Cut lengths of ribbon or braid to form the reins. Sew to gold rings at the corners of the mouth, if you wish, as shown on the illustration.

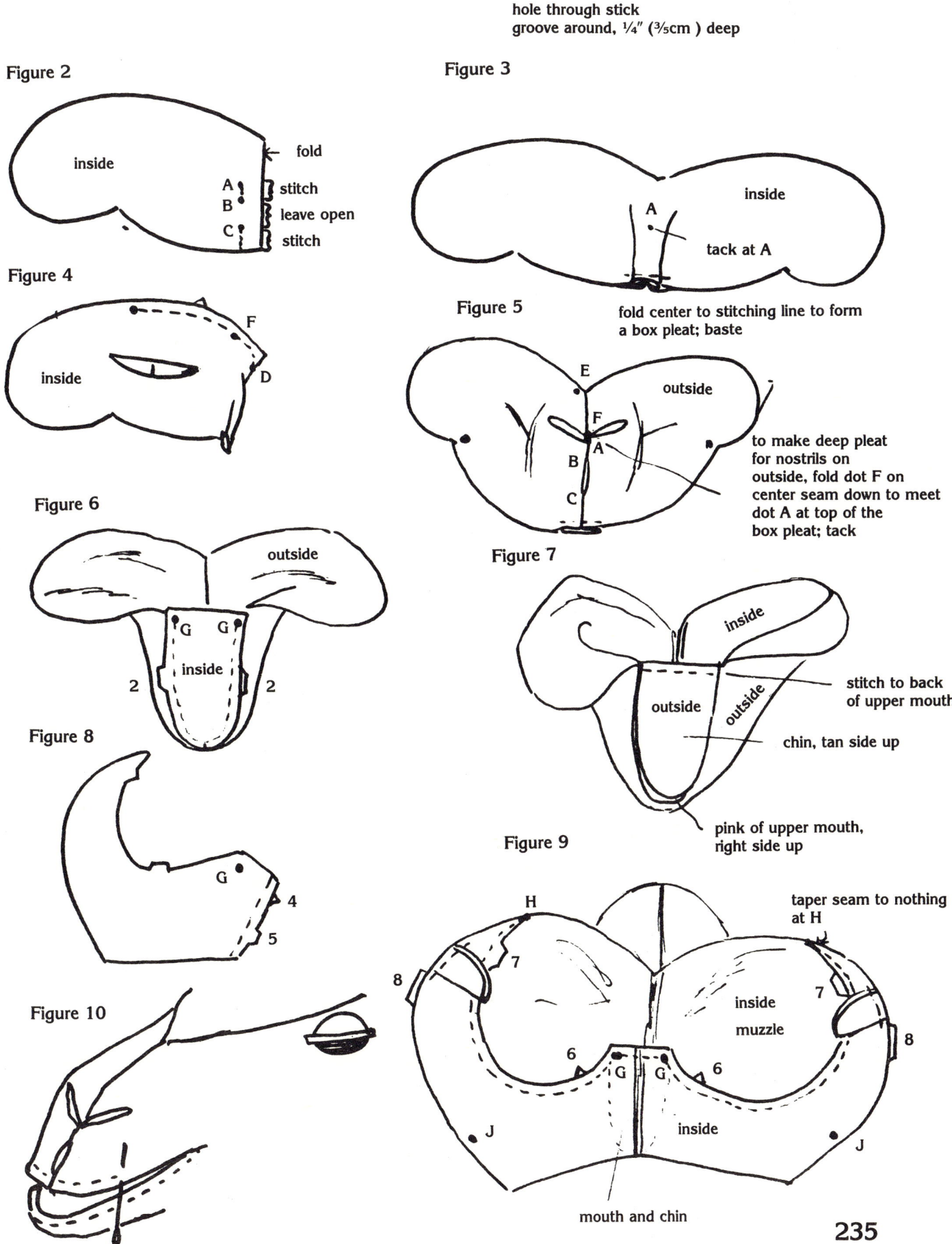

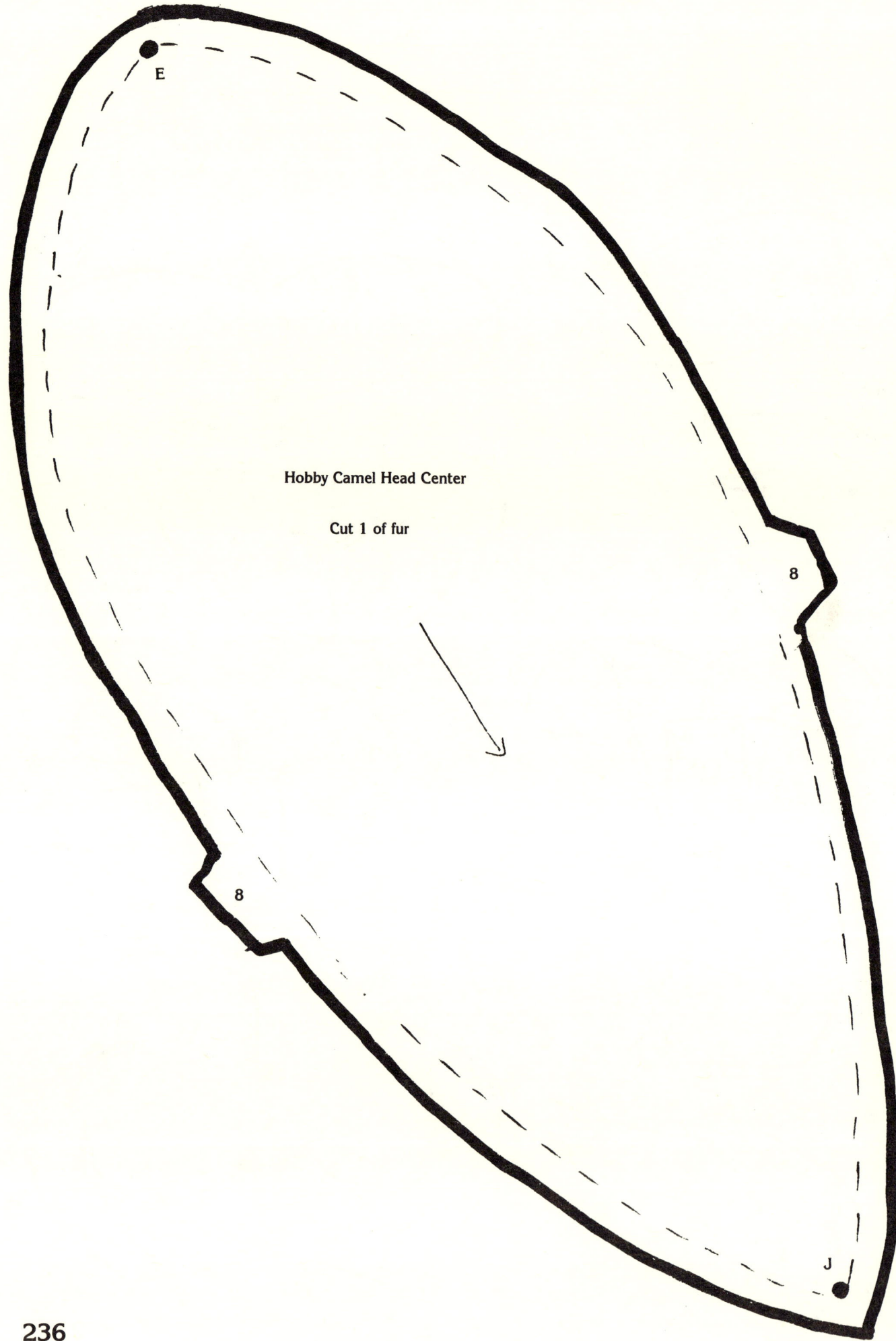

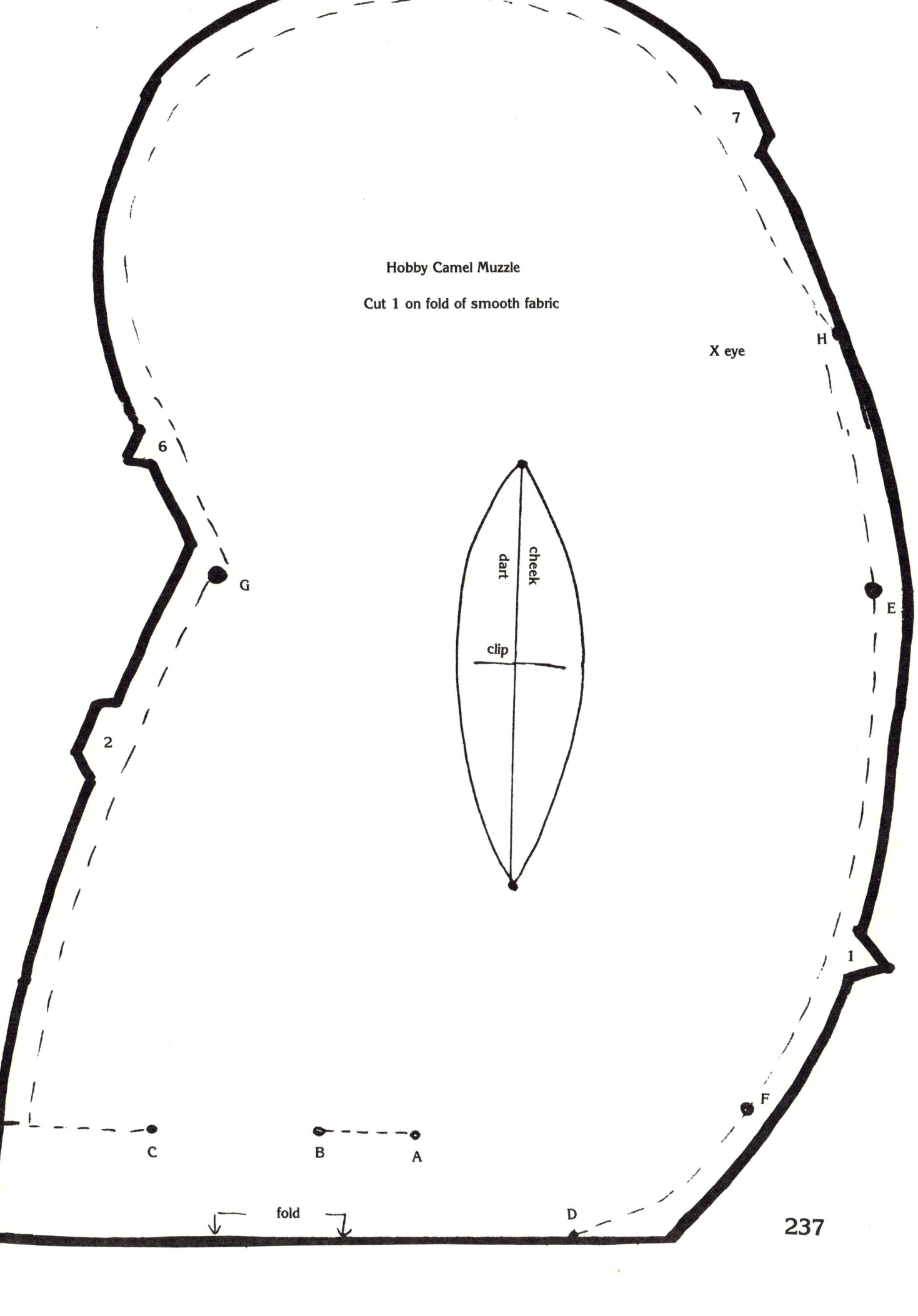

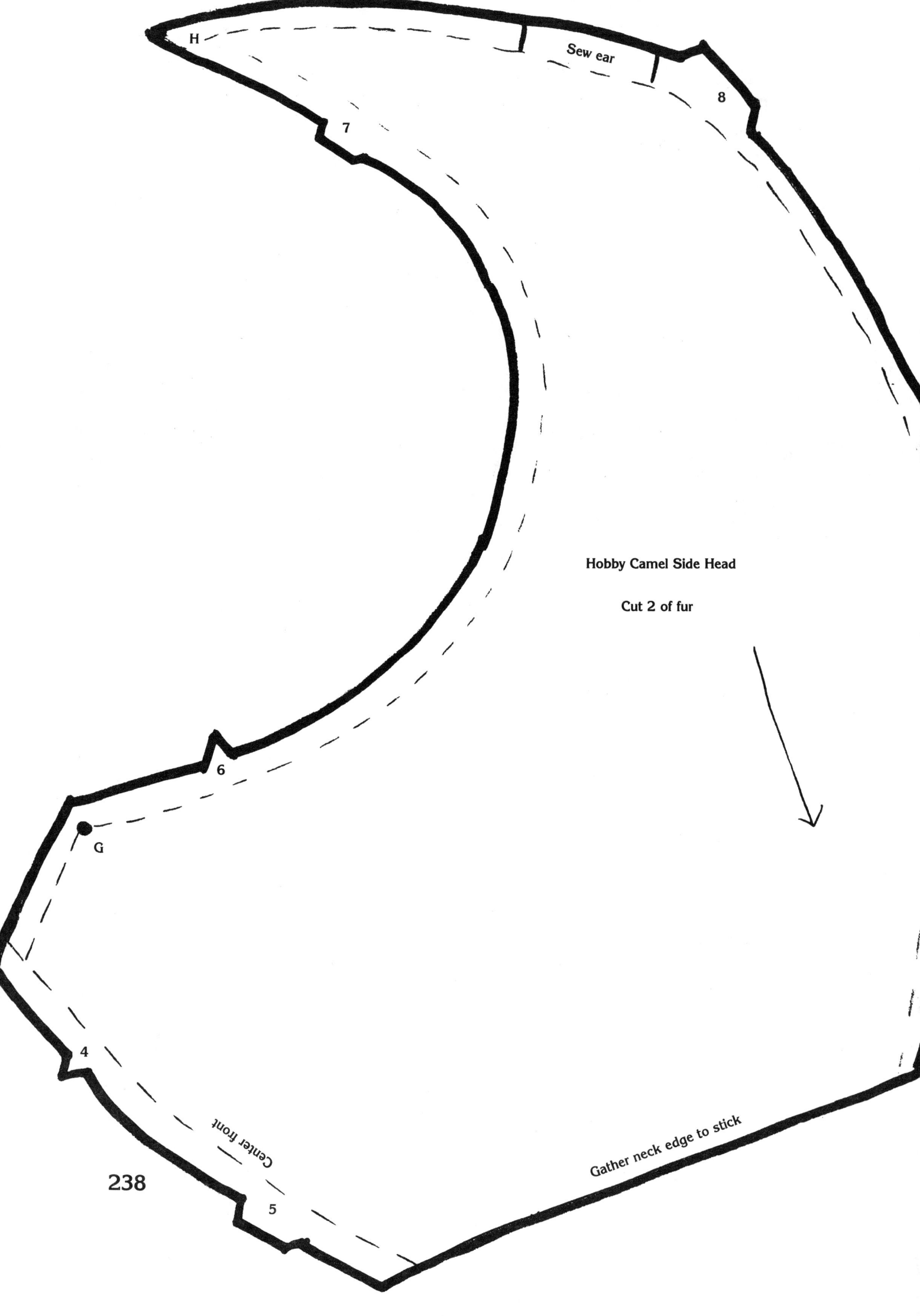

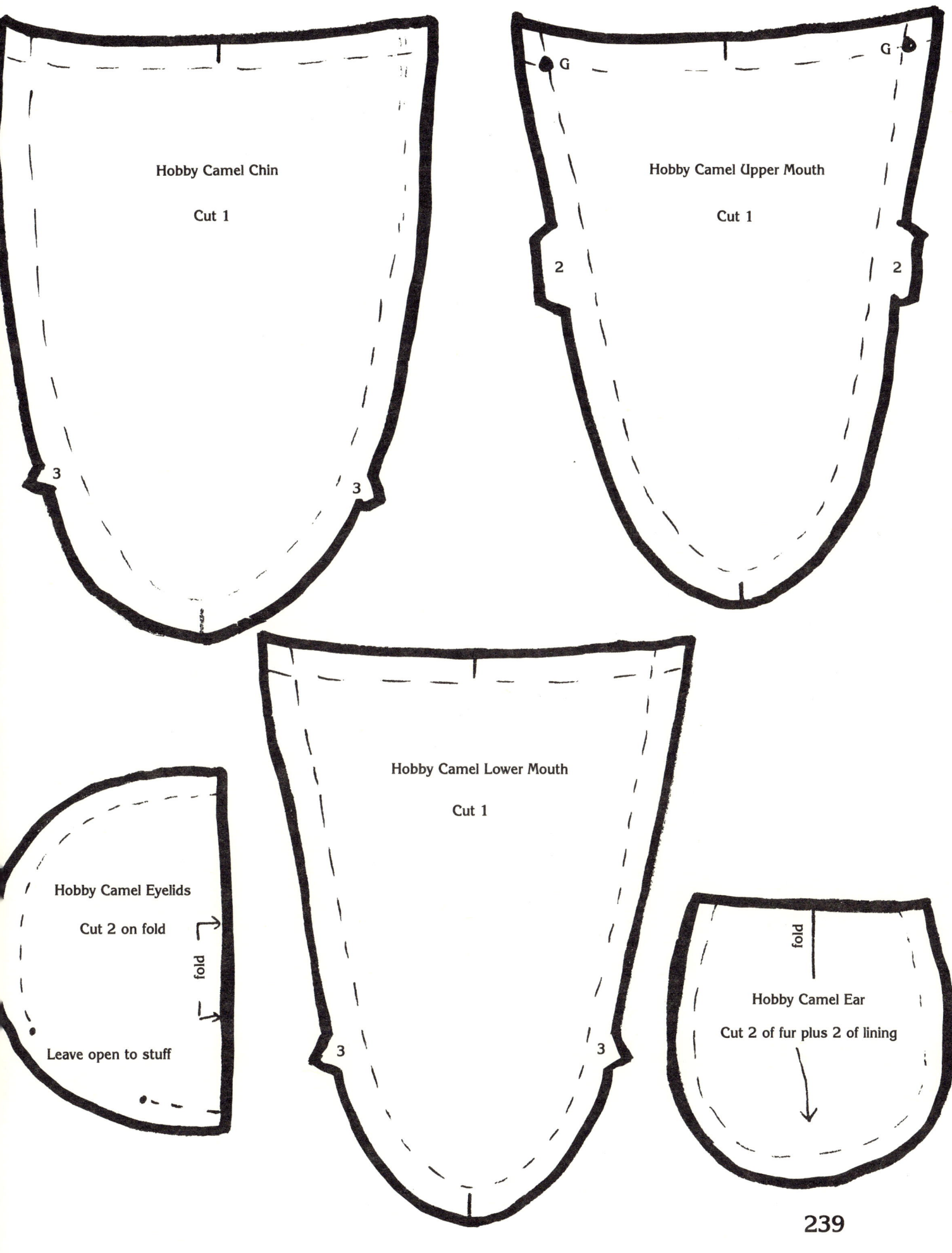

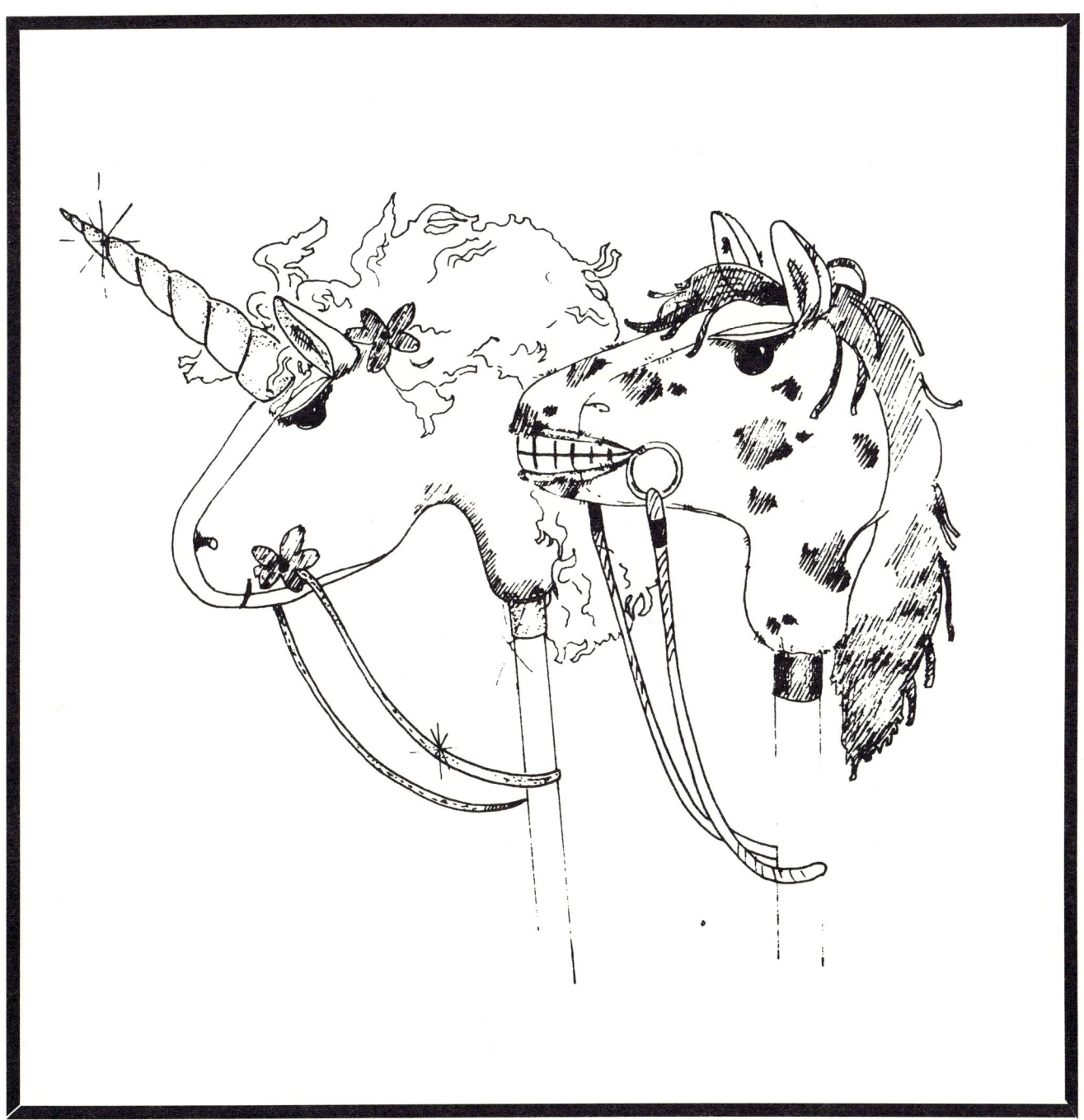

FIVE PATTERN PIECES (HORSE)
12" (30 cm) LONG (HEAD)
FOUR PATTERN PIECES (UNICORN)
12" (30 cm) LONG (HEAD)

Cutting Diagram

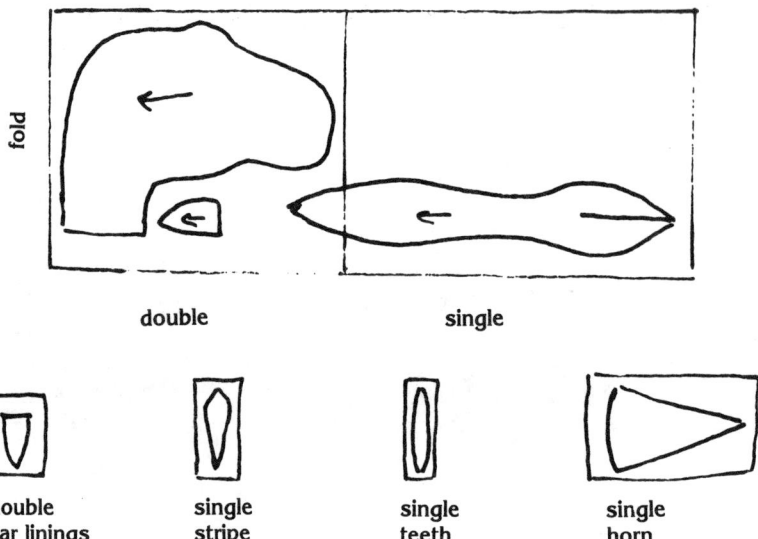

Materials ⅓ yard of 36" (⅓ m of 1 m width) pony fur, corduroy, heavy velour, satin, or other material (do not use stretch fabric)
Scrap of contrast for ear lining, if desired; scrap of white fur or felt for stripe (optional); 6½" × 10" piece (16 cm × 25 cm) for unicorn's horn
1½ ozs. (42 g) yarn for mane or 11" (28 cm) of drapery fringe
1 pair safety eyes or 2 buttons
1 each 36" (90 cm) dowel or length of broomstick, ⅞" (2 3/16 cm) diameter, prepared as shown on page 233
1 lb. (450 g) polyester fiberfill
24" (60 cm) of cable cord, braid, or rope for reins
2 gold rings (café curtain rings)
White vinyl or felt: 1½" × 7" (3¾ cm × 18 cm) for teeth (optional) or embroidery thread for mouth
Scrap of vinyl or felt to cover joint of head/stick
Heavy-duty thread to match fabric, and black heavy-duty thread

17
Hobby Horse/Unicorn

Every child should have a hobby horse, unless he or she would rather ride a unicorn. Horses can take you across the western plains or down the bridle path, but unicorns are magic and can take you anywhere in the world or out of it. Both of these make nice decorations, too. If it is for a child to ride, though, it should be made of a sturdy fabric. You might be able to find a pony-printed fur, upholstery fabric, or corduroy for the horse; or velour, velveteen, or even white vinyl for the unicorn. If you choose satin, it should be lined since satin frays easily.

Cutting Instructions—Hobby Horse

Cut two side heads, one center head, and two ears of main fabric.
 Cut two ear linings of contrast or of main fabric.
 Cut one teeth piece of white vinyl or felt (optional).
 Cut one stripe of white felt or fur (optional).

Sewing Instructions

Use ¼" (⅗ cm) seams unless otherwise stated.
 1. *Ears and nostrils.* Sew ear linings to ears, leaving bottom open. Trim tip, turn right side out. Fold on center line and stitch to side heads where indicated on the pattern and Figure 1.
 Fold pleats in to form nostrils and baste. See Figure 1.
 2. *Head center.* Cut head center along line to square. Top stitch stripe to head center if you are using a stripe. See Figure 2.
 Sew head center to side heads from dot A to dot B, matching dots at nostrils. Taper seam to nothing at dot A. See Figure 3. Turn head right side out and top stitch eyelids. See Figure 4. Turn head inside out again.

3. *Mane.* If using drapery fringe, sew it into the center back seam from neck edge, tapering to a point just below the square in the center head slit.

To make a yarn mane, wrap yarn closely around a 5" (13 cm) width of heavy cardboard for 11" (28 cm). Cut along one edge, lay flat on tissue paper and stitch down center. Figure 5. Fold the mane on the stitching line. Sew to one side of the horse's head from end of slit to near neck edge between squares. See Figure 6. Sew center back seam, enclosing mane, from neck edge, tapering to a point just beyond the square on the forehead. See Figure 7.

4. Sew center front seam from dot B to neck edge. Clip curves, and turn right side out. If you have difficulty turning through the narrow neck opening, you may open the front seam a little way up and resew it by hand after turning.

Insert safety eyes, if you are using them. If using buttons, sew on after animal is stuffed.

Stuff nose and head center as firmly as you can. Use a chopstick or ¼" (⅗ cm) dowel to push the stuffing in the far corners. Pad the top of the head with a layer of stuffing and push the painted dowel all the way to the top of the head. Stuff very firmly all around the dowel, so the head is solid. Gather the neck fabric into the groove, using heavy-duty thread. Wrap tightly into the groove, then sew fabric to stick, making a figure eight pattern through the hole in the stick. Fasten securely. Cut a strip of vinyl or felt to match the stick or the head, 1" (2.5 cm) wide and the length necessary to go around the stick. Wrap and stitch this so the raw edges, groove, and threads are covered.

5. *Finishing.* Glue or tack the teeth to the front of the head. With heavy black thread, sew across to simulate teeth. With heavy thread that matches fabric, stab stitch a ridge above and below the teeth to make lips. Catch the stuffing under the ridge. See Figure 8. (If you choose not to make the teeth, you can embroider a line for the mouth instead.)

Sew gold rings at corners of mouth. Loop cable cord or braid through each ring for reins and sew ends. The stitching may be covered with the felt or vinyl you used to cover the neck edges, or you may wrap a ring of vinyl tape around the raw ends.

Sew buttons on for eyes, if you didn't use safety eyes. Tack eyelids down over eyes. Tack ears to stand up.

Cutting Instructions—Hobby Unicorn

Cut two side heads, one center head, and two ears of main fabric.

Cut two side heads and one center head of muslin, if using satin for the outside fabric. (Satin ravels so easily; the seams must be reinforced or they will give way as you stuff.)

Cut two ears and one horn of contrasting fabric.

Sewing Instructions—Hobby Unicorn

Use ¼" (⅗ cm) seams throughout unless otherwise stated.

If using muslin lining, place muslin on wrong side of satin pieces and treat as one layer. You may want to pin or baste them to help handling.

Follow general directions for sewing the head as described for the hobby horse, omitting the stripe on the face. Stuff and mount as directed for the hobby horse. Omit the teeth and lips, if you wish, and just embroider a line for the mouth. Silk flowers at the corners of the mouth and in the mane or under the chin are pretty.

Fold the horn lengthwise and stitch along edge. Trim tip, turn right side out, and stuff firmly. Hand sew to the forehead where indicated on the pattern, turning under ¼" (⅗ cm) edge. To spiral the horn, fasten matching thread at the base of seam, wind the thread around the horn tightly to form a spiral. Take a tiny stitch as you cross the seam each time around to hold the spiral in place. Fasten thread firmly at the tip. See Figure 9.

You may want to make a little beard under the chin by sewing some strands of the yarn you used for the mane.

Figure 1

pleat nostril

Figure 2

Figure 3

taper seam to nothing at dot A

Figure 4

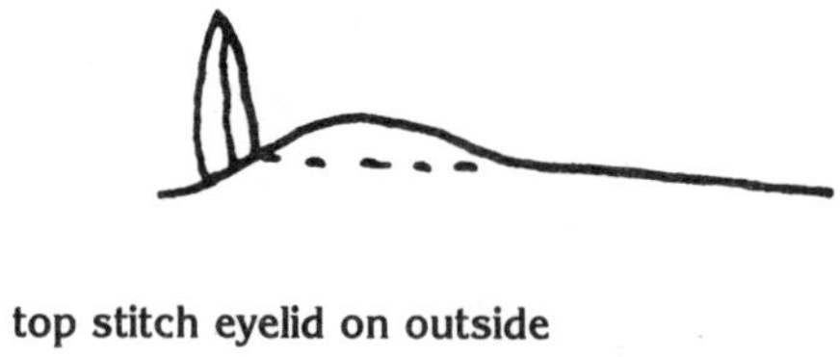

top stitch eyelid on outside

Figure 5

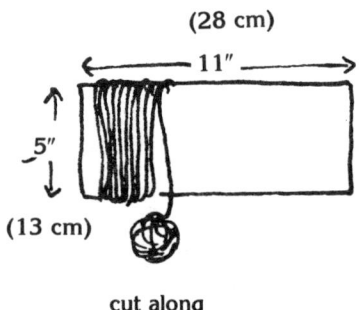

(28 cm)
11"
5"
(13 cm)

cut along one edge, open flat

10"
(25 cm)
11"
(28 cm)

stitch center

Figure 6

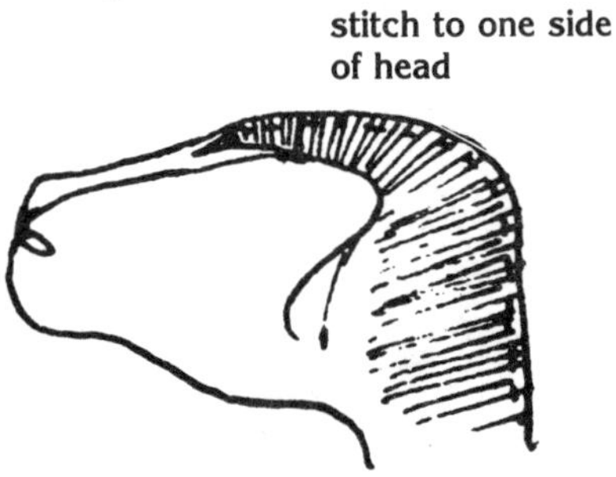

stitch to one side of head

Figure 7

Figure 8

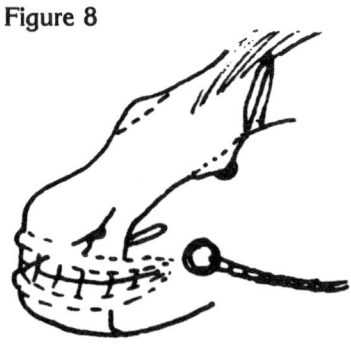

Figure 9

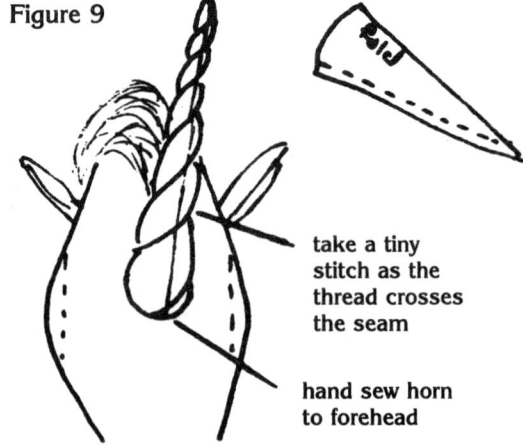

take a tiny stitch as the thread crosses the seam

hand sew horn to forehead

246

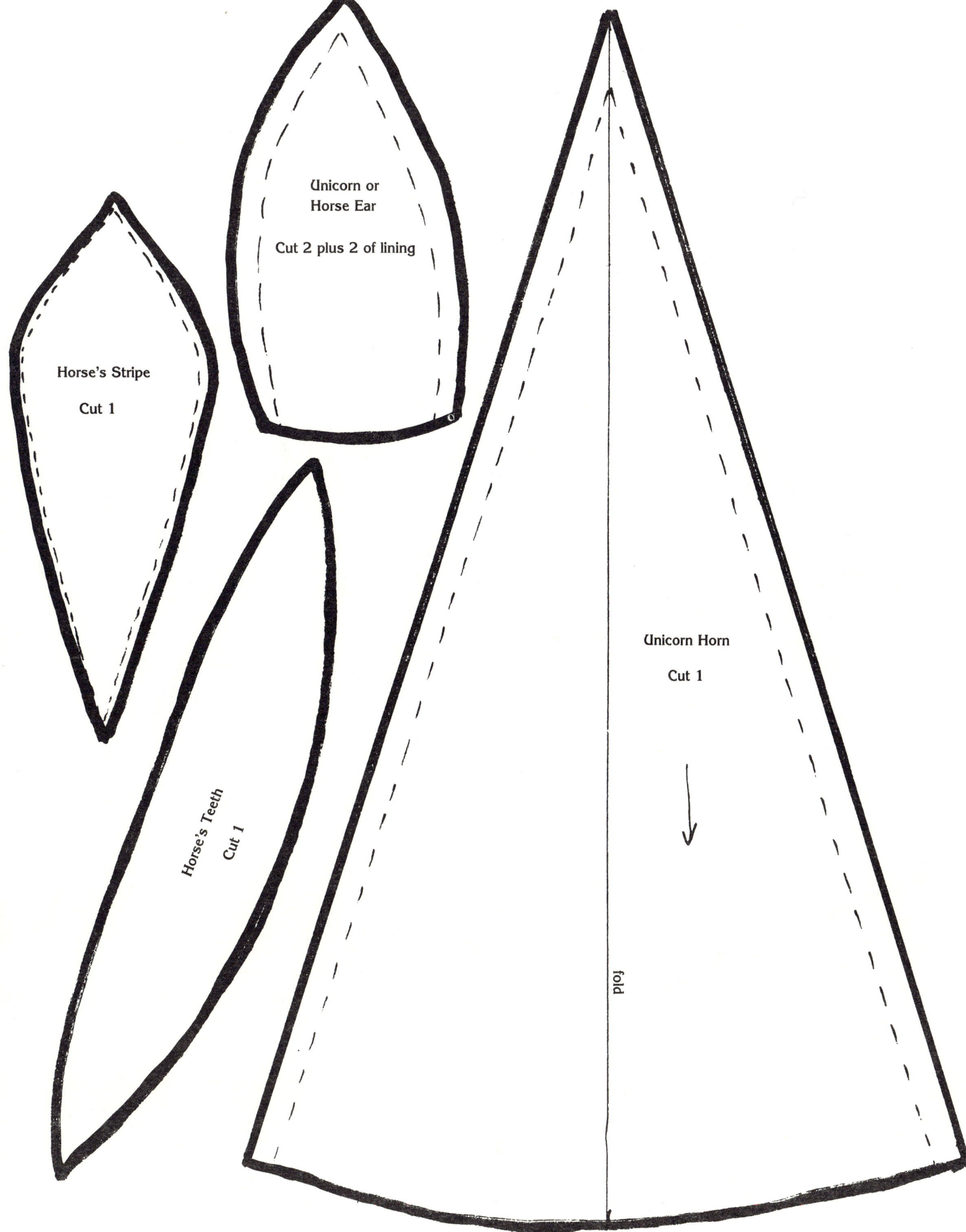

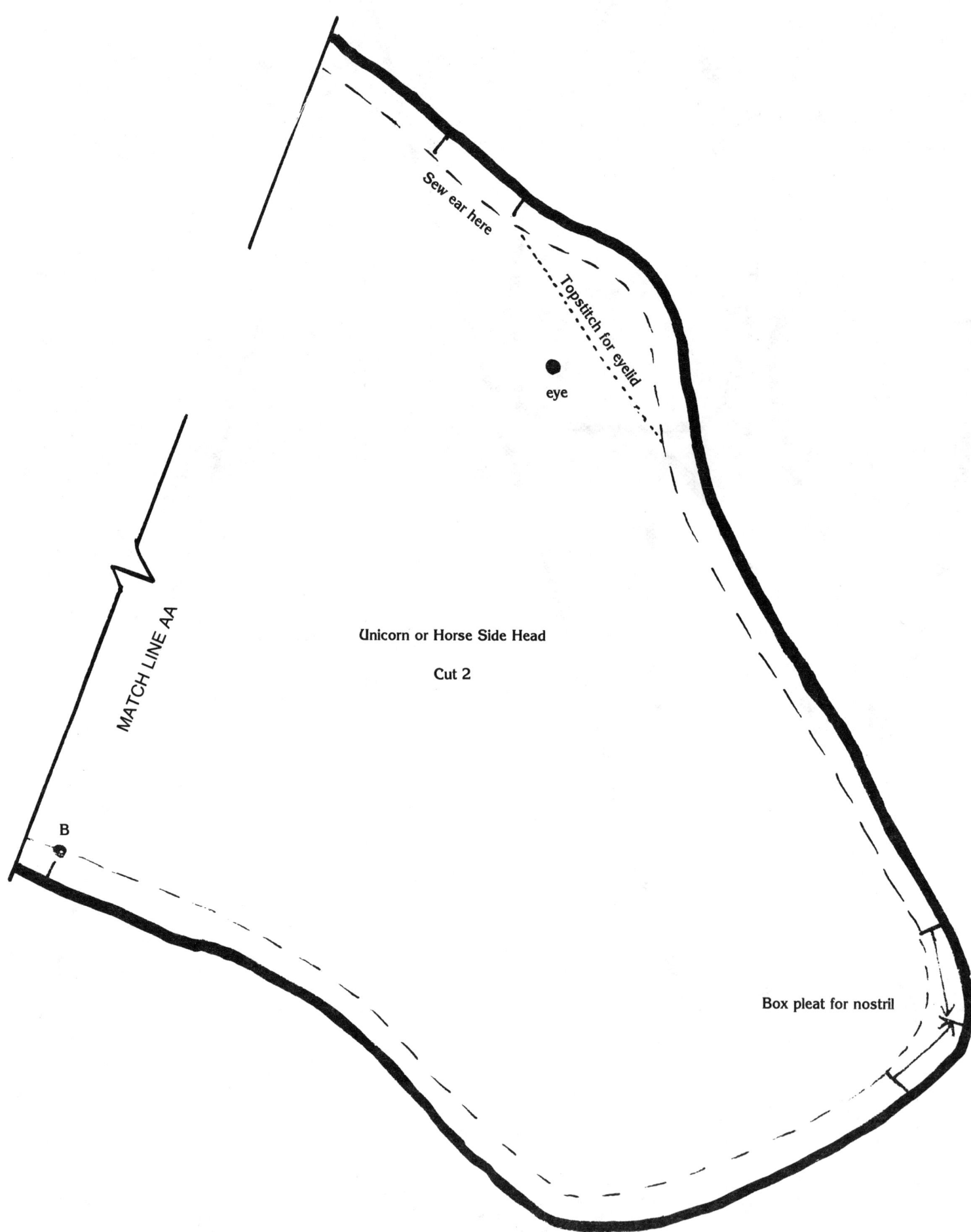

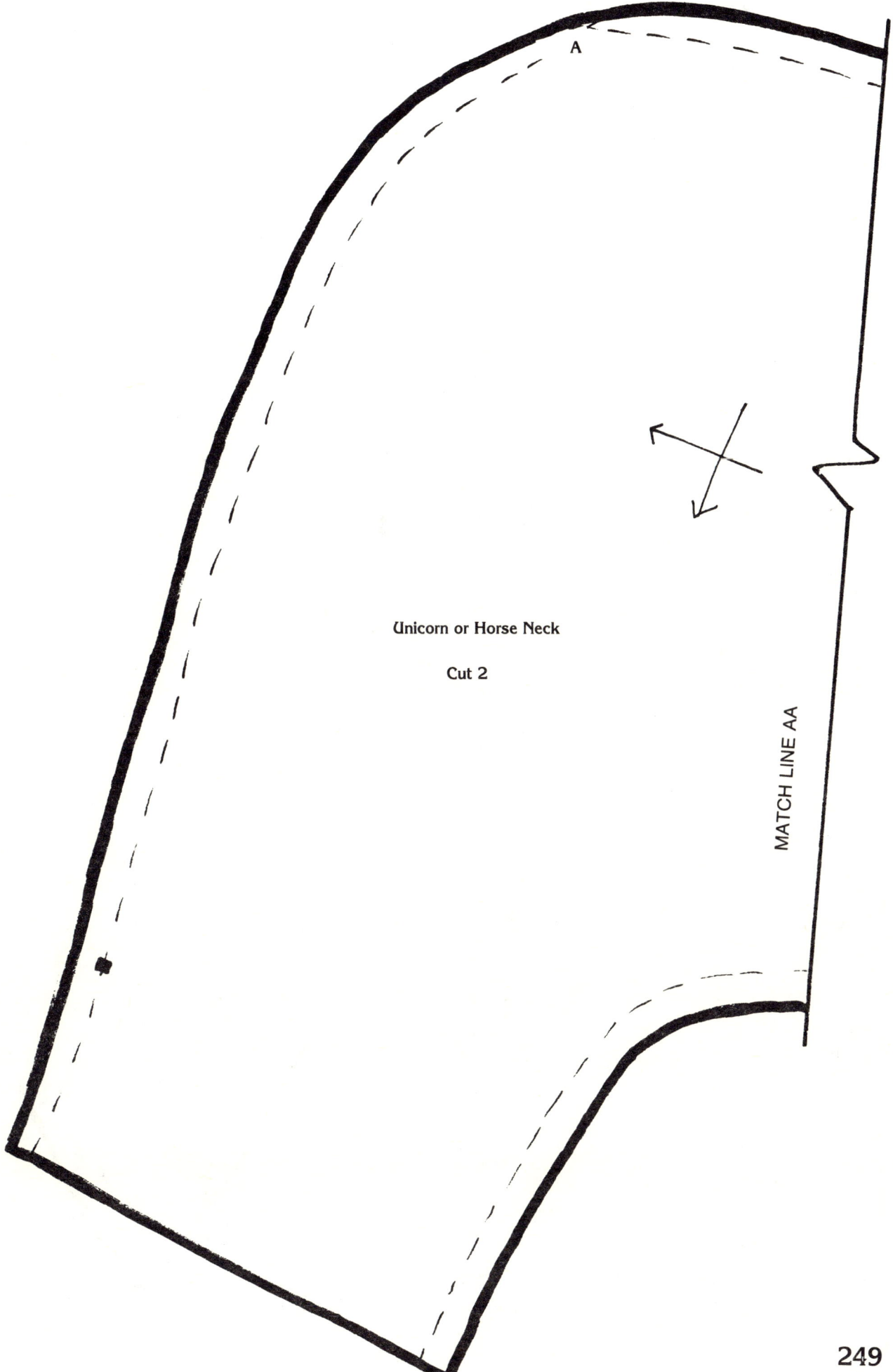

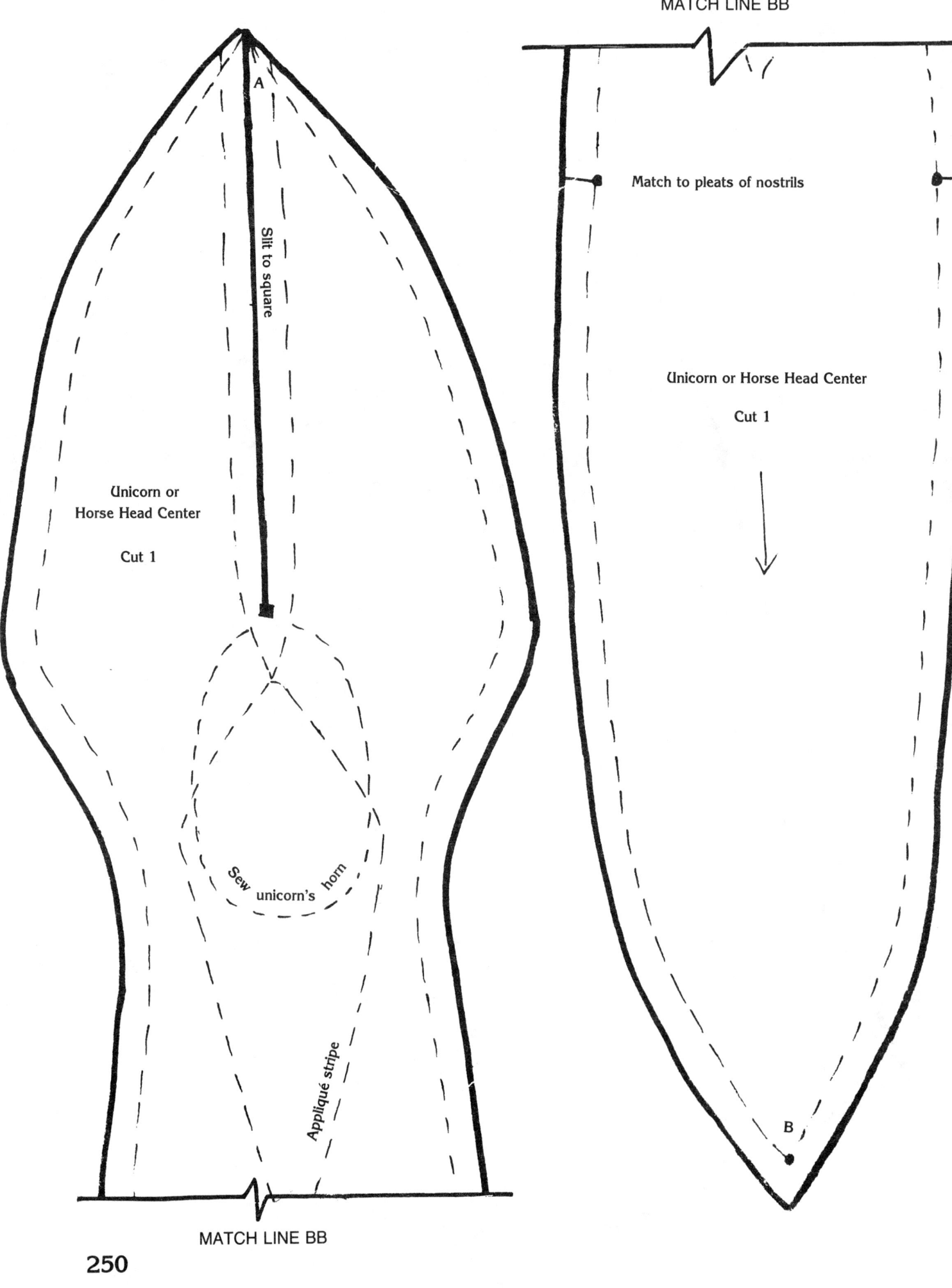

SEVEN PATTERN PIECES
9" (23 cm) LONG

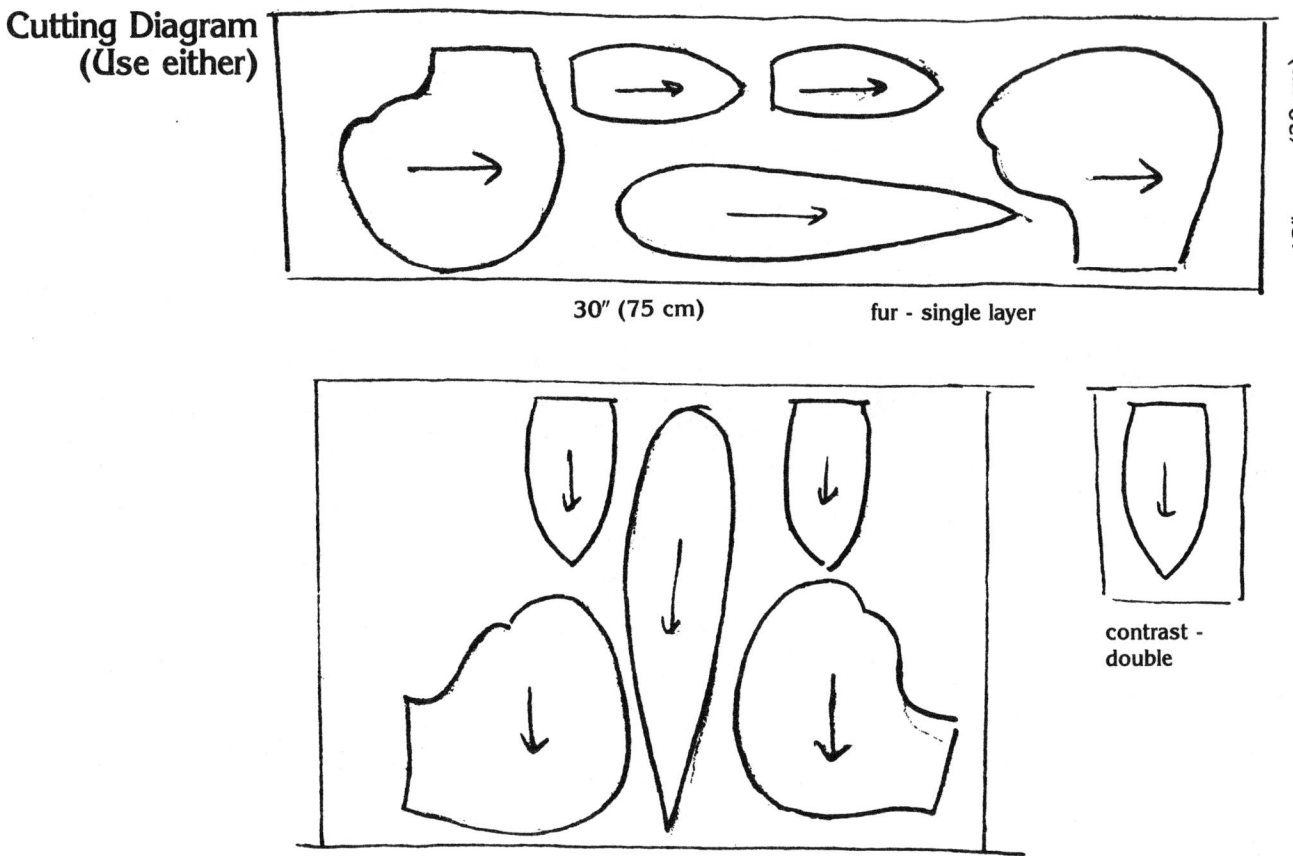

Materials   2' (60 cm) square piece or ½ yd of 45" or 60" (46 cm of 1 m 15 cm or 1 m 53 cm width fabric) of tan, gray, black, or white fur, or fabric of choice
10" × 12" piece (25 × 30 cm) of pink or contrasting fabric for ear linings plus same of interfacing or quilt batt
1 pair of safety eyes or 2 dome or half-dome buttons or scraps of felt for appliquéd eyes
One ⅞" (2 3/16 cm) diameter dowel, 3' (90 cm) long or an old broomstick, prepared as on page 233
Heavy-duty thread to match the main fabric
Scrap of white vinyl or felt for collar
9" (23 cm) of cablecord or braid for reins
5" (13 cm) of grosgrain ribbon or braid for bow tie
1 lb. (450 g) of polyester fiberfill for stuffing

18
Hobby Rabbit

There is no reason why a child should have to ride a hobby horse, when he or she can have an adorable rabbit to ride. This can be made any color, although white, black, gray, or tan are traditional. The ears can be left floppy like a lop, or stiffened and tacked to stand upright.

Cutting Instructions

See the Introduction for working with fur fabrics.
 Of main fabric, cut two side heads, one center head, and two ears.
 Of contrast fabric, cut two ear linings. For upright ears, cut two of quilt batt or heavy interfacing.
 Of white felt or vinyl, cut one collar.
 If using felt appliqué eyes, cut two large white ovals, two colored (pink, brown, or blue) small ovals, and two black circles.

Sewing Instructions

Use ¼" (⅗ cm) seams throughout unless otherwise noted.
 1. Sew ear linings to the ears (interfacing for upright ears), right sides together, leaving bottoms open. Trim points and turn right side out. Fold in half and stitch to the side heads between lines, as shown on pattern and Figure 1.
 2. Sew head center to each side head from dot A to dot B, matching notches 1 and 2. See Figure 2.
 3. Sew right and left side heads together along the center front seam from dot A to the neck edge and along the center back seam from dot B to the neck edge. See Figure 3. Leave neck edge open for turning. Clip curves and turn right side out.
 4. If using safety eyes, clip a small x (just large enough for shank of

the eye) where indicated on the pattern on each side of the head. Insert the shank of the eye from the right side and push the washer onto the shank inside the head.

If using buttons or felt appliqué eyes, sew these on after the head is stuffed.

5. Stuff the front of the head very firmly, rounding the cheek areas with extra stuffing. Pad the top of the head and insert the dowel so that the groove is at the neck edge. See Figure 4. Continue stuffing the back of the head and the neck firmly, so it is well padded all around the stick. Keep the stick centered in the neck. With heavy-duty thread, make a running stitch around the neck edge and gather the fabric into the groove. Pull the thread up tightly, wrap it around, and pull and sew the gathered fabric tightly into the groove. Sew in a figure eight through the hole in the stick, catching in the fabric on each side. Fasten off firmly.

6. Hand sew the long edge of the collar over the gathered fabric to cover the hole and threads. The collar fits around a 7/8" (2 3/16 cm) diameter stick. If you are using a stick of different diameter, you will have to adjust the pattern. Cut 9" (23 cm) of cablecord or braid. Tape or hem ends as necessary. Sew the ends to each side of the neck to form reins. Cut 5" (13 cm) of grosgrain or other ribbon and gather at the center to make a bow tie. Sew at the front of the collar to cover the ends of the reins. See Figure 5.

7. If using buttons for eyes, sew on with heavy-duty thread at the xs on the side heads.

If using felt for eyes, stitch the black circles over the colored ovals over the white ovals. See Figure 6. Embroider a white highlight on the black circles, if you desire. Hand stitch the eye patches to each side of the head where indicated on the pattern, stuffing slightly behind the white oval as you sew to make the eyes bulge out from the head.

8. The head may be further shaped by needle sculpture as shown in Figure 7. With heavy-duty thread and a long needle, pass the thread through the head in front of the eyes and pull up thread to pinch this area in. Continue back and forth across the nose area along the top of the cheeks.

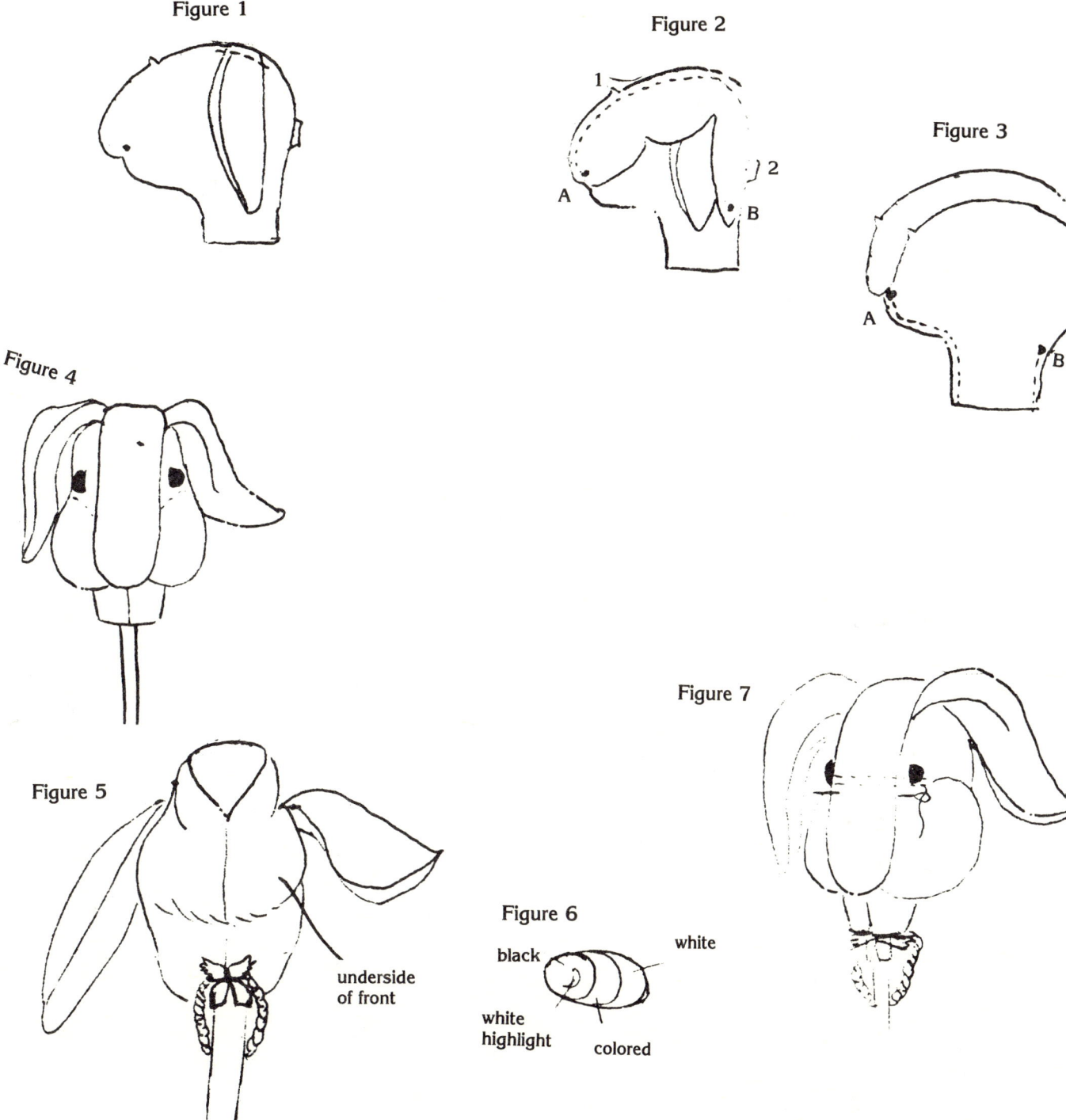

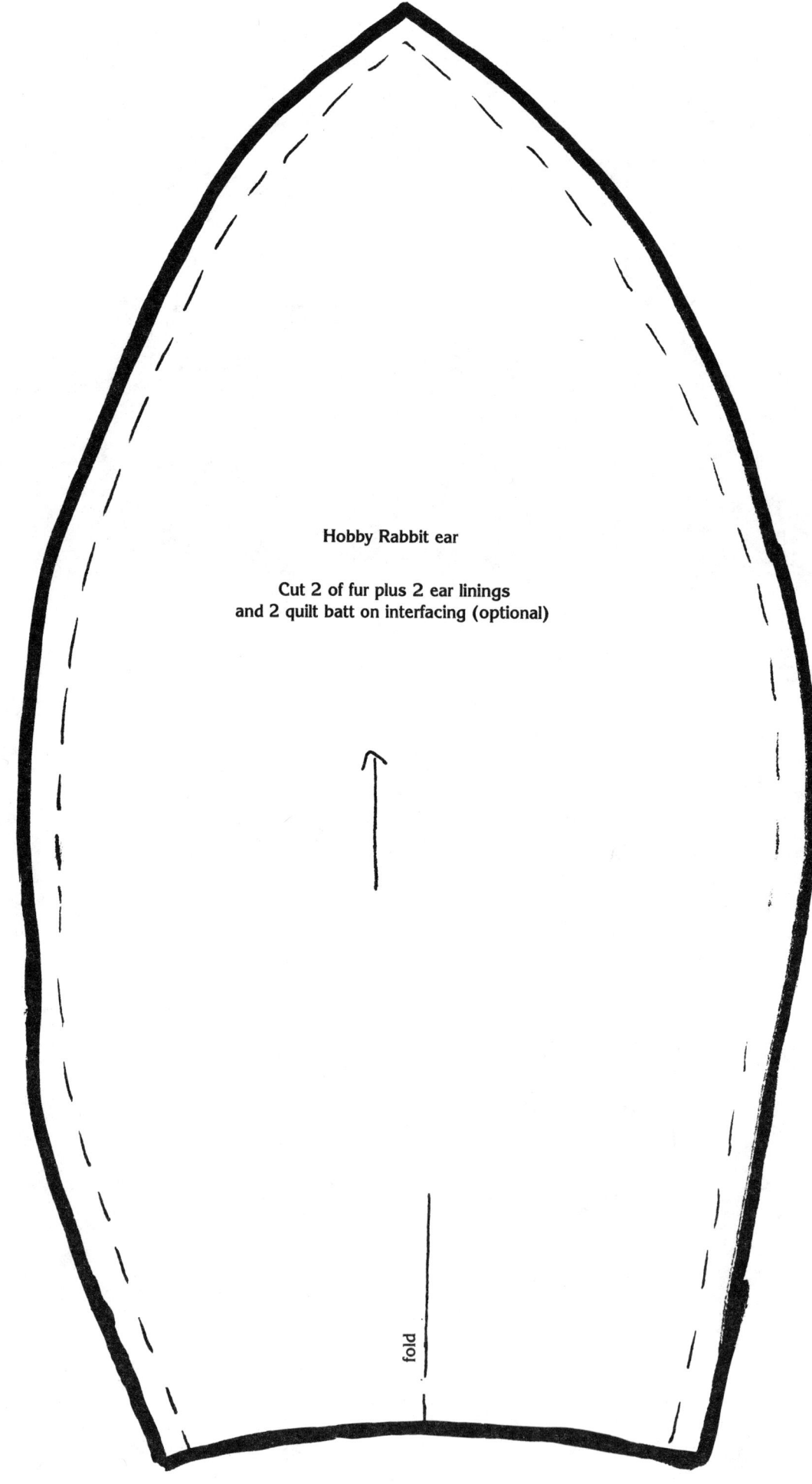

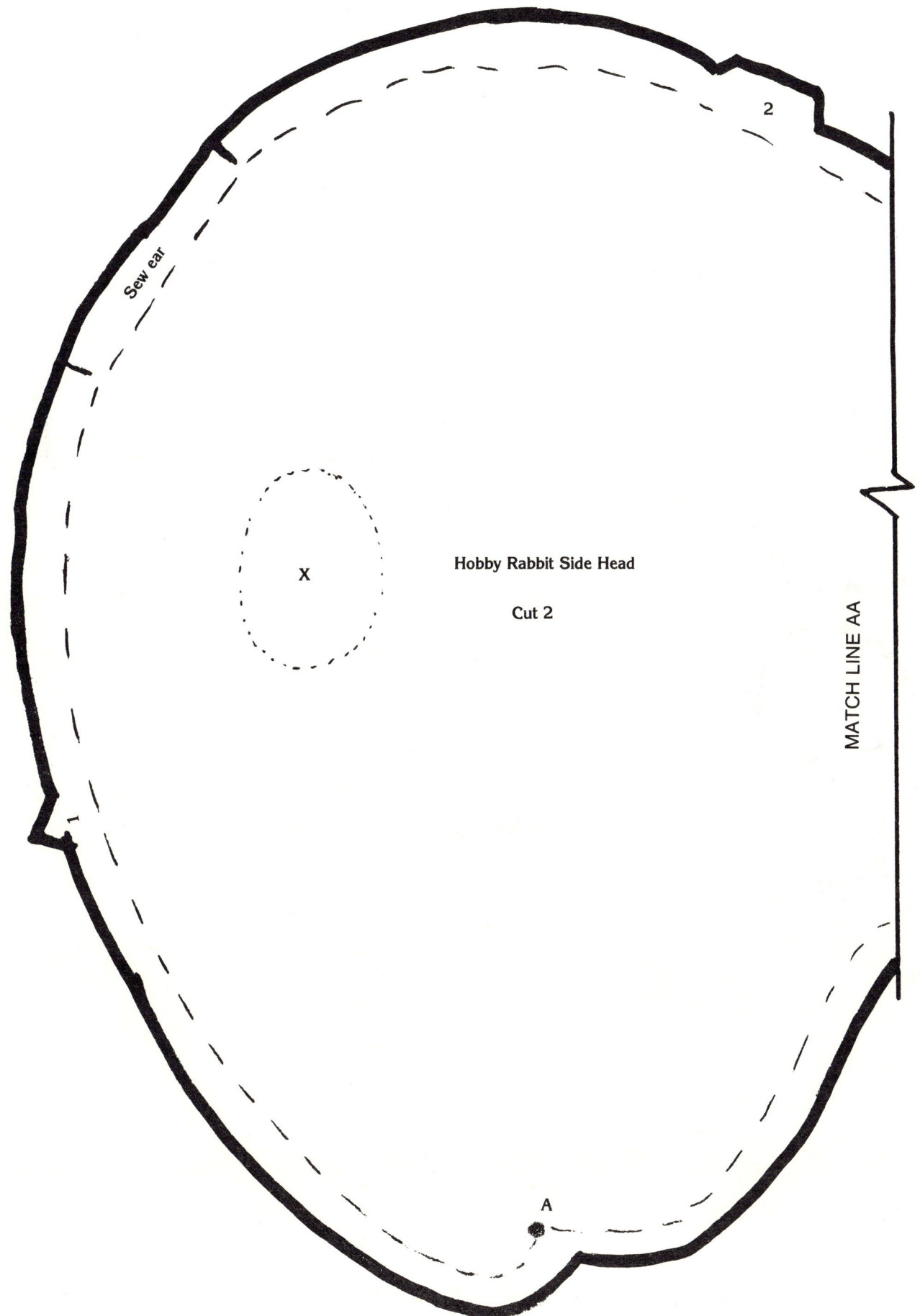

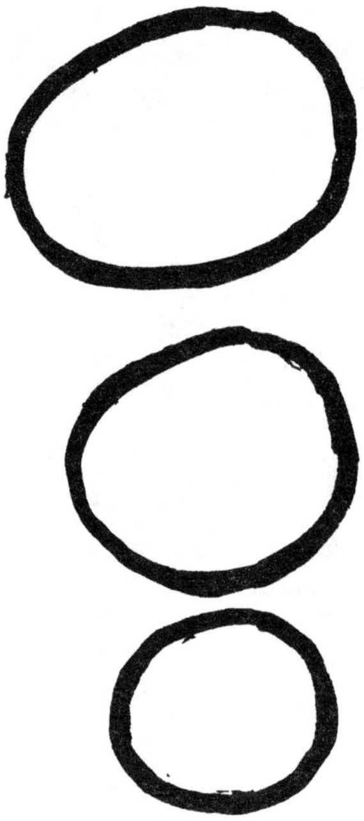

Hobby Rabbit Eye
Cut 2 of white felt

Hobby Rabbit Iris
Cut 2 of colored

Hobby Rabbit Pupil
Cut 2 black

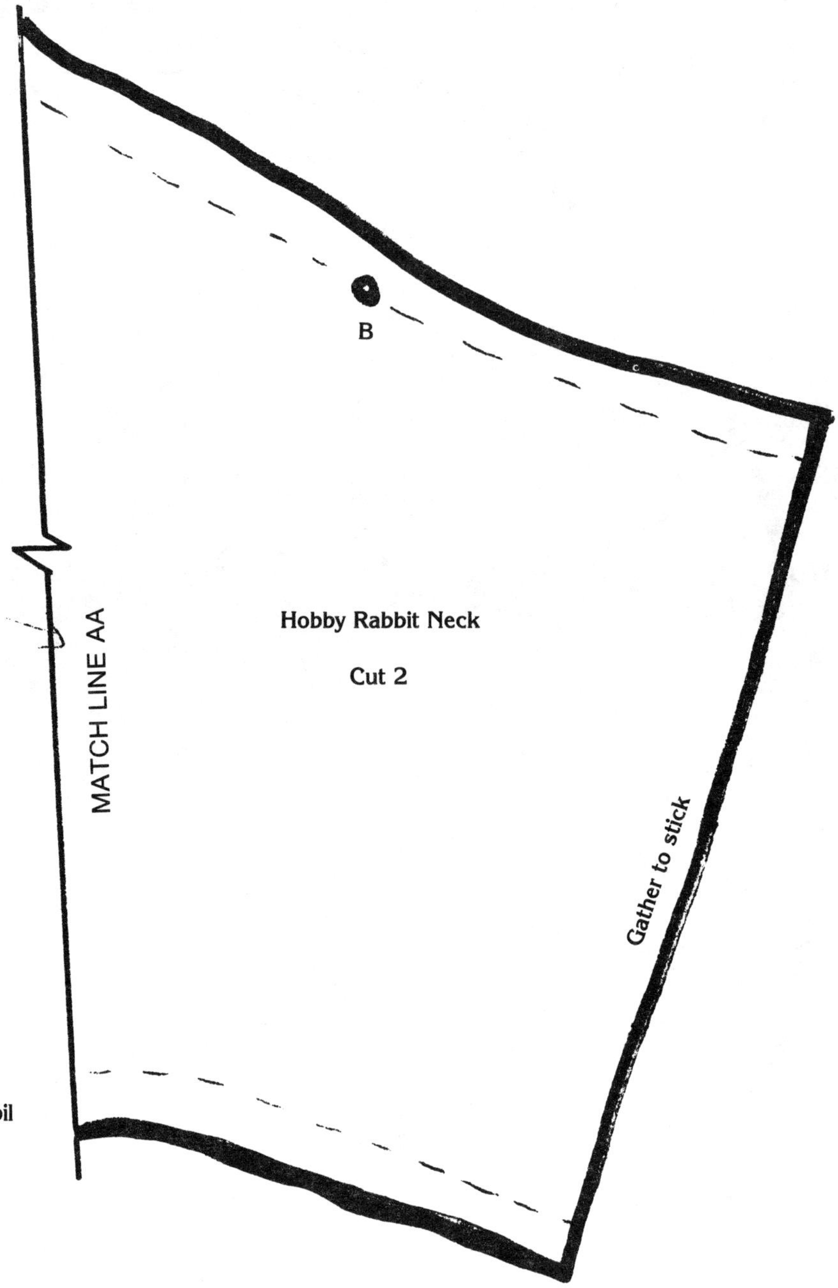

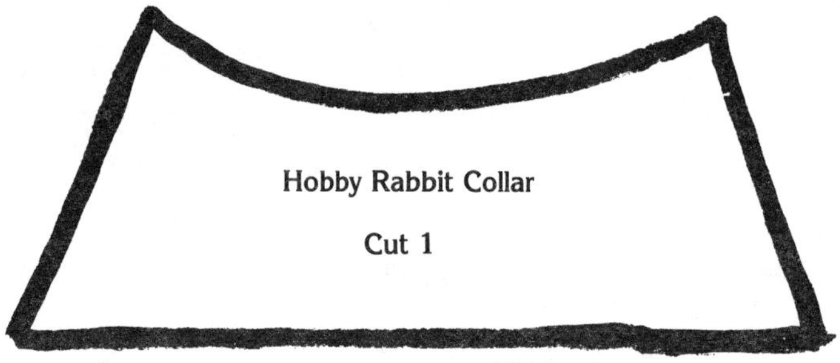

MATCH LINE AA

Hobby Rabbit Neck
Cut 2

B

Gather to stick

Hobby Rabbit Collar
Cut 1

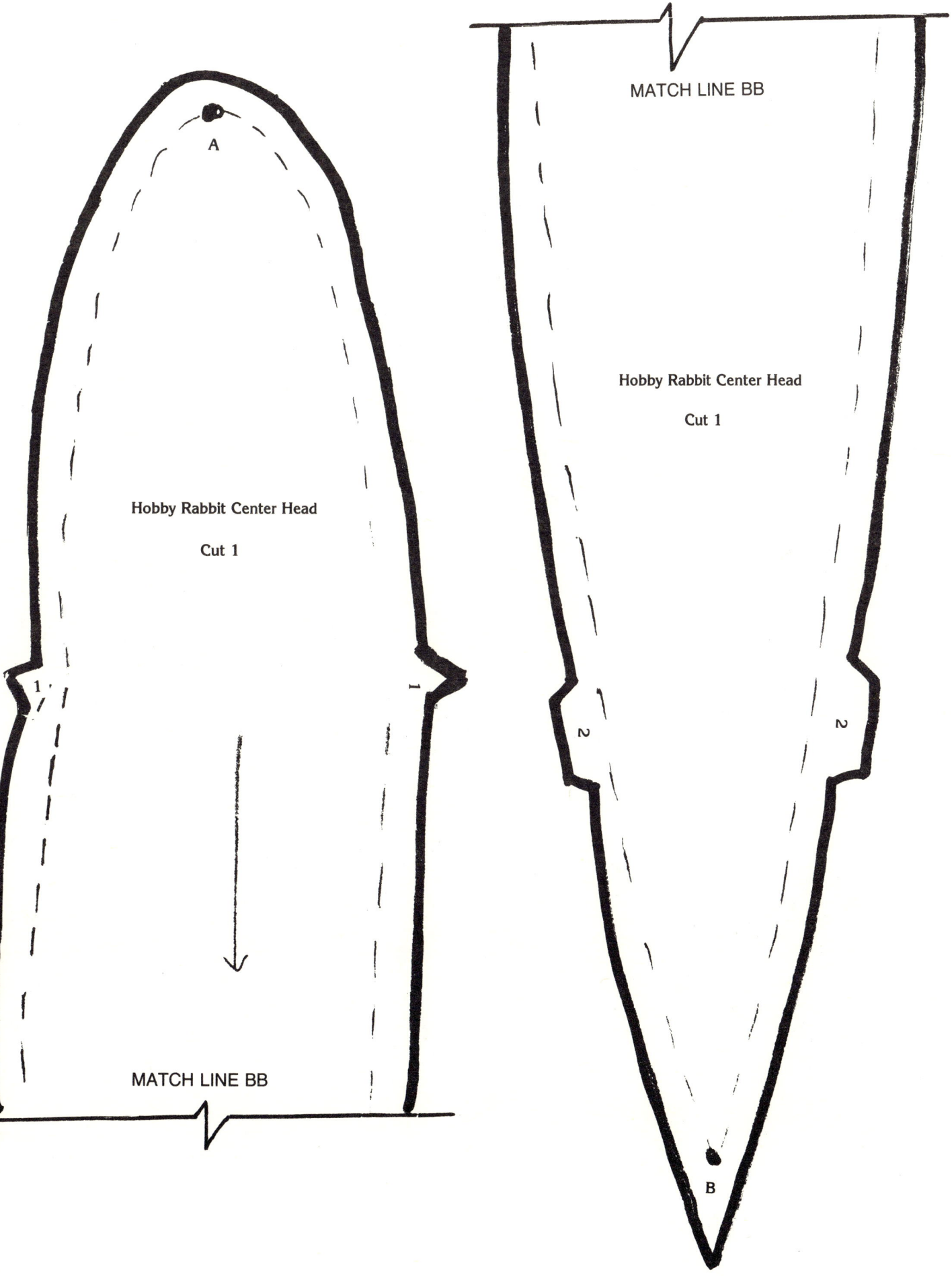